READING COMPLEX WORDS

Cross-Language Studies

NEUROPSYCHOLOGY AND COGNITION

VOLUME 22

The purpose of the Neuropsychology and Cognition series is to bring out volumes that promote understanding in topics relating brain and behavior. It is intended for use by both clinicians and research scientists in the fields of neuropsychology, cognitive psychology, psycholinguistics, speech and hearing, as well as eduction. Examples of topics to be covered in this series would relate memory, language acquisition and breakdown, reading, attention, developing and aging brain. By addressing the theoretical, empirical, and applied aspects of brain-behavior relationships, this series will try to present the information in the files of neuropsychology and cognition in a coherent manner.

The titles published in this series are listed at the end of this volume.

READING COMPLEX WORDS
Cross-Language Studies

Edited by

Egbert M.H. Assink
Utrecht University
Utrecht, The Netherlands

Dominiek Sandra
University of Antwerp
Antwerp, Belgium

KLUWER ACADEMIC / PLENUM PUBLISHERS
New York, Boston, Dordrecht, London, Moscow

Library of Congress Cataloging-in-Publication Data

Reading complex words: cross-language studies/edited by Egbert M.H. Assink, Dominiek Sandra.

p. cm. — (Neuropsychology and cognition; 22)

Includes bibliographical references and index.

ISBN 0-306-47707-6

1. Psycholinguistics. 2. Reading, Psychology of. 3. Grammar, Comparative and general—Morphology. I. Assink, E., 1944– II. Sandra, Dominiek, 1960– III. Series.

P37.5.R42R43 2003

401′.9—dc21

2002043454

ISBN 0-306-47707-6

233 Spring Street, New York, New York 10013

http://www.wkap.nl/

10 9 8 7 6 5 4 3 2 1

A C.I.P. record for this book is available from the Library of Congress

Printed in United Kingdom by Biddles/IBT Global.

CONTRIBUTORS

Darinka Andjelkovic, Laboratory for Experimental Psychology and Faculty of Philosophy, University of Belgrade, Cika Ljubina 18-20, 11000 Belgrade, Yugoslavia.

Egbert Assink, Psychology Department, Utrecht University, Heidelberglaan 2, 3584 CS Utrecht - The Netherlands.

Harald Baayen, Interfaculty Research Unit for Language and Speech (IWTS), University of Nijmegen & Max Planck Institute for Psycholinguistics, Wundtlaan 1, 6525 XD Nijmegen, (mailing address: P.O. Box 310, 6500 AH Nijmegen) The Netherlands.

Cristina Burani, Istituto di Scienze e Tecnologie della Cognizione CNR, Viale Marx, 15 - 00137 Roma, Italy.

Joanne Carlisle, Center for the Improvement of Early Reading Achievement, Univer of Michigan, School of Education, 610 East University Ave, Ann Arbor, MI 48109-1259, USA.

Aydin Durgunoglu, Department of Psychology, University of Minnesota Duluth, Bohannon Hall 320, 1207 Ordean Court, Duluth, MN 55812-3010, USA.

Laurie Beth Feldman, Department of Psychology Faculty, University of Albany, State University of New York and Haskins Laboratories, 270 Crown St., New Haven, CT 06511-6695, USA.

Ludovic Ferrand, Laboratoire de Psychologie Expérimentale, CNRS and Université René Descartes, 71, Avenue Edouard Vaillant, 92100 Boulogne-Billancourt, France.

Anne Fowler, International literacy Institute, Graduate School of Education/University of Pennsylvania, 3910 Chestnut Street Philadelphia, PA 19104-3111, USA.

Hélène Giraudo, Centre Interdisciplinaire de Recherche en Linguistique et Psychologie Cognitive, Université de Reims Champagne-Ardenne, Campus Croix Rouge, 57 Rue Pierre Taittinger, 51096 Reims cedex, France.

Jonathan Grainger, Centre de Recherche en Psychologie Cognitive, CNRS, Universite de Provence, Aix-en-Provence , France.

Paul Knuijt, Psychology Department, Utrecht University, Heidelberglaan 2, 3584 CS Utrecht , The Netherlands.

Alessandro Laudanna, Department of Communication Sciences, "Cognitive Psychology", University of Salerno, Via Ponte don Melillo - 84084 Fisciano (Sa), Italy, and Institute of Sciences and Technologies of Cognition, National Research Council (CNR), Viale Marx, 15 - 00137 Rome, Italy.

Gary Libben, Department of Linguistics, University of Alberta, 4-36 Assiniboia Hall, Edmonton, Alberta, Canada T6G 2E7.

Virginia Mann, Dept. Cognitive Sciences, University of California, SSPA5119, Mail Code: 5100, Irvine, CA 92697-5100, USA.

Harold Nefs, Psychology Department, Utrecht University, Heidelberglaan 2, 3584 CS Utrecht , The Netherlands.

Banu Oney, International literacy Institute, Graduate School of Education/University of Pennsylvania, 3910 Chestnut Street Philadelphia, PA 19104-3111, USA.

John Sabatini, International Literacy Institute, Graduate School of Education/University of Pennsylvania, 3910 Chestnut Street Philadelphia, PA 19104-3111 USA.

Dominiek Sandra, Centre for Psycholinguistics, University of Antwerp, Prinsstraat 13, B2000 Antwerp, Belgium.

Schreuder Robert Schreuder, Interfaculty Research Unit for Language and Speech (IWTS), University of Nijmegen & Max Planck Institute for Psycholinguistics, Wundtlaan 1, 6525 XD Nijmegen, (mailing address: P.O. Box 310, 6500 AH Nijmegen) The Netherlands.

Juan Segui, Laboratoire de Psychologie Expérimentale, CNRS and Université René Descartes, 71, Avenue Edouard Vaillant, 92100 Boulogne-Billancourt, France.

Joseph Shimron, Faculty of Education, University of Haifa, Mount Carmel, Haifa 31905.

Maria Singson, Department of Cognitive Sciences, University of California, School of Social Science, 3251 Social Science Plaza, Irvine, CA 92697-5100, USA.

Addison C. Stone, Center for the Improvement of Early Reading Achievement, University of Michigan, School of Education, 610 East University Ave, Ann Arbor, MI 48109-1259, USA.

Marcus Taft, School of Psychology, University of New South Wales, Sydney, New South Wales, 2052, Australia.

PREFACE

This volume on reading complex words is the spin-off of a symposium on reading morphologically complex words in different languages submitted to the Organizing Committee for the Annual Meeting of the American Educational Research Association in the late nineties. Among the participants were Joanne Carlisle, Aydin Durguloglu, Virginia Mann, John Sabatini, and Egbert Assink, who acts as the first editor of this volume. The idea to publish the scheduled presentations and to further extend and enlarge the scope of the work by inviting contributors from researchers around the world was born during a discussion with Dorien Francissen, publishing editor of Kluwer Academic. The idea to invite Dominiek Sandra as a co-editor was prompted by his own research in this field and the fact that he had already co-edited with Marcus Taft a special issue on *Morphological structure, lexical representation and lexical access* for the journal *Language and Cognitive Processes*.

Most contributions to this volume present research which was designed to shed light on the question how the mental representations of morphologically complex words are accessed in reading. It will be obvious that it is sheerly impossible to provide a short answer to this very general question. Indeed, a rich variety of facets is related to the topic, all of which deserve attention and may play a role in processing polymorphemic words. We have made an attempt to have the chapters in this book reflect this diversity. First of all, we tried to have the chapters cover a variety of languages, differing both in the richness of their morphology and in their typology. As a result, experimental studies are reported on such different languages as English, French, Dutch, Italian, Turkish, Serbian and Hebrew. Secondly, we liked to have studies on the role of morphology in different populations: children who are learning to read or are still in their first stages of reading acquisition and studies on the lexical processing of experienced readers. There is one chapter which deals with adults who are learning to read, focusing on factors that affect the reading success of participants in literacy programmes. Thirdly, we wanted the chapters to represent a variety of theoretically relevant issues with respect to morpheme-based lexical processing. Several research questions are addressed: the contribution of morphological awareness on children's reading success, the locus of morphological representations in the hierarchy of mental representations between form and meaning levels, the role of semantics in processing polymorphemic words, the role of morphosyntax in processing words consisting of more than two morphemes, the importance of the morpheme/pseudomorpheme ratio of a letter string in morphological decomposition, the role of morphology in reading aloud. Finally, two studies do not deal with the involvement of polymorphemic words in reading, but are nevertheless related to the general topic of the book. One of these studies addresses the issue of reading polysyllabic (rather than polymorphemic) words. The other one studies morphologically complex words in written language production (spelling) rather than written language recognition (reading).

The first set of chapters addresses the question of morphological awareness and its relationship to phonological awareness and later reading succes. In Chapter 1 *"Linking Morphological Knowledge to English Decoding Ability: Large Effects of Little Suffixes"* Virginia Mann & Maria Singson from the University of California, focus on the importance of morphological awareness. There is a vast literature on phonological awareness as a predictor fur success in reading. The authors show that children between grades 3 and 6 become increasingly aware of derivational suffixes. Central in their research is the question to what extent awareness of derivational morphology contributes as a predictor of reading above and beyond phonological awareness and vocabulary knowledge. Mann and Singson emphasize that English orthography is morpho-phonologically encoded and their results demonstrate that even young readers are sensitive to this fact. They conclude with the statement that from an early age children are willing and able to map the English orthography onto the morphemes of their language and that morphological awareness is an important component of reading ability.

In Chapter 2, entitled *"The Effects of Morphological Structure on Children's Reading of Derived Words in English"*, Joanne Carlisle & C. Addison Stone from Northwestern University address the question whether morphological structure positively affects reading acquisition. Carlisle & Stone are particularly interested in the question whether children benefit from the presence of embedded morphemes in words and whether their reading performance can be predicted by measures obtained in morphological awareness tasks. The answer to both questions turns out to be positive. Instead of using multiple regression techniques, as Mann & Singson did in their study, Carlisle & Stone used the factorial design technique. The authors compare poor readers with a chronological-age match group and a reading-age match group. Their major findings indicate that children indeed benefit from the morphological composition of words. This manifests itself in different ways. Measures of morphological awareness predict later reading success. High frequency words consisting of two morphemes are read more accurately than matched words consisting of one morpheme. Low frequency derived words with a phonologially and orthographically transparent morphological structure are read with a higher accuracy if their base word is more familiar. Derived words in which the vowel of the base word is altered (e.g., natural) are more difficult to read than comparable words with a phonologically transparent morphological make-up. All these results underscore the importance of morphological structure in the reading performance of young children.

Chapter 3 presents experiments probing into the precise relationship between phonological and morphological awareness, and is entitled "*Morphological and Phonological Analysis by Beginning Readers: Evidence from Serbian and Turkish*" by Anne Fowler, Laurie Beth Feldman, Darinka Andjelkovic and Banu Oney from Haskins Laboratories and research institutes in Belgrade and Turkey. The primary goal of their investigation is to find out to what extent morphological awareness contributes independently from phonological awareness to children's later reading success. In order to investigate this question they study two languages which have both a complex inflectional and derivational morphology: Serbian and Turkish. They presented children with phoneme deletion and morphological production tasks. The outcome of their experiments suggests a strong relationship between phonological and morphological awareness and further reveals that the association between these two forms of awareness increases as the phonological relationship between morphologically related forms becomes less transparent (e.g, as the result of vowel alternation). The authors conclude that their current data are compatible with several accounts, one of which being that morphological awareness is mediated by the specific phonological operations required in morphological tasks, the other one being that the importance of phonological and morphological awareness refer to the involvement of a general metalinguistic factor.

The chapter by Fowler et al is the first of several papers in which morphologically complex languages are studied that are typologically different from Indo-European languages, which are most frequently studied in the literature, like the Germanic (English, Dutch, German) and Romance (French, Italian) languages. Chapter 4, "*Recognizing Morphologically Complex Words in Turkish*", by Aydin Durgunoglu from the University of Minnesota, Duluth, studies whether children use their knowledge of the morphological structure of the language when reading words. Turkish, like Finnish, uses a morphological production system that sharply differs from the one that is used in Germanic or Romance languages. Agglutinative languages like Turkish can have many iterative loops, which can technically produce words of considerable length. A priori it seems quite likely that readers of Turkish recognize words by using a left-to-right parsing strategy. In order to find out how beginning readers of Turkish utilize morphological information, second and fourth grade children were presented with simple and complex pseudowords. Each child performed one of two tasks. They either corrected the suffixes provided by the experimenter (correction task) or they supplied the suffixes themselves (completion task) in a short paragraph about an imaginary animal with a pseudo-species name. The question of interest was whether complex pseudowords would be more difficult to handle than simple ones as the result of their length or whether this length factor would be offset by an understanding of the morphological system of the language. Indeed, it is conceivable that morphological skill facilitates word recognition, leading to the paradoxical prediction that complex items may be easier to manipulate than simplex ones. The latter possibility turned out to be the case.

In Chapter 5, "*Word Decomposition in Hebrew as a Semitic Language*", by Joseph Shimron from the University of Haifa, a language with yet another radically different morphological system is studied: Hebrew. Shimron discusses how morphological knowledge affects language performance in native speakers of Hebrew. He starts with a discussion of the basic features of Hebrew morphology as a mix of linear and non-linear morphology. Next he discusses how linguists view the morphological structure of Hebrew words, how Hebrew non-linear (non-concatenative) morphology functions, and what should be considered the morphological competence of Hebrew speakers. Here the focus is on the dispute over the ramifications of non-linear composition of morphemes and the depiction of Hebrew as a root-based morphology. Shimron finally discusses psycholinguistic studies on the effect of morphological knowledge on language performance. In his chapter he observes that whereas psycholinguistic studies suggest roots and templates to have independent mental representations involved in language behavior, some linguists reject the traditional root-based approach to Semitic languages. In the final section of this paper he argues that language users may use several representational units simultaneously and that the psycholinguistic evidence favouring the role of roots and templates does not preclude an additional role of stems and possibly other aspects of Hebrew words as well. Hence, the seemingly contradictory statements in psycholinguistic and linguistic approaches to the morphological structure of Hebrew may eventually turn out to be reconcilable.

When morphological effects can be demonstrated in written word recognition, the question arises where such effects originate. In other words: what is the locus in the representational system for language where morphology is represented? This question is tackled by Marcus Taft from the University of New South Wales in Chapter 6, "*Morphological Representation as a Correlation between Form and Meaning*". In this chapter Taft makes a predominantly theoretical analysis of the problem. One of the central tenets of the chapter is that morphological relations are captured in lexical memory by lemmas, which are abstract representations "picking up" the correlation between form and meaning. The distinctiveness of a particular lemma depends on the magnitude of this form-meaning correlation. This lemma distinctiveness is highest in freestanding morphemes (*fire*). In morphologically complex words the lemma distinctiveness of an embedded morpheme varies between high values for morphemes preserving their meaning across a large number of forms (*fire* in *fireman*) to bound morphemes that can only be found within a single word (*hench* in *henchman*). In between are cases that occur in several words (*smith* in *blacksmith, locksmith*) but not sufficiently often to be clearly considered a free morpheme. Taft discusses several theoretically possible models of the mental architecture behind processing polymorphemic words, arguing why some models inevitably run into problems and showing step by step how these problems can be solved in a different model. At the end of the chapter Taft presents his own model. In the course of his theoretical exercise Taft reports an experiment on Chinese, in which it is possible to separate effects originating at the level of form from effects whose source is situated at the lemma level (by using a character decision task and a word decision task, respectively). His data indicate a special status for bound morphemes and suggest that such morphemes have their own representations at the lemma level.

In Chapter 7, "*A Supralexical Model for French Derivational Morphology*", Hélène Giraudo and Jonathan Grainger from the University of Reims and Aix-en-Provence approach the same issue – where is morphology represented ? – on the basis of a strictly experimental approach. The vast majority of researchers adopt the sublexical account of morphological representation. They assume a general processing framework for word recognition that progressively moves from sensory codes to semantic representations, and in which morphological constituents are hypothesized to become operational before whole-word representations. In their chapter

Giraudo & Grainger challenge this dominant theoretical position in psycholinguistic research and argue in favour of a radically different alternative for the representation of derivational morphology in French. Their account, which they refer to as the supralexical account of morphological representation, stipulates that in the process of normal, fast, automatic word recognition the representations for the morphemes in a derived word are contacted only *after* the representation for the whole-word form has been accessed. They report several experimental data in favor of this alternative hypothesis. Despite the radically different localisation of morphological representations in the sublexical and the supralexical accounts, both types of account share the assumption that morphological effects cannot be explained by the joint effects of form and meaning and require an independent level of morpheme representations.

An important issue related to the processing of polymorphemic words concerns the role of the meaning of constituent morphemes. This topic cannot be neglected in any model of processing morphologically complex words, since morphemes are, linguistically speaking, the minimal forms of language with an independent meaning. As mentioned earlier, Taft's central concept had been the notion of a lemma which captures the form-meaning correlation and can thus naturally take care of morphological relationships. In chapter 8, "*Parsing and Semantic Opacity*" Robert Schreuder, Cristina Burani and Harald Baayen from the University of Nijmegen and Rome also address the topic between form and meaning in polymorphemic words. However, as can be judged by their title, their emphasis is not on how the meaning of polymorphemic words is derived from the meanings of their morphemic constituents. Rather they wonder whether the stem of a derived word is also activated when its meaning is irrelevant in the meaning of the complex word (i.e., semantically opaque word). In order to investigate this issue, they manipulate the stem frequency in derived words. The experiments show that processing semantically opaque derived words which are phonologically and orthographically regular does involve access to their stem representation, at least when the frequency of this stem is sufficiently high to boost the morphological decomposition process. This suggests that morphological decomposition is an automatic process, whose success in accessing morphemic representations is not controlled by semantic factors of the whole word but by properties of the morphemes (like stem frequency).

The issue of semantics is also addressed in chapter 9, "*Effects of Sublexical Frequency and Meaning in Prefixed Words*" by Harold Nefs, Egbert Assink and Paul Knuijt from the University of Utrecht. The central question of the paper concerns the role of prefixes in visual word recognition in Dutch beginning and skilled readers. Besides addressing the role of semantic factors, the paper also raises the question to what extent lexical processing is affected by distributional factors in the language: prefix frequency and prefix reliability. Prefix reliability is defined as the ratio of true prefix frequency to total frequency of the prefix letter string. Total prefix of the prefix letter string is the combined frequency count of an item both as true and as pseudo-prefix in the language. The data presented in this chapter allow the authors to draw two major conclusions. First, present models for decoding prefixed words are incomplete in terms of the semantic integration process, which plays a crucial role during word recognition. Current models are too narrowly focused on the isolated properties of the affix involved, neglecting the semantic relationship with the word stem. The second conclusion is that sublexical processing mechanisms contribute to the identification process mainly under conditions where relatively new or unknown words are involved. Prefixes as sublexical identification units become important when the reader cannot rely on his normally used default decoding routines.

Most researchers focus on bimorphemic polymorphemic words and mainly address the question whether or not morphological decomposition occurs during their processing. Whereas the semantic properties of these words are sometimes taken into account, the relevance of their syntactic structure has been largely neglected. This issue is taken up in chapter 10, "*Morphological Parsing and Morphological Structure*" by Gary Libben from the University of Alberta, Canada. In his chapter Libben moves beyond two-morphemic words and focuses on the processing of English trimorphemic pseudowords with the structure prefix + base + suffix (pseudoword equivalents to words like *unfillable*). In English such a structure can be left-braching, as in *[[re[fill]]able],* or right-branching, as in *[un[[think]able]].* The results presented by Libben suggest that the notion of hierarchical morphological structure does not map directly onto patterns of lexical processing time. He proposes an interactionist account of the data, more particularly, in terms of networks of associations between polymorphemic words and their constituents in the mental lexicon.

The majority of experiments reported by the authors of this book focus on "silent" single word reading, as tapped by the classical lexical-decision task. However, morphological processing may also be involved in other modes of verbal processing, such as reading aloud (i.e., naming). In chapter 11, "*Morpheme-based Lexical Reading: Evidence from Pseudoword Naming*", Cristina Burani and Alessandro Laudanna from the Institute for Psychology of the National Research Council (CNR) in Rome investigate the issue of polymorphemic word processing in a naming task. Italian is a language which at the same time has a very rich morphology and is very transparent with respect to the mapping of graphemes onto phonemes. Considering the phonological transparency of written Italian, the language is a good candidate for efficient nonlexical naming, i.e., from this perspective morphological involvement might not seem to add a special advantage in a naming task. On the other hand, despite this shallow orthography, precisely the morphological richness of the language might affect performance even in the naming task. Based on a discussion of earlier published research and new experimental data the authors conclude that a morpholexical reading routine makes for quite an efficient mechanism for reading aloud Italian.

In chapter 12, "*Word Reading Processes in Adult Learners*", John Sabatini from the National Center on Adult Literacy, University of Pennsylvania, also deals with the issue of learning to read (see chapters 1-3) but focuses on a different population than children who are learning to read: people in literacy programmes. He collected data from ninety-five American adults recruited from education programs in the mid-Atlantic region, including adult basic education classes. The aims of this study were twofold. First, what is the relationship of word recognition ability to higher-order skills such as reading comprehension? More particularly, is there a threshold above which word recognition no longer predicts comprehension measures? The second goal was to explore the relationship of component skills to word recognition ability, with an emphasis on speed of processing measures. Discrepancies between word recognition and comprehension were found toward the high end of the reading scale. As to the second issue, speed of skill application proved to be a strong predictor of word recognition and contributed above and beyond decoding accuracy.

The final two chapters do not deal with reading polymorphemic words, although each of them is closely related to the central theme of the book. In chapter 13, "*Reading aloud Polysyllabic Words*", Ludovic Ferrand and Juan Segui, from the Université René Descartes, Paris, address the issue of reading aloud a different type of complex words: words consisting of several syllables. Although a great deal is known about the naming process of monosyllabic words, very few studies have been devoted to the naming process of polysyllabic words. This is remarkable, since monosyllabic words represent less than 10% of the lexicon and therefore can be considered as the exception. In this chapter the authors explicitly address the processes involved in generating the pronunciations of polysyllabic words from their written forms. In particular, the focus of their chapter is not lexical access per se but the process of producing a phonological code for polysyllabic words. In their chapter they argue that the syllable is a likely processing unit in reading aloud polysyllabic words. After presenting empirical evidence different models of polysyllabic word reading are discussed.

In the final chapter 14, "*Homophonous Regular Verb Forms with a Morphographic Spelling: Spelling Errors as a Window on the Mental Lexicon and Working-Memory*", Dominiek Sandra from the University of

Antwerp discusses polymorphemic words from the perspective of spelling errors. Like speech errors, these errors in written language production may be used as a source of information on the structure of the mental lexicon and provide evidence on the interaction between lexically stored information and processes in working-memory. Dutch orthography offers a particular type of spelling error which can be used for this purpose. Different verb forms belonging to the same regular inflectional paradigm are homophonous but reflect their morphological structure in their spelling pattern. Even highly experienced writers of the language sometimes make spelling errors on these morphographically spelled forms. Experimental research reveals that the frequency relationship between the homophonous forms in the inflectional paradigm determines the error risk. Spellers have a tendency to spell the most frequent homophone (probabilistic spelling behaviour) and this tendency is enhanced when working-memory factors (e.g., subject-verb distance) make it more difficult for the speller to retrieve from the sentential subject the grammatical information which determines suffix selection. The error data suggest that regularly inflected homophonous verb forms have their own non-decomposed representation in the mental lexicon.

At the end of this editorial enterprise we want to thank Dorien Francissen, Christiane Roll and Mary Panarelli from Kluwer Academic for their patience and professional support. Especially, we want to express our deep gratitude to Hilde Hermans from the University of Antwerp for her excellent work in preparing the manuscript in a camera-ready form. Finally we want to thank our colleagues for their fine work and we hope that the work presented in this volume will stimulate the discussion and communication amongst the colleagues in this field.

Utrecht and Antwerp, September 15, 2002

Egbert Assink
Dominiek Sandra

ACKNOWLEDGMENTS

This book was realised in the context of a Scientific Research Network grant to Dominiek Sandra on the topic *"Psycholinguistics: Acquisition and processing aspects of reading and spelling"*, sponsored by the Fund for Scientific Research – Flanders. We are very grateful to Hilde Hermans from the University of Antwerp, who did a wonderful job in making all manuscripts camera-ready. We thank the staff members at Kluwer for their patience and their feedback at various stages during the production of this book. Finally, we thank our wives and children for their continuing support and patience with husbands and fathers who are also researchers.

CONTENTS

1. Linking morphological knowledge to English decoding ability: Large effects of little suffixes

Virginia Mann and Maria Singson 1

2. The effects of morphological structure on children's reading of derived words in English

Joanne F. Carlisle and C. Addison Stone 27

3. Morphological and phonological analysis by beginning readers: Evidence from Serbian and Turkish

Anne Fowler, Laurie Beth Feldman, Darinka Andjelkovic and Banu Oney 53

4. Recognizing morphologically complex words in Turkish

Aydin Yücesan Durgunoğlu 81

5. Word decomposition in Hebrew as a Semitic language

Joseph Shimron 93

6. Morphological representation as a correlation between form and meaning

Marcus Taft 113

7. A supralexical model for French derivational morphology

Hélène Giraudo and Jonathan Grainger 139

8. Parsing and semantic opacity

Robert Schreuder, Cristina Burani, and Harald Baayen 159

9. Effects of sublexical frequency and meaning in prefixed words

Harold T. Nefs, Egbert M.H. Assink, and Paul P.N.A. Knuijt 191

10. Morphological parsing and morphological structure

Gary Libben 221

11. Morpheme-based lexical reading: Evidence from pseudoword naming

Cristina Burani and Alessandro Laudanna 241

12. Word reading processes in adult learners

John P. Sabatini 265

13. Reading aloud polysyllabic words

Ludovic Ferrand and Juan Segui 295

14. Homophonous regular verb forms with a morphographic spelling: Spelling errors as a window on the mental lexicon and working memory

Dominiek Sandra 315

Index 331

VIRGINIA MANN AND MARIA SINGSON

LINKING MORPHOLOGICAL KNOWLEDGE TO ENGLISH DECODING ABILITY: LARGE EFFECTS OF LITTLE SUFFIXES

1. INTRODUCTION

It has long been known that an awareness of how letters correspond to speech sounds (or phones) is crucial for a child to learn to read English (Adams, 1990; Bradley & Bryant, 1985; Liberman, 1982; Mann, 1998; Perfetti, 1985). This allows young decoders of the English orthography to gain the insight that strings of letters, like *b-i-g* and *d-o-g*, can be sounded out and synthesized into words. A simplistic or 'shallow' phonemic decoding strategy, which ascribes one phoneme to each grapheme, is beneficial when the words to be decoded are orthographically regular and phonologically simple. However, by the fifth grade, more than 27 less common and more complex words (such as *methodical* and *angelic*) will be encountered each day (Anglin, 1993; Tyler & Nagy, 1989), and a more complicated decoding strategy must be used.

A more optimal strategy would need to acknowledge that the English orthography involves a linguistically complex system of grapheme-to-phoneme rules. For instance, whereas the vowel a represents one and only one sound in Spanish, it can transcribe several different vowel sounds in English (as the reading of *bake*, *hat*, *car*, and *was* will demonstrate). In English orthography, vowel pronunciation partially depends upon the following consonants.

Many of the context-contingent variations that complicate the relation between individual graphemes and phonemes are linguistically principled. Letters are complexly related to phonemes because letter sequences are transcribing linguistic units at other levels of linguistic structure beyond the mere phoneme. For example, the English orthography appears to transcribe rime-size units, thus vowel pronunciation is more closely linked to syllable final consonants than to syllable initial ones (Treiman, Mullennix, Bijeljac-Babic, & Richmond-Welty, 1995). English also appears to transcribe morphological units as well as phonological ones, as seen in the common spelling of *heal* and *health*, (Chomsky, 1964; Liberman, Liberman, Mattingly & Shankweiler, 1980).

It stands to reason that a deeper sensitivity to the various aspects of linguistic structure being represented by the orthography could be of considerable benefit to the aspiring decoder. Our interest in this paper is in the possibility that morphological awareness goes hand in hand with decoding ability. If we accept the contention that English is truly a morpho-phonological alphabet, we may expect there to be cases where the regular correspondence between graphemes and phonemes is disrupted by correspondences between letter sequence and morphological units (and vice-versa). For example, to preserve the commonality between base and derived forms, the letter *o* in *atom* is pronounced differently than in *atomic*; to preserve the identity of the plural suffix, the letter s represents the phoneme /s/ in *cats* but /z/ in *dogs*. Our question is whether children capitalize on such facts as they seek to read words aloud. From the perspective of a child learning to read, morphology has several benefits. Morphology allows new words to be created by concatenating old words with prefixes and suffixes. If we allow for the fact that new words can be formed through such affixation, a fifth grader's chance of encountering 27 new words per day begins to sound more plausible. It would be uneconomical to expect that the child would memorize how to read 27 new words everyday (as implicated by Seidenberg, 1985, for example). If, as Anglin (1993) suggests, the bulk of new words are morphologically complex, one would think that a better strategy for learning to read these words would involve drawing upon tacit knowledge of how affixes operate in word formation. It is easy to see how knowledge of word formation through derivational morphology might help reading comprehension. For example, understanding a new word (e.g., *excitement*) could be aided by recognizing the previously learned base (*excite*) and realizing that a suffix (*-ment*) has been added. Our point, however, is that morphology can also provide clues to the pronunciation of a written word. To see how morphological knowledge benefits decoding, consider suffixes that can alter the pronunciation of the base words to which they attach. For example, in word pairs *reduce-reduction*, *atom-atomic* and *personal-personality*, the derivational suffixes *-ion*, *-ic*, and *-ity* change the base's stress and pronunciation even though its spelling remains constant. Thus the simple one-to-one relationship between graphemes and phonemes is destroyed and the solution is to take morpheme-sized units into account. But if young readers must take advantage of morpheme-sized units they will need to draw upon their tacit sensitivity to morphology just as they draw on their tacit awareness of phonemes (Carlisle, 1995; Carlisle & Nomanbhoy, 1993; Fowler & Liberman, 1995). Only if they are aware of morpheme-sized units does it becomes possible to realize that attaching certain suffixes to a word can alter the word's pronunciation in regular, predictable ways.

Consider a reader who first encounters the morphologically complex word *reduction*. Although she knows the word *reduce*, what may help her in decoding and pronouncing the derived form is her awareness that the addition of the suffix *-tion* triggers a different phonemic representation of the letter string *uc*. If this is correct, we would expect that performance on another task which requires some sensitivity to morphemes would relate to the child's success in decoding *reduction* and other complex printed words. Our point, then, is that part of learning to decode necessarily involves learning the complex grapheme to phoneme correspondences of English, but another part may involve learning grapheme to morpheme correspondences as well. Morphological word formation can be generalized into two types: inflectional and derivational, both of which are transcribed in the English orthography. Mastery of inflections (e.g., past tense and plural markers) is usually accomplished relatively early in life in a fixed manner (Berko, 1958; Brown, 1973, but see Wiig, Semel & Crouse, 1973), and has been linked to reading progress during the first and second grades (Brittain, 1970; Carlisle, 1995; Carlisle & Nomanbhoy, 1993; Vogel, 1977). Mastery of derivational morphology (e.g., suffixes that do not automatically apply to each member of a syntactic category) seems to involve a longer, more open-ended course (Derwing & Baker, 1979; Nagy, Diakidoy, & Anderson, 1993; Tyler & Nagy, 1989) which coincides with the ages when children are learning to become proficient readers. There are indications that the production of derived forms is related to the ability to read English in the first and second grades (Carlisle, 1995; Carlisle & Nomanbhoy, 1993), middle elementary grades (Fowler & Liberman, 1995), as well as in the junior and high school years (Leong, 1989; Mahony, 1994; Myerson, 1976). In this chapter we review three experiments that offer a more systematic test of the role of derivational morphology in the reading ability of children in the third to sixth grades. We consider different tasks, a broader range of materials (some with more rigid frequency restrictions), and attempt to control for phonological awareness, short-term memory and vocabulary as possible confounds of our morphological measures. Because of derivational morphology's wider span of development, and because derivationally suffixed words begin to frequent the reading texts of fourth and fifth graders, we have focused our queries into the association between morphology and reading on the development of derivational suffix knowledge. We have further confined our study to derivational suffix knowledge as it relates to decoding ability from the third grade through the sixth grade level, since a relation to reading comprehension seemed more of a foregone conclusion. When we restrict ourselves to decoding, when we rule out the possibility that problems with morphological awareness are just a by-product of poor phoneme awareness or poor short-term memory, will we still obtain a relation between morphological awareness and reading ability?

Any study that considers whether morphological awareness is a factor in decoding English, must first consider the relation between knowledge of morphology and other reading-related skills. We hope to make a convincing case for an association between morphological awareness and reading in the later elementary grades when written vocabulary becomes more morphologically sophisticated. However, one possible confound to our case is the fact that being able to separate a derived form into its base and suffix-sized units may require an awareness of syllable- and phoneme-sized units and that phonological awareness is the basis of any link between morphological sensitivity and reading.

Performance on phoneme- and syllable-segmentation tasks is well documented to be related to reading ability, and there have been successful attempts to show that poor sensitivity to derivational morphology relates to reading simply because it also requires phonological awareness. Carlisle and Nomanbhoy (1993; but also see Carlisle, 1995), for example, studied first graders using separate measures of reading, phoneme awareness and morpheme awareness. Their results indicated that the two skills were related to each other and to reading ability, but that, once the contribution of phoneme awareness was considered, morpheme awareness made little additional contribution to the children's variance in reading ability. Using various phoneme and morpheme production tasks, Fowler and Liberman (1995) investigated the levels of phonological and morphological awareness in less-skilled readers aged 7.5 to 9.5 to see whether a low level in each skill correlated with poor reading ability. Their conclusions pointed more to a phonologically based deficit in poor readers, rather than a morphological one. They reasoned that morphological production tasks often draw upon a mixture of skills (ranging from orthographic knowledge to phonological sensitivity and receptive vocabulary) that are well documented to be underdeveloped in poor readers. In their view, the poor readers' low performance on morphological tasks is most likely a consequence of their deficiency in these other skills.

In yet another relevant study which administered separate phoneme- and morpheme-based tests to reading-disabled children between 7.5 and 9.5 years of age, Shankweiler et al (1995) conclude that phonological deficits and deficient production of morphologically-related forms stem from a common weakness in the phonological components of language and not from separable problems with phonology and morphology. A similar line of argument was also favored by Gottardo, Stanovich, & Siegel's (1996) results from their comparison of phonological sensitivity, working memory and syntactic processing in 112 third grade normal readers. In their study, phonological sensitivity was the strongest predictor of reading ability, while syntactic processing contributed to children's reading performance only when effects of working memory and phonological sensitivity were not controlled.

Taken together, these results suggest that any finding that morphological awareness is related to reading must be analyzed with the caveat that phonological awareness is an underlying factor. Thus, in order to investigate the true relationship between morphological awareness and decoding ability, it is clear that the contributions of other reading-related skills, such as phonological awareness, vocabulary knowledge and short-term memory, must be studied in tandem with morphological skill. It could then be resolved whether morphological awareness carries a significant contribution to decoding ability above and beyond the effects of other reading-related factors.

Having made these introductory comments, we now turn to the studies themselves. Three questions are explored in this chapter, by way of three different experiments.

First, we ask whether morphological awareness (in the form of knowledge about derivational suffixes) can account for variance in decoding ability beyond the contributions of vocabulary skill and short-term memory. Second, we examine whether morphological awareness offers an independent contribution to decoding ability above and beyond what is already furnished by phonological awareness and vocabulary. (See Singson, Mahony & Mann (in press) for a full discussion of experiments regarding these questions). Third, we investigate whether knowledge of derivational suffixes predicts decoding ability for morphologically complex words 1) when the relation between a base and its derived form is phonologically complex (opaque) as opposed to transparent, and 2) when the morphologically complex words have low base and/or low surface frequencies.

2. CAN MORPHOLOGICAL AWARENESS ACCOUNT FOR VARIANCE IN DECODING ABILITY ABOVE AND BEYOND THE EFFECTS OF VOCABULARY AND MEMORY?

It is reasonable to caution that tasks which examine morphological skills may depend on some form of short-term or working memory. All morphological awareness tasks require the parsing of multisyllabic words into their base-suffix components, and many further require the subject to evaluate the grammaticality of a sentence in reference to suffixed words. It is therefore conceivable that a child having difficulties holding words and word sequences in memory will also have problems in morphological analysis. Fowler and Liberman (1995) and Gottardo et al (1996) both reported results showing that controlling for memory factors can dissolve the significant contribution of syntactic and morphological knowledge to decoding ability. It is also well documented that poor short term memory factors in poor readers' difficulty with sentence comprehension tasks (see Mann, 1998; Brady & Shankweiler, 1991; Yuill & Oakhill, 1989, for reviews). Our question is whether problems with short-term memory contribute to poor readers' difficulties with tests of morphological awareness.

Another possible confound to studies that draw a relation between morphological skill and reading ability is vocabulary. Children may perform well on tests of morphological skill simply because they know the meaning of the test materials and not because they appreciate the separability of bases from suffixes and the independent meaning of each. To us, there seemed to be two means of controlling for this confound. One is to give vocabulary tests in tandem with the tests of morphological skills and to show that each makes a separate contribution to reading. Another is to use pseudowords that have nonsense bases adjoined to real derivational suffixes (as in bantist vs. bantic, bantly and bantify) and to use a task which requires the child to identify which of these words is a noun, verb, etc. Performance on such materials requires sensitivity to suffixes and their connotations that cannot be achieved by vocabulary knowledge alone. Should it be associated with reading ability, the role of vocabulary knowledge could be dismissed. To pursue whether morphological awareness predicts decoding ability independently from its correlation with short-term memory and vocabulary, we administered (1) the Woodcock Word Identification and Word Attack decoding tests (Woodcock 1973), (2) the WISC-R Vocabulary and Digit Span (Weschler, 1961), and (3) a morphological awareness test to 98 elementary school children. All children were native speakers of English and were without speech or hearing deficiencies.

On the morphological awareness task (as adopted from Mahony, 1994), children chose one of four derived words to best create a grammatical sentence, as in: *The doctor performed the ----operational, operationalize, operation, operate*. Our assumption was that a child's ability to make the correct choice reflects tacit knowledge of which suffix denotes an adjective, as opposed to a noun or verb. Furthermore, to make sure that correct choices were not being made simply because of word familiarity, we also included items that contained derivational forms of a nonsense word, as in: *Have you ever met a: bantist, bantious, bantify, bantize?* In this case, the child must know that *bantist* and not *bantify* fits in the blank because he or she tacitly knows that 1) a noun is required, and 2) that *-ist* is a nominal suffix but *-ize*, -ious and *-ify* are not. Wherever possible, the blanks occurred at the end of the sentence, as that is the position where the answer choices can be emphasized and compared most easily. (For a list of the test materials, see Singson et al, in press). Both real and nonsense versions of the morphological test were given in written and oral formats. The written format was a typical multiple choice test where the children read the sentences silently and circled one of four choices on their test booklet. On the oral format, the experimenter read the sentences aloud four times, each with one of the four choices, while the children followed the text silently on their test booklet. The oral format was implemented to minimize the possibility that poor performance on the morphological task may simply reflect problems with reading the test materials. Each subtest contained ten items consisting of four noun (*-ness*, *-ion/ation*, *-ity*, and *-ist*), three verb (*-ate*, *-ize* and *-ify*), and three adjective (*-ous/ -ious*, *-al* and *-ive*) suffixes.

The children who participated in this experiment can be considered reasonably good representatives of the population of normal readers at their respective grades. The average intelligence at each grade level was slightly above average for their ages based on their Vocabulary and Digit Span scores. Likewise, reading achievement for all groups was at or slightly above grade level as determined by Woodcock test results for both Word Identification and Word Attack.

On the morphological awareness task, the children's performance improved with grade level such that, by sixth grade, the children were correct on over 90% of the real word items and over 75% of the nonsense word items. As grade level increased, the differences between the written and oral presentations became less profound, and children became more able to recognize the syntactic categories of the derivational suffixes in the nonsense materials.

Correlational analyses among the reading and intelligence measures revealed significant relationships ($p < .005$) between Vocabulary and the two decoding tasks (.48 with Word ID, and .32 with Word Attack). Digit Span also correlated with Word Identification (.54) and Word Attack (.49), $p < .01$. The morphological awareness test achieved significant correlation with Word ID (.60), Word Attack (.50), Digit Span (.39), and Vocabulary (.41), $p < .05$. To see whether morphological skills predicted decoding ability independently, we conducted a multiple regression analysis using the following variables. 1) To represent morphological awareness, we used the z-scores of the averaged real and nonsense oral tests only. We chose only the oral format because it placed less demand on decoding ability and memory. 2) Memory was represented by the z-scores of the children's performance on the Digit Span. These two predictors modeled the children's decoding ability, which was represented by the age-restricted z-scores from the combined performance on Word Identification and Word Attack. Our regression of decoding ability, which entered morphological awareness after the memory factor, accounted for 21% of total decoding variance $F(2,95) = 12.91$, $p < .001$). While memory achieved a significant weight ($\beta = .33$, $p < .001$), the most note-worthy of this analysis was the significant contribution of morphological awareness to reading: Above and beyond memory's

16% contribution, morphological awareness contributed an additional 5% to total reading variance ($p < .05$).

Thus, the answer to the question we posed at the beginning of this section is positive. Morphological awareness (as tapped by our oral test of derivational suffix knowledge) offers an independent contribution to third- through sixth- graders' decoding ability. Furthermore, this contribution, although slim, is not merely due to morphological skill's association with short term memory or vocabulary.

The answer being positive, two potential confounds remain to be addressed in our next study. First, the oral format of our morphological awareness test provided a text that the children followed in their test booklet while the experimenter read the sentences aloud. It is therefore possible that children still read the test materials instead of listening to the experimenter. If so, then perhaps it was the act of reading (and, hence, reading ability), not morphological knowledge per se, that drove the correlation between decoding ability and performance on the morphological awareness test. Secondly, the possibility still remains that the relation between morphological awareness and decoding ability is only a byproduct of the association between phonological awareness and morphological awareness. As previous studies noted, controlling for the effects of phonological awareness often destroyed the significant correlation between reading and morphological knowledge in both normal and poor readers (Carlisle & Nomanbhoy 1993; Carlisle 1995; Fowler & Liberman 1995; Gottardo et al 1996). These results, premised by the fact that the English orthography is transcribed in both morphological and phonological units, warrant some caution in claiming that morphological awareness contributes to decoding separately from its relation to phonological knowledge.

3. CAN MORPHOLOGICAL AWARENESS ACCOUNT FOR VARIANCE IN DECODING ABILITY ABOVE AND BEYOND THE EFFECTS OF PHONOLOGICAL AWARENESS AND VOCABULARY?

To examine how morphological awareness is related to both phonological awareness and decoding ability, we conducted another study which administered a strictly oral version of the morphological test described above together with tests of phonological awareness and vocabulary to 101 third- through sixth grade normal readers.

The morphological awareness test was revised so that the oral version no longer provided a text for the children to follow while the experimenter read the sentences aloud. To maintain a low demand on children's verbal short term memory, we transformed each item from a multiple choice 'fill in the blank' task into a grammaticality judgment format. Thus, instead of choosing one among four derived forms of the target word, which required that all four choices be held in working memory, the children simply judged whether or not each sentence they heard sounded "right" or "wrong". For example, *He wants to colonize the moon!* was a "right" sentence, as opposed to the "wrong" sentence, *He wants to colonist the moon!*

Phonological awareness was tested using a phoneme deletion task (adopted from Rosner and Simon, 1971), where children were asked to delete initial, final or middle sounds (or syllables) from 1-3 syllable words. A 'nonse' version was also designed, where children deleted sounds from pseudowords to control any possible performance facilitation due to familiarity with the real words in the original Rosner version. Receptive vocabulary was measured by the Peabody Picture Vocabulary Test-Revised (Dunn & Dunn, 1981). To assess the children's decoding skills, we again used the Word Identification and Word Attack subportions of the Woodcock Reading Mastery Tests (Woodcock, 1973).

When we looked at the correlation among reading, morphological and phonological awareness, we found that morphological awareness (as measured strictly by the oral tasks) correlated significantly with both decoding ability (.34) and phonological knowledge (.24), p <.05. Phonological awareness, on the other hand, achieved a correlation of .44 (p <.05) with reading. To more directly answer whether knowledge of derivational suffixes plays an independent role in decoding ability above and beyond the contributions of phonological skills and vocabulary knowledge, we conducted a series of multiple regressions modeling decoding ability with morphological, phonological, and vocabulary skills. To represent morphological awareness, only the scores from the oral presentations of both real and nonsense versions were averaged and transformed into age-restricted z-scores. Phonological awareness was represented by the z-transforms of the averaged real and nonse raw scores on the phoneme deletion tasks. Vocabulary skill was represented by children's age-restricted PPVT-R scores. Decoding ability, the dependent variable, was again represented by the age-restricted z-scores from the combined raw scores on the Word Identification and Word Attack (Woodcock, 1973).

Table 1. Hierarchical Regressions of Morphological Awareness, Phonological Awareness and Vocabulary

Variables	*r^2 Increase*	*F-value*	*F-sig.*
Order 1			
Phonological Awareness	.25	F(1,99) = 33.09	p < .0000
Morphological Awareness	.09	F(1,99) = 12.80	p < .001
Vocabulary	*.06*	*F(2,98) = 10.16*	*p < .01*
Order 2			
Morphological Awareness	.20	F(1,99) = 24.21	p < .0000
Vocabulary	.11	F(1,99) = 15.18	p < .001
Phonological Awareness	*.09*	*F(1,98) = 13.97*	*p < .001*
Order 3			
Vocabulary	.24	F(1,99) = 31.57	p < .0000
Phonological Awareness	.12	F(1,99) = 18.28	p < .001
Morphological Awareness	*.04*	*F(1,98) = 6.31*	*p < .05*

Table 1 lists the results from three sets of hierarchical regressions, highlighting the amount of independent contribution of each predictor to decoding variance. In the first analysis (Order 1), a simple linear regression of decoding ability by phonological awareness accounted for 25% of reading variance. When entered after vocabulary and morphological awareness (Order 2), phonological awareness continued to significantly account for 9% of the total reading variance ($F(1,98) = 13.07$, $p < .001$). Vocabulary accounted for 24% of the reading variance in a simple linear regression (see Order 3); beyond the influence of phonological and morphological awareness (see Order 1), it contributed an additional 6% to total reading variance ($F(1,98) = 10.16$, $p < .01$). When morphological awareness was entered into a simple linear regression predicting decoding ability (Order 2), it obtained an r^2 of .20. Beyond the effect of phonological awareness (Order 1), morphological knowledge contributed significantly to reading (.09 increase in r^2, ($F(1,99) = 12.80$, $p < .001$). Order 3 offers a direct answer to our search for a separate contribution of morphological awareness (as indexed by knowledge of derivational suffixes) to decoding: When entered after vocabulary and phonological awareness, morphological skill remained a significant contributor to reading, accounting for 4% of the total reading variance, $p < .05$. Thus, at least for this particular sample, the contribution of morphological awareness (though slim) cannot be ignored.

We also performed a series of hierarchical regressions on separate grade levels in order to examine the trend of suffix awareness development as age increased (Figure 1).

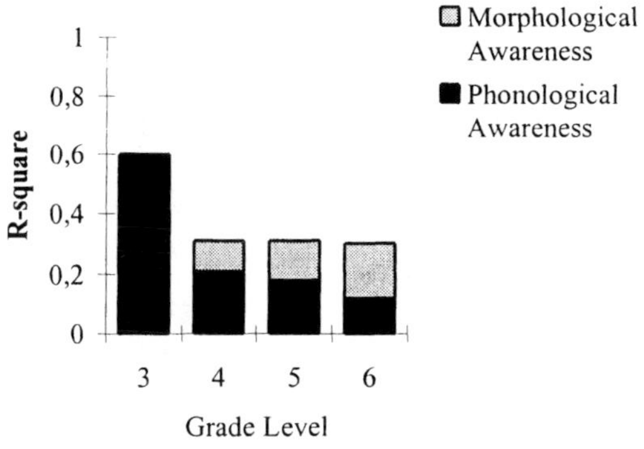

Figure 1. The relative contribution of phonological and morphological awareness to decoding ability as a function of age.

We found that: 1) Phonological awareness gradually loses its contribution to reading variance as grade level increases (ceiling effects cannot explain this result as even the oldest children made errors). In fact, when entered in a hierarchical regression after the effects of morphological awareness were controlled, phonological skill's contribution to total reading variance failed to reach significance beyond the third grade level. 2) The contribution of morphological awareness (as measured by the oral morphological tasks) to reading, on the other hand, takes an increasing trend beginning in the fourth grade level (right at the time when morphologically complex words begin to enter children's vocabulary). Above and beyond the effects of phonological awareness, performance on the oral grammaticality judgment task offers a significant contribution to reading in grade levels 5 ($F(1,24) = 4.49$, $p < .05$) and 6 ($F(1,23) = 5.85$, $p < .05$).

Thus far, we have answered some basic questions: We have shown that there is a correlation between performance on our test of derivational morphology and mid-to-late elementary school children's ability to learn to decode English. We have shown that knowledge of derivational morphology offered an independent contribution to reading ability, above and beyond the contributions of memory, phonological awareness and vocabulary. Our test of morphological knowledge (i.e., the oral tasks) focused primarily on the syntactic function of suffixes. It was administered orally to remove any immediate contribution of decoding ability. Measures of phonemic awareness and vocabulary knowledge, both of which overlapped substantially with morphological knowledge, were entered into the regression equation first. With these controls in place, we still found that morphological awareness predicted significant unique variance in children's decoding performance.

An interesting feature of our results was the indication that the relative contribution of phoneme vs. morpheme awareness is age-dependent. The contribution of phonological awareness was quite strong in the third grade, but gradually faded away, leaving in its wake a steady role of morphological awareness that persists as the reader matures. In fact, in our sample of fifth and sixth graders, the oral tests of morphological skill significantly correlated with reading ability ($p < .05$), whereas performance on the Rosner-based tests of phonological awareness did not.

However, doubt could still be cast as to whether morphological awareness truly, and not just statistically, contributes to decoding ability. Four percent of decoding variance is not a lot, and perhaps could be accounted for by many reading-related skills other than morphological knowledge. Statistically, we could confidently claim that we did control for vocabulary and phonological awareness; yet we could not quite claim that our morphological awareness measure did not heavily draw upon phonological and vocabulary skills. We concede that considerable morphological knowledge most heavily rides on phonological awareness, and that poor readers' difficulty with morphology is at least in part the expression of some phonological limitation (Fowler & Liberman, 1995, Shankweiler et al, 1995). Our regression analysis found that, when morphological awareness was coupled with phonological awareness, its contribution to decoding ability jumped from 4% to 16%. Unfortunately, we could only probe this relationship through statistical analyses, as neither of our reading and morphological awareness stimuli was designed for that purpose. One way to study the dependence of morphological awareness on phonological skill is to compose a morphological awareness task that uses phonologically "opaque" (or shifted) vs. phonologically "transparent" (or neutral) derived words. Performance on the two types of words can then be compared (as Shankweiler et al did in their study) to see how phonological complexity affects morphological processing. Our strategy is to investigate whether, among a population of normal readers, morphological awareness (measured by oral grammaticality judgments) correlates with decoding phonologically shifted words differently than decoding neutral words. This directly addresses the issue of whether morphological knowledge's prediction of decoding ability is simply due to its association with phonological awareness: If performance on the morphological awareness task significantly predicts performance on decoding the phonologically opaque items but not the transparent ones, then it can be taken as clearer evidence that the contribution of morphological knowledge to decoding is resultant of its relation to phonological awareness.

In the experiments that we have reported, we considered vocabulary as a possible correlate of decoding ability, but also as a confound due to its relation to morphological skill. In the study at hand, vocabulary (as measured by the PPVT) predicted 6% of the total decoding variance ($F(2,98) = 10.16$, $p < .01$), and correlated significantly with morphological awareness (.32, $p < .05$). We mentioned earlier how a reader might rely on his or her morphological skills to read less common, unfamiliar words. For example, already knowing the word *ocean*, a child reading *oceanic* for the first time might notice its familiar base and, thus, parse the derived form into its constituent morphemes. Yet, as with phonological knowledge, it is not clear how the relation between morphological awareness and vocabulary skill feeds into decoding ability. Do readers parse all morphologically complex words into their morphemic units, or do they reserve this strategy for when they encounter unfamiliar suffixed words only? Does parsing bases and suffixes actually help in producing a correct pronunciation, or is it unrelated to decoding ability? One strategy for resolving these questions is to compare how morphological awareness relates with highly frequent vs. infrequent derived words, as well as with words containing frequent vs. infrequent bases. What might we learn from the result of a study that compares the correlations between performance on a morphological awareness measure and decoding derivational forms that vary in word frequency? If derivational words with high frequency bases correlate with morphological awareness differently than low frequency-based words, then children must be performing morphological analysis when they decode words by paying attention to the bases, and their reading is affected by the base word's frequency. On the other hand, it is possible that children do not decompose morphologically complex words, familiar or not. If this were the case, then it would be interesting to see if performance on the morphological awareness task still correlates with decoding morphologically complex words of varying surface frequency. This leads us to the third and final question and the study it inspired.

4. WHAT HAPPENS TO THE RELATION BETWEEN DECODING AND MORPHOLOGICAL AWARENESS AS WORDS ARE VARIED IN FREQUENCY AND PHONOLOGICAL COMPLEXITY?

This inquiry elaborates on our previous findings that morphological awareness, as measured by oral grammaticality judgments, predicted decoding ability in the mid- through upper- elementary school grades. Now, we turn to stimuli that manipulate phonological and vocabulary factors in a decoding task in the hope of clarifying how morphological awareness relates to decoding accuracy. The correlation between these different factors and the morphological awareness task are compared in a recent project that we will be reporting for the first time in this chapter.

Evidence that children do not always parse morphologically complex words has been put forth in a recent study of elementary school readers: Carlisle (in press) looked into how third and fifth graders decoded morphologically complex words that differed in their surface frequency and phonological complexity. To test if children parse the base morpheme from derived words (e.g., *happy* from *happiness*), she gave them two lists of suffixed words that differed in their surface frequencies (high vs. low), but not in base frequency (both lists had high frequency bases). Similar performance on the two types of words was taken to mean that children do perceive the bases of derived words, and that knowledge of the word base does help in decoding. However, Carlisle found that the children performed less well in decoding words with low surface frequency (79%) than those with high surface frequency (95%), which suggests that children do not readily perceive the base morphemes of derived words even when those bases are highly familiar. In fact, even assuming that the children did acknowledge the base morphemes, it remains unclear that they knew how to use such information to decode the derived words.

To test the effect of phonological complexity on morphological processing and decoding, Carlisle created a third list of high surface frequency words whose base pronunciations were altered by the attachment of suffixes (i.e., opaque words). She then contrasted the children's performance on this list with performance on the previous list of high surface frequency words where base pronunciation remained the same (i.e., transparent). Worse performance on the opaque words could be attributed to phonological complexity (Carlisle, 1988; Fowler & Liberman, 1995; Leong, 1989; Tyler & Nagy, 1989). Carlisle found that children were significantly less accurate in reading opaque words (86%) than transparent words (95%). Thus, a phonological (pronunciation) change of the base in its derived form seems to affect children's performance in decoding morphologically complex words.

However, we cannot infer from Carlisle's work that word bases are not being used when children decode transparent derived words because only words with high frequency bases were considered. If a similar pattern of performance emerges when low frequency base words are included, then it lends a stronger evidence that children do not make use of the bases in derived words when decoding. The same point can be said about the comparison of transparent and opaque words: It is difficult to claim that only phonological opacity and transparency contributed to decoding performance because only high-frequency base/derived forms were compared. (In fact, performance on the transparent words reached ceiling level, which cautions that perhaps word recognition-- not decoding-- was tested). The purpose of our newest study was to ascertain the role of derivational suffix knowledge in decoding morphologically complex words that vary in phonological opacity and stem/derived frequency. It delves into the issue of the covariance between morphological skill and phonological and vocabulary knowledge by directly manipulating the decoding test. It also extends past explorations (see Carlisle, in press) in two ways: First, it includes words with low base frequencies. Second, it attempts to model the contributions of morphological awareness, phonological awareness and vocabulary to decoding morphologically complex words.

4.1 Method

4.1.1 Participants

One hundred fifty-three 3rd- through 6th-graders from elementary schools in Newport Beach, California participated in this study with written consent from their parents. All were native speakers of English and free of any reading or speech disabilities. Forty-nine children were in grade 3 (24 girls and 25 boys, with mean age of 8 years; 10 months); 38 were in grade 4 (25 girls and 13 boys, with mean age of 10;1); 38 were in grade 5 (18 girls and 20 boys, with mean age of 11;4); and 28 were in grade 6 (15 girls and 13 boys, with mean age of 12;4). All testing was completed between late March and early June of the same academic year.

4.1.2 Materials

As in our previous studies, vocabulary, phonological awareness and morphological awareness were again measured by the PPVT-R (Dunn & Dunn, 1981), the Rosner (real and nonse) tests (Rosner & Simon, 1971; Singson et al, in press), and the oral (real and nonse) derivational suffix tests, respectively.

Decoding skill was measured using a Morpheme Reading List (MRL), which consisted of 39 derivationally suffixed words factored into the following design: Phonological complexity (20 Transparent vs. 19 Opaque), base or stem frequency (20 High vs. 19 Low) and frequency of the derived form (17 High vs. 22 Low) (see Appendix for a list of all materials). Word frequencies were determined using a vocabulary corpus by Carroll, Davies and Richman (1971). "High derived" words were defined to occur more than 70 times per million in their derived form; "low derived" words occurred less than once per million words. The "high base" words contained bases that occurred 70 or more times per million in their base form, the "low base" words contained bases that occurred less than one time per million in their base form. Ten words (printed in 24-point font) were presented per page, and items were randomized. All participants read the printed words aloud, while the experimenter recorded their pronunciation on a score sheet and audiotape.

4.1.3 Procedure

Testing in the elementary schools was completed in two days in a small, quiet room. The reading, vocabulary and phonological tests were given to individual children on the first day; the second day administered the morphological awareness test to groups according to grade level.

4.2 Results

4.2.1 Decoding the Morpheme Reading List

Overall, decoding scores on the Morpheme Reading List (MRL) increased as grade level increased, ranging from 54% accuracy in third graders to 84% by sixth grade.

Below are summaries of results on the MRL according to stimulus type (see Table 2).

Table 2. Accuracy on decoding morphologically complex words

Percent Correct	*Grade 3* (n=49)	*Grade 4* (n=38)	*Grade 5* (n=38)	*Grade 6* (n=28)
Phonological Complexity				
Opaque	55.7	54.3	75.3	90.4
Transparent	61.3	67.3	75.7	82.5
Word Frequency				
Base				
High	65.8	71.2	80.1	89.0
Low	48.8	57.3	69.7	82.7
Derived				
High	77.3	88.6	95.5	98.8
Low	43.3	46.7	60.1	76.7

4.2.2 Opaque vs. Transparent Words

An ANOVA of Repeated Measures revealed a main effect of opacity ($F(1,149) = 12.75$, $p <.001$), a main effect of grade ($F(3,149) = 18.31$, $p <.001$), as well as a significant interaction ($F(3,149) = 4.76$, $p <.001$). On the transparent words, performance improved at a steady rate (about 10%) as grade level increased, reaching over 80% accuracy by the sixth grade. Scheffe's post hoc test of performance on the transparent words found significant differences among the different grade levels ($p <.05$), except between 5th and 6th grade. The opaque words, on the other hand, were difficult for the third and fourth grades (reaching only about 55% accuracy) and did not approach the same performance on the transparent words until the fifth grade, when accuracy reached 75% and over 90% after another year. Scheffe's post hoc comparison test revealed significant differences only between the lower (3 and 4) vs. upper grades (5 and 6), $p <.05$.

4.2.3 High vs. Low Frequency Bases

An ANOVA of Repeated Measures revealed main effects of base frequency ($F(1,149) = 950.95$, $p <.001$) and grade ($F(3,149) = 18.41$, $p <.001$), but no significant interaction ($F(3,149) = 1.75$, $p <.16$). Performance on both low and high frequency based words improved with age, although low frequency based words were consistently more difficult. The younger participants were significantly worse in decoding words with low frequency bases ($p <.05$), suggesting that word bases already affect decoding even in the early elementary grades.

4.2.4 High vs. Low Frequency Derived Words

An ANOVA of Repeated Measures revealed main effects of derived word frequency ($F(1,149) = 108.58$, $p < .001$) and grade ($F(3,149) = 18.53$, $p < .001$), as well as a significant grade-word frequency interaction ($F(3,149) = 9.35$, $p < .001$). Most notable was the performance on derived forms with low frequency. While performance on decoding the high frequency words started at 77% in the early grades, and approached ceiling level by 5th grade, performance on the low frequency words was more varied. Grades 3 and 4 achieved low accuracy (43% and 47%, respectively), while grades 5 and 6 could correctly decode only 60% and 77% of the words. Scheffe's post hoc comparison test yielded significant differences between younger and older children, $p < .05$.

Table 3. Accuracy on reading, vocabulary and linguistic tasks

	Percent Correct			
Grade:	*3*	*4*	*5*	*6*
Variables	(n=49)	(n=38)	(n=38)	(n=28)
Reading				
Morpheme Decoding List	53.9	68.3	77.2	84.3
Phonological Awareness				
Real	61.5	66.5	76.5	83.1
Nonse	58.7	60.4	67.9	77.4
Morphological Awareness				
Oral Real	68.6	78.8	84.6	95.3
Oral Nonse	33.8	43.7	52.7	73.6
Vocabulary				
PPVT-R (raw)	99.6	110.4	120.9	125.2
SAT-verbal				

4.2.5 Error Analysis of the Morpheme Reading List

A list of six criteria was developed to categorize the errors that the subjects made in decoding the MRL. Type 1 grouped "guessing" errors, or errors that were made when the subject was clearly guessing how to read the word, and offered another word or a phrase as a solution (e.g., *publicize* was read as *pick us up*). Type 2 included errors that had both the base and suffix wrong, but is distinguishable from Type 1 because the subject in this case resorted to a nonsense word without a suffix instead of a whole word replacement (e.g., *completeness* became *clapeney*). Type 3 errors were committed when the subject attached the correct suffix to the wrong base (e.g., *careful* was read as *creeful*). Error types 4 and 5 elicited the correct base, but either omitted the suffix (e.g., *methodical* became *method*) or used a different suffix (e.g., *imaginable* became *imagination*) and double affixations (e.g., *methodical* became methododical). Error type 6 registered pronunciation errors (e.g., methodical was read *method-ickal*). Most errors were Type 1 (17.8%), Type 3 (21.4%) and

Type 6 (23%). Children did not often volunteer a nonsense word as a decoding solution (7%), nor was it common to decode the base and disregard (4.3%) or replace (5%) the suffix.

4.2.6 Morphological Awareness

As seen in our previous experiments (see Singson et al, in press), the real word version of the morphological awareness task was easier than the nonsense version. The children's scores ranged from 69% to 95% on the real word items (M = 81%), and from 34% to 74% on the nonsense word items (M = 49%).

4.2.7 Phonological Awareness

In general, scores were slightly lower on the nonsense word phoneme deletion task than on the real word version. The third graders (i.e., the least experienced decoders) performed with only 61.5% (real) and 58.7% (nonse) accuracy, showing no effect of real vs. nonse ($F(1,36) = 1.48$, $p < .19$).

4.2.8 Vocabulary

The receptive vocabulary scores (as measured by the PPVT-R) for children ranged from 99.6 to 125.2, which is normal for third- through sixth- graders.

4.2.9 Regression Analyses

The following regression analyses investigated whether decoding different types of words required different patterns of contribution from morphological awareness (as measured by the oral derivational suffix test), phonological awareness (i.e., phoneme deletion) and vocabulary skill (as measured by the PPVT-R). The data are pooled across age to simplify the presentation and maximize the sample size, as is optimal in regression analyses.

4.2.10 Transparent vs. Opaque Words

The children's performance on phonological awareness tasks predicted the majority of the reading variance ($r^2_{transparent} = .49$; $r^2_{opaque} = .40$, $p < .001$). Vocabulary was not a significant predictor of reading either opaque or transparent words, while morphological awareness predicted both types of words, but achieved significance only in the case of opaque words ($r^2_{transparent} = .15$, $p < .07$; $r^2_{opaque} = .17$, $p < .05$).

4.2.11 High vs. Low Frequency Bases

Phonological awareness remained to be the most significant predictor of decoding words in children whether our analysis considered high or low frequency bases ($r^2_{hi\text{-}base} = .45$, $p < .001$; $r^2_{lo\text{-}base} = .42$, $p < .05$). Vocabulary and morphological awareness exerted equal weights in predicting high frequency bases although neither was significant ($r^2_{hi\text{-}base} = .14$, $p_{voc} < .06$; $p_{morph} < .10$). In the case of low frequency bases, vocabulary accounted for 8% of total reading variance ($p < .30$), while morphological awareness accounted for 18% ($p < .03$).

Table 4. Multiple regressions of Morphological Awareness, Phonological Awareness and Vocabulary, predicting the decoding of words that are varied in frequency and linguistic complexity

Variables r^2	*Beta*	*t-value*		*Sig.*
Opaque Words	.34, p <.000			
Vocabulary		.14	1.76	p < .08
Phoneme		.40	5.20	p < .01*
Morpheme		*.17*	*1.99*	*p < .05**
Transparent Words	.38, p <.000			
Vocabulary		.08	1.01	p < .31
Phoneme		.49	6.47	p < .01*
Morpheme		*.15*	*1.80*	*p < .07*
High Frequency Bases	.36, p <.000			
Vocabulary		.14	1.89	p < .06
Phoneme		.45	5.86	p < .01*
Morpheme		*.14*	*1.63*	*p < .10*
Low Frequency Bases	.33, p <.000			
Vocabulary		.08	1.03	p < .30
Phoneme		.42	5.43	p < .01*
Morpheme		*.18*	*2.14*	*p < .03**
High Frequency Derived	.38, p <.000			
Vocabulary		.08	1.01	p < .31
Phoneme		.49	6.47	p < .000*
Morpheme		*.15*	*1.80*	*p < .07*
Low Frequency Derived	.31, p <.000			
Vocabulary		-.01	-.16	p < .87
Phoneme		.46	5.83	p < .000*
Morpheme		*.16*	*1.85*	*p < .07*

4.2.12 High vs. Low Frequency Derived Words

Phonological awareness was the only significant predictor of decoding high and low frequency derived words in children ($r^2_{\text{hi-derived}} = .45$, $p < .001$; $r^2_{\text{lo-derived}} = .42$, $p < .05$). Vocabulary placed little weight in predicting high frequency derived words ($r^2 = .08$, $p < .31$), and accounted for no variance when the derived form had low frequency. Morphological awareness, like vocabulary was an insignificant predictor of derived words ($r^2_{\text{hi-derived}} = .15$, $p < .07$, $r^2_{\text{lo-derived}} = .16$, $p < .07$).

4.3 Discussion

In this experiment, we wanted to see whether the contribution of morphological awareness to decoding ability is affected by the phonological complexity and frequency of the words to be read. A special decoding test (MRL) was constructed so that the words varied in the frequency of base and derived forms, and also in phonological complexity. The predictor variables (vocabulary, phoneme deletion, and derivational suffix tests) were carefully chosen, and were found to correlate to decoding ability in previous experiments (Mahony, Singson & Mann, in press; Singson et al, in press). The investigation was once again carried out on third through sixth grade elementary school-aged children (i.e., the age range when morphological awareness seems to flourish).

Our findings mirror those of past research: A steady rise in successful decoding of transparent words, whereas accuracy in reading phonologically opaque words dramatically improved from 4rth to 5th grade. This sudden increase in accuracy of reading opaque words could reasonably follow from Anglin's (1993) observation that children's reading materials contain more morphologically complex words around the 5th grade.

Decoding also became easier as word frequency increased. Consistent with Carlisle's (in press) findings, the younger children in our study did not seem to refer to the familiar (i.e., high frequency) bases when decoding morphologically complex words, and had more difficulty reading words with low surface frequency. However, our innovation was to also hold the frequency of the derived form constant and to consider words that had high vs. lower frequency bases. In this case we found that children decoded low- frequency based words less successfully than comparable words with higher frequency bases, allowing us to arrive at a slightly different conclusion: Children are referring to word bases by the third grade. Results from our analysis of the children's decoding errors substantiate this conclusion. We found that a good portion of the children's errors involved getting the suffix right, but erring on the base pronunciation (21.4%). It is possible that such errors may have been driven by the phonological complexity (i.e., the shifted base vowel, etc.) and not the base frequency of the words, but we had controlled for phonological complexity as well. It is more likely that both phonological complexity and base-word frequency play a role because the child is trying to recover the bases of derived forms. If words are not being parsed according to bases and suffixes, then the phonological opacity of the base should not pose a problem to the reader. Likewise, if bases were not being considered in decoding words, then the lower performance on low surface frequency words could be well explained by simple word recognition factors and not by morphological awareness per se.

To directly answer our inquiry about the nature of the relation between morphological awareness and decoding ability, we highlight two aspects of our linear regression results: With the effects of vocabulary and phonological skills controlled, morphological awareness significantly predicted decoding ability only when the words were 1) opaque (i.e., phonologically complex) or 2) had low frequency bases.

The difficulty of opaque (as opposed to transparent) words points out that children's differences in morphological analysis are more likely to play a role in decoding accuracy when the base pronunciation is phonologically encrypted by the morpho-phonological rules that follow from the addition of a suffix. For some this will be viewed as support for the view that the role of morphological awareness in reading is phonologically driven (Carlisle & Nomanbhoy, 1993; Fowler & Liberman, 1995; Shankweiler et al., 1995). However, an alternative view follows from the recognition that the ability to apply the appropriate morpho-phonological rules is contingent upon stripping of the suffix. A failure to recognize the suffix would not matter for transparent suffixes which simply adjoin to a base and make no changes in pronunciation. But failure would be critical for opaque words in which you must recognize the suffix in order to know what rules apply.

A similar logic can account for the difficulty of low-frequency based words. We have argued that morphologically complex words are parsed into a base + suffix when they are being decoded. When a young decoder encounters a suffixed word with an unfamiliar base, the best (and perhaps the only) place to look for hints as to how to decode the word would be the suffix. Inspection of the suffix helps because the addition of that suffix may reconfigure the pronunciation of the base, and the reader would not know how to adjust her pronunciation of the whole word unless that suffix is acknowledged. Indeed, in Carlisle's (in press) study, it was observed that 5th graders tended to first decode a suffixed word phonetically. They seemed to restart and correct their pronunciation of the word only after they have realized that it ended with a suffix. We have also found that one of the most common mistakes in our own data was misreading the bases, even though the attached suffixes were read correctly. Both instances (i.e., Carlisle's observation and ours) suggest that suffixes are recognized and paid importance when decoding words. Part of our findings also hints that parsing words into their base and suffix components sometimes takes precedence over analyzing just the suffix and realizing fully its effects on a word's pronunciation. Even though our test of morphological awareness failed to significantly predict the decoding of morphologically complex words with high frequency bases, we speculate that the words were still parsed into bases and suffixes. However, since the bases were highly familiar, the decoder may not have had to rely on the information conveyed by the suffix to come up with a pronunciation. We informally analyzed the 23% mispronunciation errors in our children's data, and noticed that most of them were on words with opaque high frequency bases. Thus, paying more importance to the base + suffix parsing of a word than to the informational value of the suffix seems to be a more favored strategy in decoding high frequency based words, even though it may not always work (as in decoding phonologically opaque bases).

4.4 General Discussion

We started this chapter with a simple question: Does morphological awareness contribute to decoding ability? We answered this question positively in three different studies. Although morphological awareness accounted for a small variance in decoding ability, it is statistically significant above and beyond the well-known reading-related factors of phonological awareness, vocabulary knowledge and short-term memory. Moreover, we found that, as young readers mature, the role of phonological awareness in decoding decreases at the same time that morphological awareness' contribution increases. By the fifth grade, children's decoding ability is best predicted by their morphological skills, not their phonological awareness. These results - both the independent contribution of morphological awareness to reading and the apparent spurt of morphological awareness around the fifth grade - are also noted in Carlisle's and Mahony et al's (in press) studies of how morphological awareness compared to other reading-related skills (Carlisle, in press; Mahony et al, in press; Singson et al, in press).

As we mentioned earlier, studies of normal and poor readers before us had suggested that the contributions of morphological ability are highly overlapping with those of phonological skills and memory (Carlisle et al, 1993; Gottardo et al, 1996; Shankweiler et al, 1995). Carlisle and Nomanbhoy (1993) investigated the overlap of phoneme and morpheme awareness in first graders by giving separate phoneme and morpheme awareness tests. Their results indicated that morpheme awareness (measured by production of derivational and inflectional suffixes) was correlated with their measure of phoneme awareness but accounted for only an additional 4% of the variance in reading ability above and beyond the 37% of variance accounted for by phoneme awareness.

Shankweiler et al (1995) compared 7.5 to 9.5-year old learning-disabled children and normally reading controls on the Rosner phonological awareness test and a morpheme awareness test that was analogous to the production of derivational and inflectional morphemes developed by Carlisle and her colleagues (1993). Performance on both the phoneme and morpheme awareness tests was deficient among reading-disabled children, and was highly correlated with decoding ability. However, when they analyzed phonologically shifted (*five/fifth*) vs. unshifted (*four/ fourth*) words in their morphological test, they found that the shifted items resulted in greater differences between the performance of reading-disabled children and the other groups. It was further the case that when the effects of age and IQ were controlled, children's production of derivational and inflectional morphemes accounted for only 5% of the variance above and beyond that accounted for by phoneme awareness. The authors interpret these two pieces of evidence as implying that the poor readers' problems with phoneme and morpheme awareness both stem from a deficient phonological awareness.

Note that the results from our regression analysis were virtually identical to those in Carlisle and Nomanbhoy (1993) and in Shankweiler et al (1995). Although our morphological measure exclusively focused on derivational morphology and on recognition and not production, we, too, found that morpheme awareness significantly correlated with phoneme awareness. Our analysis controlled for the effects of vocabulary knowledge whereas Shankweiler et al (1995) controlled for age and IQ, yet our results were similar. When we controlled for performance on the phonological awareness and vocabulary tasks, we found that morphological awareness accounted for 4% of decoding variance; Carlisle et al found 4%, and Shankweiler et al found 5%. If what we had found was a mere statistical artifact, it would be hard to explain how at least three studies (Singson et al's, Carlisle et al's and Shankweiler et al's) arrived with the same (4 - 5%) contribution of morphological awareness to decoding ability. Rather, it would be more parsimonious to conclude that morphological awareness has a small but reliable contribution to decoding ability. Our most recent study delved more deeply into the interactions between morphological skills and phonological skills and vocabulary. Varying the phonological complexity and base/surface frequencies of the words to be decoded, we found that morphological awareness significantly predicted decoding only when the base pronunciation was altered by the attachment of a suffix, or when base frequency was low. We took such results as evidence that 1) parsing bases from suffixes occurs when young readers decode morphologically complex words, and that 2) tacit morphological awareness tasks (like our oral derivational suffix test) are sensitive to these phonological and word frequency effects. In particular, this new study gives evidence that suffixes play a valuable role in reading the English orthography because they provide clues to changes in grapheme-to-phoneme correspondence. In fact, when suffixes receive less attention than bases (e.g., in high-frequency based words), the decoder may be more likely to err in pronouncing the base portion of the morphologically complex word.

From the beginning of our inquiry, we have acknowledged that morphological awareness may feed upon phonological awareness, short term memory and vocabulary knowledge (in tune with Carlisle & Nomanbhoy, 1993; Fowler & Liberman, 1995; Gottardo et al, 1996; and Shankweiler et al., 1995). What we would like to emphasize, in closing, is that the English orthography is morpho-phonologically encoded, and young readers are sensitive to this fact. Our studies and those of Carlisle (1988; in press) and Mahony et al (in press) have shown the increasing role of derivational morphology in decoding skill during the mid-to-late elementary school years. This, we all argue, is consistent with the fact that vocabulary increases in this age range reflect an increase in morphologically sophisticated words (Anglin, 1993). That reliance upon morphological skills may be an even more widespread phenomenon in reading acquisition is suggested by two recent studies with beginning readers and preliterate children. In studying the spellings made by five and six-year-old children, Treiman and Cassar (1996) draw upon sensitivity to morphology in order to explain why children are more likely to preserve the *n* in *loaned* than in *hound*. In a study of children's initial hypotheses about how print represents spoken language, Byrne (1996) notes that pre-literate children more readily grasp the notion of grapheme-to-morpheme transcription (i.e., the plural /s/ in *bats*) than that of grapheme-to-phoneme transcription (i.e., the phonemic /s/ in *bus*). From an early age, then, it would appear that children are willing and able to map the English orthography onto the morphemes of their language. This willingness comes to their advantage as they tackle the decoding of their more and more sophisticated vocabularies.

5. APPENDIX

MORPHEME READING LIST

Word Frequency counts are in parentheses. High Frequency = 70/million or higher
Low Frequency = 1/million or lower

Transparent words

High base, High derived
- basic (85)
- careful (76)
- movement (77)
- quickly (200)
- addition (104)

High base, Low derived
- completeness (.18)
- imaginable (.25)
- quicken (.11)
- deadness (1)
- equalize (.30)
- corrective (.24)

Low base, Low derived
- seepage (.11)
- perplexity (.21)
- sparkly (.16)
- deceitful (.18)
- compliance (.25)

Low base, High derived
- equipment (70)
- information (135)
- critical (56)

Opaque words

High base, High derived
- written (176)
- familiar (70)
- easily (124)
- natural (134)

High base, Low derived
- publicize (.40)
- studious (.85)
- methodical (.24)
- oceanic (.56)
- periodic (.20)

Low base Low derived
- narration (.77)
- initiation (.12)
- inhibition (.15)
- conspiracy (.85)
- confidant (.11)
- diversify (1)

Low base, High derived
- situation (65)
- solution (60)
- population (70)
- opposite (101)

6. REFERENCES

Adams, M. J. (1990). *Beginning to read: thinking and learning about print.* Cambridge, MA: M.I.T. Press

Anglin, J. M. (1993). Vocabulary development: A morphological analysis. *Monographs of the Society for Research in Child Development*, 58, 1-166.

Berko, J. (1958). The child's learning of English morphology. *Word*, 14, 150-177.

Bradley, L. & Bryant, P. (1985). *Rhyme and reasons in reading and spelling.* Ann Arbor, MI: University of Michigan Press.

Brady, S. A., & Shankweiler, D. P. (Eds.). (1991). *Phonological processes in literacy.* Hillsdale, NJ: Lawrence Erlbaum Associates.

Brittain, M. M. (1970). Inflectional performance and early reading achievement. *Reading Research Quarterly*, 6, 34-48.

Brown, R. (1973). *A first language: The early stages.* Cambridge, MA: Harvard University Press.

Byrne, B. (1996) The learnability of the alphabetic principle: Children's initial hypotheses about how print represents spoken language. *Applied Psycholingistics*, 9, 247-266.

Carlisle, J. F. (1988). Knowledge of derivational morphology and spelling ability in fourth, sixth and eighth graders. *Applied Psycholinguistics*, 9, 247-266.

Carlisle, J. F. (1995). Morphological awareness and early reading achievement. In L. Feldman's (Ed.) *Morphological aspects of language processing.* Lawrence Erlbaum Associates, Inc, Hillsdale, NJ, p. 189-209.

Carlisle, J. F. (In press). Awareness of morphological structure and meaning: Impact on reading. *Reading & Writing.*

Carlisle, J. F., & Nomanbhoy, D. M. (1993). Phonological and morphological awareness in first graders. *Applied Psycholinguistics*, 14, 177-195.

Carroll, J. B., Davies, P., & Richman, B. (1971). *Word frequency book.* New York: American Heritage.

Chomsky, N. (1964) Comments for Project Literacy Meeting, Project Literacy report no. 2, Reprinted in M. Lester (Ed.) *Readings in applied transformational grammar* (pp. 1- 8). New York: Holt Reinhard and Winston.

Derwing, B. L., & Baker, W. J. (1979). Recent research on the acquisition of English morphology. In P. Fletcher & M. Garman (Eds.), *Language acquisition: Studies in first language development* (pp. 209-222). Cambridge: Cambridge University Press.

Dunn, L., & Dunn, L. (1981). *Peabody Picture Vocabulary Test*: Revised. Circle Pines, MN: American Guidance Service.

Fowler, A., & Liberman, I. (1995). The role of phonology and orthography in morphological awareness. In L. Feldman's (Ed.) *Morphological aspects of language processing.* Lawrence Erlbaum Associates, Inc, Hillsdale, NJ, p. 157-188.

Gottardo, A., Stanovich, K., & Siegel, L. (1996). The relationships between phonological sensitivity, syntactic processing, and verbal working memory in the reading performance of third-grade children. *Journal of Experimental Child Psychology*, 63, 563-582.

Leong, C. K. (1989). Productive knowledge of derivational rules in poor readers. *Annals of Dyslexia*, 39,94-115.

Liberman, I. Y. (1982). A language-oriented view of reading and its disabilities. In H. Mykelbust (Ed.), *Progress in learning disabilities*, 5. New York: Grune and Stratton.

Liberman, I. Y., Liberman, A. M., Mattingly, I. G., & Shankweiler, D. (1980). Orthography and the beginning reader. In J. Kavanagh and R. Venezky (Eds.), *Orthography, reading and dyslexia.* Baltimore: University Park Press, 137-154.

Mahony, D. L. (1994). Using sensitivity to word structure to explain variance in high school and college level reading ability. *Reading and Writing*, 6, 19-44.

Mahony, D. L., Singson, M. F., & Mann, V. (In press). Reading ability and sensitivity to morphological relations. Reading & Writing.

Mann, V. (1998). Language problems: A key to early reading problems. In: *Learning about learning disabilities* (2nd Ed) (B. Wong, Ed.) Academic Press. Pp163-199.

Myerson, R. (1976). A study of children's knowledge of certain word formation rules and the relationship of this knowledge to various forms of reading achievement (Doctoral dissertation, Harvard University). *University Micro-films International*, 76-130, 205.

Nagy, W., Diakidoy, I., & Anderson, R. C. (1993). The acquisition of morphology: Learning the contribution of suffixes to the meanings of derivatives. *Journal of Reading Behavior*, 25, 15-170.
Perfetti, C. A. (1985). Reading skill. Hillsdale, NJ: Erlbaum.
Rosner, J., & Simon, D. P. (1971). The auditory analysis test: An initial report. *Journal of Learning Disability*, 4, 384-392.
Seidenberg, M. S. (1985). The time course of phonological activation in two writing systems. *Cognition*, 19, 1-30.
Shankweiler, D., Crain, S., Katz, L., Fowler, A. E., Liberman, A. E., Brady, S. A., Thornton, R., Lundquist, E., Dreyer, L., Fletcher, J. M., Stuebing, K. K., Shaywitz, S. E., & Shaywitz, B. A. (1995). Cognitive profiles of reading-disabled children: Comparisons of language skills in phonology, morphology and syntax. *Psychological Science*, 6, 149-156.
Singson, M., Mahony, D., & Mann, V. (In press). The relation between reading ability and morphological skills: Evidence from derivational suffixes. *Reading & Writing*.
Treiman, R., Mullennix, J., Bijeljac-Babic, R., & Richmond-Welty, E. D. (1995). The special role of rimes in the description, use, and acquisition of English orthography. *Journal of Experimental Psychology*: General, 124 (2), 107-136.
Tyler, A., & Nagy, W. (1989). The acquisition of English derivational morphology. *Journal of Memory and Language*, 28, 649-667.
Vogel, S. A. (1977). Morphological ability in normal and dyslexic children. *Journal of Learning Disabilities*, 10, 649-667.
Weschler, D. (1967). *Weschler Preschool and Primary Scale of Intelligence*. Cleveland, Ohio: The Psychological Corporation.
Wiig, E. H., Semel, E. M., & Crouse, M. A. (1973). The use of English morphology by high-risk and learning disabled children. *Journal of Learning Disabilities*, 6, 457-465.
Woodcock, R. W. (1973). *Woodcock Reading Mastery Tests*. Circle Pines, MN: American Guidance Service.
Yuill, N., Oakhill, J., & Parkin, A. J. (1989). Working memory, comprehension ability and the resolution of text anomaly. *British Journal of Psychology*, 80(3), 351-361.

7. ACKNOWLEDGEMENT

We would like to thank Diana Mahony for her collaboration on some of the studies described in this chapter and to thank the Newport Mesa school district for their cooperation in providing participants for all three studies. We also thank the editors for their creative suggestions.

8. ADDRESS FOR CORRESPONDENCE

Virginia A.Mann
Department of Cognitive Sciences
University of California
School of Social Science
3251 Social Science Plaza
Irvine, CA 92697-5100
United States of America
Phone: (949) 824-6680
Fax: (949) 824-3548
email: vmann@uci.edu

JOANNE F. CARLISLE AND C. ADDISON STONE

THE EFFECTS OF MORPHOLOGICAL STRUCTURE ON CHILDREN'S READING OF DERIVED WORDS IN ENGLISH

1. INTRODUCTION

The English written language system represents words at the level of the morpheme as well as the phoneme. It is likely, therefore, that awareness of not only the phonological but also the morphological structure of words plays a role in learning to read. While there is a large body of research that shows the importance of phonological awareness, there are many unanswered questions about the role of morphological awareness in the acquisition of reading skill. When and under what circumstances sensitivity to morphemic structure affects the word reading of children is the focus of the present chapter.

There are practical educational reasons to be concerned about the role of morphological awareness in word reading. We know that by the late elementary years, students encounter numerous derived words in their reading. For example, Nagy and Anderson (1984) estimated that 60% of the unfamiliar words encountered by middle school children are fairly transparent morphologically complex words. Still, we do not yet know whether awareness of morphological structure affects the accuracy and speed of word reading. It is possible, for example, that the process of word reading is largely influenced by factors other than morphological structure, such as orthographic elements or syllable structure. As a result, we do not know whether programs in reading instruction should include an emphasis on morphological decomposition for children who are consolidating their word reading skills.

1.1 Morphological Structure and Skilled Word Recognition

Researchers interested in the word reading of adults have studied the effects of morphological structure on lexical decision tasks. Two persistent questions are how morphologically complex words are represented in the lexicon (as intact wholes, for example, or through their morphemic constituents) and the extent to which recognition of morphological units is part of the process of lexical access. Studies of adults' performance on lexical decision tasks (using priming) have provided evidence that morphological structure affects speed of recognition of both inflected and derived forms. Various factors play a role, including phonological, orthographic, and semantic transparency of the morphologically complex word, as well as the familiarity of the base and complex forms (Colé, Beauvillain, & Segui, 1989; Feldman & Andjelkovic, 1992; Fowler, Napps, & Feldman, 1985; Marslen-Wilson, Tyler, Waksler, & Older, 1994; Stoltz & Feldman, 1995). Once words are identified, further morphological analysis may take place, serving such purposes as determining meaning.

Recognition of the morphemic constituents of words may be part of the process of word reading not only for adults, but also for children who have acquired basic word reading skills and experience with morphologically complex words in print. Knowledge of morphemes and morphemic boundaries must be acquired over time through repeated exposures to them in different word contexts. The process of reading morphologically complex words may require recovering the lexical units from the orthographic representation. In words with suffixes, preliminary left-to right analysis of letters and syllables may activate recognition of base words that have lexical status (Schreuder & Baayen, 1995; Taft & Zhu, 1995). For full recognition, the suffix needs to be represented in conjunction with the base word (e.g., *heal* + *th* = *health*). Results of a study by Nagy, Anderson, Schommer, Scott, and Stallman (1989) suggest that for adults, the cumulative effect of morphological decomposition over time is reflected in faster and more accurate recognition of base words with high family frequencies than base words with low family frequencies. Thus, the extent to which base words are encountered in inflected and derived words affects the speed of recognition of the base word alone.

These results suggest the possibility that older children, who have had extensive reading experience, might show a stronger effect for morphological structure than younger children. Gordon's (1989) study using untimed lexical decision with children (ages 5, 7, and 9) provides support for this expectation; high frequency base words influenced the accuracy of the decisions on low frequency derived words with non-productive suffixes, especially for the older children.

1.2 Awareness of Morphological Structure in Relation to Word Reading

Morphological awareness refers to the capability to reflect on and/or manipulate the morphological structure of words. Awareness of the morphological structure of words, at least at some implicit level, may be a prerequisite for parsing words at morphemic boundaries for the purpose of reading words. The degree of explicitness of this awareness may depend on such factors as reading experience, verbal ability, and curiosity about words and word meanings. Morphologically complex words may be learned as single lexical items, without regard for the morphemic constituents (Gordon, 1989), but it is possible that awareness of morphemic structure characterizes better and more mature word readers. Two important questions, therefore, are whether children's awareness of the morphological structure of words is related to their reading of such words and, if so, what this relationship means. An oral task that taps morphological awareness may suggest the extent to which a child is aware of morphemic units and relations in words. However, such awareness is not necessarily applied in normal word reading; it may play a role only if the child encounters an unfamiliar word in which there is a familiar, readily identified base word. For skilled readers, word reading occurs as a fast and automatic process, and any decomposition into morphemic units is likely to take place without application of analytic strategies.

With regard to the development of morphological awareness, we know that English-speaking children move gradually from implicit to explicit awareness of morphological structure during the school-age years (Berko, 1958; Carlisle, 1995; Jones, 1991, Rubin, 1987). Awareness of inflections emerges somewhat earlier than awareness of derived forms, and children show sensitivity to the structure of transparent forms (in which the phonological representation of the base word is fully evident in the pronunciation of the inflected or derived form) earlier than forms that undergo a phonological shift between the base and complex form (e.g., vowel shortening, as in *nature* to *natural)*. Serbo-Croatian children (ages 7 and 8) were found to be able to substitute morphemes in words to complete sentences accurately, showing sensitivity to the formation of inflected and derived forms (Feldman & Andjelkovic, 1992). Between fourth and eighth grades, English-speaking students show increasing ability to produce as well as decompose derived forms, particularly those that are productive and transparent in terms of phonology and orthography (Carlisle, 1987; Tyler & Nagy, 1989; Wysocki & Jenkins, 1987). On both oral and written language tasks, eighth graders show more awareness of the structure of opaque or non-neutral forms than fourth graders. Younger and less able readers attend to the base word as the primary clue to the meaning of the word if it is presented in context; conversely, older and more able students make more use of the syntactic and/or semantic information in the suffixes (Champion, 1997; Tyler & Nagy, 1989).

There is quite a bit of indirect evidence that awareness of morphological structure in oral language is related to reading achievement. Carlisle (1995) found that first graders' performance on oral morphological awareness tasks accounted for a small but significant portion of unique variance in second-grade reading comprehension, although there was considerable shared variance with phonological awareness. Fowler and Liberman (1995) found that students' sensitivity to morphologically complex words on an oral production task was related to their general word reading and spelling ability. In a comparison of younger good readers matched on word reading ability with older poor readers, they found that reader group differences were most evident on words that underwent complex phonological shifts (e.g., *five/fifth*).

Further evidence that reading skill is related to awareness of morphological structure comes from Champion (1997), and Leong (1989). Both of these researchers studied good and poor readers. Leong asked students to provide derived forms or base forms, following sentence stems; response latencies showed that poor readers/spellers were slower than good readers/spellers, particularly on words that involved both phonological and orthographic changes from base to derived forms. Champion found that poor readers differed from good readers in awareness of the semantic and syntactic aspects of derived forms, but the differences were more pronounced on written than oral language tasks.

Although the findings of these studies are suggestive, they do not include direct assessment of the reading of morphologically complex words. Several researchers have provided more direct evidence of the relation of morphological awareness and reading of morphologically complex words. Elbro and Arnbak (1996) found that the correlation of morphological awareness on several oral tasks and the reading of inflected forms was significant for Danish adolescents with dyslexia but not for younger normal students. They also found that the dyslexics read semantically transparent words (e.g., *sunburn)* significantly better than opaque words, an advantage not found for the normal control group (p. 215). These and other results led the researchers to conclude that morpheme recognition may be a compensatory strategy in word decoding and comprehension for dyslexic adolescents. A second study, which involved training dyslexics on morphological awareness skills, showed modest effects on comprehension and spelling for the trained group, as compared to dyslexics receiving traditional remedial reading instruction. The researchers suggested that awareness of morphological structure may hold greater benefits for spelling, which is a more analytic process, than word reading. In terms of the developing word reading skill of third through sixth graders in English, Mann and Singson (this volume) found that morphological awareness was significantly related to reading real and nonsense derived words.

1.3 How Might Morphological Structure Affect Word Reading?

Based on our review of the literature, we considered ways in which morphological structure might affect the reading of derived forms by children. We identified four types of evidence that might suggest an effect of morphological structure on reading words with suffixes. First, a significant relation between performance on an oral task of awareness of the structure of derived words and the reading of derived words would constitute one form of evidence for morphological processing, albeit indirect evidence (Elbro & Arnbak, 1996; Fowler & Liberman, 1995). Second, if one- and two-morpheme words are similar in spelling and are high frequency (e.g., *candy* and *windy*), the two-morpheme words might be read more accurately because of recognition of familiar base morphemes. Third, for unfamiliar but transparent derived words, the morphemic constituents, particularly a familiar base morpheme, might facilitate the accuracy but not speed of word reading. The letter sequence that makes up a familiar base word should facilitate lexical access of an uncommon derived form because lexical analysis involves a left-to-right processing of successive letter combinations (Schreuder & Baayen, 1995; Taft & Zhu, 1995). Speed might not be affected because of the time needed for parsing and lexical search. The influence of the base word might be found only for older students, who have had experience processing morphologically complex words in print (Gordon, 1989; Nagy et al., 1989). Fourth, as has been found on oral tasks of morphological awareness, suffixed words with transparent structure are likely to be read more accurately than suffixed words that undergo phonological shifts (e.g., *natural)* (Champion, 1997; Gordon, 1989; Leong, 1989; Tyler & Nagy, 1989). The two studies we report hereafter consider these four types of evidence, exploring not only the possible facilitation of morphological structure for transparent words but also the possible inhibition of benefits, arising because of phonological complexities that tend to obscure morphological relations.

2. STUDY 1

The effects of morphological awareness on reading were explored in an initial study (see Carlisle, in press). Several of the ways morphological structure might affect word reading we listed above were explored in this study. First, to determine whether morphological awareness is related to reading of morphologically complex words, third and fifth graders' performance on tests of morphological awareness and of reading derived words was compared. Second, the reading task included high frequency derived words, some of which had transparent structure (e.g., *lovely*) while others underwent phonological shifts (e.g., *natural*). Because we already have evidence that students are less aware of the morphological structure of words that undergo phonological shifts, we expected to find better performance on both the oral and reading tasks on words with transparent structure than those that involved shifts. Third, we investigated students' reading of low frequency derived words whose base forms were high frequency. As has been found for monomorphemic words (see Frederiksen & Kroll, 1976), we expected high frequency transparent derived words to be read more accurately than low frequency transparent derived words. Particularly for the fifth graders, familiarity with the surface form was likely to facilitate recognition. However, the question of interest in terms of morphological processing was whether the familiarity of the base morpheme would contribute significantly to accuracy of reading the unfamiliar derived forms. We reasoned that, if the frequency of the base forms contributed significantly to reading accuracy, we would have some evidence that transparent but unfamiliar derived words may be parsed at morphological boundaries for purposes of word reading. In contrast, if word length but not base word frequency contributed to their reading of uncommon derived words, it would suggest that reading unfamiliar derived words was not facilitated by morphological composition.

The study focused on the performance of third and fifth graders, since students at these grade levels would have learned basic word reading skills. The research questions were as follows: (a) Is performance on an oral test of morphological awareness (including transparent and shift derived forms) significantly related to the accuracy of students' reading of transparent and shift derived words? (b) Are there significant differences between the reading of transparent and shift words, matched for word length and frequency? And also between transparent words, differing in surface but not base frequency? (c) Do frequency of the base word and a measure of word length (number of syllables) contribute separately to the reading of low frequency derived words with high frequency base forms?

2.1 Method

2.1.1 Subjects

The subjects were 34 third graders (16 girls and 18 boys) and 26 fifth graders (15 girls and 11 boys) who attended a private day school in a middle- to upper middle-class suburban community in the Midwest. Eight third graders and 7 fifth graders were getting special help in reading at the school; however, none of these students had Vocabulary or Comprehension scores below the 30th percentile on the school-administered Comprehensive Testing Program (Educational Records Bureau) (CTP). Mean percentiles for the third graders were Vocabulary 76.8 (15.8 SD) and Comprehension 74.9 (22.4 SD); for the fifth graders, Vocabulary 80.8 (22.4 SD) and Comprehension 79.2 (13.3 SD).

2.1.2 Materials

WORD READING TEST (WRT): this experimental test was designed to assess students' ability to read derived words of high and low frequency.[1] A list of the words is included in the appendix; for purposes of this project, several of the words from the original list used in Carlisle (in press) were eliminated because they entailed orthographic changes. The words in one set were 22 derived words with high surface frequency (HF). For 9 of these words, the base form was fully represented in the derived form (orthographically and phonologically), referred to here as transparent words (e.g., *movement*, *powerful*); for 13 words, the surface form differed from the base form in terms of phonological characteristics (referred to here as shift words)(e.g., *natural*, *easily*). For some of these, suffixation involved a change in the final letter of the base form, as the examples suggest. The suffixes were common and productive for school-age children, including nouns (*-ment*, *-ness*), adjectives (*-y*, *-ful*), and adverbs (*-ly)*. A second set was made up of 23 words with low frequency for the surface form but high base frequency (the LF set). All of the words in this set had transparent relations (e.g., *puzzlement, pailful*). There was a greater variety of suffixes in this set than in the high frequency set (e.g., *-like*, *-ist*, and *-ive)*. The words in the two sets were comparable in base word frequency, mean number of letters, and mean number of syllables. Descriptive statistics for the sets of words on the test are provided in Table 1.

Table 1. Descriptive characteristics of the word groups on the word reading test

Word Group	Number of Letters	Number of Syllables	Frequency of Surface Words	Frequency of Base Words
HF Shift	8.7	3.3	55.9	55.8
	(1.5)	(.8)	(4.2)	(5.5)
HF Transp.	7.8	2.4	58.6	58.5
	(1.1)	(.5)	(3.7)	(5.8)
LF Transp.	8.1	2.7	33.2	55.1

Word Group	Number of Letters	Number of Syllables	Frequency of Surface Words	Frequency of Base Words
	(1.2)	(.6)	(1.6)	(3.6)

Note. HF = high frequency; LF = low frequency; Transp. = transparent

TEST OF MORPHOLOGICAL AWARENESS (TMA): this experimental measure was designed to assess students' awareness of the relations of base and derived forms. The task requires a student to change a word form so that it is appropriate for the syntax and meaning of a sentence context. Such manipulation is thought to be one index of metalinguistic awareness (see Carlisle, 1995). The first part (Production) required the student to produce a derived word in order to finish a sentence (e.g., *Reason. Her argument was quite*___). The second part (Decomposition) required students to decompose a derived word in order to finish a sentence (e.g., *Variable. The time of her arrival did not* ___). The base and derived forms were equivalent in word frequency on the two parts: for the Decomposition task, the mean SFI for the base forms was 56.7 (5.0 SD) and for the derived forms was 50.2 (5.9 SD), while for the Production task, the mean SFI for the base forms was 55.8 (6.2 SD) and for the derived forms was 51.0 (5.5 SD) (Carroll et al, 1971). The two tasks contained equal numbers of words with transparent (e.g., *reason* and *reasonable*) and shift relations (e.g., *produce* and *production*). Suffixes judged to be familiar to third and fifth graders were used; these included *-th* (e.g., *growth*), *-ance/ence* (e.g., *performance*), *-er* (e.g., *teacher*), *-ity* (e.g., *equality*), *-tion/sion* (e.g., *description*), *-ous* (e.g., *famous*), *-able* (e.g., *variable*). Each suffix was equally represented on the two tasks. There were 28 items on each task.

2.1.3 Procedures

Each student was given the WRT and the TMA individually in a quiet setting. The testing took about 20 minutes. Performance on the WRT was scored during the administration of the task by the researcher or a research assistant; the students' performance was also tape-recorded. Reliability of scoring was determined by comparison of these scores with a randomly selected scoring of the tape-recorded word reading of 5 students at each grade level. Agreement of the two scorings for both grade levels exceeded 95%. The WRT was scored for both automaticity and accuracy of responses; that is, students received two points if the word was read correctly within two seconds; they received one point if there was a delay in the initiation of the response or a self-correction of any kind. The standardized reading measure (CTP) was administered to each class by school staff in the spring of the school year.

2.2 *Results*

2.2.1 *Relations of Aspects of Morphological Awareness to Word Reading*

The first question concerned the extent to which morphological awareness (TMA) was significantly related to the reading of derived words (WRT). Initial analysis of the data showed that the fifth grade had performed extremely well on the high frequency set, particularly on the transparent words, so that a ceiling effect was evident (see Table 2). As a result, the results for the fifth grade must be interpreted with caution.

Table 3 shows the correlations of the subtests of the two tasks by grade level. Of particular importance was whether awareness of structure of shift words was related to the reading of shift words. For the third grade, performance on shift words on the TMA (both Decomposition and Production) was significantly related to performance on the shift words on the WRT. Decomposition of transparent words on the oral task was also related to the reading of the LF words. For the fifth grade, production of shift words was related to the reading of HF shift words.

Table 2. Performance on the word reading test by grade level in percent correct

	High Frequency		*Low Frequency*
	Transparent	Shift	Transparent
Grade 3	94.8	75.0	74.3
	(10.2)	(21.7)	(18.9)
Grade 5	98.9	94.4	88.7
	(3.2)	(4.7)	(9.7)

Note. Standard deviations are given in parentheses

Table 3. Pearson correlations of test of morphological awareness (TMA) and word reading test (WRT) (sets A and B) by grade level

	TMA Prod		*TMA Decomp*	
WRT Word Set	Transparent	Shift	Transparent	Shift
Grade 3				
HF Trans	.12	.25	.26	.11
HF Shift	.30	.44**	.39*	.44**
LF Trans	.13	.20	.35*	.10
Grade 5				
HF Trans	.06	.26	.00	.01
HF Shift	.17	.41*	.17	.20
LF Trans	.10	.23	-.13	.42**

Note. TMA = test of morphological awareness; WRT = word reading test; Trans = transparent; HF = high frequency; LF = low frequency. * $p < .05$ ** $p < .01$

2.2.2 *Performance on the Word Reading Test*

The second question was whether the students at the two grade levels differed in their accuracy of reading HF transparent and shift words. Additionally, we wanted to know whether they performed differently on HF and LF transparent words (all with high frequency base forms). As Table 2 shows, it is evident that the students' performance was much better on the HF transparent than shift words. In addition, performance on HF transparent words was also much better than performance on the LF transparent words. Perhaps it is important to note also that the fifth graders were significantly better at reading the words than the third graders: for WRT HF words, $t(58) = 4.27$, $p <.001$, and for WRT LF words, $t(58) = 3.55$, $p <.001$. Tests of heterogeneity of variance for the three word types were significant; as a result, comparison of performance on the three word groups at each grade level was carried out using non-parametrics. Friedman ANOVA by ranks for the third grade showed that students' reading of the three groups of words differed significantly, $\chi^2(2, N = 34) = 48.7$, $p <.001$. Follow-up analysis showed that the HF transparent and shift words differed significantly, $\chi^2(1, N = 34) = 4.17$, $p <.05$; and the HF and LF transparent words also differed significantly, $\chi^2(1, N = 34) = 30.12$, $p <.001$. Similarly, the fifth-graders' reading of the three groups of words differed significantly, $\chi^2(2, N = 26) = 52.00$, $p <.001$. Follow-up tests showed that their performance on the HF transparent and shift words differed significantly, $\chi^2(1, N = 26) = 26.00$, $p <.001$; and the HF and LF transparent words differed significantly, $\chi^2(1, N = 26) = 26.00$, $p <.001$.

2.2.3 *Reading Uncommon Transparent Forms*

The third research question concerned the contribution of the base frequency and a measure of word length (number of syllables) to success in reading the LF derived forms that had high frequency base words. Two standard multiple regression analyses were carried out, one for each grade level. The results are shown in Table 4.

Table 4. Contributions of word length and base frequency to reading of low frequency derived words

	Beta	St. Error of Beta	Semipartial Correlation	t (20)	p-level
Grade 3					
Syllables	-.69	.16	-.69	-4.46	.000
Base Freq	.25	.16	.25	1.60	.130
Grade 5					

Syllables	-.49	.17	-.49	-2.86	.010
Base Freq	.44	.17	.44	2.58	.018

The analysis with third-grade reading of the words as the dependent variable showed that syllables and base frequency accounted for a significant 52% of the variance, $F(2, 20) = 10.8$, $p < .001$. The adjusted R-square was .47. Syllables contributed significantly, whereas the base frequency did not. For the fifth grade, the analysis showed that syllables and base frequency accounted for 41% of the variance, $F(2,20) = 6.94$, $p < .01$. The adjusted R-square was .35. For this group, both the base frequency and the syllables made a significant independent contribution.

2.3 Discussion

Developmental growth in students' sensitivity to morphological structure is relatively well-documented, and a relationship between this sensitivity and word reading has been reported by several researchers. However, few researchers have examined directly the relation of morphological awareness and the reading of morphologically complex words. Using a variety of tasks to assess morphological awareness in Danish, Elbro and Arnbak (1996) found a significant correlation between morphological awareness and reading inflected words for dyslexic adolescents, but not for the normally developing readers. Mann and Singson (this volume) show a significant relation of morphological awareness and the reading of real and nonsense derived words. The results of our study, also, showed a significant relation between morphological awareness and the reading of derived words for normally developing readers. It is not clear why our results differ from those of Elbro and Arnbak; differences in the language and tasks might be important to consider.

In our study, one finding of note was that the oral production task was more strongly related to reading derived words than the decomposition task. It would seem that recognition of morphological structure (as assessed by the decomposition task) might more closely resemble the morphological processing used in word reading. However, the production task shows students' ability to select an appropriate suffix, in terms of meaning and grammatical role, to add to the base word and an understanding of combinatory principles. Knowledge of both the base and the suffix might therefore play a role in accurate reading of derived forms, even at a third-grade level. In other studies, knowledge of the grammatical role and meanings of suffixes is associated with full analysis of the meaning of words and sentences (Feldman & Andjelkovic, 1992; Tyler & Nagy, 1990; Wysocki & Jenkins, 1987).

The significant relation of producing words that required a phonological shift and reading words that underwent phonological shifts may provide an important link between oral and written language aspects of morphological processing. Fowler and Liberman (1995) reported that awareness of phonological changes on an oral task was related to general word reading performance for poor but not normally achieving readers. In our study, phonological changes affected performance on both the oral morphological awareness task and the reading of derived words for normally achieving readers in third and fifth grades. Our findings are similar to those of Mann and Singson (this volume). While specific aspects of methodology (e.g., subject characteristics, selection of words and tasks) may lead to differences in research results, phonological processing clearly plays an important role in morphological processing (see Fowler and Feldman, this volume). In particular, phonological shifts may obscure the recognition of morphological structure and may also cause interference in the process of reading such words as natural.

We expected, and found, developmental differences in the reading of morphologically complex words by third and fifth graders. Earlier, Gordon (1989) found age differences in recognition of morphologically complex words on a lexical decision task, and Mann and Singson (this volume) also found significant improvement on reading derived words between third and sixth grades.

Both frequency and transparency affected students' reading of derived words. In terms of transparency, the results showed that both the third and fifth graders performed better on HF words that were transparent than HF words that entailed phonological and/or orthographic shifts. Our results are like those of Gordon (1989) and Mann and Singson (this volume), who found that younger children recognized high frequency transparent words more readily than words with opaque structure. Frequency is likely to mediate the role of transparency. Processing of the morphemic constituents is affected by transparency, which in turn is affected by the students' familiarity with the base and derived forms. We compared performance on HF and LF transparent words that all had high frequency base words. Not surprisingly, the students performed much better on the transparent words of high than low surface frequency; familiarity is a powerful factor in reading words of all kinds.

We also explored the possibility that recognition of familiar base words facilitated reading of unfamiliar derived words. The results of regression analyses were used to determine the extent to which word length and base word frequency accounted for speed and accuracy of reading the LF transparent words. The results showed that for the third grade, number of syllables contributed significantly to performance, whereas for the fifth grade, both syllables and the base frequency contributed significantly to the reading of the low frequency derived forms. This result suggests that the fifth graders made use of the base word in their reading of the derived word. The fact that the third graders' performance was affected only by word length suggests that they were likely to attempt pronunciation of the unfamiliar word without recognizing the familiar base word. The older students may have had sufficient exposure to complex words in print to provide a basis for morphological analysis in word reading, as the results of Nagy et al. (1989) would suggest.

To summarize, the results of this study, in which third and fifth graders were the participants, provided evidence of several ways in which morphological structure of derived words affected the reading of the words. Awareness of the structure of derived words was significantly related to reading such words, providing evidence that students who are sensitive to the morphological composition of words are also better at reading such words. Furthermore, transparent words were read significantly more accurately and fluently than a matched set of words with phonological shifts. The LF transparent words were read less accurately than the HF transparent words; not surprisingly, the awareness of morphological structure does not compensate fully for the difficulty of reading such words. Finally, the reading of uncommon derived words was influenced by the base word frequency for fifth graders, although not for third graders.

3. STUDY 2

A second study was designed to extend our knowledge of students' reading of transparent derived words. It seemed important to determine whether morphological structure affected word reading when complex phonological changes were not present. Fowler and Liberman (1995), as also Fowler and Feldman (this volume), have argued that it is the phonological complexities of morphologically complex words that present challenges to poor readers. However, the phonological structure is only one component of morphological knowledge that might affect the reading of complex words. As noted earlier, we had some reason to think that familiarity with written morphemes (base words and common suffixes) might play a role in the reading of words with transparent structure. Whether this effect would be evident for younger readers or students with word reading problems was a question of particular interest. To investigate the possible role of transparent structure in word reading, we compared the speed and accuracy of reading two-morpheme words to one-morpheme words matched for spelling and frequency (e.g., *hilly* as compared to *silly*). For this task we used high frequency derived words because the students with reading problems were matched for reading-age with young readers, who were in grades 2 and 3. In some theories of reading and spelling development, mastery of morphological units is a late stage that includes inflections (e.g., past tenses such as *popped*) and agentives (e.g., *gunner)* in the same stage as two-syllable mono-morphemic words, such as *plastic* and *maple* (Schlagal, 1992). In keeping with Schlagal's model, we compared reading two-syllable derived forms with two-syllable mono-morphemic words that we have termed "mock" derived forms because their word endings look like suffixes.

In a separate task, we asked the students to read low frequency derived words that had high frequency base forms, as we had in the previous study. In this way, we would gather insights into the ability of students with word-reading problems on both high and low frequency derived forms with transparent structure. As before, an important additional issue was whether, for younger and older students, the base frequency contributed significantly to the speed and/or the accuracy of reading low frequency derived forms. If the frequency of the base form contributed significantly, it would seem that processing the base word affected reading of the derived word.

In this study, unlike our previous one, we included separate assessments of speed and accuracy of word reading. The addition of a measure of speed provided data to test the automaticity of reading complex words. We were also interested in a suggestion made by Tyler and Nagy (1990) that there was likely to be a trade-off in morphological processing for word reading. In their words, "it is possible that morphological complexity speeds the process of access to the point at which the set of words which contain that base morpheme is accessed, but that further operations involved in distinguishing related forms slow subsequent processing. Thus, morphological complexity appears to facilitate some aspects of lexical access and complicate others, without necessarily resulting in a net quantitative difference in processing difficulty" (p. 31). Because word reading tends to be a fast and automatic process, the need for complex operations following initial access may be limited, and so recognition of morphological structure might result in faster word reading than for mono-morphemic words of comparable length. If no advantage is found for speed of reading morphologically complex words, we would be left without clear evidence as to whether there is a trade-off (as suggested above) or whether other factors, such as complexity of spelling or word length, play a more important role in children's word reading speed.

We compared the performance on tasks of reading transparent derived forms by students with word-reading problems to that of both chronological-age matched (CA-Match) and reading-age matched (RA-Match) groups. Elbro and Arnbak (1996, pp. 215-216) suggested that word reading by dyslexics was facilitated by the semantic transparency of words (e.g., *sunburn*) in a way that was not found for younger normal readers. We hoped to determine whether poor readers in English performed better on transparent derived words than "mock" derived words. We would have evidence of an advantage for the poor readers on transparent derived words if the poor readers but not the younger normal readers were significantly more accurate or faster on the two- morpheme words than the one-morpheme words matched for spelling and frequency (as explained above).

The research questions were as follows: (a) Do Poor Readers, CA-Match, and RA-Match groups differ in speed and accuracy of reading real versus "mock" high frequency derived forms? (b) Do Poor Readers, CA-Match, and RA-Match groups differ in the speed and accuracy of reading low frequency derived forms? and (c) For younger and older readers, do word length and base word frequency contribute significantly to speed and accuracy of reading low frequency derived words?

3.1 Method

3.2 Subjects

The subjects were drawn from a learning disabilities clinic at a suburban Midwestern university and from two near-by schools (a private school for students with learning disabilities and a parochial school). To be included in this study, a student had to have a standard score on the Peabody Picture Vocabulary Test-Revised of 80 or above. To carry out a comparison of poor readers with their chronological and reading-age matched peers, we identified a group of 15 poor readers (PR) (11 boys and 4 girls) in grades 4 through 6 who scored at or below 90 SS on a standardized word reading test (4 fourth graders, 5 fifth graders, and 6 sixth graders). The chronological-age match (CA-match) for this group was a group of 40 normally-achieving fourth, fifth, and sixth graders (11 girls and 29 boys). The poor reader (PR) group was matched to a group of second- and third-grade students on accuracy of word reading on an experimental test of word reading (described below). This reading-age match (RA-match) group included 40 second and third graders (22 girls, 18 boys).

The performance of the CA-Match, RA-Match and PR groups on standardized measures of reading and vocabulary is summarized in Table 5. While most students were given the Woodcock-Johnson Psycho-educational Battery, Letter-Word Identification and Passage Comprehension subtests, in a few cases other standardized measures of word reading or comprehension had recently been administered and were accepted as substitutes; these included the Wechsler Individual Achievement Test, Basic Reading and Reading Comprehension subtests and the Wide Range Achievement Test-3, Reading subtest. All students were given the Peabody Picture Vocabulary Test, a measure of receptive vocabulary. The groups differed significantly on the standardized reading tests: for word reading, $F(2,78) = 31.80$, $p < .001$; for reading comprehension, $F(2, 78) = 17.00$, $p < .001$. They did not differ on the vocabulary measure, $F(2,78) = 1.99$, $p = .14$. Post hoc comparisons (Tukey's Unequal *N* HSD) showed that for the standardized reading measures, the PR group was weaker than both the RA-Match and CA-Match, relative to their grade-level norms.

Table 5. Performance on reading and vocabulary measures by reading group

Group	WR	COMP	PPVT	EWRAC	EWRS
PR	83.2	89.4	96.2	81.4	1.19
	(7.8)	(12.0)	(9.9)	(16.4)	(.54)
CA-Match	110.0	103.1	105.4	97.7	.81
	(10.6)	(10.9)	(14.0)	(4.0)	(.27)
RA-Match	110.8	113.4	99.8	84.5	1.56
	(13.6)	(14.9)	(16.3)	(14.8)	(1.19)

Note. WR = word reading standard score; COMP = reading comprehension standard score; PPVT = peabody picture vocabulary test-R, standard score; EWRAC = experimental word reading accuracy (percent correct); EWRS = experimental word reading speed (in seconds). Standard deviations are given in parentheses

3.3 *Materials*

Students were given a computer-administered battery of word reading tasks. The test battery included a variety of word-reading tasks; reported here are the tasks that included monosyllabic words, high frequency derived and matched "mock" derived words, and low frequency derived words. The words used in each group are listed in the appendix.

WORD READING: the student read twelve words (randomly selected from a pool of 20 words) in each of five sets, for a total of 60 words. The sets contained increasingly complex words. The first set contained one-syllable words with closed and silent-e syllables (e.g., *hit*); the second set contained words with consonant blends and orthographic patterns such as *-ck* (e.g., *track*) ; the third set contained words with vowel teams and consonant blends and digraphs (e.g., *street, threw*); the fourth set contained two-syllable words (e.g., *master*); the fifth set contained three-syllable words (e.g., *difficult*). The three reading-ability groups differed significantly on word reading accuracy, $F(2,79) = 14.64$, $p < .001$, and speed , $F(2,79) = 7.29$, $p = .001$ (see Table 4). However, post hoc tests (Tukey's HSD for Unequal Ns) showed that the PR group did not differ significantly from the RA-Match group, and both of these groups performed less well than the CA-Match on both measures.

HIGH FREQUENCY DERIVED FORMS: because the age range of the students spanned grades 2 through 6, we selected common derived forms for this task; our choice was also constrained by difficulties finding mono-morphemic words that could be matched to derived forms on surface frequency, orthographic similarity, and word length. The derived forms (12 in all) were agentives or instrumentals (e.g., *winner)* and adjectives formed by adding the suffix *-y* to a noun (e.g., *windy*). All of the words contained two syllables. Average word length was 5.2 letters (.8 SD), mean surface frequency (SFI) was 49.6 (4.4 SD), and base frequency was 54.9 (6.7 SD). Twelve inflected forms and two derived forms with different endings (e.g., *dependent)* served as fillers to decrease the likelihood of noticing repetitions of the suffix patterns of the target derived forms; these words were not included in the data analyses.

HIGH FREQUENCY MOCK DERIVED FORMS: the student read 12 mono-morphemic words matched to the derived forms; in each case the word was as similar as possible in spelling, word length, and frequency (e.g., *dinner* matched to *winner*, *windy* matched to *candy*). All words contained two syllables. Average word length was 5.4 letters (.8 SD); mean surface frequency (SFI) was 54.2 (6.1 SD). It was not always possible to match the words for grammatical class; for example, single-morpheme words ending in *-y* are not all adjectives. For this task, fourteen additional mono-morphemic words (e.g., *ambition*) were included for variety, but performance on these words was not included in the data analysis.

LOW FREQUENCY DERIVED FORMS: the student read 23 low-frequency derived words with transparent structure and high frequency base words (e.g., *pailful*). The words were identical to those on the same task in the first study.

3.4 Procedures

The student was given standardized tests in one session lasting about 20 minutes. The experimental word reading tasks were administered in a separate session, which lasted 25 minutes. For these tasks, the student was seated before a computer screen at a comfortable viewing distance. He or she wore a pair of headphones with a microphone attached through which the student's vocalizations were recorded. The student was given a brief introduction to the computer and the reading task. The first task involved naming non-verbal stimuli (i.e., "plus" for + and "star" for *). The directions and practice items for this task introduced the student to the general procedures for all of the tasks. When one of these symbols (and in other tasks, a word) appeared on the screen, the student named it. Immediately after the student had vocalized a response, feedback on the accuracy of the response appeared in the top right corner of the screen. The purpose of the feedback was to give students a chance to regulate their responses so that they could be as quick but accurate as possible. These same directions, accompanied by appropriate practice items, were repeated before each new set of words and non-words. The word reading task was administered before the reading of real and mock derived words, which preceded the task of reading low frequency derived words. The order of presentation of the words within each task was randomly selected by the computer program. If at any time the student read six words incorrectly in a row, the examiner stopped the administration of that set.

3.5 Results

3.5.1 Performance on Real and Mock Derived Words

The first question concerned the speed and accuracy of reading real and mock derived words by PR, CA-Match, and RA-Match groups.

Table 6 shows the performances of the groups on these measures. Two ANOVAs were carried out to investigate students' reading of the high frequency real and mock derived words. For accuracy, with morphemic structure (that is, real versus mock forms) as the within-subjects variable, results showed a significant effect for group, $F(2,92) = 15.31$, $p <.001$, and a significant effect for morphemic structure, $F(1,92) = 24.58$, $p <.001$; the interaction was not significant, $F(2,92) = .02$, $p =.98$. Post hoc analyses (Tukey's HSD for Unequal N) showed that the CA-Match group differed from the PR and RA-Match groups, who did not differ from each other. All three groups were more accurate on the real than the mock derived. For speed, with morphemic structure as the within-subjects variable, results showed a significant effect for group, $F(2,92) = 14.46$, $p <.001$; the effect for morphemic structure approached but did not reach significance, $F(1,92) = 3.72$, $p = .06$, as was the case for the interaction, $F(2,92) = 2.66$, $p =.08$. Post hoc analysis of the group effect showed that the PR and RA-match did not differ in speed of reading; both were slower than the CA-Match. The RA-Match students were faster on the real than the mock forms, whereas for the older students (PR and CA-Match) there was no difference in performance on the two word types.

Table 6. Performance by reading group on the real and mock derived forms

	Real		*Mock*	
Group	Accuracy	Speed	Accuracy	Speed
Poor Readers	79.4	1.84	72.2	1.82
	(12.9)	(.94)	(15.6)	(.82)
CA Match	93.5	.91	86.4	.97
	(8.9)	(.28)	(9.6)	(.28)
RA Match	79.4	1.72	72.7	1.98
	(17.3)	(1.11)	(16.2)	(1.19)

Note. Accuracy (percent correct); speed (in seconds)

3.5.2 *Performance on Low Frequency Derived Words*

The second research question concerned performance of the groups on speed and accuracy of reading low frequency derived words. The results are shown in Table 7.

The results of an ANOVA showed significant differences in the performance of the three groups: for accuracy, $F(2,87) = 35.97$, $p <.001$; for speed, $F(2,87) = 15.62$, $p <.001$. Post hoc comparisons to explore the difference in accuracy showed that the CA-Match group performed better than the RA-Match and PR groups, whose performance did not differ significantly. Post hoc comparisons to explore the difference in speed showed that the CA-Match was significantly faster than the RA-Match group. The PR did not differ significantly from either of these groups.

Table 7. Performance on low frequency derived forms by reading group

Group	Accuracy	Speed
PR	41.63 (20.64)	2.60 (1.05)
CA-Match	80.51 (11.41)	1.47 (.56)
RA-Match	50.18 (23.0)	3.43 (2.22)

Note: Accuracy in percent correct; speed in seconds

To determine whether base frequency contributed significantly to the reading of the low frequency derived words, standard regression analyses were carried out (see Table 8). For each analysis, the question was the extent to which base word frequencies and the number of syllables in the surface form accounted significantly for variance in reading speed or accuracy.

Table 8. Contribution of word length and base frequency to speed and accuracy of reading low frequency derived forms

	Beta	Std. Error of Beta	Semipartial Correlations	t(20)	p-level
RA-Match					
Dep Var: Speed					
Syllable	.71	.16	.71	4.52	.000
Base Freq	-.004	.16	-.004	-.02	.979
Dep Var: Accuracy					
Syllable	-.73	.16	-.73	-4.84	.000

Base Freq	.20	.16	.19	1.29	.210
CA-Match					
Dep Var: Speed					
Syllable	.62	.17	.62	3.55	.002
Base Freq	-.11	.17	-.11	-.66	.520
Dep Var: Accuracy					
Syllable	-.61	.15	-.61	-3.95	.000
Base Freq	.45	.15	.48	2.92	.008

Separate analyses were run for the younger (RA-Match) and older (CA-Match) students, both for accuracy and speed of reading. (The PR group was not included in these analyses because of the small size of the group.) For the RA-Match group, the results showed that the two predictor variables accounted for 51% of the variance in reading speed (adjusted R square of .46), $F(2,20) = 10.26$, $p <.001$. However, only number of syllables contributed significantly to reading speed. For accuracy of word reading, the two variables accounted for 55% of the variance, $F(2,20) = 12.14$, $p <.001$ (adjusted R-square of .50). Again, only number of syllables made a significant contribution. For the CA-Match group, the results showed that the two variables accounted for 39% of the variance in reading speed (adjusted R-square of .33), $F(2,20) = 6.36$, $p <.001$. Only syllables made a significant contribution. For accuracy of reading, the variables accounted for 53% of the variance in word reading accuracy (.48 adjusted R-square); both syllables and base frequencies contributed significantly to the equation, $F(2,20) = 11.19$, $p <.001$.

3.6 Discussion

This study was designed to add to our knowledge about the effects of morphological structure on students' reading of derived words with transparent structure. Because there is relatively little information about developmental trends in the reading of morphologically complex words, we start by reporting that the younger (grades 2 and 3) and older (grades 4 through 6) readers differed significantly in both speed and accuracy of reading transparent derived forms and their "mock" counterparts. The older normally developing readers read both the one- and two-morpheme words in less than a second, on average, with high rates of accuracy (86% correct for mock and 94% for real derived words). The results present a slightly different picture than the one suggested by Schlagal's (1992) model, in that recognition of common, transparent derived words (e.g., *shady*) was significantly better than recognition of other two-syllable words (e.g., *lady*).

We were curious to determine whether in English word reading, poor readers would show a benefit for transparent words that was not evident for the younger normally achieving readers. This turned out not to be the case; both the RA-Match and PR groups were more accurate at reading high frequency real than "mock" derived words. The superior performance on the real derived words might be attributable to morphological parsing, leading to recognition of the high frequency base word. Because we found an advantage on the derived words for younger normal readers as well as poor readers, our results differ from those of Elbro and Arnbak (1996). An important difference in the two studies is that Elbro and Arnbak compared semantically transparent and opaque words, while we were comparing transparent derived words and monomorphemic words matched for spelling and frequency. Differences in the morphological structure of the two languages and the age of the students may also contribute to the different findings. The better performance on common transparent derived words than one-morpheme words matched for spelling and frequency suggests that the presence of one or two familiar morphemes may facilitate reading of English words.

In terms of speed of reading derived words, Tyler and Nagy (1990) suggested the speed of recognition of the morphemic units might be offset by the time it takes to process these separate linguistic units. For the poor readers and older students, the time for reading one and two morpheme words was equivalent; this may or may not represent the trade-off described by Tyler and Nagy. In contrast, the second- and third-grade readers were faster at reading the derived words (e.g., *windy*), than the single morpheme words (e.g., *candy*). It seemed unlikely that this effect would be found in the reading of words with unfamiliar surface forms, even if the base forms were familiar. In fact, the younger and poor readers performed at low levels of accuracy on the low frequency transparent words (42% and 50 % respectively). Similarly, reading low frequency transparent words was a slow process; reading these words took over two seconds, on the average, for these groups. This finding echoes the commonly reported effect of surface frequency on word reading and seems to apply to words that are complex as well as simple in structure (e.g., Frederiksen & Kroll, 1976).

As in our first study, we examined the reading of low frequency derived forms that contained very familiar base words (e.g., *puzzle* in *puzzlement*) to determine whether younger and older students would benefit from the familiar base word in terms of speed or accuracy of reading. Did only older students benefit from the presence of a familiar base form, as in the earlier study? Analysis of the contribution of word length (i.e., number of syllables) and base word frequency to accuracy and speed of reading showed that word length (but not base frequency) was significant to the speed and accuracy of the younger readers (RA-Match). For the older readers (CA-Match), however, both syllables and the base frequency contributed significantly to the accuracy of word reading, whereas only syllables contributed to speed. These results are similar to the findings of our earlier study, in which base frequency affected the accuracy of reading low frequency derived words by fifth graders, but not for third graders. They also are similar to Gordon's findings on an oral untimed lexical decision task; he too found the effect of the base word on recognition of the surface form to be more pronounced for older than younger students.

4. GENERAL DISCUSSION

Together, the results of the two studies show several ways that morphological processing affected the reading of derived forms by students between the second and sixth grades. First, we found a significant relationship between oral awareness of morphological structure and the reading of derived forms. Second, we compared the reading of familiar one- and two-morpheme words and found that the transparent derived words were read more accurately than single morpheme words matched in spelling and frequency. Third, we compared the reading of two types of derived words - those with and without transparent structure. For third and fifth graders, reading was less accurate for derived words whose base words were phonologically different, even though the word sets were matched for frequency and word length. The phonological differences may hinder students' awareness of the morphological composition of words, thereby decreasing the accuracy of word reading. This explanation is supported by the poorer performance on oral tasks of morphological awareness when decomposition or production of words involves phonological shifts, as opposed to words with transparent structure.

Finally, we found that for older students frequency of the base word, along with word length, affected the reading of low frequency derived forms; for younger students, word length but not base word frequency contributed significantly to the reading of these unfamiliar words. In both studies the effect of base word frequency on reading words such as *puzzlement* was on accuracy of word reading. The contribution of recognition of familiar morphemes to the reading of derived words may be a function of exposure to morphologically complex words in print (see Nagy et al., 1989). Students who are still learning basic word recognition skills or who are delayed in their acquisition of word reading may need to process words by letter or syllable, but without combining letters into recognizable lexical subunits. Somewhat different findings are reported by Mann et al (this volume), in that third graders on their tasks showed sensitivity to base forms in reading complex words.

We embarked on the study of students' reading of morphologically complex words with the purpose of determining whether morphological structure had a significant effect for students acquiring reading skill. We were particularly interested in aspects of morphological processing other than the sound structure of the words, as it is clear that phonological complexities affect processing of morphologically complex words in oral and written language (e.g., Carlisle & Nomanbhoy, 1993; Fowler & Liberman, 1995; Fowler & Feldman, this volume). Two of our findings concern transparent forms; these are: (a) high frequency words of two morphemes are read more accurately than matched words of one morpheme, and (b) the familiarity of the base word affects the accuracy of reading low frequency transparent derived words. Both results suggest that recognition of the base form influences correct pronunciation. Thus, aspects of morphological processing other than phonological complexities exert an influence on word reading.

Further study is clearly needed to broaden our understanding of the effects of morphology on word reading. It is important to study other types of morphologically complex words (inflections and compounds), as well as derived words with a greater variety of suffixes. In addition, further study of the reading of morphologically complex words by poor readers is clearly needed, as different studies have shown different results (Elbro & Arnbak, 1996; Fowler & Liberman, 1995). Further study is also needed to understand more fully the factors that affect processing of morphological structure. It is possible that some of the differences in research results reflect the practice of using the frequencies of individual words as indices of familiarity. The extent of exposure to base morphemes and suffixes in different combinations within words (oral and written) may exert a more powerful influence on awareness of morphological structure. The size of morphological "families" and the collective frequencies of the members of a morphological family ("family" frequency) may provide a measure of the extent to which students have had opportunities to recognize morphemes in different word contexts (Nagy et al, 1989). "Familiarity", defined and measured in this way, may help us understand the effect of morphological structure on the word reading of both normally developing readers and poor readers, who show significant gaps on both oral and written language measures of morphological awareness. It is possible that subtle language-processing difficulties, accompanied by less exposure to printed words, hinder their use of morphological awareness in reading. In many ways, we have only just begun to understand the relation of morphological awareness and word reading of children of different ages and reading abilities.

5. NOTES

[1] For purposes of matching word sets in terms of frequency in written texts, logarithmic transformations of the frequency ratings from Carroll et al (1971) were used; a value of 50 represents a word that appears once in 100,000 words of text, and a value of 30 once in ten million words in text. "High" ratings for surface frequency ranged from 50 to 63.

6. APPENDIX

6.1. Word List for Study 1 (Test of Word Reading)

High Frequency Words		Low Frequency Words
Transparent	Phonological shift	
movement	heavily	puzzlement
lovely	easily	cookery
friendly	invention	corrective
addition	direction	pailful
quickly	natural	stylish
suddenly	definition	valuation
government	explosion	organist
powerful	beautiful	equalize
harmful	moisture	wifelike
	explanation	sparkly
	solution	observable
	combination	oddity
	curiosity	preventive
		odorous
		queendom
		stardom
		dramatize
		fearsome
		idealize
		bucketful
		flowery
		beastly
		secretive

6.2. Word List for Study 2

REAL DERIVED WORDS	MOCK DERIVED WORDS	LOW FREQUENCY WORDS (see list for Study 1)
icy	mercy	
windy	candy	
shady	lady	
hilly	silly	
dirty	empty	
lucky	pretty	
lover	hover	
batter	chapter	
robber	rubber	
winner	dinner	
beggar	flavor	
mower	tower	

7. REFERENCES

Berko. J. (1958). The child's learning of English morphology, *Word,14,* 150-177.

Carlisle, J.F. (1987). The use of morphological knowledge in spelling derived forms by learning-disabled and normal students. *Annals of Dyslexia, 37,* 90-108.

Carlisle, J. F. (1995). Morphological awareness and early reading achievement. In L.B.Feldman (Ed.), *Morphological aspects of language processing* (pp. 189-209). Hillsdale, NJ: L. Erlbaum Associates.

Carlisle, J.F. (In press). Awareness of the structure and meaning of morphologically complex words: Impact on reading. *Reading and Writing.*

Carlisle, J.F., & Nomanbhoy, D. (1993). Phonological and morphological development. *Applied Psycholinguistics, 14,* 177-195.

Champion, A. H. (1997). Knowledge of suffixed words in reading and oral language contexts: A comparison of reading disabled and normal readers. *Annals of Dyslexia, 47,* 29-55.

Carroll, J.B., Davies, P., & Richman, B. (1971). *Word frequency book.* NY: American Heritage Publishing Company.

Colé, P., Beauvillain, C., & Segui, J. (1989). On the representation and processing of prefixed and suffixed derived words. *Journal of Memory and Language, 28,* 1-13.

Elbro, C., & Arnbak, E. (1996). The role of morpheme recognition and morphological awareness in dyslexia. *Annals of Dyslexia, 46,* 209-240.

Feldman, L.B., & Andjelkovic, D. (1992). Morphological analysis in word recognition. In R. Frost & L. Katz (Eds.), *Orthography, phonology, morphology, and meaning* (pp. 343-360). Netherlands: Elsevier Science Pub.

Fowler, A.E., & Liberman, I.Y. (1995). The role of phonology and orthography in morphological awareness. In L.B.Feldman (Ed.), *Morphological aspects of language processing* (pp. 157-188). Hillsdale, NJ: L. Erlbaum.

Fowler, C., Napps, S., & Feldman, L.B. (1985). Relations among regular and irregular morphologically related words in the lexicon as revealed by repetition priming. *Memory and Cognition, 13,* 241-255.

Frederiksen, J.R., & Kroll, J. F. (1976). Spelling and sound: Approaches to the internal lexicon. *Journal of Experimental Psychology, 2,* 361-379.

Gordon, P. (1989). Levels of affixation in the acquisition of English morphology. *Journal of Memory and Language, 28,* 519-530.

Jones, N.K. (1991). Development of morphophonemic segments in children's mental representations of words. *Applied Psycholinguistics, 12,* 217-239.

Leong, C.K. (1989). Productive knowledge of derivational rules in poor readers. *Annals of Dyslexia, 39,* 94-115.

Marslen-Wilson, W., Tyler, L.K., Waksler, R., & Older, L. (1994). Morphology and meaning in the English mental lexicon. *Psychological Review, 101.* 3-33.

Nagy, W. E., & Anderson, R. (1984). The number of words in printed school English. *Reading Research Quarterly, 19,* 304-330.

Nagy, W. E., & Anderson, R., Schommer, M., Scott, J.A., & Stallman, A.C. (1989). Morphological families and word recognition. *Reading Research Quarterly, 24,* 262-282.

Rubin, H. (1987). The development of morphological knowledge in relation to early spelling ability. *Haskins Laboratories Status Report on Speech Research, SR 89/90,* 121-131.

Schlagal, R. C. (1992). Patterns of orthographic development into the intermediate grades. In S. Templeton & D. R. Bear (Eds.), *Development of orthographic knowledge and the foundations of literacy: A memorial festschrift for Edmund H. Henderson (pp. 31-52).* Hillsdale, NJ: L. Erlbaum.

Schreuder, R., & Baayen, R.H. (1995). Modeling morphological processing. In L. Feldman (Ed.), *Morphological aspects of language processing* (pp. 131-154). Hillsdale, NJ: Lawrence Erlbaum Assoc.

Stolz, J.A., & Feldman, L.B. (1995). The role of orthographic and semantic transparency of the base morpheme in morphological processing. In L.B.Feldman (Ed.), *Morphological aspects of language processing* (pp. 109-130). Hillsdale, NJ: L. Erlbaum.

Taft, M., & Zhu, X. (1995). The representation of bound morphemes in the lexicon: A Chinese study. In L. Feldman (Ed.), *Morphological aspects of language processing* (pp. 293-316). Hillsdale, NJ: Lawrence Erlbaum Assoc.

Tyler, A., & Nagy, W. (1989). The acquisition of English derivational morphology. *Journal of Memory and Language, 28,* 649-667.

Tyler , A.,& Nagy, W. (1990). Use of derivational morphology during reading. *Cognition, 36,* 17-34.

Wysocki, K., & Jenkins, J. (1987). Deriving word meanings through morphological generalization. *Reading Research Quarterly, 22,* 66-81.

8. ACKNOWLEDGEMENT

We would like to acknowledge support from the Volweiler Foundation and a grant from the Alumnae of Northwestern University School of Speech. We would also like to thank the staff and students at Northwestern University Learning Disabilities Clinic, Cove School, and Immaculate Heart of Mary School for participating in this project.

9. ADDRESS FOR CORRESPONDENCE

Joanne F. Carlisle
University of Michigan
School of Education
610 East University Ave.
Ann Arbor, MI 48109-1259
United States of America
Phone: (734) 615-1267
email: jfcarl@umich.edu

ANNE FOWLER, LAURIE BETH FELDMAN,
DARINKA ANDJELKOVIC AND BANU ONEY

MORPHOLOGICAL AND PHONOLOGICAL ANALYSIS BY BEGINNING READERS: EVIDENCE FROM SERBIAN AND TURKISH

1. INTRODUCTION

Relative to the 25 years of intensive research demonstrating a central role for phonology in reading acquisition and skilled reading, efforts to understand the role of morphology are still at a preliminary stage. Ongoing research has focused on three main questions, each with clear parallels within the literature on phonology and reading.

The first question, prerequisite to the others, asks whether skilled adult readers are morphologically analytic, appreciating that morphologically complex words are made up of multiple meaningful units. A number of studies across different languages suggest that skilled readers *are* sensitive to the morphological structure of words (Caramazza, Laudanna & Romani, 1988; Feldman & Moskovljevic, 1985; McQueen & Cutler, 1997 Stanners, Neiser, Hernon & Hall, 1979), although investigators disagree as to whether the effects obtained support the view that morphology is explicitly represented in the lexicon (Caramazza et al., 1988; Marslen-Wilson, Tyler, Waksler & Older, 1994) or whether these effects emerge from the systematic mapping of form to meaning that characterizes morphologically related words (Rueckl, Mikolinski, Raveh, Miner & Mars, 1997).

The second question asks whether awareness of morphemes influences reading success in school-aged children. Whereas numerous studies indicate that awareness of *phonemes* is an important component of acquiring alphabetic literacy (for recent reviews see Blachman, 1994; Wagner, Torgesen & Rashotte, 1994), whether awareness of morphemes contributes to reading success is less solidly established. Suggestive evidence that morpheme awareness may be important derives from a small and growing number of studies indicating that skilled readers and spellers are more morphologically analytic than less skilled readers (e.g., Carlisle, 1987, 1988, 1995;

Elbro 1989; Elbro & Arnbak, 1996; Fowler & Liberman, 1995; Leong & Parkinson, 1995; Shankweiler, 1995).

Accepting that some aspects of morpheme awareness are correlated with reading success, it is a third question — what factors *influence* children's awareness of morphemes — that is the primary focus of the present research. Specifically, we ask to what extent individual differences in morpheme awareness derive from the same — or different — factors as underlie individual differences in phoneme awareness. Whereas there are reasons to believe that phonological processing abilities influence ability to gain phoneme awareness (e.g., Fowler 1991), it is possible that morpheme awareness depends on semantic factors as well. To the extent that individual differences in morpheme awareness *cannot* be attributed to the same (viz., phonological) factors as influence individual differences in phoneme awareness, it can be argued that morpheme and phoneme awareness make separate contributions to reading success. On the other hand, if morpheme and phoneme awareness are highly correlated and stem from a single underlying factor, we would argue that lack of morpheme awareness does not constitute a risk factor for reading disability separate from that posed by lack of phoneme awareness. In the present study, we turn to two languages with complex morphological systems, Serbian and Turkish, to explore semantic and phonological influences on morpheme awareness and to directly assess the association between phoneme and morpheme awareness.

Before considering factors that influence morpheme awareness, we distinguish between inflections and derivations, two types of derivation, and point out some specific facts about English morphology that limit any conclusions that can be generalized from the study of English alone. Inflectional morphemes (such as plural or past tense in English) preserve the word class of the base and have highly predictable (or 'transparent') semantic consequences, as illustrated by comparing *suggest* with *suggests*. Inflectional morphology is considered an integral part of grammatical knowledge and is typically mastered in oral language during the preschool years. In contrast, derivational morphemes (such as the agentive or diminutive in English) typically change word class, and meaning relations are less predictable, as illustrated by comparing *suggest* with *suggestive*. Whereas inflectional relatives such as *suggest/suggests* are semantically transparent, derivational relatives such as *suggest/suggestive* are semantically more 'opaque' and each is treated as a distinct lexical item. New derivational markers are more freely added to language systems than new inflectional markers (note the recent addition of -wise as in *moneywise*, *workwise* or *schoolwise*). Derivational markers also vary considerably in their productivity (contrast *-ous* and *-ation*), and continue to be acquired throughout life, with morphological gains influenced by exposure to both spoken and written vocabulary. Whereas inflectional morphology is generally considered to be part of grammatical knowledge, linguists have consigned much of derivational morphology to the lexicon (e.g., Aronoff, 1976). Given these differences between inflections and derivations, it is not surprising that adult skilled readers in a variety of languages including Italian (Laudanna, Badecker & Caramazza, 1989), Serbian (Feldman, 1994) and Hebrew (Raveh & Feldman, 1998) show more consistent evidence of analyticity when reading inflectionally complex words than when reading derivationally complex words.

In addition to differences between inflections and derivations that apply generally across languages, there are several differences that are specific to English. For one thing, English has a very limited number of inflectional markers as compared to a sizable number of derivational markers and the latter vary considerably in phonological and semantic transparency. In addition, derivations in English tend to be longer than inflections and are more likely to require phonological changes to the base form that can render the base morpheme less recognizable (e.g., compare *courage* with *courageous*). Disparities between English derivations and inflections in number, productivity, and phonological change motivate us to look at other languages, specifically Serbian and Turkish, where both inflections and derivations are numerous and productive. By studying youngsters as they gain morphological awareness in these languages, we can more systematically compare awareness of inflections and derivations, while gauging the consequences of phonological factors on morpheme awareness.

2. POTENTIAL FACTORS INFLUENCING AWARENESS OF MORPHEMES

2.1 Semantic factors

Because derivations tend to be semantically more opaque relative to inflections, comparisons of inflectional and derivational knowledge should provide some index of the role of semantic factors in morphological awareness. In English however, in which inflections and derivations differ in multiple ways, it is difficult to know how to interpret whatever performance differences are observed. In fact, due to the limited set of English inflections, few studies of morpheme awareness in beginning readers have even focused on inflectional morphology. Although there is evidence that children with specific language impairment (SLI) have some trouble generalizing the past tense or the plural marker and fail to represent these in written language (e.g., Rubin, 1988), it is assumed that most schoolchildren have little difficulty with regular inflections in English. This claim is supported in a recent study by Carlisle (1995) who found kindergarten children achieved 36.5% accuracy, and first graders 61.1% accuracy, in producing regular inflected forms. In contrast, knowledge of English derivational morphology is highly variable among schoolchildren, and there are good reasons (both theoretical and empirical) to predict that awareness of derivations would be associated with facility in reading and spelling (see Elbro 1989 or Fowler and Liberman, 1995 for a discussion).

We can turn to the productive morphological systems of Serbian to compare knowledge of derivations and inflections. To the extent that derivational tasks make greater semantic demands than do inflectional tasks and that vocabulary knowledge assesses semantic demands, we would expect that (1) children will display greater awareness of inflections than of derivations, and (2) vocabulary knowledge will correlate more closely with awareness of derivations than of inflections. If semantic factors alone account for differences between awareness of inflections and derivations, then awareness of inflections and derivations should be equivalently related to phoneme awareness once individual differences in vocabulary knowledge are partialled out.

2.2 *Phonological factors*

Vocabulary knowledge does not wholly explain the morphological insensitivity evident in poor readers of English. Carlisle (1988), for example, provides data on adolescents who know the meaning of *magic* and of *magician*, but seem not to be aware that the two words are morphologically related. Knowledge is assessed in a morpheme production task in which children hear the stem (or derived form) and a sentence frame and are asked to produce the appropriate form , as illustrated in (1).

(1) Magic. The man at the party was a wonderful –(*magician)*

There are differing accounts of morphological insensitivity. On the one hand, Carlisle attributes failure on the morpheme production task to a general lack of metalinguistic insight. In contrast, Fowler and Liberman (1995) hypothesize that the difficulty may be more specifically phonological, because the morphological relationships tested were often phonologically obscure. *Magic/magician* is a case in point, because the stem changes in both stress and consonant palatalization in the derived form. To test this hypothesis, Fowler and Liberman (1995) presented Carlisle's production task to good and poor readers (total $\underline{n} = 48$); the task was modified to include morphological pairs matched on frequency and derivational suffix, differing only in terms of phonological opacity. On phonologically "transparent pairs" (e.g., *four/fourth*), poor readers displayed as much morpheme awareness as good readers of equivalent receptive vocabulary. On "opaque" pairs with identical suffixes and word frequencies (e.g., *five/fifth*), poor readers performed significantly worse than the better readers. A similar pattern was obtained when the same stimuli were presented to a larger sample (n= 353) of 7.5 to 9.5 year olds selected to represent a wide range of learning disabilities (Shankweiler et al. 1995). In that study, there was a significant correlation between performance on phoneme deletion and overall accuracy on the morphological production task (r= .67), with morpheme awareness contributing little variance (R^2= .051) to word reading skill that was not also associated with performance on the phoneme awareness task. There was, moreover, a highly significant interaction between reading group and phonological transparency of bases in the morphological task. Although both normal and disabled readers performed less accurately on those morphological word pairs involving phonological change, the difference between the phonological change and phonological no-change performance was greater in the disabled readers than in the normal readers. Because poor readers were almost as good as good readers on morphologically complex forms that were phonologically transparent, it may be weak phonology, rather than lack of analytic skill, per se, that exacerbates the morpheme awareness difficulties of poor readers such as those studied by Carlisle (1987).

Identifying a single phonological weakness that can account for deficits in both phoneme and morpheme awareness would be consistent with the phonological deficit account of reading disability as articulated by Brady (1997), Liberman, Shankweiler, & Liberman (1989), or Stanovich (1988; 1992). According to the phonological deficit hypothesis, children may have difficulty in appreciating phonological structure not so much because they lack general metalinguistic skill, but because they have more fundamental deficits in phonological processing. The same phonological weaknesses could explain a broad range of difficulties associated with reading disability including less accurate speech perception, production, and naming and a more limited verbal memory span.

In previous research, the association between morpheme and phoneme awareness (or between morpheme awareness and reading) was evident only when stimuli included phonologically opaque stems - specifically those whose base morphemes underwent phonological changes with the addition of a derivational suffix - and this finding is consistent with a phonological interpretation. Mann & Singson (this volume) also argue that "one way to study the dependence of morphological awareness on phonological skill is to compose a ... task that uses phonologically "opaque" ... versus phonologically "transparent" ... derived words" (p. 10).

2.3 *Metalinguistic factors*

Both semantic (vocabulary) and phonological factors influence performance on a morphological awareness task. Nevertheless, insensitivity to morphological structure can arise even when vocabulary is not an issue and the relationship between derived and base forms is phonologically transparent. This finding suggests that some children are insensitive to language structures in general and thus may fail to appreciate not only the association between *five* and *fifth*, but also that between *four* and *fourth*. Such children should also have (or have had, prior to intensive intervention) difficulties isolating and segmenting phonemes. Accordingly, a general metalinguistic skill, independent of vocabulary knowledge or phonological processing weaknesses, may contribute to success in learning to read (e.g., Gleitman & Rozin, 1977; Tunmer, Herriman & Nesdale, 1988). Although insensitivity to phonemes may be the most salient weakness when children are first learning to read, insensitivity to morphemes may persist in these same children when they encounter multimorphemic words (Carlisle 1987; Mann & Singson, this volume). To the extent that a general metalinguistic skill influences morphological awareness, a significant association between awareness of phonemes and morphemes should be evident not only when the morphological stimuli are phonologically opaque (as in Fowler & Liberman, 1995), but also when the stimuli are phonologically transparent.

According to Carlisle (1987, 1988, 1995), a single underlying metalinguistic deficit may limit awareness of both phonemes and morphemes, each in turn having consequences for reading and spelling. Even in learning-disabled adolescents who had achieved phonological awareness, Carlisle (1987) observed that insensitivity to the morphemic structure of words constituted a separate and further obstacle to reading success. As evidence, she points to attempts to spell *magician* that were phonetically plausible (*magishun*, *magition*, *majision*), but failed to exploit the morphological relationship between *magic* and *magician*. Carlisle's claim is that even after phonemes are made salient, explicit instruction in morphemic analysis is required to counteract persistent underlying metalinguistic deficits (see Carlisle 1995: Carlisle & Nomanbhoy, 1993 for compelling evidence of a unique morphological factor). Carlisle notes that, "To some extent, the morphological and phonological awareness tasks (particularly production and [phoneme deletion]) may have tapped similar *metalinguistic* capabilities" (1995, p. 203, italics ours).

A somewhat different metalinguistic account derives from the data of Elbro and Arnbak (1996) who assessed the extent to which adolescent poor readers (of Danish) applied morphemic analysis in deriving meaning from written material. Intriguingly, morpheme analysis of words that were both phonologically and semantically transparent was relatively good in their adolescent poor readers, especially when compared to younger reading age-matched readers. In this group of adolescents, reliance on morpheme recognition in reading apparently served to *compensate* for persistently weak phonological skills. Although Elbro (1989) found that morpheme analysis is weaker in poor readers than in age-matched good readers, Elbro and Arnbak (1996) claim that it is possible to instill awareness of morphemes independently from awareness of phonemes — or even of syllables. Evidence derives from a morpheme awareness training program they designed for students whose phonetic skills remained weak into high school. The Elbro account is consistent with the claim that poor readers have such extreme difficulty with phoneme awareness because phonemes are most encapsulated within the linguistic processing system (Liberman et al. 1977). More recently, Byrne (1997) provides developmental data to indicate that children come prepared to recognize symbols (words) for meaningful units (morphemes), but that they are not "prepared" to consciously recognize units that lack meaning in and of themselves (phonemes and syllables). In sum, both claim that morpheme and phoneme awareness deficits derive from a common metalinguistic deficit, however it is easier to heighten awareness of morphemes.

The goal in the present study, was to assess the association between phoneme awareness and morpheme awareness in languages with complex inflectional and derivational morphology so as to identify factors that influence a child's awareness of morphology. Our first experiment focused on Serbian, which has highly productive derivational suffixes, and obligatory inflections for case, number, and gender, that are fused within one affix. Within our Serbian experimental materials, phonological predictability varies widely among derivationally related pairs, whereas most inflectionally related pairs are phonologically predictable. If phonological complexity mediates the relation between phoneme and morpheme awareness, phoneme awareness should be strongly associated only with awareness of derivationally related pairs that are phonologically opaque. On the other hand, if metalinguistic rather than phonological factors underlie morpheme and phoneme awareness, we would also expect phoneme awareness to be associated with inflectionally related word pairs and phonemically transparent derivational pairs, even after controlling for general vocabulary knowledge.

In Experiment 2, we looked at the awareness of inflectional and derivational morphology in Turkish, which is an agglutinative language with clearly separable inflectional and derivational morphemes. In Turkish, word stems remain phonologically unaltered when either derivational or inflectional affixes are added. Interestingly, affixes are influenced by the stem to which they attached, as the vowel of the affix takes on the same fronting/rounding features as the vowel of the stem. Based on these features of Turkish, our predictions were more complex. Phonological influences should be equivalent for both inflectional and derivational morphology, but it is not clear whether to expect the influence of phonology to be limited due to unchanged stems, or to be pervasive due to the varying phonological and orthographic shape of a particular affix.

As a word of caution, the results from the two experiments described below must each be interpreted independently. Our cross-linguistic comparison is probably most valuable for providing some data on the awareness of inflectional and derivational morphemes in non-English languages, but it also highlights some of the challenges inherent in constructing parallel studies across different languages, cultures and laboratories.

3. EXPERIMENT 1

In our first experiment, we examined the awareness of phonemes, inflections and derivations in Serbian, using the morphological production task employed by Carlisle (1987, 1988) and by Fowler and Liberman (1995). Because we tested both derivational and inflectional morphology, we modified the design to ensure that familiarity of a particular word form was not confounded with type of morphological relation (inflection versus derivational) or with the syntactic complexity of a particular sentence frame. In Serbian, for example, nouns can be formed from verbs (e.g., PLATA '*salary*' comes from PLATITI '*to pay*'), and verbs can be formed from nouns (e.g., PEGLATI '*to iron*' comes from PEGLA '*iron*'). In order to avoid the problem of determining the potentially ambiguous status of some morphological forms, we defined inflectional and derivational productions relative to a source word. Morphological relatives that share a base morpheme and differ only in their inflectional affixes are classified as inflectional responses. For example, if a child sees TO SWIM and produces SWIMS (3rd person singular) or sees SWIMMER and produces SWIMMERS, both responses are classified as inflectional changes. Morphological relatives that preserve the base morpheme but alter derivational (and optionally inflectional) affixes are classified as derivational responses. For example, the response SWIMMERS to TO SWIM or SWIMS to SWIMMER are derivational responses.

A preliminary question is whether beginning readers are equally able to produce the same target word when it is derivationally or inflectionally related to the source item. Although word class and other modifications should make the derivational changes inherently more challenging than inflectional changes, the fusional attributes of inflectional affixes could make the inflectional task challenging as well. For example, there is one affix in Serbian for the masculine singular dative (viz., U) and a different affix for the masculine plural dative (viz., IMA). In short, the child cannot use simple additive processes to append one inflection after another.

Our primary questions concern the relation between morphological awareness and other factors. We anticipated that morphological awareness would be importantly associated with vocabulary knowledge, especially for derivations. The critical question is whether, having controlled for the effects of vocabulary, we would still find a correlation between awareness of phonemes and morphemes, and whether it would vary as a function of morphological type and phonological transparency. If morphological type influences performance with phonology kept constant, we have evidence for a morphological factor. Similarly, if phonological factors influence performance with morphological type held constant, phonology would be implicated. If the correlation with phoneme awareness are roughly constant across morphological type and phonological complexity, results would support a general metalinguistic account of individual differences in morphological awareness.

3.1 Method

3.1.1 Participants

Forty children between seven and eight years of age who were native speakers of Serbian completed the experiment. They were all students at the Vuk Karadic elementary school in the center of Belgrade, and had reading abilities in the average or above average range. Four of these children failed to perform the task adequately after three exposures to the practice materials and were dropped from the study.

3.1.2 Materials

Thirty-six sentence pairs were constructed. Each sentence contained between four and six words. The target word was always in final position and varied with respect to word class. Sentence frames were constructed so that, depending on the source word, either an inflectional or a derivational substitution was required, and frames were paired so that for one source word both an inflectional and a derivational adjustment were necessary. For example, in one condition children were required to fit a morphological relative of the nominal source word KUVAR meaning *a cook* (agent in nominative singular) into the sentence frame

(2) Mama mi pomaže da _____.
Mother helps me to ____.

This sentence requires the first person singular verb form KUVAM which is related by derivation to the source word KUVAR[1]. In a second condition, the infinitive verb KUVATI was presented as the source word for the same sentence frame. Here the source word and the appropriate response for that sentence frame are related by inflection. The third and fourth conditions presented the same source words (i.e., KUVAR, KUVATI) in a different sentence frame thereby reversing which response was related by inflection and which was related by derivation. For example,

(3) Ovaj restoran ima dobrog _____.
This restaurant has a good_____.

requires the accusative singular form of the agent, KUVARA. The response KUVARA is inflectionally related to the noun KUVAR and derivationally related to the verb KUVATI. Subjects were instructed to "finish the sentence by changing the first [source] word"; they participated in a practice session until they could perform the task successfully for all practice items.

Across items, all four combinations of sentence frame and source word appeared equally often in each of four experimental lists. Each participant was tested on one of the four combinations of sentence frame and source word, and, across subjects, the same base morpheme appeared in all conditions. This design minimized effects due to sentence frame and to the morphological complexity and the familiarity of the source word and of the response. Morphological variants of the source word included a noun and either an infinitive, a gerund or an adjective.

In the phoneme deletion task modeled after Rosner and Simon (1971), children had to pronounce a source word aloud after deleting the designated phoneme (e.g., Can you say PLATA? Can you say PLATA without the /pe/[2]. Of the 30 source words presented, 10 were monosyllabic and 20 bisyllabic, each containing four or five phonemes. All phonemes to be deleted were consonants embedded within clusters; the clusters occurred equally often in initial, medial, and final position. All words remained orthographically legal but became meaningless sequences after phoneme deletion. For example, by deleting /pe/ from PLATA, they derive LATA; which is meaningless. Similarly, by deleting /de/ from REKORD, they arrive at REKOR. See Appendix A for the full set of materials.

3.1.3 Procedure

Children were tested individually by a native speaker of Serbian, and responses were transcribed by that experimenter. Because all materials were read aloud by the experimenter, no reading by the child was required. The morphological production task was presented first and was completed in a single 20-minute session. In the morphological task, children heard the source word, the sentence frame and the source word again; their task was to complete the sentence by adjusting the morphological affixes on the source word to make it fit semantically and syntactically with the sentence frame. All correct responses required at least one morphological substitution. The phoneme deletion task was administered one week later by the same native speaker of Serbian, who again transcribed the responses. Subjects were instructed to listen to thirty words which were also printed on cards and to pronounce each of them aloud without the designated phoneme[3]. Prior to the test, children practiced on a small set of examples until they could perform the task correctly. As noted above, all words became pronounceable but meaningless sequences after phoneme deletion.

Several weeks after the second session, the children were given general cognitive tests which served to estimate verbal (PPVT-R Form L, Dunn and Dunn, 1981) and non-verbal (WISC blocks revised as REVISK for Serbian) intelligence. The former task is a test of receptive vocabulary knowledge; children listen to a word (Serbian was substituted for English) and indicate what they think it means by pointing to one of four pictures. Both standard scores and number correct were calculated, with analyses relying on number correct. In the non-verbal task, the child duplicates a complex picture with colored blocks. Because the child must analyze the components of the block pattern in order to reconstruct it, performance is interpreted as reflecting a general analytic ability that is visual-spatial but not linguistic. Raw score correct on this task was used in the analyses.

3.2 Results and Discussion

On the test of morphological awareness, inflectional errors tended to be fewer than derivational errors ($F_1(1,39) = 37.39$, $MSe = 6.08$, $p < .001$; $F_2(1,35) = 42.32$, $MSe = 1.7$, $p < .001$). Mean errors were 5% (*SD* .08) and 19% (*SD* .15) respectively (see Table 1). The number of errors ranged between 0 and 7 out of a possible 18 on the inflectional subtest and between 0 and 9 errors out of a possible 18 on the derivational subtest. Twenty one of the forty children made no errors on inflections and 3 made no errors on derivations.[4] The mean error score on the phoneme deletion task was 6.9 (*SD* 5.9), and scores ranged from 0 to 22 errors out of a possible total of 30. The mean standard score on PPVT was 107 (*SD* 6.9) with a range of 93 to 126. The mean score on Blocks was 26 (*SD* 12.0) with a range of 8 to 50.

Table 1. Mean percent errors for sentence frames requiring inflectional and derivations adjustments

Language	*Type*	
	Inflection	*Derivation*
Serbian (Exp. 1)		
overall	5	19
no sound change	3	8
Turkish (Exp. 2)		
overall	15	33

The number of items correct on the inflectional morphology task (summed over sentence frame) was significantly correlated with phoneme deletion, $r(34) = .37$, $p < .02$ (see Table 2). Verbal intelligence (PPVT) accounted for 20% of the variance in performance on the inflectional morphology test, $r(34) = .45$, $p < .01$. In contrast, WISC Blocks accounted for only 9% of the variance on the inflectional test, $r(34) = .30$. When the PPVT score was partialled out, the correlation of inflectional score with phoneme deletion score was not significant, $r(33) = .19$.

Performance on the derivational morphology task was also significantly correlated with phoneme deletion, $r(34) = .68$, $p < .001$. Scores on verbal and non-verbal intelligence accounted for 33% and 25% of the variance on derivational morphology scores, $r(34) = .57$ and $.50$, respectively, p's $< .005$. The relationship between phonological and derivational performance remained significant when the contribution of verbal intelligence to derivational performance was removed, $r(33) = .55$, $p < .001$), as well as when the contributions of both verbal and non-verbal intelligence were both eliminated, $r(32) = .48$, $p < .01$). Performance on the phonological task accounted for a significant 23% of the variance on the derivational morphology task (see Table 3).

Table 2. Correlation matrix for Serbian. Reported are correlations and partial correlations (bottom) of inflectional and derivational productions with phoneme deletion (verbal and non-verbal IQ removed)

	phon	inflect	inflect.r	deriv	deriv.r	Blocks	PPVT	morph
phon	1.000	.373	.302	.679	.346	.568	.502	.678
inflect	.15a	1.000	.543	.337	.213	.302	.445	.714
inflect.r	.23a		1.000	.098	.382	.150	.071	.324
deriv	.48a			1.000	.419	.498	.573	.900
deriv.r	.23a				1.000	.242	.214	.410
Blocks						1.000	.438	.510
PPVT							1.000	.633
morph								1.000

Note. a refers to partial correlation with PPVT and Blocks

Table 3. Correlations and partial correlations (bottom) of inflectional and derivational productions with phoneme deletion (verbal and non-verbal IQ removed)

	PHON	*inflection*	*derivation*	*IQ.perf*	*IQ.verbal*
PHON	1.000	.569	.589	.444	-.055
inflection	.47a	1.000	.609	.450	.046
derivation	.49a		1.000	.454	.038
IQ.perf				1.000	.027
IQ.verbal					1.000

Note. a is partial correlation with IQ perf and IQ verbal removed

The uniformly high performance on the inflectional task suggests that the metalinguistic demands involved are not a source of great difficulty for these children, making it less likely that variation in performance on other morphological tasks is a simple reflection of analytic metacognitive skill. We then ask why there is such a strong association between scores on the phoneme deletion and derivational morphology tasks, but not between the phoneme deletion and inflectional tasks. In this regard, it is important to note that phonological changes to the base were more prevalent for derivational than for inflectional responses in Experiment 1.

Post-hoc inspection revealed that approximately 20% of the sentence frames entailed an idiosyncratic phonological (and orthographic) change to the base in order to form one of the correct responses in the derivational condition. When bases that required phonological changes to the base in either condition were eliminated and means and correlations were recomputed, mean errors for inflectional and derivational responses fell to 3% (*SD* .04) and 8% (*SD* .07) respectively. Moreover, with phonological change items excluded, the partial correlation of inflectional production with phoneme deletion (controlling for PPVT) did not differ significantly from that of derivational production with phoneme deletion, $r(33) = .31$ and .28, respectively; both correlations missed significance, however [p's $< .10$]. When both PPVT and BLOCKS were partialled out, the correlations were identical, in each case $r(32) = .23$. In summary, when sound change items were removed from both the inflectional and derivational conditions, the respective correlations with phoneme deletion did not differ and were not significant.

We have demonstrated that the ability to manipulate phonemic segments explicitly is associated with the ability to produce morphologically appropriate forms in a sentence completion task. More specifically, the association between morphological production and performance on a phoneme deletion task was significant only when the correct response requires a derivational adjustment and entails a phonological change to the base. The relationship exists independently of the contribution(s) of verbal (and non-verbal) intelligence. In contrast, command of inflectional morphology was quite high in this sample of children, with variation unrelated to phoneme awareness after controlling for vocabulary knowledge. Although the lack of correlation may simply reflect a limited variability in the distribution of scores, other results suggest that the minimal phonological demands on inflectional morphology may also be a factor. Specifically, when derivational items that underwent phonological change were eliminated, the partial correlations for derivational productions with phoneme deletion did not differ from those for inflectional productions with phoneme deletion. Consistent with the association that Fowler and Liberman (1995) found for phonologically opaque but not for phonologically transparent derivational forms, we interpret the results of Experiment 1 as evidence that the shared variance in the phoneme deletion and derivational morphology tasks reflects an underlying phonological skill and that this phonological skill is not required to the same extent in the inflectional morphology task. In essence, the most parsimonious way to explain the discrepancy between the results for inflections and derivations is to argue that strength of the relation between morpheme and phoneme awareness varies with sound change, and that changes to the base are more common for derivational than for inflectional responses. In Experiment 2, we again have the opportunity — unavailable in English — to explore the relation between phoneme deletion and two kinds of morphological performance. If in Turkish, as in Serbian, phoneme deletion is associated with derivational, but not with inflectional morphology where there is no viable phonological explanation, then other interpretations would need to be considered.

4. EXPERIMENT 2

In Experiment 2, we attempt to replicate the association between morphological productions and phoneme deletion performance with beginning readers of Turkish. In Turkish, phonological and orthographic changes to inflectional as well as derivational affixes are very common and this provides the basis of the critical experimental manipulation. A related advantage of studying morphological processing in a language in which changes to the base morpheme are minimal but changes to the form of the affix are common is that phonological and orthographic variations have no impact on processing the base morpheme (Chialant & Caramazza, 1995).

Turkish is an agglutinating language, combining, for example, the affix for dative (viz., A) and the affix for plural (e.g., LAR or LER) to yield the dative plural ending LARA. Although the base form is not affected by affixation, and although the affixed forms themselves are readily analyzable into distinct morphemes, Turkish is unusual in that the form of an affix can vary depending on whether it is appended to a base that ends with a vowel or with a consonant. In order to avoid sequences of vowels, in some cases a vowel is omitted; in others a buffer consonant is added (Underhill, 1976). For example, the first person singular suffix is produced as IM after a consonant and YIM after a vowel. Other changes to the form of the affix also occur. Initial consonants of some suffixes assimilate in voicing to the previous consonant. So for example, the third person singular ending is produced as TIR after a voiceless consonant and DIR after a voiced consonant. Most importantly, affixes are affected by vowel harmony rules. Although any of the eight Turkish vowels can appear in the first syllable of a word, each following vowel is conditioned by the vowel that precedes it. With respect to the vowels in affixes, for example, the vowel in TIR/DIR above can assume any of four interpretations (corresponding to /u/ (rounded) or /i/ (unrounded) that is either fronted or back). Changes in pronunciation of affixes are also captured in the spelling.

4.1 Method

4.1.1 Participants

Participants attended a public school in a middle socioeconomic community in the center of Istanbul, Turkey. Pilot testing revealed that by midyear of first grade, children were at ceiling on the phoneme deletion task, even with manipulations to stimulus materials. For this reason, we elected to work with kindergartners between five and six years of age. Thirty-two children participated, including eight children from each of four kindergarten classes within one school; all were native speakers of Turkish.

4.1.2 Materials

Sixteen sentence pairs were constructed. Each contained between four and six words and the position of the target word was at the end of the sentence. As in the previous experiment, sentence frames were paired such that in one sentence frame a particular source word needed the change of an inflectional affix and the other source word needed the change of a derivational affix but that in the second sentence frame, the word that previously needed a derivational change now required an inflectional change and vice versa.

For example, in one condition, children heard KAÇAK the agent of *run away* (viz., *fugitive*) in nominative case and had to fit it into the sentence frame

(4) Polis bugün yakalad> saklanan_____.
The police caught the ______ today.

This sentence requires the accusative singular form of the agent, KAÇT〉. Other children heard the infinitive KAÇMAK and had to fit it into the same sentence frame so as to produce KAÇA⁄›. The source word KAÇAK is related to the response KAÇA⁄› by inflection (i.e., adding the ı and changing K to ⁄. By contrast, the source word KAÇMAK is related to the response KAÇA⁄› by derivation (i.e., dropping the MAK and adding A⁄ and ›).

The third and fourth conditions consisted of the same source words (i.e., KAÇAK, KAÇMAK) with a different sentence frame thereby reversing which response was related by inflection and which was related by derivation. For example, some children were required to modify the source word KAÇAK to fit into the sentence frame

(5) Yakalanan h>rs>z dün hapisden _____.
The thief_____last week.

This sentence requires the third person singular verb form KAÇTI which is related by derivation to the source word KAÇAK (dropping the AK and adding TI) and by inflection to the infinitive source word KAÇMAK (dropping the MAK and adding TI). Stimulus materials are presented in the Appendix.

Note that in the present example, the base always appears as KAÇ. In the Turkish materials, base morphemes did not undergo phonological or orthographic change. By contrast, across items in the morphological production task, the same morphological affix could take different forms. For example, the accusative singular suffix had four different surface forms and the agent singular suffix had two.

Across items, all four combinations of sentence frame and source word appeared equally often in each of four experimental lists. Each participant was tested on one of the four combinations of sentence frame and source word, and, across subjects, the same base morpheme appeared in all conditions. As noted above, this design minimized effects due to sentence frame and to the morphological complexity and the familiarity of the source word and the response.

Ten items were included in the Turkish phoneme deletion task. Words were presented orally by the experimenter and children were instructed to pronounce the word without the final sound. Subjects were required to delete final consonants or final vowels such that the remaining portion of the word was always an unrelated real word in Turkish. Four practice words preceded the test items. In contrast to the Serbian studies, here the source word was meaningful both with and without the deleted letter in the task. Segmentation of consonant clusters was not required.

To estimate general cognitive function, each child was given verbal (similarity, arithmetic, and vocabulary) and non-verbal (Blocks, object assembly, and coding) subtests of the WISC-R intelligence tests.

4.1.3 Procedure

Subjects were tested individually by a native speaker of Turkish and responses were transcribed by that experimenter. Due to the age of the children, the size of the stimulus sets were reduced relative to Experiment 1. It is important to note that this difference in procedure is relevant only if we fail to obtain significant correlations in conditions that were significant in Experiment 1. The phoneme deletion task and the morphological production task were administered in one testing session. In the morphological task, children were orally presented with a source word before and after its sentence frame and they were asked to complete the sentence by adjusting the morphological affixes on the source word to make it fit semantically and syntactically with the sentence frame. All correct responses required at least one morphological substitution. Children participated in a practice session until they could perform the task successfully for all practice items. The test of cognitive function was conducted in a separate session approximately one week after the morphological test.

4.2 Results and Discussion

In Turkish, as in Serbian, derivational responses proved more difficult than inflectional responses (see Table 1), $F_1(1,31) = 44.64$, $MSe = 36.0$, $p < .0001$; $F_2(1,31) = 36.0$, $MSe = 36.0$, $p < .0001$. Mean error rates were 15% (*SD* .13) for inflectional responses and 33% (*SD* .8) for derivational responses respectively. The range was from 0 to 3 (out of 8) errors for inflections and from 0 to 6 (out of 8) errors for derivations. Ten of the 32 children made no errors on the inflections; two children made no errors on derivations.

Mean number of errors on the phoneme deletion task was 6.1 out of 10 (*SD* 2.0) and scores ranged between 2 and 7 errors. The mean score on the verbal IQ test was 110 (*SD* 9.8) with a range of 89 to 129. The mean score on the non-verbal performance IQ test was 115 (*SD* 8.3) with a range of 99 to 130. (Scores were prorated because not all subtests were administered.)

Results indicated a significant correlation between phonemic deletion and the inflection condition (summed over sentence frame) of the sentence completion task, $r(30) = .57$, $p < .001$. The contribution of verbal intelligence to the inflectional score was also significant, $r(30) = .45$, $p < .01$, but non-verbal intelligence accounted for less than 1% of the variance on the inflectional morphology score. When the contribution of verbal intelligence was removed, the partial correlation of the inflectional and phoneme scores remained significant, $r(29) = .46$, $p < .01$.

The pattern was quite similar for the derivational production task, with performance on the phoneme deletion task accounting for 36% of the variance in the derivation condition $r(30) =. 59$, $p < .001$. Verbal intelligence accounted for 21% of the variance and non-verbal intelligence accounted for less than 1% of the variance on the derivational morphology score. When the contribution of verbal and non-verbal intelligence was removed, the partial correlation of derivational and phoneme score was significant, $r(29) = .49$, $p < .01$. These correlations are particularly impressive because the number of items was reduced.

In summary, in Turkish, performance on the phonological task was significantly related to both production tasks, accounting for 21% and 24% of the unique variance in the inflectional and derivational completion tasks respectively. Turkish patterned differently from Serbian in that, with the effect of verbal intelligence removed, respective correlations for inflectional and derivational productions with phoneme deletion were quite comparable. Importantly, in the present experiment, the incidence of phonological change did not vary between inflectional and derivational productions. In neither condition did base morphemes undergo phonological or orthographic change; the task was phonologically complex, however, in that in both conditions, the same morphological affix could assume different phonological and orthographic forms.

5. GENERAL DISCUSSION

In the present paper, we explored the relations between phoneme and morpheme awareness in two languages with complex and highly productive morphological systems. Different subject attributes, researchers, and language structures made direct comparisons across languages impossible. Therefore, each study must be considered on its own merits. However, given the dearth of cross-language research on young children's developing awareness of language, it is useful to note similarities and differences across the two experiments and to compare the results with the patterns that have been observed in studies with English-speaking children. The large number of differences in procedure and language structure make the commonalities across Serbian, Turkish and English of considerable interest. Although our potential to unambiguously interpret differences across languages is compromised, we note these differences and consider possible explanations.

Our strongest result concerns differences in awareness of inflectional and derivational morphology. Although there is some evidence that children perform better with inflectional than with derivational morphemes in English (Carlisle, 1995), the inflectional morphology system in English differs dramatically from that of derivational morphology. Replication across languages is informative. In both Serbian and Turkish, children achieved significantly greater accuracy when asked to add an inflectional ending to a source word than when asked to add a derivational ending. In Serbian 7 to 8 year olds, this inflectional advantage was 12%; in Turkish 5 and 6 year olds, the advantage was 18%. As dictated by the experimental design, the difference between adding inflectional and derivational endings cannot be attributed to the complexity or familiarity of the final form. The accuracy advantage for inflectional over derivational morphology in a sentence completion task is consistent with the results of a lexical decision study using long term repetition priming. In a lexical decision task, skilled readers of Serbian showed greater facilitation between morphological relatives when they were related by inflection than when by derivation (Feldman, 1994). Both the present study with children and the adult study suggest a closer relation between inflected than between derived forms.

In both the Serbian and Turkish studies, we also demonstrated that children who are better at phonological analysis tend to be better at analysis of derivational morphology, even after controlling for differences in vocabulary knowledge and nonverbal intelligence. This finding seems especially robust, given that different stimulus materials were employed in Serbian and Turkish and given that the Serbian children were two years older than the Turkish youngsters. These results are consistent with other research linking facility with derivational morphology to phoneme awareness and/or reading in English (Carlisle, 1995; Fowler & Liberman, 1995; Mann & Singson, this volume; Shankweiler et al., 1995) and in Danish (Elbro, 1989; Elbro & Arnbak, 1996).

The pattern of correlations obtained across languages is consistent with several of the accounts of morphological awareness introduced above. We address each in turn. The first possibility that we considered is that morphological awareness would be strongly associated with vocabulary knowledge, especially for derivations. In fact, vocabulary knowledge was a significant predictor of morphological production in both languages, although vocabulary knowledge was equally related to performance with inflections and with derivations. We reasoned that if vocabulary accounted for most of the variance in morphological production, then a partial correlation between morpheme and phoneme awareness would not be significant. This was true, but only for Serbian stimuli that were phonologically transparent. Even after partialling out the effect of vocabulary, phoneme deletion was associated with nontransparent Serbian inflections and derivations and with all Turkish inflections and derivations. This pattern indicates that vocabulary knowledge is related to morphological production, but that it cannot account fully for the relation between morpheme and phoneme awareness (cf. Carlisle & Stone, this volume).

The second possibility we considered is that the phonological demands of a morpheme production task mediate any association between morpheme and phoneme awareness not explained by vocabulary knowledge. This was the interpretation proposed by Fowler and Liberman (1995). The results from Serbian nicely fit this hypothesis inasmuch as phoneme awareness is specifically related to morphological production (after partialling out vocabulary) only when the stimuli included derivationally related pairs involving phonological change. The findings are similar enough to those of Shankweiler et al. (1995) for us to be quite confident that, at the very least, phonological differences in the stem of morphologically related forms intensify any existing association with phoneme awareness.

The findings from Turkish do not fit so neatly into the phonological hypothesis, as originally stated. If phonological differences in the *base forms* of morphologically related pairs dictate the strength of the association between morpheme and phoneme awareness, then we would not predict the significant associations we obtained in Turkish. Morphologically related pairs shared stems that were phonologically identical in both the derivation and inflection conditions. Alternatively, phonological complexity of the *affix* may also exacerbate the skill differences in the morphological production task even when the stems are transparent. This is plausible given that accurate morphological production in the present task requires the child to produce both the appropriate stem and affixes[5].

If phonological complexity of the affix also influences the association between phoneme and morpheme awareness, then English speaking children might have more difficulty with the plural or past tense affixes (because these vary phonetically depending on the final consonant of the stem) than with the progressive marker (which is consistently /IN/). Although these predictions have not been tested directly in English, it was the past tense and plural markers that were most prone to error in the spelling and morphological production tasks with second graders reported by Rubin, Patterson and Kantor (1991).

As an alternative to the specific phonological hypothesis, investigators such as Carlisle (1987) suggest that a more general insensitivity to language structure could lead to difficulties with both phonemes and morphemes. The fact that an association between awareness of phonemes and morphemes is evident across such disparate languages as Serbian and Turkish is certainly consistent with the view that sensitivity to sublexical structures is not restricted to the phonological level, but may pertain to morphemic analysis as well. As defined earlier however, definitive support for this view depends on an association when the morphemes themselves are phonologically transparent (see also Mann & Singson, this volume). By this criterion, a metalinguistic account is not supported in the Serbian study. However, because our Turkish stimuli lack items that are phonetically transparent in *both* stem and affix, the results fail to distinguish between a phonological and a metalinguistic explanation.

A closer look at results from Shankweiler et al. (1995) and Mann and Singson (this volume) suggest that metalinguistic factors may contribute to morpheme awareness even when phonological demands are minimal, but that the contribution is quite small (5% in both studies). It is clear in those studies and the present one that phonological demands greatly intensify the association between phoneme and morpheme awareness, but the converging results across studies (and languages) suggest only a minor role for general metalinguistic skill.

Two other possible influences on morphological awareness that were not raised earlier include chronological age and exposure to written language. Regarding age effects, it may be that a general lack of language awareness in very young children leads to poor performance with both phonemes and morphemes, whereas more specific difficulties in older children may derive from factors that are not strictly metacognitive. It is possible then that the young age of the Turkish children explains why they display such a consistent pattern of performance across stimulus items.

It has been noted by several investigators that morphological awareness increases with experience with written language, because spelling often provides clues to shared morphemes (e.g., Derwing, Smith & Wiebe, 1995; Nagy & Anderson, 1984). Exposure to written language may explain why it is the association between morphological awareness and reading that increases between grades 3 and 6 in the study conducted by Mann and Singson (this volume). They suggest that morpheme awareness becomes increasingly important as students attempt to read morphemically complex words; alternatively, it may be that exposure to morphemically complex words in reading enhances morpheme awareness (see also Nagy, Anderson, Schommer, Scott & Stallman, 1989).

Although the effects of written language were not addressed directly in the present study, two features of our study make it unlikely that spelling knowledge (or experience with spelling) explains variation in morphological analysis for our sample. First, the mapping between grapheme and phoneme is relatively simple in both languages and (unlike in English) knowledge of a word's orthographic form provides little more than knowledge of its phonological form. Second, unlike the adolescents typically studied in English, the Serbian and especially the Turkish children in the present study are young and have very limited experience with the written forms of words.

Regardless of morphological type, phonological complexity enhanced the association between tasks and this finding is revealing about the nature of the underlying skill. It is well established that good and poor beginning readers differ in their ability to specify the phonological structure of a word in a variety of experimental tasks. Analysis of a word's phonological structure helps the beginning reader map unfamiliar written words into a spoken form that may be familiar even when the written form is not. Similarly, because words can be constructed from and decomposed into familiar meaningful components and those components can be recombined into new words, morphological analysis also enhances the ability to read unfamiliar words. Results of the present study can be interpreted as evidence that it is sensitivity to the componential structure of language, including phonological complexity as introduced by changes to the orthographic and phonological form of a morpheme, that is fundamental to performance on both tasks.

In summary, we have provided further evidence for an association between phoneme deletion performance and morphological production with beginning readers of two different languages. The nature of the relation between morphological and phonological analysis has not yet been unequivocally defined, however. Moreover, this relationship may be asymmetric. In particular, Byrne (1997) and Elbro and Arnbak (1996) argue that morphologically analytic skills may be present when phonological analysis is absent and that they may even serve to compensate for underdeveloped phonological decoding skills. Conversely, cross-sectional data from Carlisle and Stone (this volume) and Mann and Singson (this volume) suggest that as readers reach the middle elementary years they make greater use of morphological analysis (of derivational forms) in their reading; this arises after mastery of the phoneme analysis skills required for early decoding. Further explorations of semantic and phonological influences on morphological processes in a variety of languages with differing morphological properties will help to clarify the association between phonological and morphological awareness.

6. NOTES

[1] The literal translation is "Mother helps that I cook."
[2] The letter name of "P" in Serbo-Croatian is /pe/.
[3] The orthographic support provided in this task differs from standard procedure and was not intentional, arising only from miscommunication across continents. This may be less of a problem in Serbian than in English because written Serbian is a close phonemic transcription of the spoken language. With the exception of stress, correct pronunciation requires little orthographic knowledge other than basic phoneme grapheme correspondences (Benson, 1971). Nonetheless, visual support could have enhanced performance on this task.
[4] Contrasts between inflected and derived responses as a function of sentence frame are not reported because they are not interpretable. Differences could reflect either the children's differing familiarity with the two source words or, given the way the design was counterbalanced, with the syntactic complexity of the two sentence frames.
[5] In other tasks, such as extracting meaning from morphologically complex words, accuracy may be influenced only by the transparency of the stems. For example, in Elbro and Arnbak's (1996) study, adolescents with reading disability were able to comprehend text as long as the stems were phonologically transparent.

7. APPENDIX

Experiment 1

MORPHOLOGICAL PRODUCTION: SERBIAN

1. kuvar-kuvati
   Ovaj restoran ima dobrog kuvara.
   Moja mama pomaže da kuvam.
2. pegla-peglati
   Vesna hoće da kupi peglu.
   Sutra imaš mnogo da peglaš.
3. mašta-maštati
   Deci treba mnogo mašte.
   Deca vole da maštaju.
4. pevač-pevanje
   U razredu imamo dobre pevače.
   Ceo razred voli čas pevanja.
5. lekar-lečiti
   Tata je otišao da pozove lekara.
   Treba da počnes da se lečiš.
6. plivač-plivanje
   Treba dati nagrade dobrim plivačima
   Imao je mnogo uspeha u plivanju.
7. piće-piti
   Volim da se osvežim hladnim pićem.
   Najviše volim koka-kolu da pijem.
8. led-leden
   Staviću u sok dve kocke leda.
   Mislio sam da je voda ledena.
9. pamet-pametan
   Treba nam puno strpljenja i pameti.
   Njegova deca su bila vrlo pametna.
10. lovac-loviti
    Dobili smo patku od lovca.
    Moja braća vesti idu da love.
11. kupac-kupiti
    Ulice su bile prepune kupaca.
    Mnogo poklona moramo da kupimo.
12. odmor-odmoran
    Videćemo se na velikom odmoru.
    Za školu treba da budemo odmorni.
13. svirač-sviranje
    Na svadbi je bilo puno svirača.
    Gitara se uči samo pomoću sviranja.

14. Čudo-čudan
    U bajkama ima raznih čuda.
    Njegova kapa je vrlo čudna.
15. vozač-voziti
    Svetla služe da upzore vozače.
    Na biciklu se nismo vozili.
16. igrač-igranje
    Ovom timu su potrebni mladi igrači.
    Devijka nas je zadivila svojim igranjem.
17. trkač-trčanje
    Nove patike su potrebne mladim trkačima.
    Skola oragnizuje takmicenje u trčanju.
18. smeh-smešan
    Učionica je bila puna vike i smeha.
    Njegova nove cipele su bile smešne.
19. plata-platitit
    Na početku meseca primamo platu.
    Sve što kupiš moras da platiš.
20. pažnja-pažljiv
    Film smo gledali sa paznjom.
    Na času treba da budemo pazljivi.
21. prodavnica-prodati
    Pored škole su otvorili novu prodavnicu.
    Staru kuću u selu smo prodali.
22. kupač-kupati
    Na plaži je bilo mnogo kupača.
    Idemo na reku da se kupamo.
23. želja-želeti
    Uskoro će se ostvariti sve tvoje želje.
    Ostvarilo se ono što sam oduvek želeo.
24. Šetač- šetanje
    Njih dvoje nisu bili jedini šetaci.
    Bole me ledja od dugog šetanja.
25. pisac-pisanje
    Čitao sam knigu poznatog pisca.
    Olovku treba zaoštriti pre pisanja.
26. vrućina-vruć
    Sladoled se istopio na velikoj vrućini.
    Voda je još uvek veoma vruća.
27. sunce-sunčan
    Voda se ugrejala na jakom suncu.
    Letnji dani su uvek sunčani.
28. tuga-tužan
    Petar je osetio veliku tugu.
    Deca su bila veoma tužna.

29. sreća-srećan
    Milan je baš imao mnogo sreće.
    Zbog poklona su svi bili srećni.
30. glas-glasan
    Iz sobe su se čuli glasovi.
    Njihovo smejanje je bilo glasno.
31. buka-bučan
    Ništa se nije čulo od buke.
    Mala zabava je bila vrlo bučna.
32. mrak-mračan
    Ništa se nije videlo od mraka.
    Soba nije više bila tako mračna.
33. radnik-raditi
    Kupili su odela mladim radnicima.
    Tri žene su vredno radile.
34. Čuvar-čuvati
    Došla su tri nova čuvara.
    Nove stvari je pažljivo čuvala.
35. sijalica-sijati
    Trebalo bi da kupimo novu sijalicu.
    Njegove nove cipele su se sijale.
36. jahač-jahati
    Iz šume su došla četiri jahača.
    Branko je bio najbrži u jahanju.

PHONEME DELETION ITEMS: SERBIAN

april
balkon
banda
cirkus
cvećar
dvopek
frula
fudbal
glas
grašak
grozd
hrast
igra
izbor
jogurt
kaktus
keks
klovn
krug

marš
most
ovca
plata
princ
recept
rekord
školjka
šraf
usna
vreme

Experiment 2

MORPHOLOGICAL PRODUCTION: TURKISH

1. Kaçmak-Kaçak

    Yakalanan hırsız dün hapisden kaçtı .
    Polis bugün yakaladı saklanan kaçağı .

2. Uçmak-Uçak

    Balon az önce göğe doğru uçtu.
    Kardeşim yarın binecek uçağa.

3. Seçmek-Seçim

    Öğrenciler şimdi sınıf başkanını seçiyor.
    Beklenmeyen bir aday kazandi seçimı.

4. Sormak-Soru

    Ahmet bilmediği konuları yarın öğretmene soracak.
    Sınavdakilerin en zoru matematik sorusu.

5. Kapamak-Kapak

    Aysel şu anda o pencereyi kapıyor.
    Az önce kayboldu bu kalemin kapağı.

6. İçmek-İçki

    Bugün sabah kahvaltısında çay içtim.
    Şu adam döktü masadaki içkiyi.

7. Yakmak-Yakıt

    Dün hava soğuyunca odadaki sobayı yaktım.
    Bu kış hepsini bitirdik depodaki yakıtın.

8. Koşmak-Koşucu

    Duydum ki Ayşe dünkü yarışta çok hızlı koşmuş.
    Ahmet bizim sınıfın en hızlı koşucusu.

9. Yüzmek-Yüzücü

Ali yarın havuzda 20 dakika yüzecek.
Çok ödül verildi birinci gelen yüzücüye.

10. Silmek-Silgi

Ona söyle bu halıyı silsin.
Gene kaybettim bizim sınıfdaki silgiyi.

11. Taramak-Tarak

Ayşe her sabah kalkınca saçını tarar.
Lütfen çantama koy şu elindeki tarağı.

12. Öğretmek-Öğretmen

Bu oyunu bana Oğuz abim öğretti.
Ödevlerin hepsini vermeliyiz bizim öğretmene.

13. Yatmak-Yatak

Hasan her akşam tam saat 9 da yattar.
Kardeşim bu gece düştü odadaki yataktan.

14. Uyumak-Uyku

Bak bebek ne de güzel uyuyor.
Emre'yi kaldırmak çok zordur uykudan.

15. Durmak-Durak

Yağmur 3 günden sonra nihayet durdu.
Yağmurda koşarak vardık durağa.

16. Dalmak-Dalgiç

Ben bugün ilk kez denize daldım.
Herkes merak etmeye başlamıştı dipteki dalgıcı.

PHONEME DELETION TASK: TURKISH

1.	kale	kal
2.	geri	ger
3.	kalem	kale
4.	yalan	yala
5.	küfe	küf
6.	delik	deli
7.	derin	deri
8.	küpe	küp
9.	sinir	sini
10.	kova	kov

8. REFERENCES

Aronoff, M. (1976). *Word formation in generative grammar.* Cambridge, MA: MIT Press.

Benson, M. (1971). *An English-Serbo-Croatian dictionary.* Philadelphia: University of Pennsylvania Press.

Blachman, B. (1994) Early literacy acquisition: The role of phonological awareness. In G. P. Wallach and K.G. Butler (Eds.) Language learning disabilities in school-age children and adolescents. New York: Merrill.pp. 253-274.

Brady, S. A. (1997). Ability to encode phonological representations: A underlying difficulty of poor readers. In B. Blachman (Eds.), *Foundations of reading acquisition and dyslexia: Implications for intervention.* (pp. 21-47). Mahwah, NJ: Lawrence Erlbaum Associates.

Byrne, B. (1997). The learnability of the alphabetic principle: Children's initial hypotheses about how print represents spoken language. *Journal of Applied Psycholinguistics, 17,* 401-426.

Caramazza, A , Laudanna, A., & Romani, C. (1988). Lexical access and inflectional morphology. *Cognition, 28,* 287-332.

Carlisle, J. F. (1987). The use of morphological knowledge in spelling derived forms by learning disabled and normal students. *Annals of Dyslexia, 37,* 90-108.

Carlisle, J. F. (1988). Knowledge of derivational morphology and spelling ability in fourth, sixth, and eighth graders. *Applied Psycholinguistics, 9,* 247-266.

Carlisle, J. F. (1995). Morphological awareness and early reading achievement. In L.B. Feldman (Ed). *Morphological aspects of language processing.* (pp. 189-209). Hillsdale, NJ: Lawrence Erlbaum Associates.

Carlisle, J. F., & Nomanbhoy, D. M. (1993). Phonological and morphological awareness in first graders. *Applied Psycholinguistics,* 14, 177-195.

Carlisle, J. F. & Stone, C. A. (this volume). The effects of morphological structure on children's reading of derived words in English.

Chialant, D. & Caramazza, A. (1995). Where is morphology and how is it processed? The case of written word recognition. In L.B. Feldman (Ed). *Morphological aspects of language processing.* (pp. 55-76). Hillsdale, NJ: Lawrence Erlbaum Associates.

Derwing, B., Smith, M. & Wiebe, G. (1995). On the role of spelling in morpheme recognition: Experimental studies with children and adults. In L.B. Feldman (Ed). *Morphological aspects of language processing.* (pp. 3-27). Hillsdale, NJ: Lawrence Erlbaum Associates.

Dunn, L. & Dunn, L. (1981). Peabody Picture Vocabulary. Test-Revised. Circle Pines, MN: American Guidance Service.

Durgunoglu, A. & Öney, B. (1996). A cross linguistic comparison of phonological awareness and word recognition in Turkish and English. Paper presented at the annual meeting of the American Educational Research Association, New York.

Elbro, C. (1989). Morphological awareness in dyslexia. In C. von Euler (Ed.), *Wenner-Gren International Symposium Series: Brain and Reading.* Hampshire, England: Macmillan.

Elbro, C., & Arnbak, E. (1996). The role of morpheme recognition and morphological awareness in dyslexia. *Annals of Dyslexia, 46,* pp. 209-240. Feldman, L. B. (1994). Beyond orthography and phonology: Differences between inflections and derivations. *Journal of Memory and Language, 33,* 442-470.

Feldman, L.B. (1994). Beyond orthography and phonology: Differences between inflections and derivations. *Journal of Memory and Language, 33,* 442-470.

Feldman, L. B., & Moskovljevic;, J. (1987). Repetition priming is not purely episodic in origin. *Journal of Experimental Psychology: Learning, Memory and Cognition, 13,* 573-581.

Fowler, A., & Liberman, I. (1995). Morphological awareness as related to early reading and spelling ability. In L. B. Feldman (Ed.), *Morphological aspects of language processing.* (pp. 157-188). Hillsdale, NJ: Lawrence Erlbaum Associates.

Gleitman, L. R., & Rozin, P. (1977). The structure and acquisition of reading: Relation between orthography and the structured language. In A. S. Reber & D. L. Scarborough (Eds.), *Toward a psychology of reading* (pp. 1-53). Hillsdale, NJ: Erlbaum.

Gough, P.B., Ehri, L.C., & Treiman, R. (1992). *Reading Acquisition.* Hillsdale, NJ: Lawrence Erlbaum Associates.

Laudanna, A., Badecker, W., & Caramazza, A. (1989). Priming homographic stems. *Journal of Memory & Language, 28,* 531-546.

Leong, C. K., & Parkinson, M. E. (1995). Processing of English morphological structure by poor readers. In C. K. Leong & R. M. Joshi (Eds.), *Developmental and Acquired Dyslexia: Neuropsychological and Neurolinguistic Perspectives* . Dordrecht: Kluwer.

Liberman, I.Y., Shankweiler, D. Liberman, A.M. Fowler, C. & Fischer, F.W. (1977). Phonetic segmentation and recoding in the beginning reader. In A. Reber and D. Scarborough (Eds.). *Toward a psychology of reading.* (pp.207-226). Hillsdale, NJ. Lawrence Erlbaum Ass.

Liberman, I. Y., Shankweiler, D., & Liberman, A. M. (1989). The alphabetic principle and learning to read. In D. Shankweiler & I. Y. Liberman (Eds.), *Phonology and reading disability* (pp. 1-33). Ann Arbor: University of Michigan Press.

Mann, V. A. & Singson, M. (this volume). The little suffix that could: Linking morphological knowledge in English decoding ability.

Marslen-Wilson, W., Tyler, L.K., Waksler, R., & Older, L. (1994). Morphology and meaning in the English lexicon. *Psychological Review, 101,* 3-33.

McQueen, J. & Cutler, A. (1997). Morphology in word recognition. In A. M. Zwicky & A. Spencer (Eds.), *The handbook of morphology.* (pp. 406-427). Oxford: Basil Blackwell.

Nagy, W. & Anderson, R.C. (1984). *How many words are there is printed school English? Reading Research Quarterly, 19,* 304-330.

Nagy, W. E., Anderson, R., Schommer, M., Scott, J.A. & Stallman, A. C. (1989). Morphological families and word recognition. *Reading Research Quarterly, 24,* 262-282.

Öney, B. & Durgunoglu, A. (1997). Learning to read in Turkish: A phonologically transparent orthography. *Journal of Applied Psycholinguistics. 18,* 1-15.

Raveh, M. and Feldman, L.B. (September, 1998). The contribution of morphological relation and affix position to morphological processing: Evidence from Hebrew. Paper presented at the European Society for Cognitive Psychology, Jerusalem, Israel.

Rosner, J. & Simon, D.P. (1971). The auditory analysis test: An initial report. *Journal of Learning Disabilities, 4,* 384-392.

Rubin, H. (1988). Morphological knowledge and early writing ability. *Language and Speech, 31,* 337-355.

Rubin, H., Patterson, P. A., & Kantor, M. (1991). Morphological development and writing ability in children and adults. *Language, Speech and Hearing Services in Schools, 22,* 228-235.

Rueckl, J.G., Mikolinski, M., Raveh, M. Miner, C.S. & Mars, F. (1997). Morphological priming, connectionist networks, and masked fragment completion. *Journal of Memory and Language, 36,* 382-405.

Shankweiler, D., Crain, S., Katz, L., Fowler, A. E., Liberman, A., Brady, S., Thornton, R., Lundquist, E., Dreyer, L., Fletcher, J., Stuebing, K., Shaywitz, S., & Shaywitz, B. (1995). Cognitive profiles of reading-disabled children: Comparison of language skills in phonology, morphology and syntax. *Psychological Science, 6,* 149-156.

Stanners, R. F., Neiser, J. J., Hernon, W. P., & Hall, R. (1979). Memory representation for morphologically related words. *Journal of Verbal Learning and Verbal Behavior, 18,* 399-412.

Stanovich, K.E. (1988). Explaining the differences between the dyslexic and the garden-variety poor reader: The phonological-core variable-difference model. Journal of Learning Disabilities, 21, 59-612.

Stanovich, K.E. (1992). Speculations on the causes and consequences of individual differences in early reading acquisition. In P.B. Gough, L.C. Ehri, and R. Treiman (Eds.) Reading Acquisition. Hillsdale, NJ: Lawrence Erlbaum Associates.

Tunmer, W. E., Herriman, M. L., & Nesdale, A. R. (1988). Metalinguistic abilities and beginning reading. *Reading Research Quarterly, 23,* 134-158.

Underhill, R. (1976). *Turkish grammar.* Cambridge, MA. MIT Press.

Wagner, R., Torgesen, J., & Rashotte, C. (1994). Development of reading-related phonological processing abilities: New evidence of bi-directional causality from a latent variable longitudinal study. *Developmental Psychology, 30,* 73-87. [cited p. 2]

9. ACKNOWLEDGMENT

The research reported here was conducted at the Laboratory of Experimental Psychology at the University of Belgrade and at Bogazici University in Istanbul and was supported by funds from National Institute Of Child Health and Development Grant HD-01994 to Haskins Laboratories. Reprint requests should be sent to the first or second author at Haskins Laboratories, 270 Crown Street, New Haven, CT 06511.

10. ADDRESS FOR CORRESPONDENCE

Anne Fowler
Wesleyan University and Haskins Laboratories
270 Crown St.
New Haven, CT 06511-6695
United States of America
Phone: (203) 865-6163
email: anne.fowler@haskins.yale.edu

AYDIN YÜCESAN DURGUNOĞLU

RECOGNIZING MORPHOLOGICALLY COMPLEX WORDS IN TURKISH

1. INTRODUCTION

In order to recognize a written or spoken word, information coming through the senses has to be compared to an internal representation. There has been considerable research on the internal representation of morphologically simple words (for a review see, Balota, 1994). The length, frequency, imageability of the word, as well as the number of its neighbors in the rime family have all been found to affect how fast an internal representation is accessed. However, the recognition of morphologically complex words, especially the nature of their internal representation, has been harder to describe. Some researchers have assumed that complex words are first decomposed into their constituent morphemes and then compared with the stored representations of stems and affixes (Taft & Forster, 1975, 1976). The support for such a model comes from experiments comparing truly prefixed words (RETURN) and pseudoprefixed words (RELISH). According to this model, morphological decomposition precedes lexical access. Both truly prefixed and pseudo-prefixed words are stripped before searching the lexicon. Because pseudoprefixed words have no lexical entry once the prefix is stripped (-LISH of relish), the cognitive system needs to reassemble the components and conduct another search in the lexicon, thus producing longer reaction times for pseudoprefixed words. However, other studies have questioned whether affix stripping was an obligatory process. For example, Rubin, Becker and Freeman (1979) have shown that affix stripping was a strategic process modified by the participants, depending on the proportion of affixed items in the overall list. Also, affix stripping was assumed not to operate for high frequency words because familiar words are recognized more rapidly as a whole than by their constituent morphemes (Burani & Caramazza, 1987).

Seidenberg and his colleagues (1987; Seidenberg & McClelland, 1989) have proposed that patterns of high and low probability transitions in letter sequences can account for syllabic or morphological structure effects. According to their model, the transition (bigram) frequencies are lower for letters straddling a syllable boundary compared to letters within a syllable, creating a trough (for example, in the word har-bor, the frequency of the bigrams *ar* and *or* are higher than the bigram *rb*). Likewise, affixes have higher frequencies as letter clusters compared to letters straddling morphological boundaries (in the word *return*, *re* and *tu* are more frequent than *et*).

However, orthographic factors alone cannot explain morphological effects. As several researcher have argued (Grainger, Colé & Segui, 1991; Murrell & Morton, 1974; Napps, 1989; Stolz & Feldman 1995), the response times to a target word (e.g. *mark*) are faster when primed by a morphologically related word (*marked*) than an orthographically related word (*market*). In addition, Rapp (1992) has shown that syllable structure affected performance in a letter-color identification task regardless of bigram frequencies at syllable boundaries.

These results have encouraged several researchers (Chialat & Caramazza, 1995) to propose that word recognition can proceed by accessing either whole words or decomposed forms (stems and affixes). A more specific variation of this idea is articulated by the linguist Bybee (1995), who suggested that the words of higher frequency – even when morphologically complex – are represented as a whole, whereas lower frequency words are represented by their parts.

One common characteristic of the models discussed above is to assume a finite number of structures, yielding what Hankamer (1992) calls the Full Listing Hypothesis (FLH), and to assume that the full list is consulted when attempting to recognize a word. Such a hypothesis is possible given the languages on which most of the morphological research is based. When the most complex words involve a single root and an affix, FLH works well. However, there are many agglutinative languages around the world (for example, Finnish, Turkish) which are extremely productive. These languages can have many iterative loops which can technically produce words of infinite length. In the following example, notice how many times the plural suffix (*ler/lar*) is used: the word *kitap* (book) can be made plural *kitaplar* (books), by adding the suffix *-lar.* This can be transformed into another noun *kitaplardaki* (that present in those books), and finally pluralized again *kitaplardakiler* (those present in those books). The point of this example is to show that the presence of the suffix *-lar/-ler* does not help a Turkish speaker in decomposing a word because the same suffix can be found in different parts of words, limited only by the preceding construct. Hence, what is also needed is some knowledge of probabilistic information of when and how a suffix can be used especially in iterative contexts. To add another layer of complexity, in some agglutinating languages, morphemes can change form as a function of vowel harmony. In the previous example, one of the two different forms of the plural suffix was used depending on the nature of the preceding vowel.

For languages with complex morphological structures, Hankamer suggested a left-to-right parsing mechanism. According to that model, the root is searched in the lexicon, which presumably also includes information on its grammatical category (see lexico-functional grammars). The grammatical category then determines the suffixes that can follow. At every step, the possible choice of suffixes is narrowed down.

There is some evidence that left-to-right word parsing can exist even in morphologically simpler languages such as English and French. For example Colé, Beuvillain & Segui (1987) discovered that prefixed and suffixed words showed different patterns of processing. In that study, words were matched on surface frequency and contrasted on cumulative root frequencies (frequency of all words that share a common root, e.g., *jardin, jardinier, jardinage*), and their lexical decision times were compared. The cumulative root frequency affected lexical decision times to suffixed target words (e.g. *jardinier*), but not to prefixed words. Likewise, Hudson and Buijs (1995) found that, in Dutch, pseudoprefixed words were recognized more slowly than prefixed words, but pseudosuffixed words were not different from real suffixed words. These pattern differences have led the authors to suggest that the nature of processing may be different for prefixed versus suffixed words, and affix stripping may be valid for prefixes, but a left-to-right processing may be more likely for suffixes. In languages like Turkish, which have only suffixes, left-to-right processing may be the only alternative.

Left-to-right processing leads to the counter-intuitive prediction that "morphologically complex words should be recognized faster than matched simple words" (Hudson & Buijs, 1995, p.393). Hudson and Buijs conducted naming and lexical decision experiments in which they compared the reaction times to simple and morphologically complex words that were matched on number of letters, syllables and mean word frequency. In both tasks, complex words were processed faster than the simple words, supporting this counter-intuitive prediction.

In the current study, a parallel situation was tested in Turkish, with a group of children as participants. The paper-pencil task involved either correcting the suffix or adding the suffix in a short paragraph about an imaginary animal. The task assessed accuracy rather than reaction time. Of course, such a design does not enable us to make inferences about online processes and their duration. However, the accuracy of performance can still indicate which morphological characteristics are easier to handle, thus hinting at the nature of the underlying process.

In the current experiment, either simple or complex pseudowords were used as animal names to prevent whole-word recognition based on familiarity. However, in contrast to the Hudson and Buijs study discussed above, the simple and complex pseudowords were not equivalent in terms of number of letters or syllables. Complex items were either 1 or 3 syllables longer than the simple items, which meant they were 3 or 7 letters longer than the simple ones. These differences between simple and complex items can lead to one of two possible outcomes: if word length (number of letters and syllables) is the crucial factor, then simple words should be manipulated more accurately than complex words. Indeed, a recent study with French children showed that the word recognition performance of beginning readers was significantly impaired by increases in word length, and this effect persisted during the first five years of instruction (Aghababian & Nazir, 2000). Based on these results, one can predict that simple, short words will be manipulated more easily than complex and long words. If, however, morphological probability is the crucial factor, then complex words with fewer possible suffixes should be manipulated more accurately than simple words. In other words, complex items may be more difficult to manipulate because of their length, but this disadvantage may be offset by their morphological simplicity (i.e., the fewer number of possible suffixes that can follow their base).

2. THE CURRENT STUDY

2.1 Participants

The participants were second (n=64) and fourth-grade (n=63) children attending a private school in Ankara, Turkey. Because the school had a rigorous entrance exam, both students who were admitted based on their exam scores and children who were admitted based on a lottery system were included in the sample so as not to only have a select group of gifted students.

2.2 Tasks and materials

The children performed one of two tasks. They either corrected the suffixes (*correction task*) or supplied the suffixes (*completion task*) in a short paragraph about an imaginary animal with a pseudo-species name. For example if the imaginary animal was called a *mev,* the paragraph had the title "an animal called *mev*" and went on to describe its characteristics – which were suspiciously similar to those of a giraffe. For the correction task, the paragraph included five instances in which the target word *mev* was inflected incorrectly. For example, the correct form of the phrase "running away from the mev" is *mevden kacarken* with *mevden* meaning "from the mev". However, in the text, it was inflected as *meve* ("to the mev"). In the correction task, these errors were underlined and the children were asked to write the corrected version above the underlined target word.

The same paragraphs were used in the completion task. In this latter task, the base form of the target word was given with a blank after it (*mev*___). The children were asked to complete the word with its correct inflection given the sentence context.

The crucial manipulation was the level of the target word. In Turkish, a noun can take suffixes in the following order (Solak, 1991):

Nominal root + plural suffix + possessive suffix + case suffix + relative suffix

For example,

- nominal root: *kitap* (= book)
- plural suffix: *kitaplar* (= books) 1 possible suffix
- possessive suffix:, *kitaplarimiz* (= our books) 6 possible suffixes (expressing meanings: my, your, its …)
- case suffix: *kitaplarimizda* (= in our books) 9 possible suffixes (expressingmeanings in, at, from, with …)
- relative suffix *kitaplarimizdaki* (= those in our books) 1 possible suffix

According to Solak's computations, the number of possible suffixes becomes fewer and fewer at each level of complexity when we consider the number of possible suffixes that can be attached to a given form. (Because the relative suffix with its Persian origins has some different characteristics, it is not included in the discussion).

To make it more concrete, the target word in nominal form *kitap* (= book) can take the following suffixes [In the examples, only the following suffixes are used to make the discussion less complicated: *-imiz* (our) *-a* (to) and *-lar* (plural)]

Nominal base: (*kitap*)

(Nominal) + plural = 1 possibility (e.g. *kitaplar* = books)
(Nominal) + possessive = 6 possibilities (e.g. *kitabimiz* = our book)
(Nominal) + case = 9 possibilities (e.g., *kitaba* = to a book)
(Nominal) + plural + possessive = 1 x 6 = 6 possibilities e.g., *kitaplarimiz* = our books)
(Nominal) + plural + case = 1 x 9 = 9 possibilities (e.g., *kitaplara* = to books)
(Nominal) + possessive + case = 6 x 9 = 54 possibilities (e.g., *kitabimiza* = to our book)
(Nominal) + plural + possessive + case = 1 x 6 x 9 = 54 possibilities (e.g., *kitaplarimiza* = to our books)
Total: 139 possibilities.

Nominal + plural base: (*kitaplar*)

The number of possible suffixes is considerably reduced for the target word *kitaplar* (= books).
(Nominal + plural) + possessive = 6 possibilities (e.g., *kitaplarimiz* = our books)
(Nominal + plural) + case = 9 possibilities (e.g., *kitaplara* = to books)
(Nominal + plural) + possessive + case = 6 x 9 = 54 possibilities (e.g., *kitaplarimiza* = to our books)
Total : 69 possibilities

Nominal + plural + possessive base: (*kitaplarimiz*)

For the more complicated nominal + plural + possessive form (*kitaplarimiz* = our books), possible suffixes are further reduced.
(Nominal + plural + possessive) + case = 9 possibilities (e.g., *kitaplarimiza* = to our books)
Total : 9 possibilities

In the current experiment, each child read three paragraphs. In each paragraph the level of suffixation for the target word was varied. The imaginary animal was *mev* (nominal) for Level 1; *mevler* (nominal + plural, = mevs) for Level 2; and *mevlerimiz* (nominal + plural + possessive, = our mevs) for Level 3. Hence, the length of the base target word increased by a syllable (3 letters) at Level 2 and by three syllables (7 letters) at Level 3. In Appendix A, sample paragraphs are given to illustrate level differences. The errors were always in the case suffix since this suffix type can be added to target words at any one of the three levels of complexity. To illustrate, as discussed earlier, for Level 1, instead of *meve* the incorrect version stated *mevden.* For Level 2, when the target word was *mevler*, it was incorrectly inflected as *mevlere* rather than *mevlerden.* Finally, for Level 3, when the target word was *mevlerimiz,* it was incorrectly inflected as *mevlerimize* rather than *mevlerimizden.*

There were three different imaginary animal names with different syllable structures and requirements for vowel harmony: *mev*, *kuna* and *pelit* and the level of suffixation was counterbalanced across the three names. In addition, the order of presentation was also counterbalanced by modifying the test booklets so that each animal name appeared in each level and at each ordering of texts equally. To summarize, the experiment had a 2 (Grade level: second or fourth) x 2 (Task: completion or correction) x 3 (Suffixation level of target word: 1, 2 or 3) design. (Although a complete counterbalancing scheme required 136 participants, there were some cells missing when only 127 children could be tested. However, the missing 9 cells were distributed across all conditions). The children were tested in classrooms as a group. In each classroom, half of the children were given the completion instructions and half were given the correction instructions. The children read and worked on each paragraph at their own pace, and moved forward as they finished each paragraph. The task was completed within 20 minutes.

3. RESULTS AND DISCUSSION

The data were scored by assigning 1 or 0 to each correct suffix, and the incorrect suffixation rates were calculated. However during data analysis, an interesting pattern emerged. In some cases children used the correct suffix, but modified the target word. For example, they corrected *meve* by writing *mevlerden* rather than *mevden,* thus making the target word plural (*mevler*). These modifications were always in the direction of making the target word more complex than simple. (The same meaning can be expressed equally effectively if the target word is singular or plural, so meaning could not be the reason for making these words more complex). Because these modifications often occurred, they were also analyzed.

An overall analysis on the error rates yielded main effects of grade level and task, $F(1,123) = 28.24$ and $F(1,123) = 11.03$, respectively. (In all analyses, $p < .05$ is used). As would be expected, fourth-grade children performed better than the second-grade children. Also, correcting a suffix was easier than supplying a suffix. The level effect did not reach significance, $F < 1$. However there was a marginal effect of Grade x Level x Task, $F(2,246) = 2.02$, $p < .13$. Because of a priori reasons, the grades and tasks were analyzed separately as discussed below, even though the triple interaction did not reach conventional levels of probability.

The results for each grade and task are presented graphically in Figures 1-4, with broken lines representing the completion task and solid lines representing the correction task. The level did not affect the error rate of completions or corrections for either grade. Note that in Level 1 the correction or completion was performed on the target words which were only 3-5 letters long (e.g., *mev*). However in Level 3, the target words were much longer, 10-12 letters long (e.g., *mevlerimiz*). Contrary to the "length" explanation, shorter words were not completed/corrected more accurately than complex words. To put it in another way, even with complex words of 10 to 12 letters long, children's performance did not suffer, providing support for the counter-intuitive prediction that more complex words are just as easy to handle as simple

simple ones when their length disadvantage is offset by their fewer number of possible suffixes.

Another noteworthy effect is on the nature of modifications. When the modification rates were analyzed, grade and task were not significant. However, there was a significant effect of Level, $F(2,246) = 36.67$. For both younger and older children and also across both tasks, Level 1 words were modified more often than Level 2 and 3 words. In fact as can be seen in Figures 3 and 4, Levels 2 and 3 had no or very low modification rates. These words could have been simplified, returned to their nominal roots. However, this did not happen. The modifications were in the direction of making the nominal (Level 1) target words into Level 2 or even Level 3 target words.

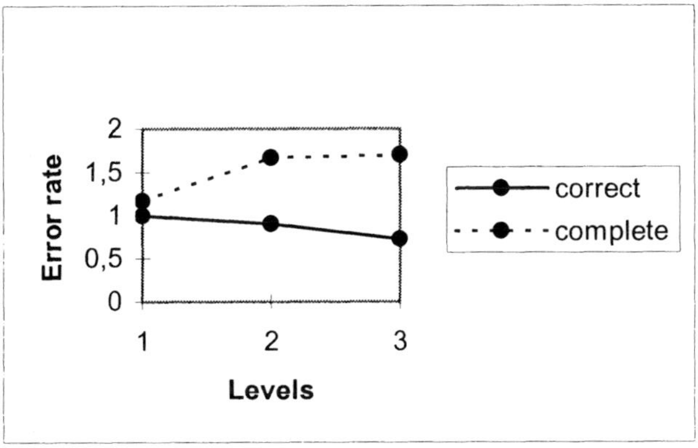

Figure 1. Grade 2 errors

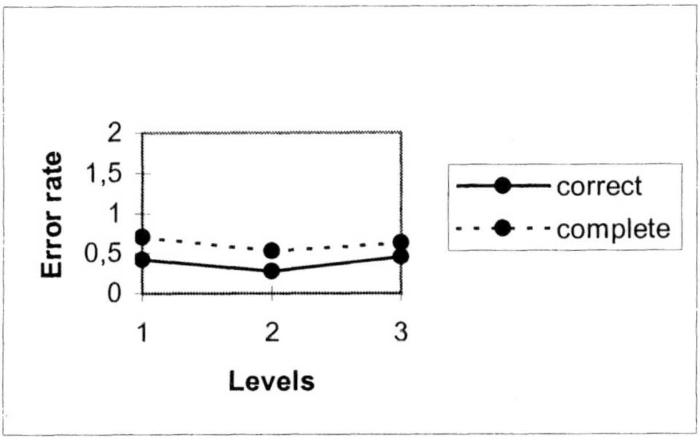

Figure 2. Grade 4 errors

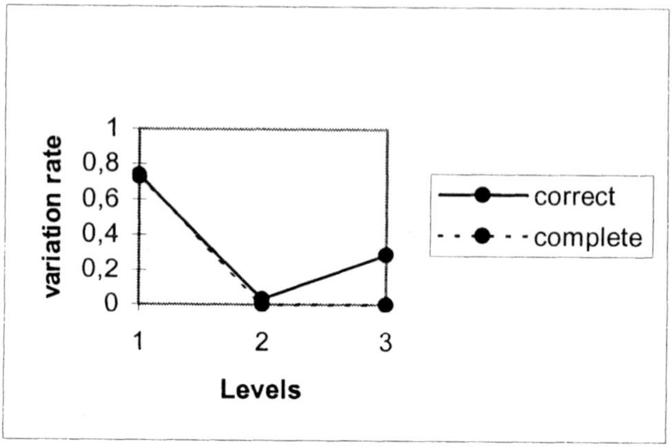

Figure 3. Grade 2 modifications

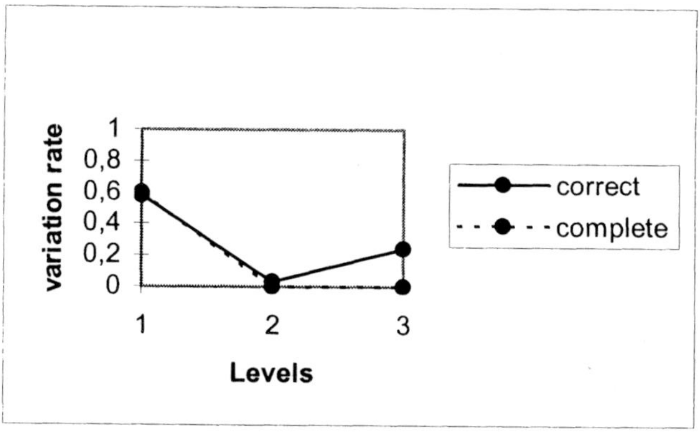

Figure 4. Grade 4 modifications

One surprising result was the similarity between Levels 2 and 3 in both errors and variations. The data indicated that since the task required the children to focus on the case suffix, they ignored the possessives and did not seem to be affected by it. (The meaning of the passage did not require any possessive information). To explain this result, a post-hoc review of the suffix probabilities was helpful. Looking back at the examples under the Method section, it can be seen that for Level 2, (*kitaplar*), the case suffix can be added to the base without any possessives. Therefore, children can completely ignore the probabilities of the possessive suffix and still perform the task correctly. In that case, the possibilities for Level 2 are reduced dramatically, from 69 to 9, if only the following branch is used to perform the task, i.e. Nominal + plural + case = 9 possibilities (e.g., *kitaplara:* to books). This, of course, was probabilistically identical to the conditions in Level 3.

4. SUMMARY

The results of the study can be summarized very simply. Even with a rough paper-pencil test, some evidence for morphological computation was found. First, morphologically complicated forms of target words were completed or corrected just as accurately as morphologically simple forms of target words. Although the complex words were longer, and orthographically complex, their lower number of probable suffixes overcame this disadvantage and facilitated the suffix correction and completion performance. In addition, children tended to make simple forms more complex before supplying or correcting the suffix, rather than vice versa. This accuracy data indicates that more complex forms were easier to handle in terms of possible suffixes.

In conclusion, although some prefix stripping and searching the full list of morphemes may be a useful strategy in languages with more manageable morphological structures such as English, in the highly agglutinating language of Turkish, a left-to-right computational strategy seems to be the mode of operation.

5. APPENDIX

(In parentheses are the correct forms of the underlined target word that the children were supposed to provide)

Level 1

Correction task

Mev adli hayvan

Mev sicak bolgelerde yasayan uzun boylu bir hayvandir. Diger hayvanlar meve (mevi) gorunce kacarlar. Mevi (meve) yaklasmak istemezler. Mevde (mevden) kacarken suya dusen bile olur. Halbuki mevden (mevde) korkutucu birsey yoktur. Cunku mevi (mev) sadece bitki yer, diger hayvanlara zarar vermez.

Completion task

Mev adli hayvan

Mev sicak bolgelerde yasayan uzun boylu bir hayvandir. Diger hayvanlar mev___ (mevi) gorunce kacarlar. Mev___ (meve) yaklasmak istemezler. Mev___ (mevden) kacarken suya dusen bile olur. Halbuki mev___ (mevde) korkutucu birsey yoktur. Cunku mev___ (mev) sadece bitki yer, diger hayvanlara zarar vermez.

The translation of the paragraph with correct suffixation

An animal named mev

Mev is a tall animal living in warm climates. Other animals run away when they see the mev. They don't want to get close to mev. Some even fall in water while running away from mev. In fact there is nothing scary in a mev, because mev only eats plants and doesn't harm other animals.

Level 3

Correction task

Mev adli hayvan

Mevlerimiz sicak bolgelerde yasayan uzun boylu bir hayvandir. Diger hayvanlar mevlerimize (mevlerimizi) gorunce kacarlar. Mevlerimizi (mevlerimize) yaklasmak istemezler. Mevlerimizde (mevlerimizden) kacarken suya dusen bile olur. Halbuki mevlerimizden (mevlerimizde) korkutucu birsey yoktur. Cunku mevlerimizi (mevlerimiz) sadece bitki yer, diger hayvanlara zarar vermez.

Completion task

Mev adli hayvan

Mevlerimiz sicak bolgelerde yasayan uzun boylu bir hayvandir. Diger hayvanlar mevlerimiz___ (mevlerimizi) gorunce kacarlar. Mevlerimiz___ (mevlerimize) yaklasmak istemezler. Mevlerimiz___ (mevlerimizden) kacarken suya dusen bile olur. Halbuki mevlerimiz___ (mevlerimizde) korkutucu birsey yoktur. Cunku mevlerimiz___ (mevlerimiz) sadece bitki yer, diger hayvanlara zarar vermez.

Translation

An animal named mev

Our mevs are tall animals living in warm climates. Other animals run away when they see (the) our mevs. They don't want to get close to our mevs. Some even fall in water while running away from our mevs. In fact there is nothing scary in our mevs, because our mevs only eat plants and don't harm other animals.

6. REFERENCES

Aghababian, V., & Nazir, T.A. (2000). Developing normal reading skills: Aspects of the visual processes underlying word recognition. *Journal of Experimental Child Psychology, 76*, 123-150.

Balota, D.A. (1994). Visual word recognition: The journey from features to meaning. in M.A. Gernsbacher (Ed.). *Handbook of Psycholinguistics*. (303-358). San Diego: Academic Press.

Burani, C. & Caramazza, A. (1987). Representation and processing of derived words. *Language and cognitive processes, 2/3*, 217-227.

Bybee, J. (1995). Diachronic and typological properties of morphology, and their implications for representation. In L.B. Feldman (Ed.). *Morphological aspects of language processing*. (pp.225-226), Mahwah, NJ: Lawrence Erlbaum Associates.

Chialat & Caramazza (1995). In L.B. Feldman (Ed.). *Morphological aspects of language processing*. (pp. 55-78), Mahwah, NJ: Lawrence Erlbaum Associates

Colé, P., Beuvillain, C., & Segui, J. (1987). On the representation and processing of prefixed and suffixed derived words: A differential frequency effect. *Journal of Memory and Language, 28*, 1-13.

Grainger, J., Colé, P. & Segui, J. (1991). Masked morphological priming in visual word recognition. *Journal of Memory and Language, 30*, 370-384.

Hankamer, J. (1992). Morphological parsing and the lexicon. In W. Marslen-Wilson (Ed.). *Lexical representation and process*. (pp. 392-408). Cambridge, MA: MIT Press.

Hudson, P.T.W. & Buijs, D. (1995). Left-to-right processing of derivational morphology. In L.B. Feldman (Ed.). *Morphological aspects of language processing*. (pp. 383-396), Mahwah, NJ: Lawrence Erlbaum Associates.

Murrell, G.A. & Morton, J. (1974). Word recognition and morphemic structure. *Journal of Experimental Psychology, 102*, 963-968.

Napps, S.E. (1989). Morphemic relationships in the lexicon: Are they distinct from semantic and formal relationships? *Memory & Cognition, 17*, 729-739.

Rapp, B.C. (1992). The nature of sublexical orthographic organization: The bigram trough hypothesis examined. *Journal of Memory and Language. 31*, 33-53.

Rubin, G.S., Becker, C.A. & Freeman, R.H. (1979). Morphological structure and its effect on visual word recognition. *Journal of Verbal Learning and Verbal Behavior, 18*, 757-767.

Seidenberg, M.S. (1987). Sublexical structures in visual word recognition: Access units or orthographic redundancy? In M. Coltheart (ed.). *Attention and Performance XII: The Psychology of reading.* Hillsdale, NJ: Erlbaum.

Seidenberg, M.S., & McClelland, J.L. (1989). A distributed, developmental model of word recognition and naming. *Psychological Review, 96*, 523-568.

Solak, A. (1991). Turkce metinlerde sozcuk yazimi kontrolunun tasarimi ve gerceklestirimi [Design and implementation of a spelling checker for Turkish]. M.S. thesis, Bilkent University, Ankara, Turkey.

Stolz, J.A., & Feldman, L.B. (1995). The role of orthographic and semantic transparency of the base morpheme in morphological processing. In L.B. Feldman (Ed.). *Morphological aspects of language processing*. (pp. 109-130). Mahwah, NJ: Lawrence Erlbaum Associates

Taft, M. & Forster, K.I. (1975). Lexical storage and retrieval of prefixed words. *Journal of Verbal Learning and Verbal Behavior , 14*, 638-647.

Taft , M. & Forster , K.I. (1976). Lexical storage and retrieval of polymorphemic and polysyllabic words. *Journal of Verbal Learning and Verbal Behavior, 15*, 607-620.

7. ACKNOWLEDGEMENT

I want to thank the head of the school Dr. Nur Otaran, and administrators Ms. Zuhal Yaman and Ms. Merih Törüner and the classroom teachers Ms. Sezen Ata, Ms. Ferah Babaoğlu, Ms. Güler Inceoğlu, and Ms. Ayten Yıldırım for welcoming me to their school, TED Ankara Koleji. My friend and colleague Dr. Füsun Akkök deserves special thanks for getting that connection established. Most of all I'm grateful to the students for their cheerful and enthusiastic participation.

8. ADDRESS FOR CORRESPONDENCE

Aydin Yücesan Durgunoğlu
Department of Psychology
University of Minnesota Duluth
Duluth, MN 55812
Email: adurguno@d.umn.edu

JOSEPH SHIMRON

WORD DECOMPOSITION IN HEBREW AS A SEMITIC LANGUAGE

1. INTRODUCTION

Most researchers of Semitic morphology refer to the principal characteristic of Semitic morphology as non-linear or non-concatenative. Namely, instead of the morphemes being placed linearly, one after the other before or after the word stem (or base), as prefixes and suffixes, as in English, the morphemic structure of Semitic words is characterized by at least two morphemes interwoven (or interdigitated) within each other in a discontinuous (or non-concatenative) manner. Thus, we have one morpheme, the root, inserted into the other (call it template, pattern or scheme) in certain slots of the word stem structure. See for example how the root MSR (מ.ס.ר) is inserted into some verbs and nominal words:

MaSaR-ti - מָסַרְתִּי (I delivered), MaSaR-ta - מָסַרְתָּ (you m. delivered)
MaSaR-nu - מָסַרְנוּ (we delivered).
e-MSoR - אֶמְסֹר (I will deliver), ti-MSoR - תִּמְסֹר (you m. will deliver)
ni-MSoR - נִמְסֹר (we will deliver).
MeSiR-a - מְסִירָה (delivery), hit-MaSR-ut - הִתְמַסְּרוּת (devotion),
MaSoR-et - מָסֹרֶת (tradition).

As two morphemes, both the root and the template are incomplete phonologically and semantically, until the morphemes are merged to form a word or a word stem. Thus the root and the template are bound morphemes, owing to the fact that it is only when a certain root and a certain template merge together that a definite word is completely specified phonologically, and semantically.

However, although roots and templates are rightly defined as bound morphemes, they are not completely void of semantic, syntactic and phonological content. Rather, they are often associated with some vague core meaning. In Hebrew, most roots are unmistakably associated with a core meaning and, in general, templatic structures (verbal *binyanim* and nominal *mishkalim*) convey certain grammatical and semantic functions. For example, the verbal structures Pu al and Huf al are generally associated with the passive voice and the Hitpa el structure indicates change-of-state incohatives, true reflexives, and reciprocals or mutuality. There are many exceptions, to be sure; some roots and templates have several meanings associated with them and some template constructions (*binyanim* and *mishkalim*) contain different denotations. Yet in most cases, the meaning of a certain novel word derived from merging a known root and a known template may be roughly guessed or quite accurately conjectured by combining the knowledge of the core meanings of the root and the template. As we shall see, this is also evident by the analysis of children's innovative word formation (Berman, 1987, 1997; Clark & Berman 1984, 1987; Ravid (1990, 1995).

Roots and templates may be easily discerned in word stems for the same reason that eyes, a nose and mouth are easily discerned in every normal face: Because they appear invariantly in different contexts, the same root appears in different templates and a single template accommodates different roots, so they stand out as independent entities. As a result, we can easily differentiate the root and the template within most Semitic words.

Roots may be seen as a common thread in the nominal, verbal, adjectival and adverbial systems of Semitic languages. For this reason, it seems justified to refer to Semitic morphology as "root-based". Yet, as we shall see, there are reasons to view the templates, not the roots, as the more influential factor in determining Semitic morphology.

As we have seen above, the verbs: MaSaRti (I delivered), MaSaRta (you mas. delivered) MaSaRnu (we delivered) as well as eMSoR (I will deliver) tiMSoR (you mas. will deliver), and niMSoR (we will deliver) have an identical stem in each of the tenses (past and future tense in this example), i.e. 'MaSaR' in the past tense and 'MSoR' in the future tense. This identical element may be referred to as the word's stem. It comprised of the root's radicals and a vocalic pattern. One could also see that the Semitic stem (the root plus its vocalic pattern) may be flanked by linearly attached affixes in producing inflected and derived forms. Thus, Semitic words should be viewed as having a mixed morphology: non-concatenative, with regard to the word's stem, and concatenative with regard to the affixes attached to it. However, researchers disagree about templates' inner boundaries, so that the dividing line between concatenativity and non-concatenativity is in dispute (Junger, 1987).

The formation of Semitic words can be viewed as a simple mechanism consisting of two lists: a relatively short list, of no more than a few hundred templates for forming nouns, verbs etc. in all their inflected forms, and a much longer list of several thousand, in fact an open list, of roots. In one sense, one can use the Periodic Table from the field of chemistry as a metaphor, as suggested by Ornan (1983): the two lists can be imagined as the two axes of a huge matrix, where words are placed in cells that correspond to a certain template on the templatic axis and a root on the root axis. The intersection between the two axes may be looked upon as a cell containing a word or a potential word. The fact that not every cell is actually occupied leaves room for the construction of new words without adding roots or templates to the matrix as a whole. In the sections to follow, I shall elaborate shortly about the features of roots and templates, then provide some evidence with regard to the linguistic and psycholinguistic reality of the roots and the templates as independent entities in the Hebrew speaker's mental lexicon.

2. THE ROOT

Although the exact role of roots in the actual use of Semitic languages is sometimes debated (Bat-El, 1994; Ornan 1971) the sheer existence of roots is never questioned. As mentioned before, roots are easily detected in most nouns and every verb, regardless of their actual role in the linguistic process. So even if it turned out that in the actual use of Semitic languages, one doesn't attend to roots and templates or process them as independent entities, say because he or she are attending to the words or the stems as wholes, it may still be true, as shall become clear from the empirical evidence enumerated below, that a Semitic speaker can easily identify roots, and if needed, can inflect them in various ways to produce derivations based on such roots even if these roots are formed from a newly borrowed root.

Roots appear in all verbs and most nouns. Thus for example, in Hebrew, KaLaT (he absorbed), niKLaT (he was absorbed), KLiTa (reception or naturalization), KaLiT (absorbable or intelligible) hiKaLTut (the process of being absorbed), and miKLaT (shelter or absorption center), all have KLT as their root, and most of the words in this group are somehow related semantically to the core meaning of absorption. Thus, as said above, although the root is a bound morpheme, and semantically vague it is loosely related to some core knowledge.

Phonologically, the root is almost invariably composed of consonants. As we have seen, these consonants may be articulated with different vowel patterns; thus, the root itself has no definite pronunciation until combined with a vocalic pattern. Yet, from a psycholinguistic vantage, it would be a mistake to perceive the bare root, (particularly upon visual presentation), as not carrying any phonological value until it is inserted in a template. Just as any visual presentation of a consonantal letter in isolation activates certain phonetic values stored in our phonological lexicon, so the cluster of consonants that makes up a root must trigger phonological realizations from some incomplete associations to the phonological mental lexicon.

An interesting question with regard to Semitic roots is whether there are any restrictions on the appearance of consonants in Semitic roots. Ever since the frequently quoted study of Greenberg (1950), we are aware of several restrictions on the appearance of consonants in triradical Semitic roots. Greenberg dealt with the identity restriction, the possibility of identical consonants in one root. There are two types of identities. One is a homogeneous identity of two consonants such as SMM or SSM or MSM, and the other is a "homorganic" identity, an identity of place of articulation such as DTN, where the first two phonemes have the same place of articulation or NPB, where the last two phonemes have the same place of articulation. A complete identity of all root consonants such as SSS never occurs. However, identity of two consonants does occur. As we are mostly dealing with triradical roots, there can be three types of such identities: first and second identical radicals, second and third identical radicals and first and third identical radicals. Greenberg (1950) suggested that for the first and second radicals, both complete identity and homorganic similarity are prohibited. A second-third identity is restricted homorganically, but not for a complete identity, and a first-third identity is partially restricted on both counts.

The restrictions on radical identity have recently aroused new interest as a result of the development of Autosegmental Phonology and its ramifications with regard to the possibility of viewing consonants and vowels as if they are separately represented on autonomous tiers and activated independently although eventually interconnectedly in normal language use. The theory of Autosegmental Phonology was initially used to describe tonal phenomena, but later expanded to cover other levels of representation (Goldsmith, 1990). The Autosegmental Phonology theory assumes that morphological elements such as stress, tone consonants and vowels are represented as independent entities as if they stand on different tiers. Moreover, the theory does not require a one-to-one correspondence between the elements on the different tiers. Elements on one tier may be linked in a one-to-many fashion to elements on another tier. Thus, rising tones or falling tones can span several phonemes, and similarly, vowels can stretch continuously, across a string of consonants. The separation of morphological elements such as consonants and vowels in the Semitic word stem may have a particular implications in Semitic languages in supporting the view that roots (almost always comprised of consonants only) are indeed a separate morpheme within the Semitic word stem. Of course, in the course of word processing, the separated tiers of consonants and vowels are eventually interconnected by a process of tier confluence to form the word skeleton – a sequence of timing units appearing as a skeletal tier, represented by the linear sequence of consonants and vowels (McCarthy, 1979).

This view of consonants and vowels as subword entities was elaborated by McCarthy (1979, 1986), who suggested that Greenberg's restrictions on radical identity of roots can be explained by a principle, which again, was first suggested for analyzing tonality, namely the Obligatory Contour Principle (OCP). The OCP (originally proposed by Leben, 1973) prohibits identical adjacent phonological elements. If we accept that a Semitic root is linguistically a separate entity (metaphorically, represented on a separate tier), then a restriction on first-second and second-third radical identity can be applied to roots exclusively, that is notwithstanding the vowels as phonological elements that enter in between root radicals.

There remains the question as to why second-third co-occurrences are not in fact restricted in a similar way as to first and second co-occurrences. McCarthy suggested an elegant theory to explain the phenomenon. He assumes that roots such as SMM are a product of an underlying biconsonantal root such as SM. However, to be aligned with the triradical template construction of Semitic words, a process of left-to-right spreading (e.g. SM > SMM), a duplication of the root's biliteral final radical, produces SMM as the output of SM. Presumably, it is only the second consonant that is free to spread because the initial consonant doesn't have an empty open slot to its right. Indeed, at least in Hebrew, the number of SSM roots is extremely rare, but SMM roots are not uncommon.

As suggested by Bat-El (1994), and corroborated by Berent and Shimron (1997), the fact that surface non-adjacent consonants seem to be controlled by the OCP in fact constitutes an argument saying that they are adjacent at some level in the grammar. This is the level where the consonants of the stem form an independent unit, known as the consonantal root. Therefore the co-occurrence restriction provides an argument for the morphologically independent existence of a consonantal root in Semitic languages.

But, obviously, if one does not accept the premises of autosegmental theory, one can think of other explanations for co-occurrences (geminations). Thus, Schwarzwald (1973-1974) accounts for Greenberg's restrictions on phonological-phonotactic grounds. Also, if one doesn't entertain the idea of separate tiers for consonants and vowels, so that all phonemes stand, as it were, on the same tier, then in most cases the OCP wouldn't hold because often, a vowel exists in between identical consonants. As for constructions where vowels do not intersperse between identical or homorganic consonants, Schwarzwald suggests that, in Hebrew, identical consonants tend to merge. As a result, the root is not necessarily a basic unit of Hebrew morphology. Rather, one should take the binyan's template or the word's base as the basic units of Hebrew words.

Note that the OCP doesn't explain the restriction on first-third radical identity, nor does it explain examples in Arabic and Hebrew, where in some constructions, a triliteral root is transformed into a quadri-literal root by duplicating (or augmenting) a middle consonant. Be it as it may, psychologically, even if we disregard McCarthy's multi-tier theory, we may still exploit the inherent restrictions on Semitic roots by examining speakers' sensitivity to these restrictions, and if such is found, we may conclude that Semitic roots as such do have a unique role in the linguistic process, cf. Berent & Shimron (1997); Deutsch, Frost & Forster (1998); Frost, Forster & Deutsch, (1997).

3. THE TEMPLATE

The Semitic template may be thought of as whatever is left of the word after the root is extracted. It always consists of a vowel pattern that accompanies the root and dictates its articulation. In most words, it also includes other consonants and vowels that may or may not be considered affixes. According to some researchers, it may be helpful to discuss template structures with regard to specific word categories (Owens, 1997; Buccellati, 1997) e.g., considering verbs and nouns in separation.

The Hebrew verbal system has seven major structural classes, traditionally called *binyanim* (singular, *binyan*). Each binyan may be inflected to mark tense, person, number and gender. That makes about 30 different word forms in each binyan. Importantly, the inflection system contains redundant elements across binyanim. For example, the suffix *-ti* is always used for marking first person singular in the past tense. Some initial elements appear in all forms of a certain binyan in a specific tense (e.g., *hit-* in past-tense of hitPa eL or *ni-* in past-tense niF aL). Invariances such as these enable us to view the *-ti* or the *hit-* components as affixes that are separable from the entire verb template. In recognizing affixes in the verbal system, we may define the verb's central component as the stem or the base, which consists of the root and its vowel pattern, while affixes are optionally placed before or after the stem/base, according to the form of inflection or the choice of *binyan*.

Apparently, this view is less suited for other lexical categories. As far as nouns are concerned, word elements beyond the root consonants and their vowel pattern may not be viewed as affixes. A more economic view of root and template, which encompasses the entire word as two bound morphemes, may seem more appropriate. Thus the word miKLaT (shelter) may be arguably represented by the root KLT and the template mi–a-, without regarding mi- as a prefix to the stem -KlaT.

An important distinction regarding templates is made by Goldenberg (1994), who emphasizes that the major characteristic of the template is its three open slots for accommodating roots. This is equally true for verbal and nominal word forms. The importance of the three-slot structure can be appreciated by observing how this basic constraint may also be applied to the minority of biliteral, quadriliteral, and quinqueliteral roots. That is, even these exceptional roots are inserted in the word template in a manner that still preserves the three open slots of the Semitic template. Goldenberg shows how quadriradical and quinqueradical roots are "pressed, as far as possible to fit in a three-place pattern" (37-39). This is done by clustering two or even three consonants into one or more of the canonical three-slots. Thus, for example, the quadriconsonantal Hebrew root GLGL is cast in Pi el, an intensive binyan, to form GiLGeL (rolled), in the same way as the triconsonantal root PKD forms PiKeD (commanded). A quinqueradical roots behave in a similar manner. Thus, TiLGReF (a loan root from the word *telegraph)* that has a five radical root, is compressed into the same template that accommodates GiLGeL and PiKeD.

In spite of Goldenberg's (1994) objection to McCarthy's propositions (see in his article), in my understanding, the original theory propounded by McCarthy (1979) is not inconsistent with the triality principle (the three slots open for root elements in Semitic templates). For example, as pointed out above, the Obligatory Contour Principle (OCP) explains the asymmetrical appearance of a considerable number of final gemination in (originally) biconsonantal roots (SM > SMM) on the one hand, and the rare initial gemination, such as SSM on the other hand. As said above, the idea is that geminations derive from biconsonantal roots via the simple mechanism of spreading or reduplication of one consonant. Because the linguistic process is presumed to proceed in a left-to-right direction, initial gemination is prevented because the spreading cannot go from right to left. However, a left-right spreading is possible. Thus, a word such as XaGaG may be created from the biconsonantal root XaG. The important point here is that the biconsonantal root XG spreads to form XaGaG because the template contains three slots that demand to be filled. Indeed there are many such examples. This theory seems compatible with the three-slot principle advocated by Goldenberg as a central characteristic of Semitic templates.

The number of noun structures, *mishkalim* (singular, *mishkal*), is not clear. According to one estimate, there are at least 285 mishkalim in Hebrew. But the actual number may be far greater (Ornan, 1983). That depends of course on the criteria for counting roots, e.g. whether we count non-productive roots (those appear in one word only). Notably, in spite of the significant differences between the nominal and the verbal structures, some researchers would consider integrating the two into one group of templates, into which roots may be inserted.

4. RESERVATIONS ABOUT THE CENTRALITY OR THE VALIDITY OF THE ROOT AND TEMPLATE CONSTRUCT

Hoberman and Aronoff (in press) point out that in a contemporary Semitic language – Maltese, "the productive verbal morphology is decidedly affixal". If that is so, they add, "Semitic is no different from any other language family: to the extent that members of a family share some peculiar trait, it is purely an accident of history ...". For them, the alternative to the root and template construct is what they call "templatic morphology". That is, "affixes occur in a fixed order, sometimes unmotivated from a syntactic or a semantic point of view...". Thus verbal patterns consist of an "inner stem with fixed vocalism and a fixed prosody, surrounded by fixed affixes (if they are present) and in some cases, different prosodies and vocalisms in different tenses, aspects or moods. Moreover, this, they suggest, "is true of modern as well as classical Semitic languages and the patterns govern the shapes of borrowing quite rigidly even in languages like Modern Hebrew".

Indeed borrowing in Hebrew has raised doubts among several linguists about the dominance of the root and template as a governing factor in modern Hebrew word formation. According to some linguists (Berman, 1987 a, b; Ornan, 1983, 1990; Scharzwald, 2000), the mechanism of inflecting or deriving a borrowed word involves (a) extracting the vowels from the borrowed word, and (b) inserting the consonants (now considered as root radicals) into a selected template. However, borrowed words often have more than three consonants. Going by the traditional way of forming denominative verbs of quadriliteral roots, they should have for example the CVCCVC structure, like MiSPeR (enumerate) from MiSPaR (number). This is so because the quadriconsonantal roots are usually conjugated either in Pi eL or hitPa eL where the middle consonant is normally augmented. Sometimes this augmentation may be conceived as gemination Ornan (1959), although it may be also viewed as a transposition of the fricatives /v/, /f/, and /x/ to their stop counterparts /b/, /p/, and /k/ respectively. On other occasions, different types of augmentation may be exhibited, including a clustering of consonants in cases where they outnumber the triradical conventional Semitic root (Goldenberg, 1994).

Most borrowed denominal verbs (verbs formed from borrowed nouns) indeed fit the traditional way of interdigitation along the lines of Goldenberg's templative restrictions. As shown above, in Hebrew, TiLFeN (telephoned) is derived from TeLeFoN (Telephone), where a four consonantal root in binyan Pi eL is inserted into the three slots. However, such a possibility is often not born out. Bolozky (1978) has pointed out a strong tendency in Modern Hebrew to preserve the source cluster. Thus, the segmentation of denominatives such as PRiKLeT (advocated) derived from the noun PRaKLiT (advocate) does not adhere to the expected placement of roots inside the template, i.e. *PiRKLeT. Similarly, the verb hitPRakLeT (became a lawyer) in the hitPa L binyan, is conventionally expected to become *hitPaRKLeT. Apparently, some denominations are affected by factors related to their borrowed source rather than playing their role as independent morphological elements (roots and templates, in this context). According to Bat-El (1994): "[T]he model of Semitic verb formation suggested so far cannot account for cluster transfer without some ad hoc lexical marking." (579). She then adds: "It is necessary to abandon [root] Extraction plus Root-to-Template Association and to consider Stem Modification as the appropriate approach."

On the root as the governing element of Hebrew word formation, Bat-El suggests that "what is crucial is the bisyllabic structure". Such an approach demonstrates that the number of consonants is actually irrelevant. Note, however, that Bat-El's objection to the traditional view is not inconsistent with the three-slot principle in Hebrew because, in practice, the bisyllabic structure is compatible with the three slot principle.

Additional opposition to the traditional root-based view is presented by Rose (1998) with regard to the Ethiopian languages, and in analyzing it, she reaches the conclusion that neither templates and roots nor word-based models of derivation are capable of capturing the range of possibilities in this domain. Benmamoun (1999, in press) in discussing Arabic suggests that "the two fundamental assumptions, namely, the central role of the root in deriving words and the status of the template as the realization of grammatical forms are not empirically valid." Moreover, "lexical relations in Arabic are based on derivations involving words/lexemes and morphemes, very much like in English."

Benmamoun is not the first to suggest that we need to abandon the assumption that only the root is central to the derivation of lexical relations. McCarthy (1993) also proposes a mechanism that requires both the vocalic and the consonantal properties of the base form as one unit to derive other lexical forms. Thus it is not only the root that is central to the derivation of lexical relations. As an alternative to the root and template model of word formation, Benmamoun suggests viewing the Arabic imperfective as a default form of the verb when it does not carry temporal or aspectual features. In addition, it acts as input to Arabic word formation processes used to derive other verbal and nominal elements. The imperfective is then affixed to encode person and number features. From a syntactic point of view, the imperfective, according to Benmamoun, is the unmarked syntactic form. A similar suggestion for derivations in Hebrew is suggested by Ussishkin (to appear, a, b).

Finally, Heath (1987) suggests that, while a case might be made for consonantal roots in strong verbs in Moroccan Arabic, it will not hold for weak or hollow stems. As for nouns, Heath finds no reasonable way to separate consonants and vowels into different levels because the vowels cannot be grammatically motivated. Thus, like Benmamoun, he suggests that Arabic has a core of underived stems, such as the singular of simple nouns and the imperfective of simple verbs. These underived stems can be fed into derivational processes that produce derived stems by ablaut, affixation, or both. The input to the derivation processes is often an underived stem, but can also be the output of an earlier ablaut derivation.

Note that both Heath and Benmamoun do not argue that Arabic is not productive. They suggest, it seems, that different patterns of productivity are applied to particular language domains. They nonetheless insist that the idea of a generative master plan made of a word template that contains a stem composed of a root and a vocalic melody doesn't work for too many linguistic domains. At times the stem or even the word as a whole is the input for further derivations.

5. PSYCHOLINGUISTIC EVIDENCE

The issue in question appears quite differently when psycholinguistic data is considered. Two groups of psycholinguists discuss the root vs. word-based controversy; one dealing with evidence derived from language acquisition data and the other from experimental laboratory data. Among the language acquisition researchers, Berman (1987 a, b) collected her data from Hebrew speaking children's lexical innovations. She argues that "for speakers of Hebrew, the consonantal root has definite psychological reality as both the structural and the semantic basis for new-word formation. Moreover, this is true not only for more erudite literate members of the Hebrew speaking community, it applies to those naively "natural" of speakers, preliterate, preschool children who do not have access to the orthographic representation of the words they know and who have not been explicitly introduced to the grammatical notion of *shoresh*, 'root' in the formal school study".

Berman collected her data by presenting children with existing words and asking them to innovate words with the same roots, but in patterns that are not normally inflected or derived with these roots although they could have been; in a sense, they were asked to innovate words that fit those empty cells in the above mentioned root-template matrix. New verbs can be derived from nouns, adjectives, or from other verbs. In order to do so, one needs, as said above, to perform two kinds of operations: root extraction and pattern assignment. With root extraction, the speaker identifies the consonantal skeleton out of which a word is formed. With pattern assignment, the speaker assigns a suitable affixal pattern with this root so as to produce a verb that is structurally well formed and semantically appropriate. The critical question is whether these processes will conceive a verb that would be faithful to classical Hebrew verb formation in spite of the fact that currently and historically it is a non-occurrent verb.

Generally speaking, the variability of responses recorded by Berman was found to be negatively correlated with age, and the less canonic or transparent the consonantal base and syllabic structure of the source noun, the poorer the match between the base consonants of the source noun and those used in contrasting novel verbs. Yet the data of coining such new verbs shows that children from a young age are able to identify and isolate the consonantal skeleton (success rate of about 80% among preschoolers and above 90% among school-age children). In verb innovation, Berman found that children of 3-4 year old were less successful in innovations; they gave far more varied, often idiosyncratic, responses to most items. But the 4-5 year old reached over 80% of success. However, even the 3-4 year olds produced very few items, which violate Hebrew verb-structure constraints.

Berman concludes that "Hebrew-speaking children can perform consonantal root extraction from as young as age three years both in interpreting and producing novel verbs in relation to familiar nouns and adjectives. Moreover, as soon as they are able to derive novel verbs, they do so in the classical Semitic way."

6. EVIDENCE FROM EXPERIMENTAL STUDIES OF SEMITIC MORPHOLOGY

Experimental studies on Hebrew morphology are only a decade old. They were apparently triggered by the increasing interest in word recognition, often referred to as "word comprehension" or "lexical access" (cf. Balota et al, 1990; Taft, 1991; Feldman, 1995; Pinker, 1999). The early studies (beginning with the pioneering studies of Taft & Forster, 1975, 1976), none of them dealt with Semitic languages, investigated European languages. Basically, they can be seen as an attempt by psycholinguists to examine issues of generativity or productivity of morphological processes that are involved with word formation and comprehension. In the language of psycholinguists it is often referred to as an issue of representation, in this case, the representation in the mental lexicon. As Gural & Obler (in press) put it, the question is whether the mental lexicon is organized by "full listing" or by "separate storages". The full listing hypothesis assumes that all words, simple or complex, derived, inflected or not, are listed in the mental lexicon as whole units regardless of their internal structure. The decomposition hypothesis suggests that words containing more than a single morpheme are listed in the lexicon in a way such that word stems and affixes are stored separately, thus providing a more economical system for the construction or comprehension of complex words. If the latter hypothesis is closer to reality, it requires the word recognition process to operate at times through a process of word decomposition. Thus the comprehension of a complex word requires word decomposition, identification of the word stem and its meaning, the identification of the affixes or other morphemes, and finally, synthesizing the complex (comprehensive) word meaning.

Between the two poles of "full listing" vs. "separate storage", there have emerged a number of models which take a mid-way position which I will not describe here (cf. Gural & Obler, in press). In Hebrew, the issue was first studied about a little more than ten years ago by Bentin (1989); Bentin & Feldman (1990); and Feldman & Bentin, (1994). The initial studies were designed to investigate the possibility of word decomposition in Hebrew with an experimental paradigm known as "repetition priming". With this paradigm, the participants are asked to read aloud a list of strings of letters comprising of words and nonce-words and their task is to decide as fast as possible whether these strings of letters are legitimate words or not. Their reading time from the stimulus onset to the marking of their decision by pushing a button is recorded. A priming effect is found when a particular word makes the reading of another (target) word, later on the list, faster. In Bentin and Feldman's studies, taking advantage of the large number of words in which a Hebrew root may appear, some of the primes consisted of Hebrew words which were related to the target words by a common meaning, others, by a common morphology, and still others by both semantic and morphological relationships. When the primes preceded the targets by a short lag, a priming effect was obtained in all three conditions although the semantic and the semantic+morphological priming had a significantly larger effect than the morphological priming alone. However, with long lag repetitions, only the morphological or the morphological+semantic relationship obtained a priming effect. Because the morphological relationship was based on the repetition of the root, the results support the claim stating that Hebrew speakers are sensitive to the root during the process of word recognition.

In another experimental paradigm, known as "segment shifting", Feldman, Frost and Pnini (1995) asked Hebrew speakers to take a segment of a 'source word' and attach it to a target, thus forming a morphologically complex word, they were then asked to name the resulting word as fast as possible. The source words were always legitimate voweled words like מַזְכֶּרֶת maZKeRet. Their roots were either productive (roots that appear in many Hebrew words) or non-productive (roots appearing in only one Hebrew word). The target stimuli were strings of consonant letters, forming neither real words, nor even legitimate roots. The participants' task was to name the string of consonants using the word pattern of the source (prime) word, e.g. maCCeCet. That is to extract the pattern of the source word and to merge it with the target stimulus as if the target stimulus is a root. The researchers hypothesized that it should be easier to detach word patterns associated with productive roots than from patterns associated with non-productive roots. As predicted, the targets were named faster when the roots of the source word segments were productive. The authors interpret these findings to mean that Hebrew word identification includes a stage in which roots and word patterns are decomposed in spite of their being interwoven.

Gural and Obler (in press) continue the experimental tradition of Taft and Forster (cf. Taft, 1991). In a lexical decision task, dealing with verbs only, they examine word decomposition in Hebrew by comparing the word recognition latency of words and two types of non-words. One type of non-words was similar to (real) pseudo-affixes in English, whereby the Hebrew non-words was composed of a normal Hebrew word template but the roots consisted of a string of consonants that did not constitute an existing Hebrew root. The other type of non-words were composed of real roots inserted in a legitimate templates, not the templates that are usually used with such roots (remember the empty cells in the root-template matrix discussed above). They expected that if the non-words composed of real roots are decomposed, and the real roots will be recognized as such, they would slow down the "No" response in the lexical decision task. If, on the other hand, words are fully accessed, all non-words should be rejected equally fast.

The results suggest that overall, it was indeed more difficult for the participants to reject non-words comprising a legitimate root. The error rates were higher and the response times were longer in the real root non-word condition. Thus, this study again supports word decomposition in Hebrew, or at least the assumption that roots are extracted in the process of word recognition.

Frost, Forster & Deutsch (1997) and Deutsch, Frost & Forster (1998) report more research in (an improved) repetition priming task and other experimental paradigms, which allow more refined evidence with regard to word decomposition in Hebrew, and Hebrew speakers' sensitivity to roots and patterns. In their recent studies, they investigated the power of the root and the template as organizing factors in the processing of Hebrew words. The improved priming paradigm known as "masked priming" (developed by Forster and Davis, 1984) allows a very brief presentation of the prime preceded and proceeded by forward and backward masking. In this paradigm, the prime is presented so briefly, and its trace in our memory is circumscribed by the backward and forward masking, so that it is unavailable to conscious processes, although may still affect word perception. Owing to the task conditions, such priming is not sensitive to semantic factors and has its effect on the sheer perceptive, presumably automatic, processes that are affected by either word orthography or morphology or both. In a series of studies (Deutsch, Frost and Forster, 1998, and Frost, Forster and Deutsch, 1997), they found a clear priming effect when the prime was a root and the target word had a nominal or a verbal form derived from that same root.

One contribution of the studies reported by Deutsch and Frost is in demonstrating that the sensitivity to the roots is not necessarily related to their meaning. Rather, the root as a morpheme has an independent effect unconstrained by semantic mediation. This conclusion is further supported by eye movement studies conducted by the authors in collaboration with Rayner and Pollatsek (in preparation). It is inconsistent, however, with earlier findings of Bentin and Feldman (1990). Altogether, this series of studies suggests that the root is independently represented in the mental lexicon, and perhaps governs the process of lexical access in Hebrew, unrestricted by semantic factors.

Deutsch, Frost and Forster also report that with different word patterns as primes, investigated with the same experimental method, a different pattern of results is found for verbs and nouns. Whereas no priming effect of word templates was found for nouns, there was a significant priming effect of templates for verbs. Such findings are perhaps explained by the fact that the number of verb patterns is much lower than the number of nominal patterns. But one should also remember the caveat mentioned above that the role of roots and templates may not be the same in different word groups (e.g. verbs and nouns).

Interestingly, when a special kind of verb was examined (weak verbs in which one consonantal root is not pronounced) with the same experimental paradigm, to assess Hebrew speakers' sensitivity to their constituent morphemes, the priming effect of the roots was not found even with verbs. It thus appears that roots, which deviate from the canonical three-slot pattern, are less powerful as a morphologically organizing factor. If this is so, the force of the word pattern which dictates the syllabic structure of Hebrew words seems highly important as a basic structure (template, pattern) that subsumes the root, and its importance is perhaps equal or at least no smaller than that of the root in governing the process of word recognition.

Berent and Shimron (1997) examine word decomposition in Hebrew from another angle with a different experimental paradigm. Basically, they assume that if Hebrew speakers are sensitive to the root as an independent constituent of Hebrew words, they should ipso facto be sensitive to the morpheme's idiosyncrasies or restrictions. As far as the root is concerned, Berent and Shimron take the consonant gemination constraints discussed above as their starting point for examining the sensitivity of Hebrew speakers to roots as independent morphemes in Hebrew words.

It is important to keep in mind that there is a marked asymmetry in the location of geminates in the root. Root final gemination is highly frequent, while root initial gemination is extremely rare. In fact, there are only five roots with root initial gemination (*mmn, mmš, ddh, kkb*, and *nns*), of which only two are productive (*mmn* and *mmš*). Berent and Shimron apply McCarthy's OCP theory (McCarthy, 1979, 1986) as an explanation for the asymmetry. The advantage of such explanation is that it is based on a fundamental principle of phonology, not tailored particularly for the Hebrew phenomenon. In the Berent and Shimron studies, the asymmetry of gemination patterns was exploited to assess Hebrew speakers' sensitivity to the Hebrew root. The question asked was whether Hebrew speakers judge roots with a restricted frequency as less appropriate for novel Hebrew word formation.

We used two tasks: a production task and a rating task. In the production task, speakers were asked to generate words from existing roots. They were presented with a novel root and a word example. Their task was to conjugate the non-root by analogy to the presented exemplar word. To accomplish the task, the participants had to extract the root from the word exemplar and to replace it with the non-root. Among the non-roots some were triradical roots comprised of different consonants, to which no constraints were applied. Other non-roots had just two radicals. In such cases, in order to accomplish the task considering the three-slot structure of the Hebrew template, subjects would normally add one consonant. They could either add a new consonant or geminate one of the two consonants presented to them. According to the constraints discussed above and the OCP theory, we expected Hebrew speakers to geminate one of the radicals. In addition it was predicted that the number of final root gemination should be far more frequent than root initial gemination. Indeed, these predictions were fully born out. Root initial gemination corresponded to less than 1% of the correct responses, whereas root final gemination corresponded to about 46%.

In the rating task, speakers assessed the acceptability of words derived from three types of non-roots, one with root initial gemination, one with root final gemination and one with no gemination at all. Our participants were asked to rate the acceptability of the non-word patterns in which these three types of non-roots were inserted, as if these were candidates for new Hebrew words. The results of the rating task show significantly lower ratings for the root initial gemination compared with the root final gemination. This pattern emerged regardless of the location of the root in the word in three mishkalim and a variety of conjugation types. Thus the rejection of the root initial gemination cannot be explained by its location in the word. Instead, the findings suggest that the speakers attend to the root structure. In conclusion, both methods provided strong support for the OCP theory on the one hand, and the word decomposition hypothesis, on the other hand, by demonstrating that Hebrew speakers are sensitive to the roots' constraints. Such results are consistent with a root decomposition hypothesis. Importantly, when participants in these studies were asked to explain their rejection of root initial gemination they were unable to explain their behavior. Thus there is no reason to attribute a conscious awareness or a schooling effect to these findings.

Because root gemination restrictions have nothing to do with meaning, the studies of Berent and Shimron also support the view that the Hebrew root is an independent structural force in addition, or perhaps, above and beyond its semantic power. Deutsch, Frost and Forster (1998) corroborate such a position regarding the independent psychological reality of the root as a structural unit although not by earlier studies such as Bentin and Feldman (1990), and Feldman and Bentin (1994).

Importantly, by stressing the morphological role of the root or any other morpheme, one cannot fully deny the semantic role of the root (cf. Bentin & Feldman, 1990; Marslen-Wilson, Tyler, Waksler, & Older, 1994). Feldman and Raveh (in press) examined this issue while applying a crosslinguistic approach. They suggest that opposing data originate from different experimental paradigms. Thus the question is whether differences are related to the semantic role of basic morphemes as language specific factors or whether they can be attributed to variations across experimental procedures.

As mentioned above, Bentin & Feldman (1990) did not find a semantic effect in Hebrew in a simple repetition priming paradigm after a long lag, as was similarly the case in a study with English words (reported in Feldman, 1992). However, in studies investigating a priming effect after a short lag, a semantic effect was found in some experimental settings but not in others. For example, Bentin & Feldman (1990) found a semantic priming effect after a short lag, and in this volume, Feldman and Raveh report a significant semantic priming effect with Hebrew (and Serbian) verbal inflections and derivations. Importantly, in a series of studies conducted by Feldman and her associates in English, it was found that the time interval between the presentation of the prime and the target dramatically influences the results. After being exposed to a very short prime duration, a semantic effect does not surface. Possibly, they suggest, when prime visibility is relatively limited and time to process the prime is restricted, there is no effect of semantic priming. Such a conclusion is consistent with the observations reported by Deutsch, Frost and Forster. Based on their review of studies involving a variety of priming techniques, Feldman and Raveh thus conclude that there is no evidence that semantic priming is determined by language specific factors. More likely, it depends on the specific experimental setting of the priming procedure.

In summary, while some linguists argue against the traditional root-based approach to Semitic languages, and prefer a word- or a stem-based approach, the experimental psycholinguistic data supports the claim that is consistent with the decomposition hypothesis or at least with the notion that roots and templates have an independent status in our mental lexicon. As can be seen in this volume, the root and the template may prime the whole word, perhaps to a different degree, in both verbs and nouns. On the one hand, the template by itself, when accompanied by a non-root, delays a lexical decision. On the other hand, subjects are clearly sensitive to the internal characteristics of the root as demonstrated by the manipulation of the restrictions on consonant gemination. In addition, children from a very early age can successfully demonstrate their knowledge of legitimate template structures such as mishkalim and binyanim as well as their ability to produce new words while obeying the linguistic rules.

How should one explain the differences between the observations of linguists, presented earlier in this chapter, which in a sense reject the role of roots and templates as governing the linguistic behavior of Semitic speakers, and the psycholinguistic data that imply at least a definite sensitivity to roots and templates among Semitic language speakers? I suggest that we should first verify that the two parties are focusing on the same facets of the linguistic phenomenon. That may not be the case. While linguists are interested in examining the variety of mechanisms of word formation consistent with the input-output principles of morpho-phonemic generativity, most experimentalists, intrigued by the possibility of word decomposition as part of the general process of word comprehension, investigate speakers' sensitivity for the main morphemes of Semitic words, the root and the template, their independent power to prime a word or to affect a lexical decision. These concerns are somewhat different.

Let me explain by an analogy. You may enter a room where there are some people doing whatever they do. If you know the people in the room you will be naturally become aware of their presence. Yet that awareness may or may not dictate your behavior unless the situation causes you to interact with the people in this room. Generally speaking, what psycholinguists find is that (a) speakers of Semitic languages are aware of the morphology of their language, and (b) that under the conditions and requirements of a specific task in the laboratory, they tend to behave in a way that is consistent with their linguistic knowledge. That by itself doesn't mean that in all other conditions and for all other purposes, Semitic language speakers will be following these very rules. What linguists show us is that for other purposes, and under different conditions, Semitic languages speakers may apply additional linguistic rules in a way that has little or nothing to do with the speakers' knowledge of or sensitivity to roots and templates.

More specifically, the converging evidence obtained from the psycholinguistic data: that the root and the template prime the whole word, and the template by itself, even when accompanied by a non-root, delays a lexical decision; or that subjects are sensitive to the internal characteristics of the roots, as demonstrated by the manipulation of consonant gemination; and, finally, that children from a very early age can successfully demonstrate their knowledge of legitimate template structures such as mishkalim and binyanim and are able to produce new words while obeying morpho-phonemic rules, all that data clearly imply that roots and templates probably exist as special entities in the mental lexicon of the Semitic languages speakers examined in these studies. Yet none of this evidence precludes the possibility that other parts of Semitic words, segments that are perhaps larger or different than roots and templates may have their own independent status in our mental lexicon.

Among these larger elements, the word's stem may be particularly important. In Hebrew, many stems are words by their own right, but they may also serve as input for producing other words. As said already, when the vowels are stripped from stem/words we normally get the bare root. Then, allowing ablauts to play their role by transforming vocalic patterns and /or affixing the stem in different manners we arrive at the central mechanism of word formation.

I suggest that if we agree to see stems as independent morphological elements, alongside roots and templates, as well as a variety of affixes, then, the process of word decomposition may sometimes stop at the stem level, at other times it may go deeper to the root and template level or even deeper – in verbs – to the level where the root consonants may be identified as an independent entity separated from the vocalic pattern. The word decomposition process may also reach the level where affixes may be stripped or added. Thus the evidence attesting that Semitic languages speakers are sensitive to roots and templates does not mean that such sensitivity has a role to play in every linguistic process and doesn't preclude sensitivities to other types of morphological elements.

My suggestion differs from the model suggested by Deutsch and Frost (in press). Deutsch and Frost suggest a Dual-Route model for morphological processing of Hebrew words. One route is used for the search or activation of whole words, the other leads towards the extraction of the root and/or the word pattern. In view of the variety of the linguistic data mentioned above, I find Deutsch and Frost's model that takes into account only words, roots and templates, too restrictive. I suggest a more versatile model of word decomposition – to account for the multiple sorts of data uncovered by linguists and psycholinguists.

To sum it all, yes, roots and templates are likely to be independent entities in our mental lexicon, but they perhaps exist alongside stems vocalic patterns, words (or a certain part of them), and all sort of affixes. At this point, we cannot be certain because research on this issue has just been started.

In addition, in the attempt to reconcile the gap between the conclusions of linguists and psycholinguists it should be pointed out that some linguists examine processes of word formation of very special types of words – often, borrowed (loan) words. Indeed they have found that speakers are affected by features of the source words, sometimes at the expense of obeying the general structural rules of Semitic inflections and conjugations. Nevertheless, it may not be preposterous to suggest that violations such as these are to be found in every natural language. They do not necessarily rule out general principles. As Pinker (1999) suggests, psychologically, we may make room for parallel systems to work simultaneously side by side in processing the variety of lexical items in our lexicon.

7. REFERENCES

Bat-El, O. (1994). Stem modification and cluster transfer in Modern Hebrew. *Natural Language and Natural Linguistic Theory*. 12: 571-596.

Balota, D. A., Flores D'Arcais, Giovanni, B., & Rayner, K. (1990) (Eds.). *Comprehension processes in reading*. Hillsdale, NJ: Erlbaum.

Benmamoun, E. (1999). Arabic Mophology: the Central Role of Imperfective. *Lingua*, 108: 175-201.

Bentin, S. (1989). Orthography and phonology in lexical decision: Evidence from repetition effects at different lags. *Journal of Experimental Psychology: Learning, Memory, and Cognition, 15*. 61-72.

Bentin, S. and Feldman, L.B. (1990). The contribution of morphological and semantic relatedness to the repetition effect at long and short lags: Evidence from Hebrew. *Quarterly Journal of Experimental Psychology* 42A: 693-711.

Berent, I., and Shimron, J. (1997). The representation of Hebrew words: Evidence from the obligatory contour principle. *Cognition* 64 (1): 39-72.

Berman, R. A. (1987a). Productivity in the lexicon: New-word formation in Modern Hebrew. *Folia Linguistica* 21: 425-461.

Berman, R. A. (1987b). A developmental route: Learning about the form and use of complex nominals. *Linguistics* 27: 1057-1085.

Berman, R. A. (1997). Preliterate knowledge of language". In *Writing Development: An Interdisciplinary View*, C. Pontecorvo (ed.), 61-76, Amsterdam: John Benjamins.

Berman, R. A. (1998). "Children's innovative verbs versus nouns: Structured elicitations and spontaneous coinages." In *Methods in Studying Language Production*, L. Menn and N. Bernstein-Ratner (eds.). Mahwah, NJ: Lawrence Erlbaum.

Bolozky, S. (1978). Word formation strategies in the Hebrew verb system: denominative verbs. *Afroasiatic Linguistics* 5.3: 111-135.

Buccellati, G. (1997). In R. Hetzron (Ed.) *The Semitic languages*. New York: Routledge (69-99).

Clark, E.V. & R. A. Berman, (1984). Structure and use in the acquisition of word-formation. *Language* 60: 542-590.

Clark, E. V. & R. A. Berman, (1987). Types of linguistic knowledge: Interpreting and producing compound nouns. *Journal of Child Language* 14: 547-568.

Deutsch, A. & Frost, R. (in press). Lexical organization and lexical access in a non-concatenated morphology: Mapping the mental lexicon.

Deutsch, A., Frost, R., and Forster, K. (1998). Verbs and nouns are organized and accessed differently in the mental lexicon: Evidence from Hebrew. *Journal of Experimental Psychology: Learning, Memory, and Cognition* 24: 1238-1255.

Deutsch, A., Frost, R., Rayner, K., and Pollatsek, A. (in preparation). Early morphological effects in word recognition in Hebrew: Evidence from parafoveal preview benefit effect.

Feldman, L.B. (1992). Morphological relationships revealed through the repetition priming task. In: N. Moonan, P. Downing & S. Lima (eds.), *Literacy and linguistics*. Amsterdam/Philadelphia: John Benjamins Pub. Co.

Feldman, L. B. (1995) (Ed.). *Morphological aspects of language processing*. Hillsdale, NJ: Erelbaum.

Feldman, L. B. & Bentin, S. (1994). Morphological analysis of disrupted morphemes: Evidence from Hebrew. *Quarterly Journal of Experimental Psychology*.

Feldman, L.B., Frost, R., & Pnini, T. 1995. Decomposing words into their constituent morphemes: Evidence from English and Hebrew. *Journal of Experimental Psychology: Learning, Memory, and Cognition* 21: 947-960.

Feldman, L.B. & Raveh. M. (in press). When degree of semantic similarity influences morphological processing: cross language and cross task comparisons.

Forster, K.I., & Davis, C. (1984). Repetition priming and frequency attenuation in lexical access. *Journal of Experimental Psychology: Learning, Memory, and Cognition, 10*, 680-698.

Frost, R., Forster, K.I., & Deutsch, A. (1997). What can we learn from the morphology of Hebrew: a masked priming investigation of morphological representation. *Journal of Experimental Psychology: Learning Memory, & Cognition* 23: 829-856..

Goldenberg, G. (1994). Principles of Semitic word-structure. In *Semitic and Cushitic Studies*, G. Goldenberg and S. Raz (eds.), 29-64. Wiesbaden: Harrassowitz.

Goldsmith, J. (1990). *Autosegmental & metrical phonology*. Cambridge: Basil Blackwell.

Goral, M. & Obler, L.K. (in press). In: Shimron, J. (ed.) *Language processing and language acquisition in root-based (Semitic) languages*. Amsterdam: John Benjamins.
Greenberg, J. (1950). The patterning of root morphemes in Semitic. *Word,* 6, 162-182.
Heath, J. (1987). *Ablaut and Ambiguity: Phonology of a Moroccan Arabic Dialect*. Albany NY: SUNY Press.
Hoberman, R.D. & Aronoff, M. (in press). The verbal morphology of Maltese: From Semitic to Romance. In: Shimron, J. (ed.) *Language processing and language acquisition in root-based (Semitic) languages*. Amsterdam: John Benjamins.
Junger, J. 1987. *Predicate Formation in the Verbal System of Modern Hebrew*. Dordrecht: Foris.
Leben, L. (1973). *Suprasegmental phonology*. Cambridge, Mass: MIT Press dissertation.
Marslen-Wilson, W., Tyler, L. K., Waksler, R., & Older, L. (1994). Morphology and meaning in English mental lexicon. *Psychological Review, 101*. 3-33.
McCarthy, J. (1979). *Formal problems in Semitic phonology and morphology*.
Cambridge, Mass: MIT Ph. D. dissertation. Distributed by Indiana University Linguistics Club. New York: Garland Press.
McCarthy, J. (1986). OCP effects: Gemination and antigemination. *Linguistic Inquiry, 17*, 207-263.
McCarthy, J., 1993. Templatic Form in Prosodic Morphology. *Proceedings of FLSM* III.
Ornan, U. (1959). *Dikduk Ha-pe Ve-ha-ozen* (the grammar of the mouth and the ear) Jerusalem: Inbal.
Ornan, U. (1971). Binyanim u-bsisim, netiyot u-gzarot (Verbal structures and bases, inflections and derivations) *Ha'universita, 15*, 2.
Ornan, U. 1983. How do we build a new Hebrew word?. In. M. Bar-Asher, A. Dotan, G. B. Sarfatti and D. Tene (eds), *Hebrew Language Studies* 13-42. Jerusalem: The Magnes Press (in Hebrew).
Ornan, U., Machinery for Hebrew word formation, In M. Golumbic (Ed.), *Advances in Artificial Intelligence*. Springer Verlag, pp. 75-93, 1990.
Owens, J. (1997). The Arabic grammatical tradition. In R. Hetzron (Ed.) *The Semitic languages*. New York: Routledge (46-58).
Pinker, S. 1999. *Words and rules: The ingredients of language*. New York: Basic Books.
Ravid, D. (1990). Internal structure constraints on new-word formation devices in modern Hebrew. *Folia Linguistica* 24: 289-346.
Ravid, D. (1995). *Language change in child and adult Hebrew: A psycholinguistic perspective*. New York: Oxford University Press.
Ravid, D. & R. Farah. 1999. Learning about noun plurals in early Palestinian Arabic. *First Language .19*, 187-206.
Rose, S. (1998). Triple take: Tigre and the case of internal reduplication. Paper given at the 4th Conference on Afroasiatic Languages, SOAS, London.
Schwarzvald, O. (1973-1974). Roots, bases and the structure of morphemes. *Leshonenu, 38*, 131-136.
Schwarzwald (Rodrigue), O. (1996). Syllable structure, alternations, and verb complexity: Modern Hebrew verb patterns reexamined. In S. Isre'el and S. Raz (Eds.) *Israel Oriental Studies, XVI. Studies in Modern Semitic Languages* (95-112).
Schwarzwald (Rodrigue), O. (2000). Shoresh ha-po'al ve-zikat ha-shem la-po'al. (The verb's root and the relation of the noun to the verb). In O. Schwarzwald (Rodrigue), S. Blum-Kulka, and E. Olshtein (Ed.), *Sefer Refa'el Nir*. Jerusalem: Carmel.
Taft, M. (1991). *Reading and the mental lexicon*. Hillsdale, NJ: Erlbaum.
Taft, M. & Forster, K. I. (1975). Lexical storage and retrieval of prefixed words. *Journal of Verbal Learning and Verbal Behavior, 14*. 683-647.
Taft, M. & Forster, K. I. (1976). Lexical storage and retrieval of polymorphemic and polysyllabic words. *Journal of Verbal Learning and Verbal Behavior, 15*. 607-620.
Ussishkin, A. to appear a. The inadequacy of the consonantal root: Modern Hebrew denominal verbs and output-output correspondence. *Phonology 16,* 3
Ussishkin, A to appear b. Root-and-pattern morphology without roots and patterns. *Proceedings of NELS,* 30.

8. ADDRESS FOR CORRESPONDENCE

Joseph Shimron
University of Haifa
Faculty of Education
Mount Carmel
Haifa 31905
Phone: 04-824373
email: shimron@construct.haifa.ac.il

MARCUS TAFT

MORPHOLOGICAL REPRESENTATION AS A CORRELATION BETWEEN FORM AND MEANING

1. INTRODUCTION

Lexical memory exists for the purpose of mapping meaning onto word form. It interfaces with the world via a level of representation that corresponds to the presented form of the word (either orthographic or auditory), and access to this representation makes available the semantic information associated with it. Such a form-to-meaning association has been built up over repeated occurrences of the same form referring to the same thing. That is, the lexical system captures the correlation that can be found between a form and the context in which it occurs. For example, the word form *cat* is consistently found in a context that refers to a furry, whiskered pet that says "miaow", even though this context might vary markedly in other ways (e.g., when referring to a cat stuck up a tree, a cat owned in one's childhood, or a cat chasing a mouse).

The ability to capture a correlation between two levels of stimulus characteristics (e.g., form and meaning) is a feature of connectionist models where weightings on connections between the two levels are strengthened in response to the correlations between those levels. Whether each of the units found at the different levels of analysis represent a complete identity (i.e., are "localist representations") or contribute to a pattern of activation across a number of units (i.e., are "distributed representations"), the correlation between levels can still be captured (see e.g., Page, 1999). The framework to be used here is a version of the connectionist approach that is localist (e.g., Grainger & Jacobs, 1996; Norris, 1994; Schreuder & Baayen, 1995; Taft, 1991) rather than distributed (e.g., Plaut, McClelland, Seidenberg, & Patterson, 1996; Seidenberg & McClelland, 1989). The reason for this is that the localist version provides a more concrete metaphor for lexical processing in that the units of activation can be explicitly described. Even if it turns out that the brain works in a distributed fashion, the localist framework presented here might be thought of as a model of this distributed system that allows one to understand the nature of the lexical representation in more concrete terms.

Such a framework is presented in Fig 1, which depicts how the system might represent the correlation between form and meaning, at least for visually presented words that are the focus of this paper. In this figure, each form representation constitutes a unit that is activated by the presence of relevant orthographic features in the stimulus. Each concept unit represents the coalition of a set of semantic features.

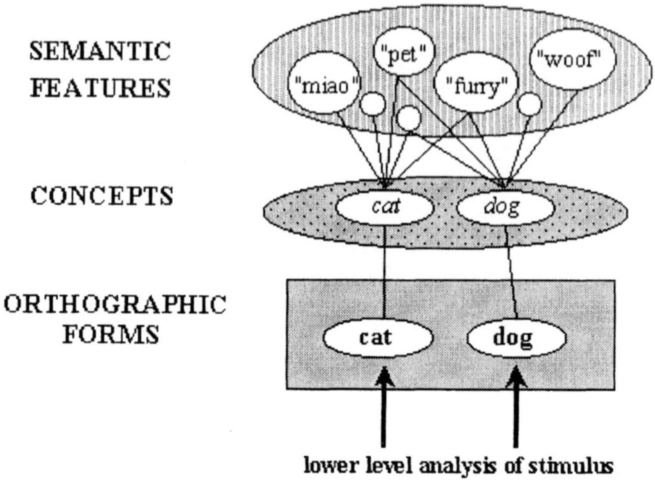

Figure 1. A depiction of the connection between form and meaning in lexical memory.

Note that it is possible for a single form unit to be associated with more than one concept unit, namely, when it is an ambiguous word. For example, the word *dog* can refer to a verb that means "to follow closely", which has few, if any, semantic features in common with its "animal" meaning. Therefore, there must be some way of keeping these two sets of features separate from each other and this is achieved by the existence of two separate concept units, one for each meaning of the word *dog*. If semantic features were linked directly to the form units, there would be no way of distinguishing features that are relevant only to the "animal" meaning from those relevant only to the "follow" meaning. The ability to distinguish between the two meanings of an ambiguous word provides one important reason for proposing the existence of a concept level separate from the level of semantic features. In other words, it is the concept unit that brings together a set of semantic features and links it to the word form.

The alternative to this would be the postulation of two separate but identical form units for each meaning of a word (e.g., two form representations for *dog*), but this would seem to be unnecessarily redundant. Of course, redundancy is not always a bad thing in and of itself, because it might provide a back-up mechanism should there be disruption to the system. However, it is hard to see the advantage of having two identical form representations if they are relevant to different meanings. That is, the redundant information does not in this case provide an alternative route to the same information.

Concept units (or lemmas, cf. Baayen, Dijkstra, & Schreuder, 1997; Schreuder, Burani, & Baayen, *this volume*) can actually be seen as the units that capture the correlation between form and meaning. As such, they take on the role of the "hidden units" that are proposed in distributed models to mediate between input and output (e.g., Seidenberg & McClelland, 1989), and are equivalent to what Plaut et al describe as "attractor patterns". What this means is that lemmas can vary in their precision depending on the degree of correlation between form and meaning. The greater the variation of meaning that a word has in different contexts, the less distinctive its lemma representation will be (i.e., the more widely tuned the attractor pattern will be). Such a proposal is consistent with the finding that concrete words, whose meaning is very precise, are recognized more readily than abstract words (e.g., Bleasdale, 1987; Schwanenflugel & Shoben, 1983).

2. REPRESENTATION OF POLYMORPHEMIC WORDS

The concern of this chapter, however, is the role of morphology in lexical processing. To examine this issue, attention will first be turned to the nature of the form representation in visual word recognition. Does each form-level unit really represent a word, or does it represent a morpheme or even a syllable? Most connectionist models of lexical processing are based solely on monosyllabic words, like *dog* or *cat* (e.g., Coltheart, Curtis, Atkins, & Haller, 1993; Grainger & Jacobs, 1996; Plaut et al., 1996; Seidenberg & McClelland, 1989), where word, morpheme and syllable are the same thing. When modeling the processing of more complex words, however, the nature of the form representation needs to be established because the three possibilities are quite different, as depicted in Figs 2a, 2b, and 2c.

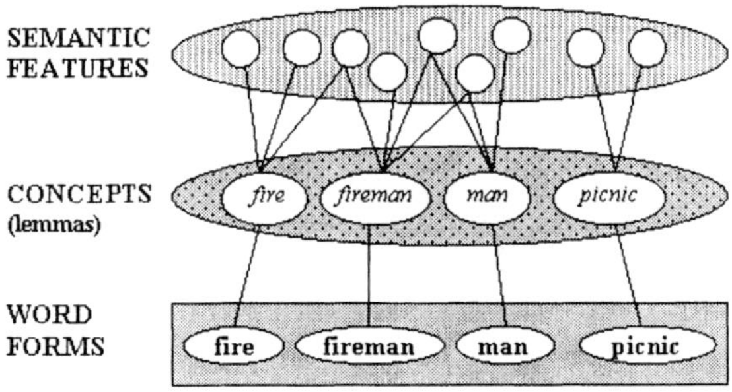

Figure 2a. The representation of polymorphemic and polysyllabic words when the orthographic form level represents whole words.

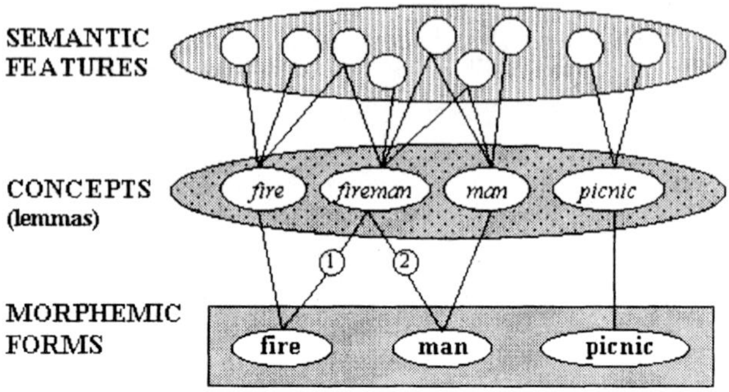

Figure 2b. The representation of polymorphemic and polysyllabic words when the orthographic form level represents morphemes.

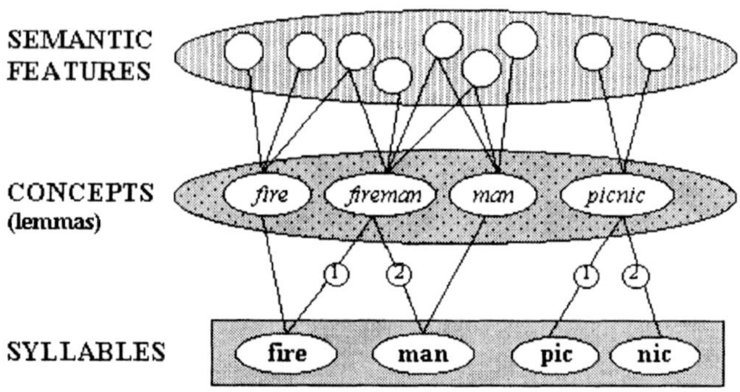

Figure 2c. The representation of polymorphemic and polysyllabic words when the orthographic form level represents syllables.

If the form representations are those of whole words (Fig 2a), then polymorphemic words (like *fireman*) and monomorphemic polysyllabic words (like *picnic*) will be represented in full. Alternatively, if the form representations are morphemic in nature (Fig 2b), then only monomorphemic words will be represented even when they are polysyllabic (like *picnic*). The concept unit for a polymorphemic word will be activated by the combined activation of the form units for each morpheme, with the combination of activation following a particular order (or else *gunshot* could not be differentiated from *shotgun*). This is arbitrarily depicted in the figure as numbered links. Polysyllabic monomorphemic words (like *picnic*) will be broken down further only if the form units represent syllables (Fig 2c).

An additional possibility is a hierarchy of units such that, for example, a syllabic level sends activation up to a morpheme level which in turn sends activation up to a whole word level (see e.g., Taft, 1994). This, however, will lead to considerable redundancy in representation with, for example, *man* existing at all three levels. Some of this redundancy could be eliminated by specifying that the morpheme level is only for morphemes that are not free standing words (i.e., bound morphemes like the *hench* of *henchman*). In this way, *man* will have a representation at the word level, but not at the morpheme level. Nevertheless, if a syllable level also exists, there would still be redundancy between this and the other two levels.

In fact, the way in which bound stem morphemes are represented is an important issue because it addresses the relationship between the representation of morphemes and syllables, as well as that between morphemes and words. That is, a bound stem morpheme can be distinguished from a purely form-based syllable because some sort of meaning can be ascribed to it, and it can be distinguished from a word because it cannot stand alone. For this reason, bound morphemes are the central focus of the present inquiry into lexical representation.

3. REPRESENTATION OF BOUND MORPHEMES

The existence of a form-level representation for bound morphemes has been proposed for a long time (e.g., Emmorey, 1989; Taft, 1994; Taft & Forster, 1975), and is supported by the finding that bound morphemes are relatively hard to classify as non-words. For example, difficulties encountered in making a lexical decision to *vive* compared to *lish* (Taft & Forster, 1975) can be interpreted as evidence that *vive* is represented in lexical memory for the purposes of recognizing *revive*, while the *lish* of *relish* is not. Such an interpretation dismisses any model that fails to incorporate any morphological analysis such as that depicted in Fig 2a (which will therefore not be considered further), but is consistent with the "morpheme" model depicted in Fig 2b, which readily incorporates bound morphemes by simply allowing the form representations to be either bound or free. In such a way, bound morphemes (e.g., *vive*, *hench*) have a status that syllables (like *pic* and *nic*) do not have.

In contrast, according to the "syllable" model depicted in Fig 2c, bound morphemes and syllables would have the same status within the form-based representations. This does not mean, however, that bound morphemes and syllables are necessarily represented in the same way in the lexical processing system. In particular, one could argue that bound morphemes are associated with a meaning and, therefore, will have a lemma representation, whereas syllables will not. Thus, bound morphemes and syllables can potentially be differentiated at the lemma level of representation in Fig 2c.

This raises the question of whether knowledge does exist in the lexical processing system that a syllable functions as a bound morpheme or not. Do language users draw a distinction between letter-strings like *hench* and those like *pic*? The research by Taft and Forster (1975) and Taft (1994) suggests that they do, in that the non-morphemic word parts (e.g., *lish*) were often syllables. This was particularly true in the Taft (1994) study where the bound stem items (e.g., the *peccable* of *impeccable*) were matched on stress pattern with the non-stems (e.g., the *tinerary* of *itinerary*), yet were harder to classify as non-words. It may well be, though, that the first syllable is the most important in recognizing a polysyllabic word, and we do not know whether such syllables (like *pic*) are treated any differently to bound morphemes (like *hench*). Although Taft and Forster (1976) found a delay in classifying first syllables as non-words relative to non-syllables, they did not compare syllables to bound morphemes. Indeed, some of the syllable items used by Taft and Forster (1976) were actually bound morphemes (like *hench*).

When considering a comparison of bound morphemes and syllables, however, one must confront the difficulties that exist in defining both of these terms. In relation to the syllable, it is possible to give either a phonological or an orthographic definition. If a phonological definition is adopted, there will often be a conflict with morphemic structure (e.g., the syllable structure *ea* + *ten*, *ac* + *tor* is incompatible with the morphological structure *eat* + *en*, *act* + *or*). For this reason, Taft (1979, 1987) supported the idea that an orthographically defined syllable is important in reading, where the first syllable includes all consonants after the first vowel without creating an illegal final consonant cluster. So, while the first syllable of *picnic* would be taken to be *pic* (because *cn* is not a permissible final cluster), the first syllable of *police*, *tiger*, and *winter* would be *pol*, *tig*, and *wint* respectively even though these violate the phonological syllable structure. This orthographically based unit was labeled the Basic Orthographic Syllable Structure (or BOSS). However, because others have failed to find support for the BOSS (e.g., Lima & Pollatsek, 1983), it is unclear what the appropriate choice of definition should be when examining the role of the syllable. There do exist clear cases that are consistent with any definition of syllabification (like the *pic* of *picnic* or the *zig* of *zigzag*), but the number of such words, at least in English, is very restricted.

Furthermore, even if syllabification were clear-cut, it is not always obvious whether such a subunit should be considered a bound morpheme or just a meaningless syllable. Being a bound morpheme is not an all-or-none phenomenon; there are degrees of meaningfulness. A letter-string is clearly a bound morpheme when it does not stand on its own as a word, but forms a constituent in a number of different words with a shared meaning. An example might be *smith,* which is not a free-standing word in most people's vocabulary, but which recurs in several words that have overlapping meanings, like *blacksmith*, *goldsmith*, *locksmith* and *silversmith*. Thus, some sort of meaning can be extracted out for *smith* (i.e., something to do with "working with metal"), thus making it morphemic in nature.

Less clear cases are letter-strings like *hench* that only occur in a single word, but where the accompanying constituent (*man*) is used as a morpheme. That is, a henchman is a man and, therefore, *hench* might be taken to refer to "the thing that a man does in order to be a henchman". In this way, it might be possible to work out what a *henchwoman* or *henchdog* mean if those words were coined (whereas *talis-woman* or *talisdog* would be non-sensical because *man* does not function as a morpheme in the word *talisman*, being semantically unrelated to it).

There are other cases that have an even more dubious status as a bound morpheme, namely, where a syllable may be considered to have some level of meaning as a result of sound symbolism. For example, it could be argued that *zig* refers to "a sharp movement in one direction" in contrast to *zag*, which refers to "a sharp movement in the other direction", thus creating a *zigzag*. So, is it appropriate to consider that the syllables *zig* and *zag* have a morphemic status?

In the "morpheme" model of "syllable" model of Fig 2c, it is relevant to the lemma level. However, if the representation of morphemic information arises from the correlation between form and meaning, neither model needs the reader to make a conscious decision about the morphemic status of any sublexical unit. In fact, a decision about whether a sublexical unit should be classified as a morpheme or not simply becomes a taxonomic exercise and not of crucial concern for the establishment of representations in the lexical processing system. The development of such representations will be based purely on the statistical relationships that exist between form and meaning.

To be more specific, the form units that develop according to the "morpheme" model, will be the smallest units that can be abstracted out from the correlation with meaning. So, *smith* would develop as a form unit because its appearance in a word is consistently associated with the idea of "working with metal". *Hench* would also develop as a form unit because it constitutes the remnant of the word *henchman* after the meaningful *man* has been abstracted out as a unit. It is unclear whether form units for *zig* and *zag* would develop on the basis of sound symbolism. However, pure syllables, like *pic* and *nic*, definitely would not. Although the existence of the letter-string *pic* is correlated with the occurrence of the meaning "an outdoor meal", this correlation will be identical with that for the unit *nic* and, therefore, having separate units would achieve nothing beyond what can be captured in a single unit for *picnic*.

While form units represent morphemes according to this model (as depicted in Fig 2b), we need to also consider the nature of the units at the lemma level. A unit at the form level that represents a free morpheme (e.g., *fire* or *picnic*) will be associated with its own lemma as well as with any lemmas for polymorphemic words in which it occurs (e.g., *fireman*). However, when a form unit represents a bound morpheme (e.g., *hench*), it may or may not develop its own lemma as a link to semantics. Fig 3 shows what the system would look like if bound morphemes were not associated with a lemma unit, but rather, linked solely to the relevant polymorphemic word lemma. By this version of the "morpheme" model, to consider a bound morpheme (like *hench* or *smith*) as being at all meaningful, there must be generalization from the meaning activated via the polymorphemic word/s in which it occurs.

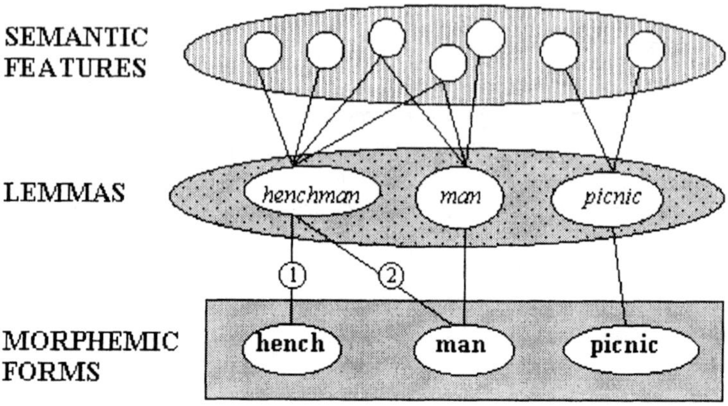

Figure 3. The representation of polymorphemic and polysyllabic words when the orthographic form level represents morphemes and bound morphemes have no lemma-level representation.

Turning now to the "syllable" model depicted in Fig 2c, the units that develop as a result of the correlation between form and meaning are at the lemma-level. That is, the form-level units are defined purely on a structural basis, independent of meaning, with the lemmas being the units that capture the correlations. So, lemmas are not restricted to free morphemes, because bound morphemes also display a correlation between form and meaning, even if not very precisely. When a letter-string occurs in several semantically related words (like *smith*), a lemma unit will develop with a precision greater than that developed when the associated semantic features are less obvious, namely, when the letter-string occurs in only one relevant context (e.g., *hench*). In the latter case, semantic features are associated with the constituent essentially by default. That is, the lemma units for *henchman* and *man* will be linked to semantic features that overlap, and this provides the possibility for *hench* to develop its own lemma unit on the basis of the non-overlapping features associated with *henchman.* In other words, a lemma for *hench* would bring together the semantic features that are linked specifically to *henchman* and which are not relevant to the fact that it refers to a "man". Finally, because form units are based on structural grounds alone, *pic* and *nic* will be represented at the form level but not at the lemma level. This is its crucial contrast with the "morpheme" model, where pure syllables are represented at neither the form nor lemma level.

According to the pure "syllable" model, then, form units are defined entirely on form-based grounds, and these units can then participate in the correlation with meaning. However, it is easy to refute this proposal. Take, for example, the polymorphemic word *weekend*. Here, the lemmas for the constituent morphemes will be activated via the form units *week* and *end*. If form units are to be set up without any influence from higher level knowledge, there must therefore be a way of identifying these two units on a purely orthographic basis. In fact, a BOSS analysis provides the appropriate structure because the *k* would be included in the first unit. However, what then of *beekeeper*? It would have to be represented as *beek* + *eep* + *er* and this would provide no avenue to the lemmas for *bee* and *keep*. Hence it is apparent that higher level knowledge must have an impact on the form units that are stored. Indeed, it was for this reason that Taft (1979, 1987) incorporated morphology into the definition of the BOSS (i.e., "include all consonants following the vowel of the stem morpheme").

Does the fact that functional information can influence form-level representation entail that Fig 2b is correct and Fig 2c is wrong? Not entirely. It may be that a combination of the two is possible. In particular, efficient form-level representation can be seen as one that breaks complex words down into smaller, manageable units. Correlation between form and meaning provides the primary basis for this breakdown of the word, such that morphemic analysis dominates over purely form-based analysis (giving *week* + *end* and *bee* + *keeper*). Nevertheless, form-based analysis might occur when there is no morphemic basis for the analysis (as with *picnic*). This is exemplified in Fig 4, where the existence of lemma units for bound morphemes is also depicted. The structure of this model is the same as that shown in Fig 2c. The only difference is that morphemic considerations can override syllabic ones in determining the form-level representations (as in *weekend* and *beekeeper*). For this reason, the orthographic units have been re-labeled with the general term "form" (rather than "syllables"), in order to capture the fact that the form units not only represent syllables for the recognition of monomorphemic words, but can represent morphemes for the recognition of polymorphemic words as well. Thus the model is a hybrid of a morpheme and syllable account. Morphemic considerations lead to the first form unit of *weekend* being *week* and the first form unit of *beekeeper* being *bee*, whereas syllabic considerations lead to the first form unit of *picnic* being *pic*. The basis for *hench* being a form unit is ambiguous since it is both the first syllable and first morpheme of *henchman*. However, the example of *henchman* is given in the figure in order for it to be compared directly to Fig 3.

According to this hybrid model, syllables are represented at the form level in exactly the same way as are monosyllabic bound and free morphemes, but they differ by virtue of the fact that a syllable is not associated with its own individual lemma. In contrast, according to the model depicted in Fig 3, syllables differ from morphemes inasmuch as the former have no form-level representations, while bound morphemes differ from free morphemes inasmuch as the former have no lemma-level representations.

What is being suggested, then, is that we can reject the "syllable" model of Fig 2c on logical grounds, but that the idea of pure syllabic analysis in lexical processing can still be incorporated if a hybrid model (Fig 4) is adopted. Whether purely syllabic representations are actually present in the word recognition system is still an open question, though research supporting the existence of the BOSS (e.g., Taft, 1979, 1987) favors such an idea.

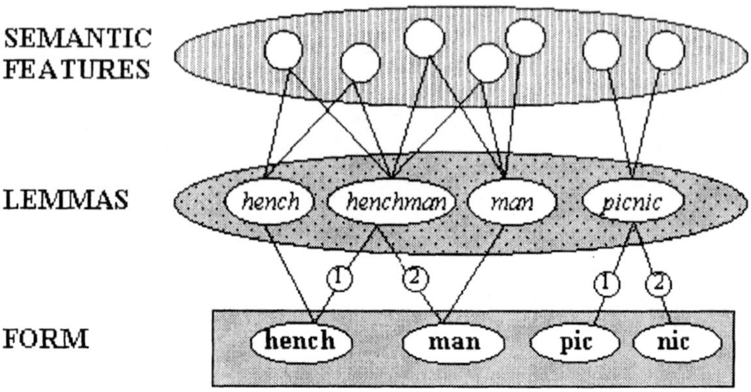

Figure 4. The representation of polymorphemic words when the orthographic form level represents both syllables and morphemes and bound morphemes have a lemma-level representation.

4. MORPHEME RETRIEVAL

In the hybrid model (as well as in the morpheme models of Fig 2b and Fig 3), higher level knowledge influences the nature of the form-level representations: In the example of *weekend* and *beekeeper*, the form units are determined on the basis of the fact that the meaning of each unit is relevant to the meaning of the whole word. However, even if morphological considerations influence the nature of the form unit, it must be emphasized that it is still possible to activate that unit purely on a physical basis. For example, if the "beekeeper" lemma is activated via the form units for *bee*, *keep* and *er*, while the "weekend" lemma is activated via *week* and *end*, the appropriate form units will be activated simply because they are congruent with the letter groupings contained in the stimulus word.

What this means is that a number of irrelevant form units might be activated when a word is presented, but these will eventually be inhibited by virtue of the fact that they fail to activate an appropriate lemma. For example, *beetroot* contains the letter-string *bee* and, therefore, the form unit for *bee* will be activated. However, the remaining letters *troot* will fail to activate any form unit, so the alternative analysis as *beet* and *root* will eventually be accepted because it succeeds in activating the lemma for *beetroot* (see also Libben, 1994; Taft, 1979). Thus, while functional knowledge might influence the storage of form-level representations, the actual retrieval of those representations during reading can occur without the direct involvement of such higher-level information.

5. AN EXPERIMENT THAT DISTINGUISHES FORMAL AND FUNCTIONAL PROCESSING

It was stated earlier that being a bound morpheme is not an all-or-none phenomenon and that this is captured within the notion of correlation between form and meaning. That is, morphemes vary in their precision or clarity of representation depending on the strength of this correlation. This variation in clarity is readily captured within lemma units because they develop as a means of characterizing the correlation between form and meaning. It was suggested earlier that lemmas representing bound morphemes like *smith* that occur in many different semantically related contexts have a reasonably precise representation, and may even be hard to distinguish from free morphemes (which also, of course, occur in a wide range of contexts). Bound morphemes like *hench*, on the other hand, which only exist within a single context, might have only an indistinct lemma representation because their meaning is harder to determine independent of the single word in which they occur.

The question that arises, however, is whether form-level units that are regulated by morphemic information (i.e., the "morpheme" model of Fig 2b and Fig 3, or the hybrid model of Fig 4), also vary in their clarity depending on their morphemic status. That is, is the form unit for *smith* "clearer" than that for *hench* which in turn is "clearer" than that for *pic*? In fact, it is not necessary to assume that this is the case as long as the variations in clarity are already captured at the lemma level. That is, form-level representations might only be influenced by their frequency of usage, whereas at the lemma level they differ in terms of the strength of correlation between the form and meaning. So, by this account, form-level representations will exist equally for *smith*, *hench*, *pic*, and even *fire*, as long as their frequency of usage is matched. Where they will differ, though, is at the level of the lemma where they vary in terms of their association with meaning. Support for this idea comes from a set of experiments that I recently conducted using Chinese characters.

Chinese words are composed of one or more physically separated characters, though a two-character structure is the most common. There were several reasons for using Chinese to examine the distinction between form-level and lemma-level processing. First, many characters exist that are bound morphemes, either occurring in many contexts, i.e., in many two-character compound words (equivalent to *smith*) or occurring in only one context (like *hench*). There are also quite a few meaningless syllables (equivalent to *pic*) that only ever occur in combination with another syllable which, in turn, only ever occurs in that same word (as is the case with *zig* and *zag* in English). Second, and most importantly, because each character in Chinese is a physically distinct unit, there are two types of judgement that can be made about such characters that cannot be differentiated if using alphabetically scripted words.

In English, one is able to say that *bench* and *pit* are words while *hench* and *pic* are non-words. However, it is unclear whether this judgement is based on the fact that the letter-strings *bench* and *pit* exist as word forms while *hench* and *pic* do not (i.e., a form-based explanation), or on the fact that *bench* and *pit* have clearly defined meanings while *hench* and *pic* do not (i.e., a function-based explanation). Any confusion in classifying *hench* as a non-word relative to *pic* could similarly be given a form-based or a function-based explanation. That is, the morphemic status of *hench* could have its impact either at the form-level or at the lemma level. In Chinese, on the other hand, these two possibilities can be differentiated because a character can be classified in two distinct ways; one focusing on form and the other on function.

In a "Character Decision Task" (or CDT), existing characters are discriminated from non-existing characters. Non-characters are composed of real components which are combined in non-existing ways, while real characters are either free morphemes, bound morphemes, or pure syllables. The CDT could be potentially performed purely at the form level because real characters have an orthographic representation while nonsense characters do not. Note that character frequency may well have an effect on the CDT, arising from the likelihood that activation of a form unit is affected by its frequency of usage.

In contrast to the CDT, however, it is also possible for a Chinese reader to decide whether a character exists as a free-standing word or not (a "Word Decision Task" or WDT). Here, the response is "yes" for free morphemes and "no" for the other types of characters, namely, bound morphemes and pure syllables. Thus, it can be seen that the Word Decision Task requires the processing of functional information, which is not necessary in the Character Decision Task.

The CDT and WDT tasks can therefore be contrasted to determine what is important in form-level processing and what is important at the higher functional level. First, according to the hybrid model of Fig 4 (as well as the rejected "syllable" model of Fig 2c), pure syllables, bound morphemes and free morphemes should all be equally well classified as real characters in the CDT as long as frequency is well matched. In the WDT task, on the other hand, the pure syllables should be easier to reject than the bound morphemes (because the former have no lemma representation). Moreover, the bound morphemes should be distinguishable from the free morphemes in the sense that the latter will have a more precise lemma representation (because of their more consistent meaning across contexts). The distinction between bound and free morphemes, then, should be seen in the greater likelihood of classifying the latter as a "word" rather than a "non-word" in the WDT, even though they are equally classifiable as characters in the CDT.

As mentioned, in testing these predictions, it is important that frequency be well-matched and this raises the issue of what the appropriate frequency should be. Specifically, should the frequency of a character be the number of times that that character occurs regardless of context (i.e., token frequency) or should one take into account the number of compound words in which that character occurs (i.e., type frequency)? An answer to this would be needed if one were wanting to compare "clear" bound morphemes that occur in many compound words (like *smith*) with "unclear" ones that occur in only one compound word (like *hench*). However, because one cannot know if a token frequency based on the frequency of a single compound word (like *henchman*) is equivalent to the same token frequency based on the summed frequencies of a number of different compound words (like *blacksmith*, *goldsmith*, *locksmith* etc), a direct comparison of clear and unclear bound morphemes was not carried out. On the other hand, *hench*-like bound morphemes can unquestionably be compared to *zig*-like[1] syllables because the frequencies of both sorts of item are based on the token frequency of a single word (i.e., *henchman* and *zigzag* respectively) and are therefore necessarily matched on type frequency. In addition, free morphemes (like *fire*) can be compared to *smith*-like bound morphemes because it is possible to match them on both character frequency (token frequency) and the number of compound words in which they occur (type frequency).

Two experiments were therefore carried out using native Chinese speakers as participants. Fifteen such participants were given a Character Decision Task and another 15 were given a Word Decision Task. The same experimental characters were used in both tasks, though in the CDT there were also an equivalent number of non-characters used as distracters. The experimental characters included 20 bound morphemes that occur in only one word (*hench* items) matched on token frequency (about 6 per million) with 20 pure syllables that also occur in only one word (*zig* items). The distinction between these two types of item is that the character that accompanies it in the word in which it occurs either has its own meaning (as in *henchman*) or it does not (as in *zigzag*).

The other comparison was between 20 bound morphemes that occur in several semantically related words (*smith* items) and 20 free morphemes (*fire* items) that occur in just as many compound words. Thus the bound and free morphemes were matched on type frequency (a mean of 5 words), and they were also matched on token frequency (about 22 per million). The decision that a character could or could not be a free morpheme was based on whether or not it was found as a single character in Table 1 of the *Modern Chinese frequency dictionary* (1985) where word frequencies are listed.

In the WDT, the expected results were obtained. It was significantly harder to say that *hench* items were non-words than to say the same of *zig* items (with 24.3% "yes" responses vs 10.7%, and a mean reaction time for the correct "no" responses of 882 ms vs 854 ms). In addition, although it proved difficult for readers to classify the putatively free morphemes (*fire* items) as free-standing words (with only 65.4% "yes" responses), this was nevertheless significantly different to the responses to *smith* items (with 40.6% "yes" responses)[2].

It is apparent from the results of the WDT that the lexical processing system represents bound morphemes differently from pure syllables (*hench* items vs *zig* items) and also from free morphemes (*smith* items vs *fire* items). Importantly, analysis of the results of the CDT indicated that this difference in representation is not at the form level. In particular, there was no significant difference in either of the comparisons when status as a character was to be determined: The error rate comparison in the CDT for *hench* and *zig* was 12.0% vs 10.7% with reaction times of 620 ms vs 618 ms; and for *fire* and *smith*, 5.0% vs 4.9% with reaction times of 568 ms vs 575 ms.

The contrast between the results from the two tasks is quite informative. First, it suggests that Fig 3 is wrong because, if a bound morpheme has no lemma, then any difference between bound morphemes and syllables must arise at the form level and, therefore, such a difference should be found in both the CDT and WDT. The fact that it is only found in the WDT, indicates that the difference between these two types of item must arise from a level higher than the form level, namely, the proposed lemma level. So, it is suggested that a bound morpheme does develop a lemma representation, but one that is typically less precise than that for a free morpheme. Thus, even though free and bound morphemes are equally represented at the form level (as shown in the CDT), they can be discriminated at the lemma level, albeit with some difficulty (as shown in the WDT). Such a conclusion is compatible with the model presented in Fig 4.

The question can be raised, however, whether the conclusions drawn here might be specific to Chinese and not generalizable to alphabetically scripted languages. In particular, one of the features of Chinese is that its individual characters can be determined on the basis of physical features alone, i.e., on the basis of their physical separation from each other. For this reason, one does not need any familiarity with Chinese to isolate each form-level unit (i.e., each character) and, therefore, knowing what to store at the form level is simple. In contrast, one needs to understand English to know that *weekend* should be stored as *week* and *end* rather than as *wee* and *kend*. What this means, though, is that even in a script where form units are readily isolated (i.e., Chinese), there is still evidence that higher level units develop with a level of precision related to the correlation between the occurrence of these form units and a particular meaning.

It seems highly likely that the strength of this correlation also affects the ease with which English readers can decide whether a letter-string is a free standing English word or not (as in the standard Lexical Decision Task). Unlike the situation in Chinese, it is hard to come up with examples in English where a unit recurs in several words that are all semantically related. The example of *smith* has been used here, but it would not be ideal as a non-word item in an experiment because there is the potential for confusion with the surname *Smith*. However, one can imagine readers mistakenly classifying *venge* as a free morpheme far more than they would *ceive*, for example, because there is a clear difference in the consistency of the semantic relationship between the words in which they occur: That is, the constant meaning associated with *revenge*, *avenge*, *vengeful*, and *vengeance* is obvious, while that between *receive*, *deceive*, *perceive* and *conceive* is not and, therefore, the lemma abstracted out for the former will be more precise than that for the latter.

Furthermore, it is not hard to imagine that lexical decision responses to bound morphemes would take longer than those to initial syllables in English just as they did in Chinese. Some indication of this can be found by looking at the items used by Taft and Forster (1976) who demonstrated a delay in classifying syllables as nonwords relative to letter-strings that were not part of a word. The few items that might be considered to be bound morphemes (i.e., *hench*, *voy*, *cran*, *yester*, *caval,* and *plat*) showed a larger RT difference relative to their controls than did the purely syllabic items (a 127 ms difference versus a 31 ms difference).

So, it seems that the results obtained in Chinese, at least for the WDT, are likely to be generalizable to alphabetic scripts as well. This therefore suggests that the notion of units that capture the correlation between form and meaning (i.e., lemmas) is a fruitful way in which to conceptualize morphological representation.

6. MORPHOLOGICAL TRANSPARENCY

Although the hybrid model of Fig 4 appears to be a useful framework for understanding morphological processing, there are still several theoretical issues that need to be considered. As it stands, the difference between the representation and processing of a polymorphemic word (e.g., *fireman*) and that of a monomorphemic polysyllabic word (e.g., *picnic*) is whether or not there is concomitant activation of lemmas associated with the sublexical form units. That is, there are lemmas associated with *fire* and *man*, but not with *pic* or *nic*. However, it sometimes happens that the syllables of a monomorphemic word coincide with real words (e.g., the *cart* and *ridge* of *cartridge*) and, in such circumstances, lemmas for those constituents will be activated just as they would be for a polymorphemic word (see also Schreuder et al, *this volume*).

It is important, though, to explain how a difference might arise in processing a complex word whose constituent meanings are transparently related to its whole word meaning (as with *fireman*) relative to one where they are not (as with *cartridge*), because there is evidence that such transparency does have an impact on lexical decision responses (e.g., Marslen-Wilson, Tyler, Waksler, & Older, 1994, in English; Sandra, 1990, Zwitserlood, 1994, in Dutch; Taft, Liu & Zhu, 1999 in Chinese). Within the current conceptualization, the difference lies in the overlap between the semantic features associated with the lemma for the whole word and those associated with the lemmas for its constituents. That is, the semantic features associated with both *cart* and *ridge* will be entirely different to those associated with *cartridge*, while there will be an overlap between the semantic units activated by *fire* and *man* and those activated by *fireman*. The transparency of a word's morphemic structure is indeed defined in terms of this overlap.

Any demonstration of the impact of transparency on lexical processing would therefore need to be explained in terms of the involvement of overlap at the semantic level. For example, if recognition of *man* is facilitated more by the prior presentation of *fireman* than is the recognition of *ridge* by the prior presentation of *cartridge* (Zwitserlood, 1994), this could be explained in terms of the semantic units activated via the lemma for the complex word feeding activation back to the constituent lemmas in the case of *fireman* but not in the case of *cartridge*.

Now, while it is obvious that *fireman* is semantically related to its constituent morphemes, one cannot say that its meaning is entirely predictable from the combination of the meanings of those morphemes. In particular, one needs access to information that a fireman puts out fires rather than sets fires, or that firemen wear a special uniform, and so on. This fact justifies the need for a lemma to exist for the polymorphemic word *fireman*. That is, there needs to be a unit that is associated with the semantic information specific to *fireman* because its meaning cannot be accurately generated from the meanings associated with its individual morphemes. Some of its meaning can be extracted from that of its constituents (e.g., features relevant to the fact that a fireman is a man), but other information is needed as well. If a polymorphemic word were entirely predictable from its constituents, on the other hand, there would be no need for a lemma to exist for that word. Is such a thing possible?

This extreme form of transparency would seem to exist most clearly in the case of inflected words. For example, the meaning of *cats* is entirely predictable from the meaning of its stem *cat* and the plural function of its suffix *s*. This implies that the inflected word *cats* will be recognized via both the form units and the lemma units associated with its constituent morphemes *cat* and *s*[3]. The more interesting cases are irregularly inflected words, like *men*. Would such words require their own lemma? Not necessarily. While there would need to be independent form units for *men* and *man*, the former might simply be associated with the *man* lemma and the "plural" lemma, as depicted in Fig 5 (where the regular plural is also shown).

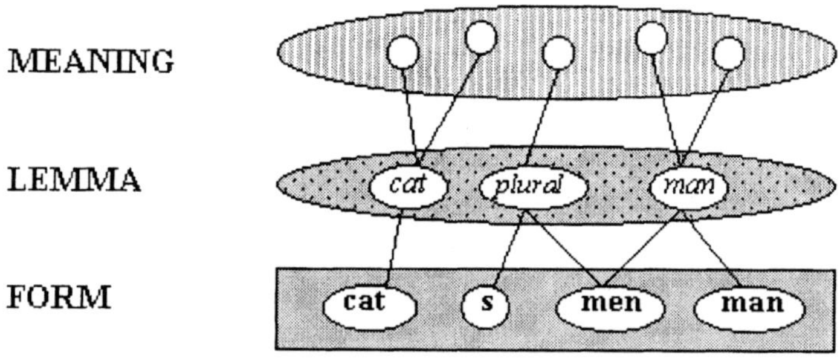

Figure 5. The representation of regularly and irregularly inflected words.

However, it should be noted that if the "plural" lemma can be activated via a form unit that does not represent *s*, the idea of lemmas capturing the correlation between form and meaning is lost. That is, a "plural" lemma should develop explicitly out of the correlation that exists between plurality and the presence of a final *s*, so it should only be activated when a final *s* is present. If it were also activated by units that are entirely unrelated in form (as with *men*), one would have to say that units representing grammatical function, such as plurality, are of quite a different nature to those representing semantic function. In fact, they may not have a representation at the lemma level at all, perhaps being represented by a single unit in a separate syntactic module which is directly activated by the appropriate form-level representations (cf Taft, 1994). Such an idea is compatible with the conceptualization of lemmas as being the means by which a number of different semantic features are brought together and linked to the form level. If there is no set of semantic features to unite, as in the case of a syntactic function like "plural", then there is no need for a lemma.

7. MORPHEME FREQUENCY

The difference between a complex word with transparent constituents, like *fireman*, and one with opaque constituents, like *cartridge*, is described in terms of semantic overlap between lemmas. However, there is a modification to the model that seems to be required and which potentially provides another way of differentiating them. In particular, there is a problem with the idea that a monomorphemic lemma unit can be directly activated by more than one syllable unit, as in the example of *picnic* being activated via *pic* and *nic*. There is at least one logical problem with this, having to do with the influence of morpheme frequency on polymorphemic word recognition.

Experiments have demonstrated that polymorphemic words containing high frequency stems are easier to recognize than those containing low frequency stems (e.g., Andrews, 1986; Burani, Salmaso, & Caramazza, 1984; Taft & Forster, 1976; Taft, Huang, & Zhu, 1994; Zhang & Peng, 1992). In terms of the current framework, recognition of the word *fireman* would not only be influenced by the weighting on the links that connect the form units for *fire* and *man* with the lemma for *fireman* (i.e., based on the frequency of *fireman*), but also by the ease with which the form units can be activated in the first place (i.e., based on the frequency of the individual constituents). The latter gives the morpheme frequency effect.

The problem arises, however, when a constituent of the polymorphemic word has more than one syllable. Take *policeman* for example. Activation of the lemma for this word will emanate directly from the form units for *pol*, *ice,* and *man* (assuming a BOSS analysis). Thus, it is the frequency of *pol* (and *ice* and *man*) that will affect the ease of access to *policeman*, and not the frequency of *police*. The frequency of *pol* does incorporate the frequency of *police*, but also that of *policy*, *polite*, *politics*, *polish*, etc. So, the prediction from the model is that the morpheme frequency effect will only hold for monosyllabic morphemes, and this is highly unlikely to be true.

One way to avoid this situation would be to incorporate a hierarchy of units at the form level, with representations for polysyllabic monomorphemic words in addition to their syllable representations. That is, there would exist a form unit for *police* that is activated through the form units for *pol* and *ice* and, therefore, the lemma for *policeman* would be activated via the units for *police* and *man*. In this way, the frequency of *police* can have an impact on the recognition of *policeman*.

What is being suggested by this modification, then, is that the form units that interface with the lemma units are always morphemic in nature and never purely syllabic. It also means that the form units for *cart* and *ridge* would together activate the form unit for *cartridge*, but also each independently activate their own lemmas. This is different to the situation with transparent complex words, like *fireman*, which would not have their own whole-word form unit.

By incorporating whole word form units, however, the issue of redundancy arises. There is actually no apparent processing advantage for the system to include such units given that the lemma for the polysyllabic word can be effectively activated without it (i.e., directly from the syllable units). While it might be argued that redundancy is not necessarily a bad thing (e.g., Sandra, 1994), there is an alternative modification that avoids it. In particular, one can suggest that it is the lemma units that are hierarchically structured, and this is illustrated in Fig 6.

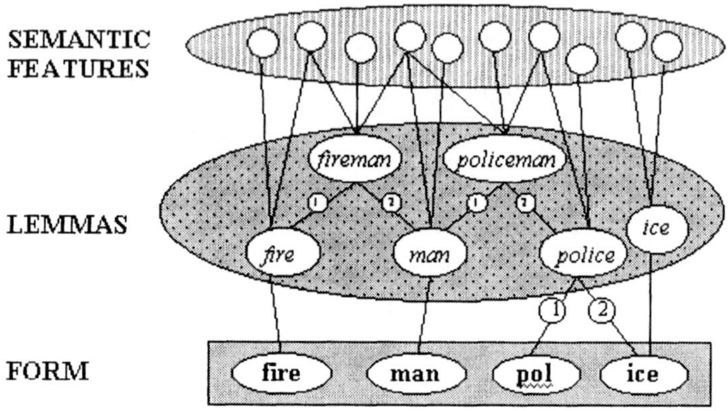

Figure 6. The representation of polymorphemic and polysyllabic words when lemmas are hierarchically represented.

It can be seen from the figure that the lemma for a polymorphemic word is activated via the lemmas for its constituent morphemes. In this way, when a polymorphemic word is presented, the lemma for a constituent morpheme is not activated merely in parallel with the lemma for the whole word, but as a crucial step in activating the lemma for the whole word. On the other hand, activation of the lemma for a polysyllabic word (e.g., *police* or *cartridge*) does not involve any lemma that might be activated by its constituent syllables (e.g., the *ice* of *police*, or the *cart* and *ridge* of *cartridge*).

While one might expect the frequency of use of a form unit to have some impact on recognition times, the morpheme frequency effect will primarily arise in this hierarchical model from the lemma level. That is, recognition of *fireman* will be influenced by the ease with which the lemma units for *fire* and *man* are activated (as determined by their frequency), and recognition of *policeman* will be influenced by the activation of the lemma units for *police* and *man*.

Previously it was suggested that lemma processing is influenced by the precision of the form-meaning correlation. How is this compatible with the idea that lemma activation is also influenced by frequency? There are various possibilities. One is that both contribute additively to the "strength" of the lemma and, therefore, only frequency effects will emerge if lemma precision is matched (as might be the case, on average, for two randomly chosen free morphemes). A second possibility is that frequency and precision are confounded for free-standing words in that the more commonly a word occurs, the greater the variety of contexts in which it is likely to appear. This, in turn, would provide more information about which semantic features are consistently associated with the word form and which vary with context.

Another alternative is to suggest that the precision of a lemma has its effects in terms of its activation threshold, whereas frequency has its effects in terms of weightings on the links between units. For example, regardless of how precise the meaning of *fire* or *man* is, activation of their lemmas will be influenced by the weighting on the connections from their form representations to their respective lemmas. Furthermore, the frequency of *fireman* will also affect recognition responses, regardless of the precision of its lemma, as a result of the weightings on the connections to it from the *fire* and *man* lemmas. That is, the connection between *fire* and *fireman* will be stronger than that between *fire* and *firewall* because the former is more frequently used.

Note that by postulating a hierarchy of lemmas, there is the opportunity to explain the results of experiments that fail to observe morpheme frequency effects under certain conditions (e.g., Bertram, Schreuder, & Baayen, 2000). In particular, there is the possibility to introduce a second route to the lemma for a polymorphemic word, namely, one that goes directly from the form level units to that lemma (as in Fig 4). In other words, a combination of Fig 4 and Fig 6 can be suggested whereby there are two pathways to the recognition of a polymorphemic word: Via the lemmas for the constituent morphemes (giving morpheme frequency effects) and directly from the relevant form units (giving form frequency effects). Form frequency may or may not be the same as morpheme frequency depending on what other units are activated by the same form, but they will not be as marked as the effects obtained via the hierarchical route, which arise from activation at both the form and lemma levels. Whether or not strong morpheme frequency effects are observed will therefore depend on which pathway succeeds in activating the whole word lemma first, and this could depend on a number of different factors (see e.g., Bertram et al, 2000).

What is being suggested here, then, is that results that appear to reflect whole-word processing rather than morphological decomposition do not necessarily require the postulation of a whole-word form representation in addition to the morphemic representations (e.g., Bertram et al, 2000; Schreuder et al, *this volume*). Instead, it might be possible to explain such results within the suggested framework whereby form units are always smaller than the whole word when that word is polymorphemic, or even just polysyllabic. Whole word information is found at the lemma level and it is here that "whole-word" effects are potentially explained. If there is a "race" between whole-word processing and morphological decomposition, the suggestion being made is that it takes place within the lemma system rather than between different sized form units.

8. THE INVOLVEMENT OF PHONOLOGY

The correlation between form and meaning has been talked about here in terms of orthographic form. The reason for this was because the focus has been upon visual word recognition. However, speech is the fundamental form of language and, therefore, the correlation between spoken form and meaning may well be more important in setting up the lexical processing system than the correlation between visual form and meaning. It is possible that lemmas are developed solely on the basis of exposure to the spoken word and that orthographic forms are merely appended to these. However, it is also likely that the introduction of orthography actually modifies the system in some way.

This is particularly clear in the case of Chinese where there is an enormous amount of homophony at the syllable level. In other words, a spoken syllable might be associated with a wide range of meanings because a number of different morphemes are pronounced in the same way. However, much of this ambiguity is resolved by the introduction of orthographic information, because the different homophonic morphemes are represented by different characters. So, the involvement of orthographic information serves to greatly increase the correlation between form and meaning in Chinese.

In an alphabetic script it is possible for orthographic information to similarly increase the correlation between form and meaning. The internal form analysis of a visually presented word is not forced upon the language user by the stimulus itself, unlike the spoken word, which physically defines its syllabic structure. For this reason, a morpheme may be disguised by the syllable structure or phonetic realization of a spoken word, but orthographically available in the visually presented version of the word. For example, the morpheme *act* does not form a unit in the spoken version of *actor*, *active*, or *action,* where the first unit is the syllable /æk/. Obviously, any correlation between form and meaning will be lower if it were based on /æk/ rather than /ækt/, since the former will include unrelated words like *accurate*, *acne*, *accent*, *accident*, and *axis*. The orthographic version of the word, on the other hand, invites the optimal correlation between form and meaning because it allows the consistent presence of the letter cluster *act* to be detected in the semantically related words.

So, the suggestion is that phonological and orthographic information both participate in the correlation with meaning, leading to a single lemma that represents the linkage between all three types of information. This means that the pathway from orthography to phonology, and vice versa, is mediated by a lemma unit, though it may also be that there are additional direct linkages between the two modalities.

9. CONCLUSIONS

The aim of this chapter has been to consider the implications of an attempt to incorporate polysyllabic and polymorphemic words into a lexical processing system that captures the correlations between form and function. It is suggested that morphemic information is primarily captured in lexical memory in the guise of units (i.e., lemmas) that mediate between form and meaning, with lemma distinctiveness depending on the magnitude of this correlation. The range of lemma distinctiveness goes from free-standing morphemes (e.g., *fire*) and polymorphemic words (e.g., *fireman*) that have a constant meaning within a huge number of contexts, through to bound morphemes that can only be found within a single context (e.g., *hench*). In between are cases that occur in many contexts (e.g., *smith*), but not enough to be clearly considered a free morpheme. Such a view was supported by experimental data obtained with Chinese, which were claimed to be generalizable across all languages.

Clearly, there are a number of issues that need to be explored further, like the syllabic nature of the form units, the mechanisms underlying morphemic frequency effects, and the relationship between orthography and phonology. However, what is provided here is another stage in the evolution of a framework that might prove optimal in understanding morphological representation and processing.

10. NOTES

1 Terminologically speaking, analogy to *zig* is preferred over analogy to *pic*, even though the former has a dubious status as a pure syllable in English. This is because the criterion for inclusion in this condition is the fact that the item exists in only one word (true of *zig*, but not of *pic*), as does its accompanying constituent (true of *zag*, but not of *nic*).

2 Reaction times were not measured because the correct response was different for the free morphemes ("yes") and bound morphemes ("no").

3 In fact, there would exist two lemmas activated by the presence of a final *s*: One for the plural inflection and one for the verbal inflection (as in *sees*), but the former will be determined to be the relevant one on the basis of the fact that the stem is a noun rather than a verb.

11. REFERENCES

Andrews, S. (1986). Morphological influences on lexical access: Lexical or non-lexical effects? *Journal of Memory and Language, 25*, 726-740.

Baayen, R. H., Dijkstra, T., & Schreuder, R. (1997). Singulars and plurals in Dutch: Evidence for a parallel dual route model. *Journal of Memory and Language, 37*, 94-117.

Bertram, R., Schreuder, R, & Baayen, R. H. (2000). The balance of storage and computation in morphological processing: The role of word formation type, affixal homophony, and productivity. *Journal of Experimental Psychology: Learning, Memory, & Cognition, 26*, 489-511.

Bleasdale, F. A. (1987). Concreteness-dependent associative priming: Separate lexical organization for concrete and abstract words. *Journal of Experimental Psychology: Learning, Memory, and Cognition, 13*, 582-594.

Burani, C., Salmaso, D., & Caramazza, A. (1984). Morphological structure and lexical access. *Visible Language, 18*, 342-352.

Coltheart, M., Curtis, B., Atkins, P., & Haller, M. (1993). Models of reading aloud: Dual-route and parallel-distributed-processing approaches. *Psychological Review, 100*, 589-608.

Emmorey, K. (1989). Auditory morphological priming in the lexicon. *Language and Cognitive Processes, 4*, 73-92.

Grainger, J., & Jacobs, A. M. (1996). Orthographic processing in visual word recognition: A multiple read-out model. *Psychological Review, 103*, 518-565.

Libben, G. (1994). How is morphological decomposition achieved? *Language and Cognitive Processes, 9*, 369-391.

Lima, S. D., & Pollatsek, A. (1983). Lexical access via an orthographic code? The Basic Orthographic Syllabic (BOSS) reconsidered. *Journal of Verbal Learning and Verbal Behavior, 22*, 310-332.

Marslen-Wilson, W., Tyler, L.K., Waksler, R., & Older, L. (1994). Morphology and meaning in the English mental lexicon. *Psychological Review, 101*, 3-33.

Modern Chinese frequency dictionary [Xianda huayu pinlu zidian] (1985). Beijing, China: Beijing Language Institute Press.

Norris, D. (1994). A quantitative multiple-levels model of reading aloud. *Journal of Experimental Psychology: Human Perception and Performance, 20*, 1212-1232.

Page, M. (1999). Connectionist modelling in psychology: A localist manifesto. *Behavioral and Brain Sciences, 23*.

Plaut, D. C., McClelland, J. L., Seidenberg, M. S., & Patterson, K. (1996). Understanding normal and impaired word reading: Computational principles in quasi-regular domains. *Psychological Review, 103*, 56-115.

Sandra, D. (1990). On the representation and processing of compound words: Automatic access to constituent morphemes does not occur. *Quarterly Journal of Experimental Psychology, 42A*, 529-567.

Sandra, D. (1994). The morphology of the mental lexicon: Word structure viewed from a psycholinguistic perspective. *Language and Cognitive Processes, 9*, 227-269.

Schreuder, R., & Baayen, R. H. (1995). Modelling morphological processing. In L. B. Feldman (Ed.), *Morphological aspects of language processing* (pp. 131-154). Hillsdale, NJ: Lawrence Erlbaum Associates.

Schreuder, R., Burani, C., & Baayen, R. H. (*this volume*) Parsing and semantic opacity.

Schwanenflugel, P. J., & Shoben, E. J. (1983). Differential context effects in the comprehension of abstract and concrete verbal materials. *Journal of Experimental Psychology: Learning, Memory and Cognition, 9*, 82-102.

Seidenberg, M. S., & McClelland, J. L. (1989). A distributed, developmental model of word recognition and naming. *Psychological Review, 96*, 523-568.

Taft, M. (1979). Lexical access via an orthographic code: The Basic Orthographic Syllabic Structure (BOSS). *Journal of Verbal Learning and Verbal Behavior, 18*, 21-39.

Taft, M. (1987). Morphographic processing. The BOSS re-emerges. In M. Coltheart (Ed.), *Attention and performance, XII*. London: Lawrence Erlbaum Associates Limited.

Taft, M. (1991). *Reading and the mental lexicon*. Hove, UK: Erlbaum.

Taft, M. (1994). Interactive-activation as a framework for understanding morphological processing. *Language and Cognitive Processes, 9*, 271-294.

Taft, M., & Forster, K. I. (1975). Lexical storage and retrieval of prefixed words. *Journal of Verbal Learning and Verbal Behavior, 14*, 638-647.

Taft, M., & Forster, K. I. (1976). Lexical storage and retrieval of polymorphemic and polysyllabic words. *Journal of Verbal Learning and Verbal Behavior, 15*, 607-620.

Taft, M., Huang, J., & Zhu, X. (1994). The influence of character frequency on word recognition responses in Chinese. In H. W. Chang, J.-T. Huang, C.-W. Hue, & O. Tzeng (Eds.), *Advances in the study of Chinese language processing* (Vol. 1, pp. 59-73). Taipei: National Taiwan University.

Taft, M., Liu, Y., & Zhu, X. (1999). Morphemic processing in reading Chinese. In A. Inhoff, J. Wang, & H.-C. Chen (Eds.), *Reading Chinese Script: A cognitive analysis* . New Jersey: Lawrence Erlbaum Associates.

Taft, M., & Zhu, X. (1997). Using masked priming to examine lexical storage of Chinese compound words. In H.-C. Chen (Ed.), *The cognitive processing of Chinese and related Asian languages* (pp. 233-241): Chinese University Press.

Zhang, B. Y., & Peng, D. L. (1992). Decomposed storage in the Chinese lexicon. In H.-C. Chen & O. J. L. Tzeng (Eds.), *Language processing in Chinese* (pp. 131-149). Amsterdam: North-Holland.

Zwitserlood, P. (1994). The role of semantic transparency in the processing and representation of Dutch compounds. *Language and Cognitive Processes, 9*, 341-368.

12. ACKNOWLEDGEMENT

The research reported in this paper was supported by a grant awarded to the author by the Australian Research Council. The technical assistance of Zhu Xiaoping is gratefully acknowledged.

13. ADDRESS FOR CORRESPONDENCE

Marcus Taft
School of Psychology
University of New South Wales
Sydney New South Wales 2052
Australia
Email: M.Taft@unsw.edu.au

HÉLÈNE GIRAUDO AND JONATHAN GRAINGER

A SUPRALEXICAL MODEL FOR FRENCH DERIVATIONAL MORPHOLOGY

1. INTRODUCTION

Today there is a growing consensus among psycholinguists that morphological information plays a critical role in the highly automatized process of word recognition. At a linguistic level of analysis, morphology describes the word formation rules of a given language. A morphologically complex word, such as *banker*, represents the combination of at least two morphemes: the root *bank* and the suffix *–er* in the given example. As a consequence, from each root morpheme (e.g., *bank*) one can derive numerous morphologically complex words by adding another morpheme to the root (i.e., *-er*, *-ing*, *-s*, *-rupt*... to form the words *banker, banking, banks, bankrupt...etc.*). Thus, from a linguistic point of view, the accent is often placed on productivity when discussing the role of morphological information. Morphemic components (roots and affixes) can be used to create new word forms in production and to understand novel forms in comprehension. For example, someone who had never heard or read the word *dimness* before, but has knowledge of the root *dim* and the suffix *-ness*, could derive the meaning of the novel whole-word from the meaning and function of the component morphemes.

The fact that morphology is the basis of language productivity at the word level, has lead the vast majority of researchers interested in word recognition (cognitive psychologists and psycholinguists alike) to propose what we will refer to as the sublexical account of morphological representation. Within a general processing framework for word recognition that moves from sensory codes to semantic representations, morphological codes are hypothesized to intervene before whole-word form representations. Two variants of this hypothesis, a single-route and a dual-route version, are presented in Figure 1.

In both variants of the sublexical account of morphological representation, depicted in Figure 1, morphemes are directly activated from sublexical representations of the stimulus (e.g., letters or phonemes), and are therefore form-based representations (i.e., they code the presence of a given string of letters or a given string of phonemes in the stimulus). In this approach, it is phonologically and orthographically specified stems and not abstract roots that are the morphological units of representation, along with affixes. The various authors of these sublexical accounts often speak of a morphological parsing mechanism that automatically extracts morphemes from the stimulus without reference to whole-word representations. In the single route account (e.g., Taft, 1994), a given word stimulus is first parsed into its morphological components before the word can be recognized as a whole. In the dual-route account (e.g., Caramazza, Laudana, & Romani, 1988; Schreuder & Baayen, 1995), there is both a direct whole-word route from sensory representations to meaning, and a morphological parsing route that extracts morphemes from the incoming signal before assigning meaning to these components.

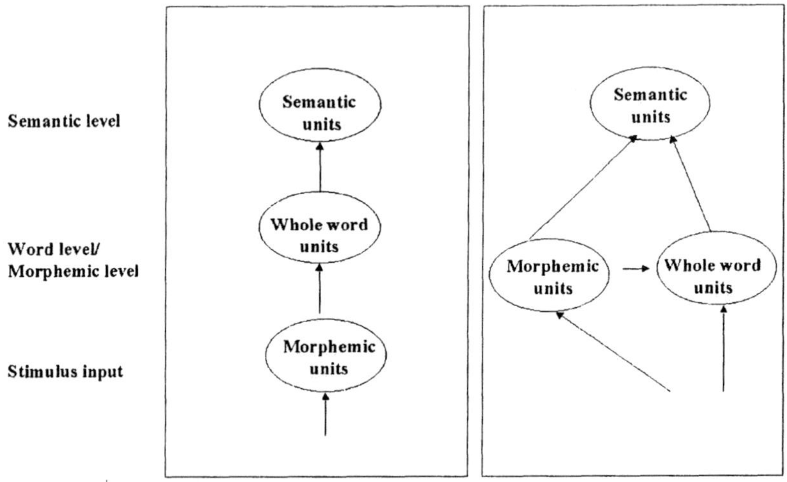

Figure 1. Two variants of the sublexical account of morphological representation. The left-hand panel represents a single route version, the right-hand panel a dual route version.

The great majority of current research on morphological processing provides an interpretation of observed empirical data within a variant of this sublexical framework. However, in this chapter we present what we believe to be a viable alternative for the representation of derivational morphology in French, and we examine some recent data in favor of this alternative hypothesis. The alternative account, referred to as the supralexical account of morphological representation, stipulates that in normal, fast, automatic word recognition, morphemic representations present in derived complex forms are only contacted after some initial processing of whole-word form representations.

Common to both the sublexical and supralexical accounts of morphological representation is the assumption that morphology is explicitly represented in long-term memory, over and above the representation of form and meaning. So first let us summarize what we believe to be the critical empirical data in favor of the representation and use of morphological information during word recognition.

2. EVIDENCE FOR THE ROLE OF MORPHOLOGY IN PRINTED WORD PERCEPTION

Over the last two decades, numerous studies have been performed in order to examine morphological influences on word recognition using various experimental techniques tested in different languages. These studies can be classified according to the type of manipulation: priming studies (including long-lag priming, and the more recent masked priming research); morpheme frequency effects (including manipulations of cumulative root frequency, and the more recent variable referred to as morphological family size, Schreuder & Baayen, 1997); and pseudo-morpheme manipulations (most predominantly pseudo-prefixation).

Some of the most critical evidence, in our opinion, has been obtained using the masked priming paradigm which has gradually been adopted in recent years as an important tool for uncovering the fast and highly automatized processes that underlie printed word perception. Masked priming combined with the lexical decision task (Forster & Davis, 1984) has helped define the relative role played by orthographic, phonologic, morphologic, and semantic information in this process. Using prime exposures of around 60 ms, it has been shown that, while morphologically related primes facilitate processing relative to unrelated word primes (e.g., Deutsch, Frost & Forster, 1998; Drews & Zwitserlood, 1995; Forster, Davis, Shocknecht, & Carter, 1987; Frost, Forster & Deutsch, 1997; Grainger, Colé & Segui, 1991), orthographically related primes tend to inhibit target word processing, generating longer response times (RTs) and/or more errors compared to an unrelated prime condition (Drews & Zwitserlood, 1995; Grainger & Ferrand, 1994; Segui & Grainger, 1990). Some recent work has also demonstrated that masked morphological priming is not just a combination of effects of form and meaning. For example, Rastle, Davis, Marslen-Wilson, and Tyler (2000) tested priming with "portmanteau" words (e.g., smog - smoke) and phonaesthemes (e.g., glitter – glisten) where there is both form and meaning overlap in the absence of morphological overlap. At 72 ms prime exposures, these stimuli produced no significant priming effect, while morphological priming was highly robust. Furthermore, in a study of morphological priming in Hebrew (Frost, Deutsch, Gilboa, Tannenbaum, & Marslen-Wilson, 2000), facilitatory priming was obtained with morphologically related but semantically unrelated words. Finally, research carried out by the present authors using the masked priming technique has systematically failed to find any evidence for semantic priming in conditions (60 ms prime exposures with the lexical decision task) where robust morphological priming is obtained. Recent research therefore suggests that a purely semantic account of morphological priming is not a viable option.

Thus, there is currently an impressive amount of evidence from masked priming studies in favor of the explicit representation of morphological information in memory. However, there is still little agreement as to precisely how such information is stored in long-term memory. In this chapter, we discuss two main alternatives (the sublexical and supralexical hypotheses) that differ in terms of where, in the processing hierarchy from form to meaning, morphological codes are situated.

The results of all of the above-cited studies using the masked prime paradigm are easily accommodated by the sublexical account of morphological representation. When primes share the same morphological stem as targets, target recognition is facilitated by preactivation of the stem representation during prime processing. However, the supralexical account of morphological representation, to be described in more detail below, can also account for morphological priming effects via the preactivation of morphemic representations. We first present the supralexical hypothesis, before describing some critical tests of these alternative accounts of morphological representation.

3. THE SUPRALEXICAL HYPOTHESIS

The supralexical hypothesis is once again expressed within the framework of a hierarchical activation model of language comprehension that includes whole-word form representations and morphemic representations that intervene between lower-level form analyses and higher-level semantic representations (Figure 2).

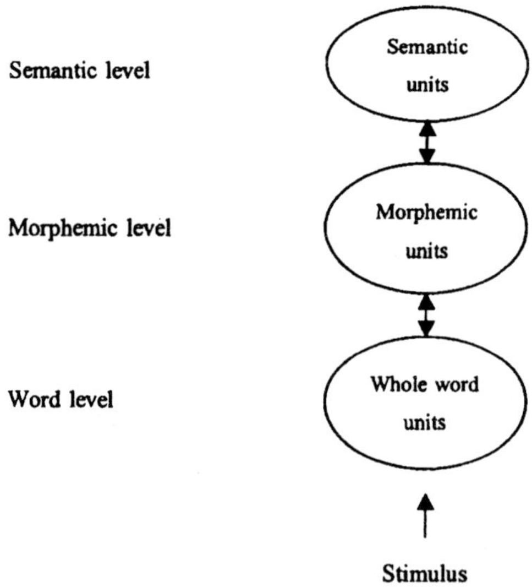

Figure 2. The supralexical model of morphological processing. In this architecture, morphemic representations are situated at the interface between form analyses and semantic representations.

According to the supralexical account, morphemic representations receive activation from whole-word form representations and act as a partial interface between form-representations and semantics. Within this framework, morphemic representations are form- and modality-independent. Accordingly, we refer to root rather than stem representations, to reflect their abstract nature. All whole-word forms that share a given root are connected to that root representation, and activated root representations send activation back to all compatible whole-word forms. On presentation of a complex word such as *remake*, units corresponding to the root *make* and the affix *re* will receive activation from the whole-word representation, and send back activation to all whole-word representations that are compatible with either the root or the affix. In this way, root representations impose an organization on the lower-level form representations in terms of so-called morphological families (Butterworth, 1983; Lukatela, Gligorijevic, Kostic, & Turvey, 1980; Manelis & Tharp, 1977).

Both the sublexical and the supralexical accounts of morphological representation propose morphemic representations as the locus of masked morphological priming effects. Thus, all words that share a given morpheme are hypothesized to be linked to a common representation that corresponds to that morpheme. Prime stimuli that contain the same morpheme as target stimuli (i.e., morphologically related primes) generate facilitatory priming via pre-activation of the shared morphemic representation. Prime presentation leads to growth of activation in a given morphemic representation thus conferring an advantage in the processing of target stimuli that contain the same morpheme. Here we assume that the size of morphological priming effects are proportional to the activation level of the critical morpheme after prime word presentation.

4. PRIMING WITH SIMPLE AND COMPLEX WORDS

Although, both the sublexical and the supralexical accounts of morphological representation propose morphemic representations as the locus of masked morphological priming effects, they differ in terms of where the morphemic codes are located relative to whole-word representations. The precise location of these units has a direct implication on how morphologically complex words are accessed relative to simple words. If a complex word is first parsed into its constituent morphemes (the sublexical hypothesis), then in the masked prime paradigm with brief prime exposures, root primes should be more effective than derived word primes, since the former do not require parsing. Here the basic assumption is that there is some extra computation involved in isolating a root in a derived word compared to recognizing a root presented on its own. This extra computation should slow down the processing of derived word primes leading to less priming. The predictions of this particular version of the sublexical hypothesis are summarized at the top of Table 1.

Alternatively, the sublexical view could stipulate that morphemic representations are activated as soon as an appropriate string of letters is detected in the stimulus, regardless of the status of the remaining letters (i.e., morpheme or not). This is an example of obligatory morphological decomposition where, at least in initial stages of processing, the system is blind to the compatibility of morphological constituents. In this way, there is no extra computation involved in processing a derived word prime, since no attempt will be made to check if the remaining letters form an appropriate affix. If this is how the morphological parser operates, then the sublexical hypothesis is led to predict that pseudoroot primes (word primes containing a string of letters corresponding to a root without having the status of a root in that particular word) should be just as effective as true derived word primes. This leads to the experimental predictions given in Table 1 for the second variant of the sublexical hypothesis.

According to the supralexical hypothesis, on the other hand, derived word primes should be just as effective as root primes. Both types of prime will lead to similar levels of pre-activation of supralexical morphological units. The bi-directional excitatory links between a supralexical representation of the root and all words containing that root will facilitate the recognition of a target word sharing the same root as the prime. Furthermore, the supralexical hypothesis predicts a significant advantage for derived word primes compared to pseudoroot primes. Since morphemic representations only receive activation via whole-word form representations, only truly complex word stimuli can generate significant activation in the appropriate morphemic units. These predictions are summarized at the bottom of Table 1.

Table 1. Logic of the predictions for the experiments reported in Giraud & Grainger (2001), generated from the sublexical and supralexical accounts of morphological representation.

Model variant	Experimental predictions
Sublexical hypothesis:	
- 1. Parser checks that remaining letters form an affix	root > derived morpheme > pseudo-morpheme
- 2. Parser does not check that remaining letters form an affix	root = derived morpheme = pseudo-morpheme
Supralexical hypothesis:	root = derived morpheme > pseudo-morpheme

These predictions were tested in two series of masked priming experiments. In the first series, we examined morphological priming effects on lexical decision latencies to simple and complex word targets using primes that were either free roots or suffixed words (Giraudo & Grainger, 2001). One critical result obtained in these experiments is presented in the left-hand panel of Figure 3. Here we see that responses to suffixed word targets were facilitated (relative to form-related control primes) by both free root primes and suffixed word primes sharing the same root as the target. The free root and suffixed word prime conditions did not differ significantly. It should be noted that the unrelated prime condition (not shown in the figure) was not significantly different from the orthographic control prime condition (mean RT = 798 ms compared to 795 ms for the orthographic condition). Finally, in another experiment in this series, responses to free root targets were significantly faster when preceded by related suffixed word primes (608 ms) than unrelated primes (635 ms).

Our observation of statistically equivalent priming for free root and derived word primes falsifies the first version of the sublexical morphological parser described above. According to this version, root primes should have been more effective than derived word primes, since the derived word primes require additional computation to check for the affix status of the remaining letters, once the root has been identified. This therefore suggests that, if there is some form of sublexical morphological parsing mechanism, then it operates just as efficiently on complex and simplex stimuli. As noted above, this would be the case if the parsing mechanism were blind to surrounding context. In other words, strings of letters that correspond to roots would be extracted from the stimulus independently of the remaining letters in the string. In such a system, a sublexical root representation will be activated whenever a sequence of letters corresponding to the orthographic description of that root is activated. This alternative version of the sublexical hypothesis was tested in a further experiment comparing masked priming from true derived word primes and pseudo-root primes.

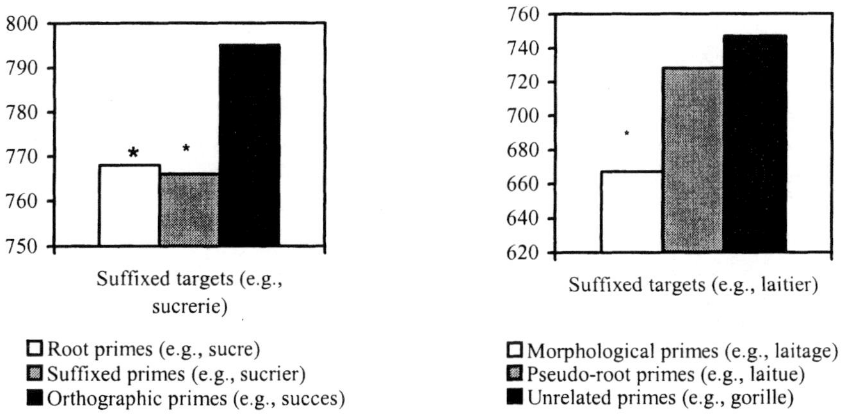

*Figure 3.Principal results of Giraudo & Grainger (2001). Lexical decision latencies to derived word targets (*indicates a significant priming effect relative to the unrelated condition, $p<.05$ by subject and item).*

The results of the second experiment are presented in the right-hand panel of Figure 3. It can be seen that only true derived word primes (e.g., *laitage-laitier*), were found to produce facilitation, while morphologically simple primes containing a pseudo-root (e.g., *laitue-laitier*) did not influence performance relative to the unrelated prime condition. These results falsify the second version of the sublexical hypothesis presented in Table 1. According to this version, a subset of letters corresponding to a potential root should activate the corresponding morphemic representation irrespective of the status of the other letters in the string. This should have produced significant morphological priming from primes containing such sequences, as in the pseudo-root primes tested in the above experiment.

5. EFFECTS OF PRIME WORD FREQUENCY AND CUMULATIVE ROOT FREQUENCY IN MASKED MORPHOLOGICAL PRIMING

Another prediction on which the two proposed architectures for morphological representation differ, concerns the effects of prime word frequency and cumulative root frequency in masked priming. In a supralexical architecture, morphological facilitation is hypothesized to arise via shared morpheme units located above the level of whole-word form representations. When primes and targets share the same root, the activation of the root representation by the prime stimulus facilitates processing of the target word via excitatory connections between morphemic representations and appropriate whole-word representations.

Thus, according to the supralexical account of morphological representation, a morphologically related prime generates two conflicting effects: within-level inhibition acting across simultaneously activated word forms, and top-down facilitation from shared morphemic representations. Both of these mechanisms are fundamental to the family of interactive-activation models of word recognition (McClelland & Elman, 1986; McClelland & Rumelhart, 1981). On presentation of a given stimulus, all whole-word representations that share lower-level form representations (e.g., letters) with the stimulus, receive bottom-up activation. These whole-word representations that receive support from the stimulus then enter a competitive process that allows only a single representation to dominate processing, via inhibitory connections across all units at that level. In the masked priming paradigm, form-related primes (e.g., *blue-blur*) can generate inhibition compared to unrelated primes (Segui & Grainger, 1990) by increasing the competitivity of the target word's natural competitors (i.e., those that receive the most bottom-up support from the stimulus, apart from the target itself).

Now, since form overlap across morphologically related items is generally much lower than in situations where form-related inhibitory priming is observed (Segui & Grainger, 1990), this allows the facilitatory morphological component to dominate in masked morphological priming (Grainger et al., 1991). Keeping target frequency as high as possible will further help morphological facilitation to dominate over form-level inhibition. The higher the surface frequency of the target word, the greater its resistance to within-level inhibition. This first prediction was tested in a series of masked prime experiments where the printed frequency of morphologically complex prime words (their surface frequency) was varied while maintaining both target frequency and cumulative root frequency (the summed frequency of all derived words sharing the same root) constant (Giraudo & Grainger, 2000).

According to the supralexical model of morphological representation, more frequent morphologically related primes should enhance effects of morphological priming. In this model, morpheme unit activation is a function of the activation of all whole-word representations that share that morpheme. During prime word processing under the brief temporal conditions of masked priming, the only significantly activated word unit is the prime word itself, whose activation level is a function of its surface frequency (McClelland & Rumelhart, 1981). Thus, the activation level of supralexical morphemic representations will be a function of the surface frequency of the prime word. Grainger et al. (1991) found that prime word frequency (medium or low) did not interact with effects of morphological priming. However, target word frequency varied with prime frequency in this experiment (medium frequency targets were primed with low frequency words, while low frequency targets were primed by medium frequency words).

The results of a series of masked prime experiments (Giraudo & Grainger, 2000) are presented in Figure 4. The results show that, as predicted by the supralexical hypothesis, prime-word surface frequency influences the size of masked morphological priming effects obtained with free root targets in the lexical decision task. On the other hand, the orthographic prime condition did not differ significantly from the unrelated prime condition in either the RT or the error analyses, and prime word frequency did not modulate this absence of priming effects.

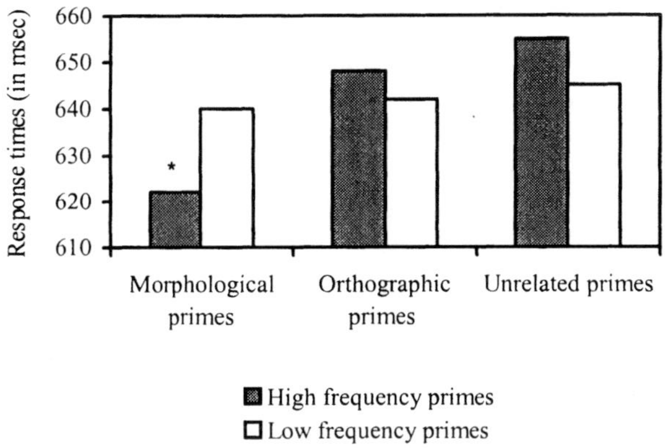

*Figure 4. Principal results of Giraudo & Grainger (2000). Lexical decision latencies to free root targets (*indicates a significant priming effect relative to the unrelated condition, p<.05 by subject and item).*

The results of another experiment in this series showed no influence of the cumulative root frequency of complex prime words on the size of masked morphological priming. Free root targets were primed equally well by suffixed word primes with either a high or a low cumulative root frequency. The predictions of the sublexical and supralexical architectures relative to effects of cumulative root frequency, will be examined within an activation framework where connections strengths are a function of the frequency with which the two connected units have indeed been co-activated in the past. Within such a system, the connection strengths between letter representations and morpheme representations in a sublexical architecture will be a function of cumulative root frequency (indexing the number of times that a given root appears independently of surface forms). On the other hand, in a supralexical architecture, the connections strengths between whole-word representations and morphemic representations will be a function of surface frequency (indexing the number of times a given whole-word form has been processed). In the experiment run by Giraudo and Grainger (2000), priming effects compared to unrelated primes were 38ms for low cumulative frequency primes and 46ms for high cumulative frequency primes. Needless to say, there was no interaction between cumulative frequency and priming effects.

Taken together, the results of this study fit with the predictions of a supralexical architecture where morphemic units are situated above whole-word representations such that morphemic representations only receive activation from low-level stimulus analysis via whole-word representations. As a consequence, the surface frequency of morphological primes affects the size of morphological priming and the effects of morphology necessarily depend on processing of a whole-word form that gives rise to effects of surface frequency.

Looked at from another angle, the results of this study are difficult to reconcile with a dual-route version of the sublexical hypothesis (e.g., Caramazza, et al., 1988; Schreuder & Baayen, 1995). According to this variant of the sublexical approach, the morphological parsing route mainly influences the processing of low frequency words, since high frequency words will be rapidly processed by the direct (non-decompositional) route. This therefore predicts that morphological priming effects should be eliminated with high frequency targets. Since all the targets in the Giraudo and Grainger (2000) study were high frequency free roots, the presence of robust morphological priming falsifies the dual-route variant of the sublexical hypothesis.

6. THE REPRESENTATIONAL STATUS OF DERIVATIONAL AFFIXES

One key result most often cited against the supralexical account of morphological representation, is the pseudo-prefixation effect. Indeed, the vast majority of studies investigating the role of affixes in the recognition of morphologically complex words have used what is commonly referred to as a pseudo-affixation manipulation. Within this set of studies, practically all have focused on the processing of prefixes (see Henderson, Wallis & Knight, 1984, for an exception). Pseudo-prefixed words are morphologically simple words that contain an initial letter sequence that corresponds to a prefix but does not function as a prefix in that word (e.g., the *pre-* in *precipice* does not function as a prefix and the remaining letters in the word, *-cipice*, do not form a legal stem). Several studies have examined lexical decision performance to pseudo-prefixed words and non-words. The pseudo-prefixation manipulation with non-word targets distinguishes morphologically non-decomposable non-words (e.g., *depertoire*) from morphologically decomposable non-words (i.e., non-words such as *dejuvenate* that are formed by the illegal combination of a stem and an affix). It has been shown that the latter category of non-words were more difficult to reject than the former, yielding longer RTs and more errors (Caramazza et al., 1988; Laudanna, Cermele & Caramazza, 1997; Taft & Forster, 1975). Concerning performance to word targets, it has been shown that pseudo-prefixed words like *precipice* are processed more slowly and produce more errors than both prefixed words and non-prefixed words (Pillon, 1998; Taft, 1981). This pseudo-prefixation effect was interpreted as direct evidence in favor of the sublexical hypothesis of morphological representation. According to one specific view of morphological processing within the sublexical framework, the recognition of any morphologically complex word induces an obligatory affix stripping procedure by which the complex word is stripped of its affix, and the stem is used as the entry for lexical access (Taft, 1981). Because pseudo-affixed words contain a letter string that resembles an affix, the model predicts that the pre-lexical parsing procedure will fail and this procedural deadlock will delay lexical access.

However, several researchers have leveled the argument of computational inefficiency against a prefix-stripping procedure. Schreuder and Baayen (1994), for example, argued that pseudo-affixation is so common in languages like Dutch and English that applying a compulsory pre-lexical parsing procedure would lead to a substantial decrease in processing efficiency (see Colé, Beauvillain, Pavard & Segui, 1986, for the same argument relative to French). Empirical evidence against a mandatory prefix-stripping procedure was provided by Laudanna, Burani and Cermele (1994). These authors demonstrated that lexical decision latencies to prefixed non-words varied according to the distributional properties of affixes in the language (the ratio between truly prefixed and pseudo-prefixed words beginning with the same orthographic sequence). The more likely a given letter string would occur as a prefix compared to a pseudo-prefix, the harder it was to reject non-words containing such strings at their beginnings.

One unavoidable problem with all pseudo-prefixation studies is that they involve between-item comparisons that unfortunately leave the door open for possible confounding variables. In a study to be summarized here, we used a priming paradigm to study affix processing, thus allowing within-item comparisons. The effects of affixed prime words that share an affix with a complex target word were compared to a pseudo-affix prime condition (the pseudo-affix condition provides a form priming baseline against which true affix priming can be measured) using the masked prime paradigm (Giraudo & Grainger, 2002). In these experiments, the same affixed target words were tested with affixed and pseudo-affixed primes (as well as an unrelated prime condition). Thus each target word (prefixed and suffixed words) was preceded by a morphologically related word sharing the same affix, a pseudo-affixed word, and an unrelated word.

The results of one experiment using a prime exposure duration of 57ms, are presented in Figure 5. Here we see strong effects of prefixed primes relative to both pseudo-prefixed and unrelated control primes, while suffixed primes produced non-significant effects. These results clearly establish that morphological priming effects can be obtained between two words sharing the same prefix. Most important, these prefix priming effects were obtained relative to a pseudo-prefixed prime condition as well as relative to an unrelated prime. The pseudo-affixed primes served as a form control allowing morphological priming effects to be interpreted as being more than just effects of orthographic or phonologic overlap between prime and target. However, the pseudo-prefixed priming condition did not differ significantly from the unrelated priming condition, suggesting that the low degree of form overlap (on average 40% letters shared) was not sufficient to produce measurable priming in the present testing conditions. The contrast between the effects of real prefixes and pseudo-prefixes also stands in contradiction to any model that applies an obligatory prefix-stripping mechanism. If a masked prime sharing a prefix with the following target word can facilitate processing of the latter, then this facilitation should have occurred for both the prefixed and the pseudo-prefixed primes.

As can be seen in Figure 5, there was no hint of priming from suffixed word primes in this experiment. Further attempts to obtain significant suffix priming effects all failed. These experiments included manipulations that i) increased the surface frequency of the suffixed word primes, ii) increased the length of the suffix in letters, and iii) used suffixed word primes whose morphological boundary corresponded to a syllable boundary (e.g., the prime-target pair *rou.AGE - pli.AGE*, where the dot represents a syllable boundary and affixes are in upper case letters). It was critical to test this third condition, since in our previous experiments the great majority of the prefix primes had such a syllable-compatible morphological structure (e.g., *EN.jeu - EN.vol*), while this was generally not the case for the suffixed primes that had been tested (e.g., *ju.pON - ra.tON*).

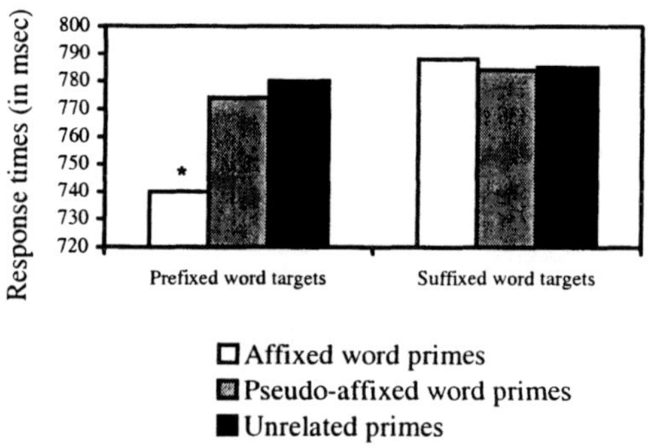

*Figure 5. Principal results of Giraudo & Grainger (2002). Lexical decision latencies to derived word targets (*indicates a significant priming effect relative to the unrelated conditon, p<.05 by subject and item).*

The prefix priming effect observed in these experiments complements the root priming advantage relative to pseudo-root primes reported in Giraudo and Grainger (2001). Following our interpretation of the root vs. pseudo-root effect, we once again argue that the simplest interpretation of the prefix vs. pseudo-prefix effect is in terms of a supralexical representation of prefixes. Thus all prefixed words containing the same prefix are hypothesized to be connected to a unit coding the presence of that particular prefix. Such prefix representations receive activation from whole-word form representations, and feed-back activation to these representations. Thus only true prefixed word primes will generate significant levels of activation in prefix representations, and these pre-activated representations facilitate the processing of target words containing the same prefix.

However, in the study reported above (Giraudo & Grainger, 2002), a distinct asymmetric pattern of priming effects was obtained for prefixes and suffixes: strong prefix priming was observed, but there was no hint of a suffix priming effect. This absence of suffix priming effects can be interpreted in terms of a left-to-right processing bias in word recognition. This type of mechanism has already been used to explain asymmetries in effects obtained across prefixes and suffixes. Colé, Beauvillain, and Segui (1989) tested for effects of whole-word (surface) frequency and cumulative root frequency in French derived words. They found surface frequency effects for both prefixed and suffixed words, whereas only suffixed words showed a cumulative frequency effect (see also Beauvillain, 1996, and Meunier & Segui, 1999). According to these authors, suffixed words but not prefixed words are accessed via the representation of their stem, hence giving rise to the asymmetric effects of cumulative frequency. This processing bias could result from the specific structure of spoken language, spoken words being delivered to the lexical processor gradually from beginning to end. Thus, the processing of suffixed words could be dominated by their stem representation (at the beginning of the word) while prefixed words would be processed with more equal weight given to prefix and stem (e.g., Schriefers, Zwitserlood, and Roelofs, 1991).

Other possible differences between prefixes and suffixes might underlie the asymmetric pattern of affix priming obtained in the present study. A number of important distinctions between prefixes and derivational suffixes have been noted by linguists (e.g., Gardes-Tamines, 1988, for French). Prefixes have a more predominantly compositional character than suffixes. Rather than simply transforming the meaning of the stem to which it is attached, prefixes often add meaning in the same manner as combining two roots in compound words (note the tendency to hyphenate after prefixes but never before suffixes). Prefixes have an exclusively semantic function whereas derivational suffixes have both semantic and syntactic functions. Finally, prefixes never phonologically or orthographically transform the stem to which they attach, whereas suffixes do. These different factors may provide the basis for a different representational status for prefixes compared to suffixes. Only further experimentation will help uncover the mechanisms underlying this distinct dissociation in masked prefix and suffix priming observed in the above study.

7. CONCLUSIONS

All the findings presented above provide support for a supralexical account of morphological representation for derivational morphology in French. It has been shown that (1) there is no extra computation involved in processing derived word primes compared to free root primes, (2) no priming effects can be obtained with word primes containing a pseudo-morpheme (whether a pseudo-root or a pseudo-affix) compared to unrelated primes, and (3) only the surface frequency, and not the cumulative root frequency, of morphologically complex primes affects the size of morphological priming, The key results are summarized in Table 2 along with an evaluation of how they agree with the predictions of the sublexical and supralexical architectures.

According to the supralexical account of morphemic representation, representations corresponding to roots and affixes are activated by any whole-word representation containing such units. Activation then feeds back from morphemic units to whole-word representations hence providing a mechanism that accounts for the morphological priming effects observed in the present study (for roots and prefixes) and other masked prime experiments (for roots). The fact that morphemic representations only receive activation from whole-word representations (in comprehension), allows this approach to capture the results summarized in Table 2. Activation of morphemic representations corresponding to the root of a stimulus occurs in exactly the same way for free root and derived word stimuli. On the other hand, the presence of letter sequences that correspond to roots without having such a status in reality (i.e., pseudo-roots), will not lead to activation of the corresponding morphemic representation. Similarly, when the surface frequency of derived word stimuli is too low, activation of the component morphemes is negligible in the conditions of masked priming. Finally, while increasing the surface frequency of derived words increases the connection strengths between the whole-word representation and its corresponding morphemic representation, variations in cumulative root frequency have little influence. If one assumes that modifications of connection strengths occur once the network has stabilized, in an interactive activation network this implies that only the connection between the stimulus word and its corresponding morphemes are reinforced. Whole-word representations that are partially activated in early phases of stimulus processing (and these are likely to include morphologically related words) are assumed not to participate in the adjustment of connection strengths.

Table 2. Summary of the key results obtained in masked morphological priming experiments

Result	Model	Agreement
No difference in priming	Sublexical	?
from free root and derived word primes.	Supralexical	Y
No priming from monomorphemic	Sublexical	?
primes containing a pseudo-root.	Supralexical	Y
No priming from derived word primes	Sublexical	N
with low surface frequencies.	Supralexical	Y
No influence of the cumulative root frequency	Sublexical	N
of derived word primes.	Supralexical	Y

The supralexical account of morphological representation can be thought of as a whole-word based solution to the problem of morphological parsing. The crucial question then is how novel complex forms can be recognized as such. The solution to this problem can be found in hierarchical activation networks that allow significant levels of activation to develop from partial form overlap with the stimulus (e.g., Grainger & Jacobs, 1998). For example: given the novel stimulus XNESS, and given prior knowledge of words such as Yness, Zness, and Xer, Xed, then partial overlap with the stimulus allows activation of these whole-word forms and then activation of the X and NESS morphemes. At the whole-word level, no single representation will reach a critical activation level for identification, and so no learning will proceed on the basis of existing whole-word representations. This is a situation where the system that controls learning in a network can dedicate a new representational unit to the stimulus being processed. This newly recruited representation is then connected to those units that are most active at the morpheme level. This is a classic example of Hebbian learning applied in various areas of cognitive science (e.g., Burton, 1998).

This solution for the processing of novel complex forms also provides part of the answer as to how supralexical morphemic representations might be learned in the first place. Once whole-word representations have developed and are connected to their corresponding semantic representations, then morphemic representations can develop via the correlated activity of a specific semantic representation (a set of semantic features, for example) and the simultaneous activation of words sharing bottom-up information derived from the stimulus. Thus, on presentation of a complex word such as *reprint*, all words sharing the same prefix will be activated and will activate in turn the semantic representation of this prefix (assuming systematicity in the meaning of the prefix across the different prefixed words). Each specific case of correlated activity in form and meaning can be represented by a morphemic unit that codes that specific relationship. Thus, the representation for the prefix RE can then be thought of as a node that codes the link between all whole-word forms that contain this prefix and that also activate some common semantic representation.

Now, given that the great majority of linguistic input (particularly in the early years of language use) arrives through the auditory modality, the specific constraints imposed by spoken language will shape the above learning process. More specifically, it is now assumed by several models of spoken word recognition (e.g., McClelland & Elman, 1986; Norris, 1994) that phoneme sequences that are possible word beginnings will activate such words even when not aligned with the beginning of the stimulus. Prefixes, and the stems of suffixed words are at the beginning of complex words, hence simplifying the detection of correlated activity in these cases. Free stems (as opposed to bound stems) of prefixed words also constitute legal word beginnings and will therefore be activated even when not aligned with the beginning of the stimulus. On the other hand, suffixes by definition never form the possible beginning of a word (suffix-like sequences such as *ment* at the beginnings of words are totally unrelated to real suffixes). This implies that only prefixes, stems (free or bound) of suffixed words, and the free stems of prefixed words offer the appropriate conditions for detecting form-meaning correlations that are necessary for the development of morphemic representations. This leads us to predict a further dissociation in masked morphological priming: whereas free stems of prefixed and suffixed words should show priming, bound stems should only produce priming in suffixed words. On this point, it is interesting to note that in French there are many cases of bound stems occurring in suffixed words, while none occur in prefixed words. The French language may have evolved in a way that reflects the difficulty in detecting the morphemic status of such bound stems in prefixed words.

In this chapter we have summarized some recent research on the processing of French derivational morphology using the masked prime paradigm. The results confirm that morphological codes are rapidly and automatically extracted from printed strings of letters, even in conditions where no morphological decomposition is required (i.e., with free stem targets). Current evidence suggests that this automatic activation of morphological codes operates via whole-word forms: the lexical processor first detects the presence of a given word form, and then activates its component morphemes. Future research should examine the limits of this alternative *supralexical* approach to morphological representation, particularly across different languages.

8. REFERENCES

Beauvillain, C. (1996). The integration of morphological information and whole-word form information during eye fixations on prefixed and suffixed words. *Journal of Memory and Language, 35,* 801-820.

Burton., A.M. (1998). In J. Grainger & A.M. Jacobs, *Localist connectionist approaches to human cognition*. Mahwah, NJ: Erlbaum.

Butterworth, B. (1983). Lexical Representation. *Language Production, 2,* 257-295.

Caramazza, A., Laudanna, A., & Romani, C. (1988). Lexical access and inflectional morphology. *Cognition, 28,* 297-332.

Colé, P., Beauvillain, C, Pavard, B., & Segui, J. (1986). Organisation morphologique et accès au lexique. *L'Année Psychologique, 86,* 349-365.

Colé, P., Beauvillain, C., & Segui, J. (1989).On the representation and processing of prefixed and suffixed words: A differential frequency effect. *Journal of Memory and Language, 28,* 1-13.

Deutsch, A., Frost, R., & Forster, K. I. (1998). Verbs and nouns are organized and accessed differently in the mental lexicon: Evidence from Hebrew. *Journal of Experimental Psychology: Learning, Memory and Cognition, 24,* 1238-1255.

Drews, E., & Zwitserlood, P. (1995). Morphological and orthographic similarity in visual word recognition. *Journal of Experimental Psychology: Human Perception and Performance, 21,* 1098-1116.

Forster, K. I., & Davis, C. (1984). Repetition priming and frequency attenuation in lexical access. *Journal of Experimental Psychology: Learning, Memory and Cognition, 10,* 680-698.

Forster, K. I., Davis, C., Schoknecht, C., & Carter, R. (1987). Masked priming with graphemically related forms: Repetition or partial activation? *The Quarterly Journal of Experimental Psychology, 39,* 211-251.

Frost, R., Deutsch. A., Gilboa, O., Tannenbaum, M. & Marslen-Wilson, W. (2000). Morphological priming: Dissociation of phonological, semantic, and morphological factors. *Memory & Cognition, 28,* 1277-1288.

Frost, R., Forster, K., & Deutsch, A. (1997). What can we learn from the morphology of Hebrew ? A masked priming investigation of morphological representation. *Journal of Experimental Psychology: Learning, Memory and Cognition, 23,* 1-28.

Gardes-Tamines, J. (1988). *La grammaire: phonologie, morphologie, lexicologie, Tome 1*. Paris: Armand Colin.

Giraudo, H., & Grainger, J. (2000). Effects of prime word frequency and cumulative root frequency in masked morphological priming. *Language and Cognitive Processes, 15, 421-444.*

Giraudo, H., & Grainger, J. (2001). Priming complex words: Evidence for supralexical representation of morphology. *Psychonomic Bulletin & Review*, in press.

Giraudo, H., & Grainger, J. (2002). On the role of derivational affixes in recognizing complex words: Evidence from masked priming. *Manuscript submitted for publication.*

Grainger, J., Colé, P., & Segui, J. (1991). Masked morphological priming in visual word recognition. *Journal of Memory and Language, 30,* 370-384.

Grainger, J. & Ferrand, L. (1994). Phonology and orthography in visual word recognition: Effects of masked homophone primes. *Journal of Memory and Language, 33,* 218-233.

Grainger, J., & Jacobs, A., M. (1998). *Localist connectionist approaches to human cognition*. Mahwah, NJ: Erlbaum.

Henderson, L., Wallis, J., & Knight, D. (1984). Morphemic structure and lexical access. In H. Bouma & D. Bouwhuis (Eds.), *Attention and Performance, X* (pp.221-224). Hillsdale, N. J: Lawrence Erlbaum Associates, Inc.

Laudanna, A., Burani, C., & Cermele, A. (1994). Prefixes as processing units. *Language and Cognitive Processes, 9,* 295-316.

Laudanna, A., Cermele, A., & Caramazza, A. (1997). Morpho-lexical representations in naming. *Language and Cognitive Processes, 12,* 49-66.

Lukatela, G., Gligorijevic, B., Kostic, A., & Turvey, M.T. (1980). Representation of inflected nouns in the internal lexicon. *Memory & Cognition, 8,* 415-423.

Manelis, L., & Tharp, D. (1977). The processing of affixed words. *Memory & Cognition, 5,* 690-695.

McClelland, J. L. & Elman, J. L. (1986). The TRACE model of speech perception. *Cognitive Psychology, 18,* 1-86.

McClelland, J.L., & Rumelhart, D.E. (1981). An interactive activation model of context effects in letter perception: Part 1. An account of basic findings. *Psychological Review, 88*, 375-405.

Meunier, F. & Segui, J. (1999). Frequency effects in auditory word recognition: The case of suffixed words. *Journal of Memory and Language, 41*, 327-344.

Norris, D. (1994). Shortlist: A connectionist model of continuous speech recognition. *Cognition, 52*, 189-234.

Pillon, A. (1998). The pseudo-prefixation effect in visual word recognition: A true-neither strategic nor orthographic-morphemic effect. *The Quarterly Journal of Experimental Psychology, 51*, 85-120.

Rastle, K., Davis, M.H., Marslen-Wilson, W.D., and Tyler, L.K (2000). Morphological and semantic effects in visual word recognition: A time-course study. *Language and Cognitive Processes, 15*, 507-538.

Schreuder, R., & Baayen, R. H. (1994). Prefix stripping re-revisited. *Journal of Memory and Language, 33*, 357-375.

Schreuder, R., & Baayen, R. H. (1995). Modelling morphological processing. In Feldman, L. B. (Ed.), *Morphological aspects of language processing*. (pp. 131-154). Hillsdale, NJ: Erlbaum.

Schreuder, R., & Baayen, R. H. (1997). How complex simplex words can be. *Journal of Memory and Language, 37*, 118-139.

Schriefers, H., Zwitserlood, P., & Roelofs, A. (1991). The identification of morphologically complex spoken words: Continuous processing or decomposition? *Journal of Memory and Language, 30*, 26-47.

Segui, J. & Grainger, J. (1990). Priming word recognition with orthographic neighbors: Effects of relative prime-target frequency. *Journal of Experimental Psychology: Human Perception and Performance, 16*, 65-76.

Taft, M. (1981). Prefix stripping revisited. *Journal of Verbal Learning and Verbal Behaviour, 20*, 289-297.

Taft, M. (1994). Interactive-activation as a framework for understanding morphological processing. *Language and Cognitive Processes, 9*, 271-294.

Taft, M., & Forster, K. I. (1975). Lexical storage and retrieval of prefixed words. *Journal of verbal Learning and verbal Behavior, 14*, 638-647.

9. ACKNOWLEDGEMENT

The first author was supported by a grant from the Fyssen Foundation, Paris, while preparing this chapter. The authors thank the editors of this volume for their helpful comments on an earlier version of this chapter.

10. ADDRESS FOR CORRESPONDENCE

Hélène Giraudo
Centre Interdisciplinaire de Recherche en Linguistique et Psychologie Cognitive
Université de Reims Champagne-Ardenne
Campus Croix Rouge
57 Rue Pierre Taittinger
51096 Reims cedex
France
Email: helene.giraudo@univ-reims.fr

ROBERT SCHREUDER, CRISTINA BURANI, AND HARALD BAAYEN

PARSING AND SEMANTIC OPACITY

1. INTRODUCTION

The Dutch low-frequency morphologically complex word *branding*, 'surf, the rolling and splashing of the waves' (7 occurrences per million), consists of two high-frequency constituents, *brand*, 'fire, to burn' (111 occurrences per million), and the nominalizing suffix *–ing* (13330 occurrences per million. Semantically opaque words such as *branding* pose an interesting challenge for dual route models of morphological processing in word recognition that allow complex words to be recognized by means of both a direct route and a parsing route (Baayen, Dijkstra, Schreuder, 1997; Burani Laudanna, 1992; Frauenfelder & Schreuder, 1992; Laudanna & Burani, 1995; Schreuder & Baayen, 1995).

Consider the question how the meaning of opaque complex words such as *branding* might be accessed. Do the constituents of such words play a role during word recognition even though the meaning of the complex word cannot be computed from the meanings of the constituents? The simplest solution is to assume that their full-form access representations provide pointers to their stored meanings (which are unpredictable by rule) and that the parsing route does not play a role (see, e.g., Frauenfelder and Schreuder, 1992). This solution would be consistent with the results of Marslen-Wilson, Tyler, Waksler, and Older (1994), who, in a cross-modal priming task, observed effects of morphological structure for semantically transparent words only. Thus, it would seem that constituent structure is irrelevant for opaque complex words.

However, although in general opaque complex words tend to have high frequencies of use, guaranteeing efficient direct access, it is not self-evident for low-frequency words such as *branding* that the direct route is fast enough to complete lexical access before the parsing route. Complex words with low full-form frequencies and high constituent frequencies are optimal candidates for being effectively processed on the basis of their constituents (Burani & Laudanna, 1992; Baayen, Dijkstra, & Schreuder, 1997). This holds for transparent complex words and opaque complex words alike. If the parsing route applies autonomously to its input irrespective of semantic transparency, as expected in a modular bottom-up architecture, then the parsing route may be expected to lead to the activation of the morphological constituents of *branding*, and hence to the activation of the semantic and syntactic representations of these constituents. Given a large frequency imbalance between the full-form frequency of the complex word as a whole on the one hand, and the frequencies of its constituents on the other, in favor of the latter, parallel dual route models predict that the transparent, unintended, reading ('burning' for *branding*) would become available before the opaque, intended, reading ('surf' for *branding*). The challenge for parallel dual route models is to establish empirically whether their predictions for low-frequency opaque complex words find empirical support.

This study is an attempt to come to grips with the role of the parsing route for low-frequency opaque words with high-frequency constituents by asking the following questions. First, does identification of the constituents of opaque complex words take place? This question is addressed in Experiment 1. Second, does activation of the semantic representations of these constituents take place? And if so, in which order do the meanings of the constituents and the opaque meaning of the complex word as a whole become available? These issues are addressed in Experiment 2. Finally, Experiment 3 considers the question whether the observed effects are crucially dependent on the presence of productive morphology.

2. EXPERIMENT 1

Experiment 1 investigates the role of semantic transparency for the processing of low-frequency morphologically complex words by orthogonally contrasting Semantic Transparency (opaque versus transparent) with Constituent Frequency (high versus low frequency of the base word). If the base word is identified in low-frequency complex words and plays a role in lexical processing, then we may expect that complex words with a high-frequency base word are responded to more quickly in visual lexical decision than comparable complex words with low-frequency base words. If semantic opacity effectively decreases the relevance of the constituents for lexical processing, as suggested by Frauenfelder and Schreuder (1992) and Schreuder and Baayen (1995), then the effect of constituent frequency should be small or absent for opaque complex words compared to transparent complex words. Conversely, if semantic transparency is in fact irrelevant so that constituent identification takes place for opaque and transparent complex words with a high-frequency base word alike, then opaque and transparent words should show a similar effect of constituent frequency.

Other studies on the role of constituent frequencies (Andrews, 1986; Burani & Caramazza, 1987; Colé, Beauvillain & Segui, 1989; Taft, 1979 have shown that lexical processing is indeed sensitive to Constituent Frequency. However, these studies have not addressed the role of semantic transparency in relation to the constituent frequency effect. There are several ways in which the frequency of a constituent such as *brand* in *branding* can be assessed. First, we may consider the frequency of the word form *brand* itself in isolation. We will refer to this frequency count as the Base Word form Frequency. Second, there is evidence suggesting that the frequencies of inflected variants of a given base form accumulate with the Base Word form Frequency (Baayen, Dijkstra, & Schreuder, 1997; Baayen, Burani, & Schreuder, 1997). We will refer to this cumulated count as the Base Lemma Frequency. Finally, a word such as *brand* also occurs in many derived words and compounds (e.g., *brandbaar*, 'burn-able', 'inflammable'). The summed frequencies of such derived words and compounds, excluding the Base Lemma Frequency itself, will be referred to as the (morphological) Family Frequency. Taft (1979) presents data suggesting that the Family Frequency also affects lexical processing. On the other hand, Schreuder and Baayen (1997) have observed that for monomorphemic Dutch nouns Family Frequency is irrelevant. By contrast, a type count of the number of different derived words and compounds in the morphological family of monomorphemic nouns, the (morphological) Family Size, was found to be a crucial codeterminant of response latencies in visual lexical decision.

For morphologically complex words, the respective roles of Family Size and Family Frequency have not yet been teased apart. Bertram, Baayen, and Schreuder (1999) report that a high family size of the base word of a complex word, henceforth the Base Family Size, may also speed up response latencies in visual lexical decision, depending on the kind of word formation involved. In their experiments the Base Family Size co varies with Base Family Frequency, however. In the present experiments, we therefore constructed our materials such that the contrast in Constituent Frequency reflects all three frequency contrasts at the same time: a contrast in Base Lemma Frequency, a contrast in Base Family Frequency, and a contrast in Base Family Size. A low Constituent Frequency thus denotes a low score on all three counts, and a high Constituent Frequency denotes a high score on all three counts. In this way, we maximalize our chances of observing an effect of Constituent Frequency.

2.1 Method

2.1.1 Participants

Eighty participants, mostly undergraduates at Nijmegen University, were paid to participate in the experiment. All participants were native speakers of Dutch.

2.1.2 Materials

We have selected our word materials from a low surface frequency range of 10 to 500 per 42 million word tokens, using the CELEX lexical database (Baayen, Piepenbrock, & Gulikers, 1995. Four sets of words were created, varying with respect to the design factors Transparency and Constituent Frequency. The set of opaque words contained fourteen words with a high constituent frequency (Base Lemma Frequency: 13198; Base Family Frequency: 13113; Base Family Size: 82) and fourteen words with a low constituent frequency (Base Lemma Frequency: 397; Base Family Frequency: 378; Base Family Size: 15). The set of transparent words likewise contained fourteen words with a high constituent frequency (Base Lemma Frequency: 8751; Base Family Frequency: 8887; Base Family Size: 115) and fourteen words with a low constituent frequency (Base Lemma Frequency: 536; Base Family Frequency: 351; Base Family Size: 15).

Appendix A lists our experimental materials. Each set of words contains two words with the suffix *-ing*, eight words with the suffix *-ig*, one with the suffix

-achtig, two with the suffix *-er*, and one with the suffix *-lijk*, so that the sets are matched for the distributional properties of the affixes (see, e.g., Burani, Dovetto, Thornton, & Laudanna, 1997, for the relevance of distributional properties of affixes for lexical processing). For each target word, it lists the relevant frequency measures, as well as the English translation equivalents of the base word and the complex word as a whole. We have used the morphological properties of translation equivalents as an objective means to confirm that our opaque and transparent words differ substantially with respect to semantic compositionality. Transparent, compositional words will tend to translate into complex words that are likewise compositional on a morpheme-by-morpheme basis. For instance, Dutch *stof+ig* translates straightforwardly into English *dust+y* with full translation equivalence between base, affix, and full form, and full compositionality in both languages. Conversely, opaque complex words tend to have morphologically unrelated translation equivalents. For example, Dutch *brand+ing* is derived from the verb 'to burn', but has a translation equivalent in English the monomorphemic noun surf, morphologically unrelated to the English verb *burn*. Of course, the two languages occasionally use the same morphemes to express the same opaque meaning, which occurs in two instances in our opaque set (e.g., *kat+ig* and *cat+y* (both denote an unpleasant character trait using the same animal as point of departure for the same idiomatic metaphorical extension). Generally, however, opaque complex words require morphologically unrelated translation equivalents. The general principle of compositional translation equivalence between related languages is clearly reflected in our materials. The pairs of translation equivalents for the base word and the complex word in the set of transparent words make use of the same English stem in 25 out of 28 pairs. For the opaque set, only 2 out of 28 pairs do so. These counts provide a strong objective indication that our two sets of words differ considerably with respect to semantic transparency.

Each participant was exposed to 14 target words, all of which were either opaque or transparent. This between-subject design ensures that it is impossible for participants to become aware of the extreme transparency contrast in the materials. Half of these words had a low constituent frequency, and half a high constituent frequency. Affix types were equally distributed over the two sets. In addition, 36 morphologically complex words with constituents that did not appear in the target words, as well as 150 monomorphemic words were added as filler materials. Orthographically legal nonwords corresponding to the words with respect to length and morphological constituency were constructed. For the nonwords matching the complex real words, half consisted of a pseudo-stem with an existing suffix, and half of a real stem followed by a pseudo-suffix. For the set of monomorphemic filler words, monomorphemic nonwords were constructed. Thus, the experiment contained 200 word trials and 200 nonword trials. The experiment was preceded by a practice session with 20 word trials and 20 nonword trials.

2.1.3 Procedure

Participants were tested in groups of three in individual noise-proof experimentation booths. They received standard lexical decision instructions. Each trial consisted of the presentation of a fixation mark (asterisk) in the middle of the screen during 500 ms, followed after 50 ms by the stimulus centered at the same position. Stimuli were presented on Nec Multisync color monitors in white upper-case 36 points Helvetica letters on a dark background. Stimuli remained on the screen for 1500 ms. Time-out occurred 2000 ms after stimulus onset. Three pauses were included, one of which directly followed the practice session. The other two pauses divided the items in three equally sized sets of roughly 133 trials. The total duration of the experiment was approximately 35 minutes.

2.2 *Results*

For each participant, the proportion of incorrect responses was calculated for all trials in the experiment. The data of two participants performing with an error score greater than 10 percent were discarded in the analyses. Four of our critical experimental words elicited error scores higher than 30 percent, and were also discarded. Table 1 summarizes the mean reaction times and error scores for the different experimental conditions using the remaining observations.

Mean reaction time by participant as a function of Transparency and Constituent Frequency (Experiment 1). Error percentages between parentheses.

Table 1. Mean reaction time by participant as a function of Transparency and Constituent Frequency (Experiment 1). Error percentages between parentheses

	transparent	opaque
High Constituent Frequency	582 (6.0%)	584 (3.6%)
Low Constituent Frequency	608 (4.4%)	631 (8.8%)

By-item and by-participant analyses of variance were carried out on the reaction times with the two factors, Transparency and Constituent Frequency. Transparency was a between-subjects factor in the analysis by participants. No significant effect of Transparency was obtained (F_1, F2 <1). The effect of Constituent Frequency was significant both by participant and by item ($F_1(1,76) = 21.7, p < .001$, $MSE = 2396.7$, $F_2(1,48) = 6.8, p < .01$, $MSE = 2549.5$). The interaction of Transparency and Constituent Frequency was not significant ($F_1(1,76) = 1.9, p < .2$, $MSE = 2396.7$, $F_2 < 1$). The error scores suggest a slight speed-accuracy trade-off in the transparent condition. However, the difference between the two conditions (1.6%) is not statistically reliable ($t(37) = .93$, $p > .3$).

2.3 *Discussion*

Experiment 1 addressed the question whether the base word constituent of opaque morphologically complex words plays a role during visual word recognition. For the transparent words, we observe the expected pattern of results. Transparent words with a high Constituent Frequency are processed faster than words with a low Constituent Frequency while matched on Surface Frequency. This suggests that the morphological constituents are identified. This possibility is supported by post-hoc by-item correlational analyses, which reveal significant correlations of RT and the (logarithmically transformed) frequency measures related to the base word, and no correlation with the (logarithmically transformed) frequency of the word as a whole (Surface Frequency $r = .28$, $t_2(24) = 1.41$, $p > .15$, Base Frequency: $r = .54$, $t_2(24) = 3.16$, $p < .01$, Base Family Size: $r = .59$, $t_2(24) = 3.56$, $p < .01$, Base Family Frequency: $r = .42$, $t_2(24) = 2.28$, $p < .05$). Although this experiment was not designed to detect Surface Frequency effects, the fact that we have observed effects of Surface Frequency with other Dutch materials in the low frequency range (see, e.g., Baayen, Schreuder, De Jong, & Krott, 2001) leads us to hypothesize that these low-frequency transparent words are primarily processed on the basis of their constituents.

To our surprise, the effect of Constituent Frequency for opaque words is at least as large as that for transparent words. After all, processing of opaque words is generally assumed to proceed on the basis of full-form representations, since rules cannot, by definition, provide access to irregular, opaque meanings. However, post-hoc correlation analyses show neither reliable correlations of RT with Surface Frequency, nor any such correlation with Base Lemma Frequency, Base Family size, or Base Family Frequency (Surface Frequency: $r = .06$, $t_2 < 1$; Base Frequency: $r = .21$, $t_2(24) = 1.06$, $p > .25$; Base Family Size: $r = .28$, $t_2(24) = 1.44$, $p > .15$; Base Family Frequency: $r = .17$, $t_2(24) < 1$). Apparently, Constituent Frequency has some role to play, as shown by the factorial results, while at the same time the correlation analyses suggest that some additional process may also be involved that superimposes extra variability, masking the correlations between Constituent Frequency and the response latencies on an item by item basis. We will return to this issue in the discussion of Experiment 2.

These results show that, at the very least, the access representations of the (high-frequency) constituents of our low-frequency opaque words are activated. We now turn to consider the question whether the base words of opaque complex words are only activated at the access level, without further activation of their semantics, or whether their semantics become available as well, together with the idiosyncratic semantics of the complex words as a whole. Of special interest is the relative time course of the possible activation of these two distinct meanings. This issue is addressed in Experiment 2.

3. EXPERIMENT 2

To investigate whether the semantics of the base word in an opaque complex word are activated, we made use of a semantic priming design. We used opaque complex words (consisting of a formally completely regular combination of an existing stem and an affix subcategorized for that stem) with a low Full-Form Frequency and a high Constituent Frequency as critical primes. For each of these primes, two targets were chosen, one transparently related to the meaning of the base, and one related to the idiomatic opaque meaning of the derived word. In addition, monomorphemic control primes were selected that were unrelated to both kinds of target words. Thus we have the following four conditions, exemplified for the critical prime *branding*, derived from the verbal base *brand*, 'fire, burn'.

Condition	Prime	Target
base-related	branding ('surf')	vuur ('fire')
full-form-related	branding ('surf')	zee ('sea')
base-related control	schuchter ('shy')	vuur ('fire')
full-form-related control	schuchter ('shy')	zee ('sea')

To investigate the time course of the activation of the opaque and transparent meanings, we presented the prime-target pairs with two different stimulus onset asynchronies (SOA).

3.1 Method

3.1.1 Participants

One hundred nineteen participants, mostly undergraduates at Nijmegen University, were paid to participate in the experiment: 58 for SOA 150, and 61 for SOA 500. All were native speakers of Dutch.

3.1.2 Materials

We selected seventeen critical primes and the corresponding control primes and target words. These words are listed in Appendix B.1, together with the frequency characteristics of the critical primes and the English translation equivalents of the base and the full form. For all prime-target pairs, semantic relatedness ratings were obtained (see Appendix B.2). Only one condition, the full-form-related condition, received a high relatedness rating, indicating that the forty participants in the rating experiment were aware of the idiomatic meaning of primes such as *branding*. In addition, familiarity ratings were obtained for all primes and targets (see Appendix B.2). Although the primes had a low surface frequency, they were rated as reasonably familiar (approximately 5 on a seven-point scale), indicating that they are not from too low a frequency range. Despite a difference in their Full-Form frequency, the two kinds of targets were nevertheless rated as roughly equally familiar.

We constructed four experimental lists, selecting one condition from each set and rotating over conditions, so that each list contained exactly 17 different items. Three conditions were represented by four items, and one condition by five items. The condition with five items was rotated across the lists. For each of the 17 prime-target pairs, a word -nonword pair was constructed. In addition to these 34 word and nonword pairs, 17 word-word pairs and 17 word-nonword pairs were selected as filler materials. None of the word-word fillers were semantically related in any way. Finally, 10 word-word and 10 word-nonword practice items were created. The total number of items in the experiment was 88.

3.1.3 Procedure

Participants were tested in groups of four in individual noise-proof experimentation booths. They received lexical decision instructions that made explicit that they had to respond to the second stimulus in each trial. Each trial consisted of the presentation of a fixation mark (asterisk) in the middle of the screen during 500 ms, followed after 50 ms by the prime centered at the same position. After 50 ms, or after 400 ms, the prime disappeared, and 100 ms later the target was displayed centered at the same position. The target remained on the screen for 1500 ms. Time-out occurred 2000 ms after stimulus onset. Stimuli were presented on Nec Multisync color monitors in white upper-case 36 points Helvetica letters on a dark background. The total duration of the experiment was approximately 15 minutes.

3.2 Results and Discussion

The data of participants with error scores exceeding 10% were removed from the analysis (two for SOA 150, and two for SOA 500). For each SOA, we carried out one-tailed t-tests across participants and across items to ascertain whether the difference between the prime and control conditions was reliable. Table 2 summarizes our results. For SOA 150, a significant priming effect was obtained for the Full-Form related condition ($t_1(56) = 2.6$, $p = .006$, $t_2(16) = 2.8$, $p = .007$). No priming effect was observed for the Base-related condition (both t-values less than 1). For SOA 500, the priming effect for the Full-Form related condition was marginally significant by participants ($t_1(59) = 1.5$, $p = .065$) and significant by items ($t_2(16) = 2.4$, $p = .015$).

Table 2. Mean reaction time by participant to morphologically complex opaque derived words as a function of Stimulus Onset Asynchrony, Relatedness (related versus unrelated) and Transparency (related to Base, transparent; related to Full Form, opaque) in Exp. 2

	stimulus onset asynchrony			
	150		500	
unrelated	518	(.01)	538	(.02)
base-related	511	(.01)	512	(.02)
unrelated	542	(.03)	528	(.06)
full-form related	515	(.03)	516	(.02)

Note. Error proportions between parentheses.

At this SOA, the effect of Base-related priming was significant both by participants and by items ($t_1(59) = 2.2$, $p = .017$, $t_2(16) = 2.0$, $p = .034$). Further inspection of our items revealed two outlier items with mean difference scores greater than the cell mean plus two standard deviations in the opposite direction expected for priming. One such item occurred in the Base-related condition for SOA 150, and the other item occurred again in the Base-related condition but now at SOA 500. T-tests for these two conditions after removal of these two outliers resulted in a non-significant effect for the Base-related condition in the short SOA ($t_2(15) = 1.64$, $p = 0.12$) and a solid effect for the Base-related condition in the long SOA ($t_2(15) = 3.39$, $p = 0.004$). Using Bonferroni's inequality and focusing on the item-analyses, we conclude that the priming effect is reliable at SOA 150 for the Full-Form related condition only and that it is reliable at SOA 500 for the Base-related condition only (all p-values $< 0.05/4.0 = 0.0125$).

Apparently, the opaque meaning is already activated at the short SOA of 150 ms. At the longer SOA of 500 ms, there appears to be some activation left, but the t-tests do not suggest that this late activation is completely reliable. Conversely, the meaning of the base is not activated at all for the short SOA, while it is clearly activated at the long SOA.

We can now answer our original questions concerning semantic activation and its relative time course for base word and full form. Experiment 1 revealed that a high Constituent Frequency influences response latencies to both opaque and transparent complex words. The factorial results of Experiment 1 suggest that, apparently, the constituents of low-frequency complex words are at the very least identified irrespective of their transparency. Experiment 2 shows that the constituents of opaque words are not only identified, but that their meaning becomes activated as well.

With respect to the time course of semantic activation, we observe that, surprisingly, the opaque meaning of the full form of a morphologically complex word is activated long before the meaning of its base, despite the high Constituent Frequency of the base word and the low Full-Form Frequency of the complex word itself. The observed pattern is the exact opposite of what might be expected on the basis of the frequency relations between full form and base. It is also unexpected in the light of the absence of any indication of a full-form frequency effect in Experiment 1.

On the other hand, the present results are similar to those obtained for monomorphemic homonyms. For words such as bank, the dominant reading becomes available earlier in time than the non-dominant reading. In our present data, we likewise observe that the dominant meaning, the one related to the full form, becomes available long before the non-dominant reading, a reading that is a possible reading morphologically but that is not used in Dutch at all. What remains remarkable is that the non-dominant reading becomes activated at all, given that speakers of Dutch never use the word in that sense.

How can we explain this crossover pattern of activation over time of the two meanings? One possibility is to assume that the direct route would have such an advantage over the morphological parsing route that access to the idiosyncratic meaning would be completed long before the parsing route completes activation of the meaning of the base word. Under this assumption, segmenting the input into base word and affix would be a very time-costly operation. Whereas the full form would activate the opaque meaning within 150 ms, parsing the input into base word and affix would require more time.

This explanation, however, is incompatible with the absence ($r = 0.06$) of a correlation of Surface Frequency of the opaque words and the response latencies in Experiment 1, and it is also at odds with a series of studies modeling experimental results. The computational models suggest that the segmentation time, the time required for parsing the input into its constituents, is much shorter than 100 ms. For Dutch verb plurals, segmentation appears to be completed within 20 ms (Baayen, Dijkstra, en Schreuder, 1997), and segmentation times for Italian noun plurals appear to be of the same order of magnitude (Baayen, Burani, and Schreuder, 1997). These findings suggest that segmentation by itself is not time-costly at all.

If *branding* is rapidly segmented into *brand* and *ing*, why then does it take such a long time for *brand* to activate its meaning ('fire')? And why do the post-hoc analyses of Experiment 1 not reveal any reliable correlations between our measures of Constituent Frequency and the response latencies for opaque words, in contrast to transparent words? If the base word is indeed rapidly segmented out, how then is it possible that the meaning of the full form is activated more quickly than the meaning of the base, initially biasing the competition process completely to the advantage of the opaque meaning? Is this due to the high speed of the direct route? Given the low frequency of the full form and the high constituent frequencies, the likelihood that the direct route is the first to complete lexical access is small, however. How can we resolve this paradox?

The solution that we would like to offer here hinges on the concept of integration nodes introduced by Schreuder (1990) for the processing of particle verbs in Dutch. Particle verbs such as *op-vallen* (up-fall, 'to attract attention') and *af-vallen* (off-fall, 'to loose weight') have highly idiomatic meanings that pose a special problem for lexical processing as the particle (*op, af*) can occur separated from the base: *zij valt niet genoeg af*, 'she doesn't loose enough weight'. To allow the correct but unpredictable meaning 'to loose weight' to be accessed on the basis of the separated constituents *valt*, 'falls' and *af*, 'off', Schreuder (1990) introduced the notion of the integration node. Integration nodes require input from two constituents (e.g., *valt* and *af*) to reach threshold activation level. Once threshold has been reached, the integration node will activate the idiosyncratic meaning of *afvallen*, 'to loose weight', and at the same time inhibit the regular meanings of these constituents ('fall' and 'off'). Thus, the integration node serves the purpose of redirecting the activation of the constituents to the correct opaque meaning, effectively pre-empting rule-based semantic composition.

Within the framework developed by Schreuder & Baayen (1995), we can understand the present results along very similar lines. Figure 1 shows an outline of the representations and the connections between representations that might be involved in the processing of opaque words such as *branding*. At the layer of access representations we find orthographic units for the stem *brand* and the suffix *-ing*, as well as for the full form *branding*. Upon encountering a low-frequency word such as *branding*, these three access representations become active, the access representation for the full form slowly, the access representations of the high-frequency constituents *brand* and *ing* quickly.

The access representations activate their corresponding lemma nodes, the middle layer in Figure 1. These lemma nodes mediate between the access representations and the semantic and syntactic representations in the central lexicon, the top layer in Figure 1. The dummy markers 'SURF', 'FIRE', and 'ING' have glossed these central representations. For fully transparent derived words such as *snelheid*, 'quickness', i.e., 'speed', there are no links between the access representations of the constituents and the lemma representation of the full form. In the case of words such as

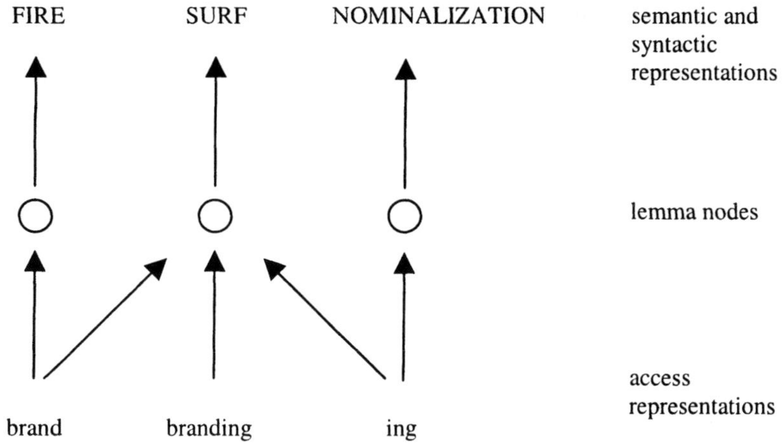

Figure 1. Representations for branding in a spreading activation model of morphological processing

branding, however, such links are posited. Their functionality is similar to the functionality of the links between access representations and the integration nodes of Schreuder (1990). In fact, the lemma node of *branding* has the same function as the integration node proposed in that study, i.e., to redirect activation to the appropriate unpredictable meaning. Thus, upon activation of *brand* and *-ing*, the lemma node of *branding* receives sufficient activation to access the opaque meaning 'surf', see Figure 1. We assume that the access representation of the suffix *-ing*, which has a much higher frequency than the base word *brand* and the full form *branding*, reaches activation threshold before the access representations of *brand* and *branding*. Because the access representation of the high-frequency suffix *-ing* reaches threshold first, the lemma node of *branding* is pre-activated by the time that the access representation of *brand* reaches activation threshold. Once the access representation of *brand* has reached threshold, it will in turn activate the lemma representations of *brand* and *branding*. Since the lemma representation of branding is pre-activated, in contrast to that of *brand*, the lemma node of *branding* will reach threshold activation before the lemma node of *brand*. Hence, the meaning 'surf' becomes available before the meaning 'fire'.

We suspect that the absence of reliable correlations of our measures of Constituent Frequency with the response latencies for the opaque words in Experiment 1 is due to the pre-activation of the lemma nodes of the full forms by the various different affixes used in that experiment. Each affix has its own resting activation level proportional to its frequency of use and its distributional properties (Laudanna & Burani, 1995). Consequently, the amount of pre-activation of the lemma nodes of the opaque full forms differs for words with different affixes. Hence the contribution of the base to the activation of the lemma node of the opaque full form is no longer a simple function of the frequency of the base. Pre-activation introduces additional variability, masking the way in which item-specific frequency-determined resting activation levels influence lexical processing within the high and low Constituent Frequency sets of target words. As a result, a reliable correlation between constituent frequency and response latencies can no longer be observed, although the correlation still is in the predicted direction.

Experiments 1 and 2 show that base words in complex words play a role in morphological processing independently of their semantic transparency. All complex words studied in these experiments contain productive affixes that attach to independently occurring words. In the next Experiment, we investigate whether opaque complex words with unproductive affixes and bound stems that do not occur in isolation also reveal a role for the bound base word in lexical processing.

4. EXPERIMENT 3

In Experiment 3 we compare complex words from the Germanic and Romance strata of the Dutch lexicon. The larger part of the Dutch lexicon falls into the Germanic stratum, and it is here that most productive word formation rules are found. These word formation rules take as their input freely occurring words to yield new words. For instance, the suffix -baar ('-able') attaches to the verb form brand ('burn') to yield *brandbaar* ('inflammable').

The Romance stratum contains a range of words historically borrowed from French, Latin, and to some extent Greek. Word formation in this stratum is not based on freely occurring words, but on bound stems, forms that do not occur in isolation. For instance, *dictie*, 'diction', can be analyzed into the bound stem dict- and the suffix *-ie*. Most word formation patterns in this stratum, which in Dutch is much more restricted than in English, are not productive, due to the absence of regular form-meaning correspondences (Van Marle, 1985. The majority of the complex words in the Romance stratum is semantically opaque.

Nevertheless, complex words in the Romance stratum vary on the dimensions of Base Family Size and Base Family Frequency, defined on the basis of their etymologically determinable bound stems. Hence, just as in Experiment 1, we proceed to contrast Constituent Frequency, but now for the Romance stratum as well as for the Germanic stratum. Note that Constituent Frequency consists of the Base Lemma Frequency, Base Family Size, and Base Family Frequency for the Germanic Stratum, and of Base Family Size and Base Family Frequency only for the Romance Stratum- the Romance stratum makes use of bound stems that do not occur in isolation. Also note that the difference in Stratum is correlated with a difference in register and age of acquisition. Words from the Romance stratum occur primarily in formal styles (officialese, scientific prose), and they are generally acquired after primary school.

The overall properties of Germanic and Romance words suggest that Stratum will emerge as a main effect with Romance words being responded to somewhat more slowly. Our interest, however, is not in this main effect, which can be traced to a great many different possible sources. The focus of our attention is the behavior of Constituent Frequency across the two strata. What we expect to find is that the effect of Constituent Frequency is larger for the Germanic stratum than for the Romance stratum.

It is important to note that our predictions are specific for Dutch and other Germanic languages such as German, Norwegian, Swedish, and Danish, which, unlike English, make only very restricted use of Romance morphology. Dutch morphology is word-based, in the sense that freely occurring forms are input to morphological rules. The learned words from the Romance stratum are exceptional, and the likelihood that their etymological structure has psychological relevance is small for the average speaker of Dutch. We do not claim that bound stems as such cannot be active processing units. In languages such as French and Italian, productive morphology is based on bound stems, and not on free forms as in Dutch. We have opted for studying bound stems in Dutch not because they are bound, but because they are part of the unproductive part of the Dutch lexicon.

4.1 Method

4.1.1 Participants

Fifty-five participants, mostly undergraduates at Nijmegen University, were paid to participate in the experiment. All were native speakers of Dutch.

4.1.2 Materials

We have selected our word materials from the low Surface Frequency range of approximately 25 on 42 million occurrences, using the CELEX lexical database. This allowed us to make a maximal contrast between Surface and Constituent Frequency, as it is especially in the lower frequency ranges that we expect parsing to be effective, and hence for Constituent Frequency to play a role.

We have constructed two sets of materials, one containing only words from the native or Germanic stratum of the Dutch lexicon, the other containing only words with a Romance origin. The words from the Germanic stratum were fully transparent complex words with undisputed Germanic affixes. The words from the Romance stratum were opaque and contained unproductive formatives that on etymological grounds can be argued to be affixes. Within each set, we contrasted two further sets that differed as maximally as possible with respect to Constituent Frequency.

For the Germanic stratum, the contrast in Constituent Frequency is realized in terms of Base Family Frequency, Base Family Size, and Base Lemma Frequency. For the Romance stratum, this contrast is carried only by Base Family Size and Base Family Frequency, as the base words of Romance complex words are bound forms with no independent frequency of their own. For each of the four cells of our orthogonal design (Constituent Frequency x Stratum, using a complete within-subject design), we obtained a total of 14 words. The contrasts in Constituent Frequency in the Germanic and Romance strata were of the same order of magnitude, as shown in

Appendix C. The overall ratio of string familiarity, evaluated in terms of the sum of Surface Frequency, Base Family Frequency, and Base Lemma Frequency, was similarly balanced between the Constituent Frequency conditions (9930/928 =10.7 for Romance, 15996/1538 =10.4 for Germanic). Appendix C lists our materials, their frequency characteristics, and the English translation equivalents of the constituents and the full form. Note that 3 out of 28 Romance words have English translation equivalents sharing the same Romance root. This contrasts with the Germanic words, for which 27 out of 28 cases translate with the same stem. This shows that the Romance and Germanic words differ substantially with respect to their semantic transparency.

In addition to the critical target words, we included 114 filler words in the experiment. This set of filler words contained both monomorphemic and morphologically complex words from the medium frequency ranges. The experiment was preceded by a practice session with 30 low and high frequency Germanic and Romance words.

For each word in our experiment, an orthographically and phonotactically legal pseudoword was constructed of approximately the same length and of similar morphological complexity. Thus, we used pseudowords resembling Romance words (e.g., *confreus*, compare with existing words such as *confronteer*, 'confront', and *affreus* ('awful'), and pseudowords resembling Germanic complex words (e.g., *druinlijk*, consisting of a pseudostem and the Dutch Germanic suffix *-lijk*, '-like').

The total number of trials in the experiment including the practice trials was four hundred.

4.1.3 Procedure

The procedure was identical to that of Experiment 1. The total duration of the experiment was approximately 35 minutes.

4.2 Results

For each participant, the proportion of incorrect responses and missing data was calculated over all word trials in the experiment. Overall, the participants performed the task accurately, with less than 10% errors. All observations were therefore used to calculate item and participant mean reaction times and error scores for the different conditions. It turned out that several experimental words elicited high numbers of errors. We removed 11 Romance words and four Germanic words that showed error rates exceeding 30% from the data set (see Appendix C for details).

Table 3. Mean reaction time by participant as a function of Stratum and

	Germanic	Romance
High Constituent Frequency	610 (6.6%)	665 (20.0%)
Low Constituent Frequency	641 (12.2%)	637 (14.1%)

Removal of these items did not affect the matching for Surface Frequency, nor were the ratios of string familiarity between the high and low Constituent Frequency conditions effected substantially (Romance: 8419/714 =11.8; Germanic: 16104/1636 =9.8). Table 3 shows the mean reaction times and error scores for the different experimental conditions using the remaining data points.

By-participant and by-item analyses of variance were carried out on the response latencies. No significant effect of Constituent Frequency was observed ($F_1(1,54) < 1$, $F_2(1,37) < 1$). The effect of Stratum was significant by participant and marginally significant by items ($F_1(1,54) = 13.3$, $p < .001$, MSE =2543; $F_2(1,37) = 2.8$, $p < .10$, MSE =2201. The interaction of Stratum and Constituent Frequency was significant by participants ($F_1(1,54) = 16.0$, $p < .001$, MSE =3326) and marginally significant by items ($F_2(1,37) = 3.6$, $p < .07$, MSE =2201). The error analysis revealed a similar pattern of results.

The difference of 28 milliseconds (in the wrong direction for a frequency effect) between the Romance high (665 ms) and low (637 ms) Constituent frequency conditions was significant by participants but did not receive any support in the by-items analysis ($t_1(54) = 2.1$, $p < 0.05$; $t_2(15) < 1$, two-tailed t-tests). By contrast, the difference of 31 milliseconds between the Germanic high (610 ms) and low (641 ms) Constituent Frequency conditions was significant in the predicted direction both by participants and by items ($t_1(54) = 4.5$, $p < .001$; $t_2(22) = 2.0$, $p < .03$, one-tailed t-tests).

Post-hoc analyses of the correlations of our measures of Constituent Frequency with the response latencies for the Germanic and Romance subsets of words revealed the following pattern, supporting the results of the analysis of variance. For the Romance words, the only significant correlation concerned Surface Frequency ($r = -0.53$, $t(15) = 2.4$, $p < .03$). For Base Family Frequency and Base Family Size, the correlations were less than .06 ($t < 1$ in both cases). For our Germanic words, by contrast, Base Lemma Frequency and Base Family Frequency revealed significant correlations (Base Lemma Frequency: $r = .41$, $t(22) = 2.1$, $p < .05$; Base Family Frequency: $r = .48$, $t(22) = 2.6$, $p < .02$) while Surface Frequency did not reveal a significant correlation ($r = .31$, $t(22) = 1.5$, $p < .15$). Base Family Size also did not reveal a significant effect ($r = .30$, $t(22) = 1.5$, $p < .15$).

We further computed the orthographic string familiarity of the affixes in the Germanic and Romance cells of the experimental design, restricting ourselves to the words included in the above analyses, to make sure that our results are not driven by the orthographic form properties of our target words. For the Germanic affixes, the affixal string familiarity (the summed frequencies of all words in the CELEX lexical database containing the orthographic affix string) in logarithmic units was 11.12 in the High Constituent Frequency condition, and 10.26 in the corresponding Low condition. (Note that the log affixal string familiarity is much higher than that of the base: 9.22 (log 10169) in the High and 7.48 (log 890) in the Low Constituent Frequency condition.) Log affixal string familiarity did not reveal any correlation with the response latencies ($p > .3$). For the Romance words in this experiment, log affixal string familiarity was 12.36 for the High Constituent Frequency condition and 12.63 for the Low Constituent Frequency Condition. (As before, the string familiarity of the base words is lower, 9.03 (log 8389) for the High and 6.52 (log 683) for the Low

Constituent Frequency condition.) Again, log affixal string familiarity did not reveal any reliable correlation with the response latencies (p >.7).

4.3 Discussion

The question we have addressed by means of Experiment 3 is whether morphological productivity is a necessary condition for the Constituent Frequency effect as observed in Experiment 1. We have addressed this question by comparing the effect of Constituent Frequency for the Romance and Germanic strata. For the Germanic stratum, we observe the expected effect of Constituent Frequency: Words with a high Constituent Frequency are processed faster than words with a low Constituent Frequency. By contrast, Constituent Frequency did not reveal any effect for the Romance stratum. We conclude that indeed full productivity is required for the effect of Constituent Frequency to emerge.

The orthographic string familiarity of the affixes in this experiment did not reveal any significant correlation with the response latencies, not for the Germanic words nor for the Romance words. This is in line with the predictions of a parallel dual route model for morphological processing. Whenever the full-form route wins the race, the constituents, their frequencies, and the time they need to reach threshold activation level do not determine the response latencies. In this case, response latencies will correlate with the frequencies of the full forms. When the parsing route wins the race, a response can only be executed after both constituents have reached threshold activation level. Given the much higher frequencies of the affixes in our experiment compared to the frequencies of the base words, the affixes will on average reach threshold activation level before the base words. Hence, response latencies for items recognized via the parsing route will correlate with the frequency of the base word, and not with that of the affix. Irrespective of which route wins the race, differences in affixal string familiarity are irrelevant to the pattern of results in the response latencies. We understand the results of the present experiment as indicating that the Romance words are recognized via the direct route only, while for the Germanic words the parsing route is predominantly used.

The results of Experiment 3 seem to contradict the results reported by Bergman, Hudson, and Eling (1988). In their Experiment 3, they compared Romance prefixed words with Romance monomorphemic words in a lexical decision task. They found that the prefixed words required longer response latencies than their monomorphemic controls. This, they argued, is evidence for obligatory prefix stripping for their Romance prefixed words. Apart from some theoretical and statistical shortcomings of any theory of obligatory prefix stripping (see Schreuder and Baayen, 1994), we find the conclusion reached by Bergman et al. (1988) counterintuitive. Why would morphological processing take place for words the form and meaning of which are often completely unpredictable, such as *recept*, 'recipe' and *decreet*, 'decree'?

Inspection of the materials listed in Bergman (1988, pp. 207-208), the doctoral thesis on which the paper by Bergman et al. (1988) is based, suggests that there is a confound in their experiment. Their critical and control groups differed substantially with respect to the abstractness or concreteness of the words they used. For both groups, we counted the number of words denoting a picturable, concrete, physical object. For instance, *citroen*, 'lemon', and *horloge*, 'watch', were classified as concrete, while we classified *comfort*, 'comfort', and *illusie*, 'illusion' as abstract. It turned out that for their complex words, three out of 24 words were concrete. Conversely, 16 out of 24 words in the control set denoted concrete objects ($X^2(1) = 12.5, p < .001$. This strongly suggests that the difference in response latencies between the prefixed and control sets is due to a difference in concreteness (see, e.g., James, 1975).

Our conclusion that no morphological processing is involved for the Romance words in our Experiment 3 nor in any of the Romance words in Experiment 3 of Bergman et al. (1988) does not imply that no morphological processing can be involved for the complete nonnative stratum of the Dutch lexicon. As we have argued elsewhere (Schreuder and Baayen, 1995), morphological processing depends crucially on factors such as semantic and phonological transparency, frequency, productivity, affixal homonymy, and the extent of pseudo-affixation. The Romance materials in Experiment 3 are phonologically highly irregular and unpredictable, and semantically they are also quite opaque. This is characteristic for the Romance stratum as a whole, although there are some pockets of regularity where the parsing route might have some role to play (e.g., the suffix *-atie*, comparable to English *-ation*, which attaches to Romance verbs with the verbal suffix *-eer*). What Experiment 3 shows is that in the absence of morphological productivity a high Constituent Frequency by itself is not sufficient to give rise to effects of morphology in lexical processing.

5. GENERAL DISCUSSION

We have addressed the question how low-frequency opaque complex words with high-frequency constituents are processed. Are the constituents of semantically opaque complex words identified just as for transparent words? If so, is this effect a genuine morphological effect, or does it arise irrespective of morphological productivity? If morphological decomposition is involved, how then might the unpredictable meanings of opaque complex words be accessed?

Experiment 1 contrasted low-frequency complex words with respect to their Constituent Frequency. Words with a high Constituent Frequency (i.e., with a high Base Lemma Frequency, a high Base Family size, and a high Base Family Frequency) were found to elicit shorter response latencies in visual lexical decision than words with a low Constituent Frequency. Surprisingly, this effect was equally large for opaque and transparent words. Interestingly, the opaque words did not show reliable correlations of our measures of Constituent Frequency with the response latencies, in contrast to the transparent words. At the same time, the opaque words also did not reveal any correlation of Surface Frequency with the response latencies.

Experiment 2 addressed the question whether the constituents of opaque words, which are apparently identified, also activate their meanings, and if so, in what order the meaning of the base word and the opaque meaning of the complex word become available. A semantic priming experiment with opaque complex words as primes revealed that both the usual opaque meaning as well as the meaning of the base becomes available. Surprisingly, despite the low surface frequency of the complex word itself, and despite the absence of a Surface Frequency effect in the correlations of Experiment 1, the first meaning to become active is the opaque one. Conversely, the meaning of the base becomes available relatively late, only after the activation of the opaque meaning has already entered decay. We have interpreted these results by adding an integration mechanism to the lemma nodes of the activation model proposed by Schreuder & Baayen (1995). The functionality of this integration mechanism is to redirect activation to idiosyncratic meanings on the basis of activated constituents when the direct route fails to do so efficiently.

In the case of particle verbs, for which the integration mechanism was first proposed (Schreuder, 1990), the direct route fails due to the separation of the particle from its base by intervening materials. In the present case of low-frequency opaque complex words with high-frequency constituents, the direct route fails due to the frequency imbalance. In both cases, an integration mechanism allows efficient access to idiosyncratic meanings. The integration mechanism depends on the output of the segmentation process, which leads to the activation of the access representations of the constituents. Since high-frequency constituents are activated more quickly than low-frequency constituents, we observe an effect of Constituent Frequency in Experiment 1 irrespective of whether complex words are semantically transparent. However, since integration is involved in the processing of opaque words, extra variability is introduced, leading to the absence of reliable correlations of our measures for Constituent Frequency with the response latencies for the opaque words in Experiment 1.

Experiment 3 considered the possibility that the effect of constituent frequency observed in Experiments1 and 2 might arise only for complex words with productive constituents. To this end, the effect of Constituent Frequency was examined for productive morphology in the Germanic stratum of Dutch and for unproductive morphology in the Romance stratum of Dutch. We found an effect of Constituent Frequency only for the productive morphology. This shows that morphological productivity is a necessary condition for the effect of Constituent Frequency.

We are not the first to call attention to effects of the morphological structure of opaque words in visual lexical processing. Bentin and Feldman (1990, see also Stolz & Feldman, 1995) observed repetition priming both at short and long repetition lags for morphologically but not semantically related words. Unfortunately, repetition priming is a task that does not allow the researcher to disentangle effects of morphological structure that occur during lexical access itself and effects due to shared morphological representations in the central lexicon that become available after completion of lexical access. Our experiments suggest that the early stages of lexical processing already reveal effects of morphological structure for opaque words with productive constituents.

At first sight, our results contrast with those obtained by Zwitserlood (1994), Sandra (1990), and Marslen-Wilson, Tyler, Waksler, and Older (1994). Zwitserlood (1994) studied the role of semantic transparency in the processing of nominal compounds in Dutch. Using the same priming technique as in our Experiment 2 she observed no priming effect for target words semantically related to one of the constituents of opaque compounds. Zwitserlood concludes that the constituents of opaque compounds are not identified and do not activate their meaning. However, Zwitserlood used an SOA of 300 ms. We observed a solid priming effect at a later SOA of 500 ms. Our findings suggest that the SOA of 300 ms used by Zwitserlood is perhaps too small to allow effects of priming to become visible. In our interpretation, the meaning of the constituent is still inhibited by the meaning of the complex word as a whole.

Sandra (1990), using similar techniques for the study of nominal compounds, also observed no effect of priming on target words that are semantically related to one of the constituents of opaque compounds. As pointed out by Zwitserlood (1994), the specific experimental procedure used by Sandra resulted in SOAs of approximately one second. Sandra also concludes that the constituents of opaque compounds do not play a role in lexical processing. We suspect that at this long SOA used by Sandra, the meanings of the constituents of opaque complex words have fully decayed. But at an SOA of 500 ms, we observe reliable effects of priming. Thus it appears that Zwitserlood and Sandra have studied possible effects of morphology for opaque complex words using SOAs that are either too short or too long. Clearly, a wider range of SOAs is required in further studies of opaque compounds.

Marslen-Wilson et al. (1994) studied transparent and opaque derived words using cross-modal priming. They observed effects of priming for transparent derived words with respect to their stems (e.g., *punishment* – punish) but not for opaque derived words (*casualty* – casual). Their conclusion is that morphological structure is irrelevant for the processing of opaque complex words (but see Burani, 1993). We suspect that also in the auditory modality the first meaning to become available is the meaning of the opaque derived word itself. When visual targets are presented at the offset of the auditory primes, the meaning of the base constituents might well not be available yet, just as in the visual modality at short SOAs. Of course, the temporal nature of auditory presentation of the prime might affect the extent to which the meaning of the base word is still available at word offset, i.e., after the suffix. Further experimental research with a broader range of SOAs is required to ascertain whether and when the meanings of the constituents of opaque words are activated in the auditory modality.

What our results indicate is that morphological structure has some role to play even for opaque complex words, contrary to our own expectations (Baayen, 1993; Frauenfelder & Schreuder, 1992; Schreuder & Baayen, 1995). In fact, the evidence presented here converges with other evidence that morphology is not a-priori irrelevant for opaque complex words. Schreuder, Grendel, Poulisse, and van der Voort (1990) using an intramodal visual short SOA partial priming technique, observed effects of morphological structure for particle verbs, irrespective of their semantic transparency. Particle verbs in Dutch (e.g., *aanval*, 'on-fall', i.e., 'attack') are compounds the constituents of which can also occur with intervening words depending on the syntactic context. Syntactic flexibility enforces morphological parsing for particle verbs, irrespective of whether they are semantically opaque or not.

Similarly, Fleischeuers (1997) observed for idiomatic adjective-noun combinations such as *red herring* activation of both the meanings of the constituents as well as the meaning of the idiomatic combination as a whole, using visual priming tasks. As in our Experiment 2, constituent meanings are activated that are irrelevant to the meaning of the combination of constituents as a whole. Moreover, the time course of semantic processing of idioms seems to follow a similar pattern as we have observed in Experiment 2: It has often been observed that the idiomatic meaning of idiomatic phrases becomes available either first or in parallel with the literal meaning (see, e.g., Schweigert & Moates, 1988, and Swinney & Cutler, 1977).

Summing up, the constituents of opaque complex words can play a role in lexical processing in language comprehension. The experiments reported here for the visual modality suggest that in the case full-form access representations have too low resting activation levels to allow the direct route to complete lexical access before the parsing route, the parsing route is indeed involved. The parsing route activates the constituents, after which the integration mechanism of the lemma nodes in the central lexicon takes over the task of activating the required opaque meanings. Our conclusion is that, paradoxically, opaque words reveal more about morphology than we had ever thought.

6. NOTES

[1] The verb *branden*, 'to burn', and its nominalization *branding*, 'surf', originally derive from the Indo-Germanic root *bhere(u)-*, 'to move vehemently'. In the verb, this meaning aspect applies to the flames, in the noun, it applies to the waves. See De Vries de Tollenaere, 1958.

[2] Note that these results cannot be attributed to backward priming, as backward priming effects in lexical decision tasks typically do not decrease with increasing SOA, as shown by Peterson & Simpson (1989).

[3] In other words, the integration mechanism is an implementation of the knowledge that the language user has of conditional probabilities. The probability that *vallen* means 'to fall' is high, but the conditional probability that *vallen* means 'to fall' in the context of *af* is low.

7. APPENDIX A

Word	RT	Fsurf	FBase	Vf	Nf	Base Meaning	Word Meaning
Opaque, high Constituent Frequency							
achterlijk	630	260	24378	151	21703	behind	retarded
beeldig	508	58	8362	155	20613	image	gorgeous
bondig	629	109	847	44	2373	federation	terse
branding	608	307	4679	123	5348	burn	surf
geestig	515	307	8375	76	5277	ghost	funny
hartig	511	58	8059	123	6906	heart	tasty
kattig	557	37	3054	35	439	cat	catty
klinker	571	160	8209	21	972	sound	vowel
mondig	501	82	9798	39	1819	mouth	mature
roerig	608	79	1499	22	3164	rudder	turbulent
statig	683	374	12305	130	5014	state	solemn
waarachtig	646	448	69252	117	101846	true	truly
zekering	666	16	24640	72	8781	sure	fuse
zuiger	540	39	1312	40	1666	suck	piston
Means	584	167	13198	82	13280		

Opaque, low Constituent Frequency							
drachtig	627	34	78	5	260	garb	with young
jachtig	565	72	1104	40	931	hunt	hectic
krampachtig	623	467	326	20	787	spasm	frenetic
kranig	646	115	629	18	289	tap	brave
mollig	588	308	116	3	327	mole	plump
morsig		(69)	(212)	(5)	(98)	spill	messy
scheutig		(25)	(346)	(4)	(139)	splash	lavish
schichtig	694	308	47	3	402	flash	nervous
schutting	536	229	95	16	799	lock	fence
slijter	618	18	310	15	768	wear	liquor merchant
stamper	663	40	581	7	258	stamp	pistil
stierlijk	641	23	545	10	161	bull	beastly
tering	692	58	697	34	1127	tar	consumption
vinnig	630	222	234	8	318	fin	caustic
Means	627	158	397	15	536		

8. APPENDIX A (CONTINUED)

Word	RT	Fsurf	FBase	Vf	Nf	Base Meaning	Word Meaning
Transparent, high Constituent Frequency							
bangig		(11)	(7921)	(9)	(420)	afraid	somewhat afraid
bloedig	510	336	5801	115	4418	blood	bloody
bouwer	571	145	4840	243	14939	build builder	
eindig	595	89	6599	12	10236	end	finite
hoekig	566	205	5059	54	2912	edge with edges	
houtig	582	20	2056	113	4795	wood	woody
meting	642	285	1918	69	12059	measure	measurement
puntig	588	245	8842	136	11768	point pointed	
roodachtig	639	162	7055	59	2474	red	reddish
stoffig	535	443	4422	138	6161	dust	dusty
trekking	557	45	22587	126	32984	draw drawing	
vaderlijk	571	278	24412	50	4475	father	fatherly
waterig	556	249	15497	282	5863	water	watery
werper	641	70	4882	51	4816	throw	thrower
Means	582	198	8767	111	9069		

Transparent, low Constituent Frequency							
ijverig	548	498	576	16	941	diligence	diligent
moerassig	638	86	481	14	162	swamp	swampy
nukkig	624	77	37	2	84	quirk	quirky
ridderlijk	615	45	565	22	336	knight	knightly
roeier	623	45	537	13	794	row	rower
romig	642	159	240	21	624	cream	creamy
schimmig	585	98	513	10	218	shadow	shadowy
splijting		(20)	(248)	(8)	(164)	split	splitting
splitsing	633	200	429	8	363	bifurcate	bifurcation
spookachtig	565	207	856	15	659	spook	spooky
venijnig	719	258	64	2	270	venom	venomous
vettig	546	374	1604	45	1002	fat	fatty
wollig	574	83	423	22	671	wool	woolly
zaaier	635	45	642	15	615	sow	sower
Means	612	167	536	16	518		

Materials for Experiment 1: RT: response latency; Fsurf: Surface Frequency, FBase: Base Lemma Frequency; Vf: Base Family Size; Nf: Base Family Frequency. Means per group after removal of error-prone items, the items listed without a mean RT.

9. APPENDIX B.1

Relatedness	Prime	Freq	Target	Freq	English Translation Base	Word	Target
base	branding	307	vuur	4646	burn	surf	fire
derived	branding		zee	6056	burn	surf	sea
-	schuchter	316			vuur	timid	fire
-	schuchter		zee			timid	sea
base	kattig	37	poes	3054	cat	catty	pussy
derived	kattig		snibbig	49	cat	catty	snappish
-	krokant	21	poes			crusty	pussy
-	krokant		snibbig			crusty	snappish
base	beeldig	58	scherm	981	image	gorgeous	screen
derived	beeldig		mooi	15065	image	gorgeous	beautiful
-	secuur	79	scherm			secure	screen
-	secuur		mooi			secure	beautiful
base	hartig	58	bloed	5801	heart	tasty	blood
derived	hartig		zout	2121	heart	tasty	salt(y)
-	egaal	87	bloed			smooth	blood
-	egaal		zout			smooth	salt(y)

10. APPENDIX B.1 (CONTINUED)

Relatedness Prime Freq Target Freq English Translation							
base	lijvig	69	lichaam	12378	body	corpulent	body
derived	lijvig		dik	6724	body	corpulent	fat
-	bruto	140	lichaam			gross	body
-	bruto		dik			gross	fat
base	potig	71	been	8098	paw	burly	leg
derived	potig		fors	805	paw	burly	sturdy
-	alert	134	been			alert	leg
-	alert		fors			alert	sturdy
base	roerig	79	boot	2835	rudder	turbulent	boat
derived	roerig		druk	13117	rudder	turbulent	busy
-	ultiem	93	boot			ultimate	boat
-	ultiem		druk			ultimate	busy
base	mondig	82	lip	4594	mouth	mature	lip
derived	mondig		weerbaar	92	mouth	mature	able-bodied
-	robuust	151	lip			robust	lip
-	robuust		weerbaar			robust	able-bodied
base	houterig	88	boom	5862	wood	stiff	tree
derived	houterig		stijf	1806	wood	stiff	stiff
-	accuraat	96	boom			accurate	tree
-	accuraat	stijf				accurate	stiff

11. APPENDIX B.1 (CONTINUED)

Relatedness	Prime	Freq	Target	Freq	English Translation		
					Base	Word	Target
base	beestachtig	104	dier	7990	beast	bestial	animal
derived	beestachtig		gruwelijk	657	beast	bestial	gruesome
-	plausibe	1 154	dier			plausible	animal
-	plausibel		gruwelijk			plausible	gruesome
base	bondig	109	club	956	federation	terse	club
derived	bondig		kort	14846	federation	terse	short
-	subliem	162	club			sublime	club
-	subliem		kort			sublime	short
base	achterlijk	260	voor	293908	behind	retarded	before
derived	achterlijk		gek	5822	behind	retarded	idiot
-	clandestien	238	voor			clandestine	before
-	clandestien		gek			clandestine	idiot
base	geestig	307	spook	856	ghost	funny	phantom
derived	geestig		leuk	4026	ghost	funny	funny
-	discreet	443	spook			discrete	phantom
-	discreet		leuk			discrete	funny
base	huiselijk	364	deur	15927	house	homely	door
derived	huiselijk		knus	157	house	homely	cozy
-	continue	355	deur			continuous	door
-	continue		knus			continuous	cozy
base	statig	374	land	18637	state	solemn	country
derived	statig		deftig	647	state	solemn	dignified
-	attent	383	land			attentive	country
-	attent		deftig			attentive	dignified
base	jarig	382	maand	9727	year	birthday	month
derived	jarig		feest	2606	year	birthday	feast
-	ijdel	310	maand			vane	month
-	ijdel		feest			vane	feast
base	gangbaar	584	hal	1278	corridor	valid	hall
derived	gangbaar		gewoon	13509	corridor	valid	normal
-	vitaal	493	hal			vital	hall
-	vitaal		gewoon			vital	normal

Materials for Experiment 2: primes, targets, and their Surface Frequencies.

12. APPENDIX B.2

Type	Example	Familiarity Rating	Frequency
prime	branding	5.2	191
target stem	vuur	6.9	21980
target derived	zee	6.4	7765
prime control	schuchter	4.5	215
stem	brand	6.5	9691

Mean familiarity ratings (7-point scale) and mean surface frequency for the materials of Experiment 2.

Condition	Example	Relatedness Rating
Stem-related	branding- vuur	2.36
Derived-related	branding- zee	6.09
Stem-related control	schuchter- vuur	1.15
Derived-related control	schuchter- zee	1.94

Mean relatedness ratings (7-point scale) for the materials of Experiment 2.

13. APPENDIX C

Romance, high Constituent Frequency						
Word	RT	Fsurf	Vf	Nf	English translations constituents	 full form
ab+ject		(14)	(97)	(9802)	off+throw	despicable
ad+struct+ie		(24)	(142)	(8979)	to+build+ion	substantiation
af+fect	565	44	77	8453	to+grasp	affect
con+vent	636	36	27	5912	together+come	monastery
de+cept+ie	662	7	56	5288	off+take+ion	deception
de+duct+ie	663	53	66	13714	off+lead+ion	deduction
de+termin+ist	743	11	44	7209	off+border+ist	determinist
gener+iek	695	17	60	7210	generate+ic	generic
in+finit+ief	669	4	31	5516	un+finite+ish	infinitive
part+ikel		(20)	(214)	(20390)	depart+ie	particle
port+o	626	98	154	9924	carry+o	postage
re+vis+or		(46)	(140)	(11943)	re+see+or	corrector
su(s)+spect		718	4 80	12275	under+see	suspect
tra+verse		(8)	(17)	(12011)	across+turn	arcade
Means	664	30	66	8389		
Romance, low Constituent Frequency						
al+lus+ie		(26)	(14)	(1608)	to+play+ion	allusion
cant+ate		(25)	(6)	(40)	sing+ IMP	cantata
de+script+ie	605	13	12	954	off+write+ion	description
de+sert+ie	620	46	7	340	off+leave+ion	desertion
dict+ie		(15)	(33)	(1506)	say+ion	diction
fract+uur	578	34	20	797	break+ure	fracture
nov+iteit	738	9	19	356	new+ity	novelty
pend+ant	679	75	8	231	hang+ant	counterpart
pict+o+gram	679	4	3	56	picture+o+write	pictogram
puls+ar		(13)	(12)	(995)	throb+er	pulsar
re+cid+ive		(11)	(12)	(1069)	back+fall	relapse
re+flect+or	629	19	6	480	back+bend+er	reflector
tract+ie		(2)	(37)	(1963)	pull+ion	traction
voc+aal	621	51	29	2250	call+al	vocal
Means	644	31	13	683		

14. APPENDIX C (CONTINUED)

Word	RT	Fsurf	Fbase	Vf	Nf	English Translations: constituents	English Translations: full form
Germanic, high Constituent Frequency							
be+hoeft+ig	595	51	10297	16	7223	be+need+ish	needy
draag+baar	550	47	11963	81	20209	bear+able	bearable
eis+er+es		(8)	(5691)	(19)	(8883)	claim+er+FEMALE	claimant
gekk+erd	643	11	5822	17	6401	foolish+er	fool
groei+sel	645	14	8425	50	11397	grow+ee	growth
handel+baar	558	20	6942	251	26220	trade+able	tradeable
her+kies+baar	653	4	7973	80	11955	re+elect+able	re-electable
klaag+ster	667	9	1544	29	3113	complain+er FEM	complainer
leeg+heid	553	36	5451	29	6948	empty+ness	emptiness
leuk+heid	602	3	4026	3	4057	jolly+ness	jollity
on+kund+ig	627	101	103	141	6783	un+knowledge+ish	unknowledgeable
proev+er	575	17	2223	46	4819	taste+er	taster
toon+der	666	43	9400	56	18515	show+er	someone who shows
wend+baar	601	24	2613	17	4551	turn+able	turnable
Means	611	29	5906	63	10169		
Germanic, low Constituent Frequency							
bad+er		34	558	4	637	bathe+er	bather
ge+zwets	648	26	24	2	60	ing+blather	blathering
gluiper+ig	45	0	3	73		shifty-eyed person+ish	like a ...
goei+erd	628	13	1312	3	894	good+er	kind soul
griep+erig	697	9	284	7	342	flue+ish	ill with flue
hut+achtig		(2)	(1635)	(18)	(1955)	hut+like	hutlike
krui+er	621	76	19	2	290	carry+er	carrier
ribbel+ig	699	7	53	2	60	rib+ish	ribbed
scharrel+aar	637	19	379	8	545	rummage+er	rummager
snoep+erij	581	9	353	12	524	eat sweets+ery	the eating of sweets
splijt+baar	674	24	248	8	412	split+able	splitable
stevig+heid	575	53	3299	3	3561	firm+ness	firmness
viez+ig	658	15	1157	6	1312	dirty+ish	dirty-ish
voogd+es	691	26	807	16	1786	guardian+FEM	female guardian
Means	647	25	721	6	890		

Materials for Experiment 3: RT: response latency; Fsurf: Surface Frequency, FBase: Base Lemma Frequency; Vf: Base Family Size; Nf: Base Family Frequency. Means per group after removal of error-prone items, the items listed without a mean RT.

15. REFERENCES

Andrews, S.: 1986, Morphological influences on lexical access: lexical or non-lexical effects?, *Journal of Memory and Language* 25, 726-740.

Baayen, R. H.: 1993, On frequency, transparency, and productivity, in G. E. Booij and J. van Marle (eds), *Yearbook of Morphology 1992*, Kluwer Academic Publishers, Dordrecht, pp. 181-208.

Baayen, R. H., Burani, C. and Schreuder, R.: 1997, Effects of semantic markedness in the processing of regular nominal singulars and plurals in Italian, in G. E. Booij and J. v. Marle (eds), *Yearbook of Morphology 1996*, Kluwer Academic Publishers, Dordrecht, pp. 13-34.

Baayen, R. H., Dijkstra, T. and Schreuder, R.: 1997, Singulars and plurals in Dutch: Evidence for a parallel dual route model, *Journal of Memory and Language* 36, 94-117.

Baayen, R. H., Piepenbrock, R. and Gulikers, L.: 1995, *The CELEX lexical database* (CD-ROM), Linguistic Data Consortium, University of Pennsylvania, Philadelphia, PA.

Baayen, R. H., Schreuder, R., De Jong, N. H. and Krott, A.: 2001, Dutch inflection: the rules that prove the exception, in S. Nooteboom, F. Weerman, and F. Wijnen (eds), *Storage and computation in the language faculty*, Kluwer Academic Publishers, Dordrecht (in press).

Bergman, M. W., Hudson, P. T. W. and Eling, P. A. T.: 1988, How simple complex words can be: Morphological processing and word representation, *Quarterly Journal of Experimental Psychology* 40A, 41-72.

Bertram, R., Baayen, R. H. and Schreuder, R.: 1999, Effects of family size for derived and inflected words, *Journal of Memory and Language* yy, xx.

Burani, C. and Laudanna, A.: 1992, Units of representation for derived words in the lexicon, in R. Frost and L. Katz (eds), *Orthography, Phonology, Morphology, and Meaning*, Elsevier, Amsterdam, pp. 361-376.

Col\' e, P., Beauvillain, C. and Segui, J.: 1989, On the representation and processing of prefixed and suffixed derived words: A differential frequency effect, *Journal of Memory and Language* 28, 1-13.

Fleischeuers, M.: 1997, *Lexical representations and processing of idiomatic adjective-noun combinations*, PhD- Thesis, University of Nijmegen, The Netherlands.

Frauenfelder, U. H. and Schreuder, R.: 1992, Constraining psycholinguistic models of morphological processing and representation: The role of productivity, in G. E. Booij and J. v. Marle (eds), *Yearbook of Morphology 1991*, Kluwer Academic Publishers, Dordrecht, pp. 165-183.

James, C. T.: 1975, The role of semantic information in lexical decisions, *Journal of Experimental Psychology: Human Perception and Performance* 104, 130-136.

Marle, J. v.: 1985, *On the Paradigmatic Dimension of Morphological Creativity*, Foris, Dordrecht.

Marslen-Wilson, W., Tyler, L. K., Waksler, R. and Older, L.: 1994, Morphology and meaning in the English mental lexicon, *Psychological Review* 101, 3-33.

Peterson, R. R. and Simpson, G. B.: 1989, Effect of backward priming on word recognition in single-word and sentence context, *Journal of Experimental Psychology: Learning, Memory, and Cognition* 15, 1020-1032.

Sandra, D.: 1990, On the representation and processing of compound words: automatic access to constituent morphemes does not occur, *Quarterly Journal of Experimental Psychology* 42A, 529-567.

Schreuder, R.: 1990, Lexical processing of verbs with separable particles, *Yearbook of Morphology* 3, 65-79.

Schreuder, R. and Baayen, R.: 1997, How complex simplex words can be, *Journal of Memory and Language* 36, 118-139.

Schreuder, R. and Baayen, R. H.: 1994, Prefix-stripping re-revisited, *Journal of Memory and Language* 33, 357-375.

Schreuder, R. and Baayen, R. H.: 1995, Modeling morphological processing, in L. B. Feldman (ed.), *Morphological Aspects of Language Processing*, Lawrence Erlbaum, Hillsdale, New Jersey, pp. 131-154.

Schreuder, R., Grendel, M., Poulisse, N., Roelofs, A. and Voort, M. v. d.: 1990, Lexical processing, morphological complexity and reading, in D. A. Balotta, G. B. Flores d'Arcais and K. Rayner (eds), *Comprehension Processes in Reading*, Lawrence Erlbaum Associates, London.

Taft, M.: 1979, Recognition of affixed words and the word frequency effect, *Memory and Cognition* 7, 263-272.

De Vries, J. and de Tollenaere, F.: 1958, *Etymologisch Woordenboek*. Het Spectrum, Utrecht.

Zwitserlood, P.: 1994, The role of semantic transparency in the processing and representation of Dutch compounds, *Language and Cognitive Processes* 9, 341-368.

11. ACKNOWLEDGEMENT

We wish to thank Leonore Biegstraten for her help in running the experiments. This study was financially supported by the Dutch Research Council NWO grant to the first author). Requests for reprints should be addressed to R. H. Baayen, Interfaculty Research Unit for Language and Speech, University of Nijmegen, P.O.Box 310,6500 AH Nijmegen, The Netherlands.

12. ADDRESS FOR CORRESPONDENCE

R. Harald Baayen
Interfaculty Research Unit for Language and Speech (IWTS),
University of Nijmegen & Max Planck Institute for Psycholinguistics
Wundtlaan 1, 6525 XD Nijmegen
The Netherlands
Mailing address: P.O. Box 310, 6500 AH Nijmegen
Phone: 0031-24-3521510
Fax: 0031-24-3521213
email: baayen@mpi.nl

HAROLD NEFS, EGBERT M.H. ASSINK,
AND PAUL P.N.A. KNUIJT

EFFECTS OF SUBLEXICAL FREQUENCY AND MEANING IN PREFIXED WORDS

1. INTRODUCTION

Since the early seventies, when Taft and Forster (1975) started their research, the question has been raised how morphologically complex words are recognized by skilled and beginning readers. Several morphological word processing models have been proposed. Broadly speaking, three frameworks can be distinguished: the Prelexical Morphological Decomposition model (Taft & Forster, 1975), the full-listing model (Butterworth, 1983; Henderson, 1985), and the interactive models (AAM model (Caramazza, Laudanna & Romani, 1988), and the Interactive Activation model (Taft, 1994)).

In this paper, we argue that the interactive models are flexible and can therefore work as either a prelexical morphological decomposition model or as a full listing model, since languages are not uniform in morphological complexity. We conducted three experiments to investigate whether prefix-specific characteristics are relevant for the recognition of prefixed words. More specifically, we investigated the effects of prefix reliability, which is defined as the ratio of true to total (true and pseudo-prefixes) frequency of the prefix-unit. Before we describe these experiments, we discuss the three frameworks mentioned above and elaborate the ideas underlying this study.

2. MODELS OF MORPHOLOGICAL COMPLEX WORDS

2.1 *The Prelexical Morphological Decomposition Model*

It is assumed in the Prelexical Morphological Decomposition model (Taft & Forster, 1975) that the first step in the identification process of a prefixed word consists of stripping the prefix from the rest of the word. Since the stem is considered to be the primary access-unit to the lexicon, the prefix is temporarily set apart, while the stem is looked up in the lexicon. This model is accordingly referred to as the 'prefix-stripping model'. If the word stem is not found in the lexicon, the procedure is repeated with the whole word as an access unit. According to this model, words are stored in a 'decomposed lexicon' in which no redundant storage is allowed; that is, prefixes and word stems are represented separately, and only once, in the lexicon.

A drawback of this method is that words containing a pseudo-prefix are incorrectly stripped. Pseudo-prefixes are initial syllables that orthographically resemble a prefix, but are, in morphological terms, not true prefixes; for example, *re-* in *relish* is a pseudo-prefix. Incorrect stripping of pseudo-prefixes complicates word identification, and is especially disadvantageous for readers of languages with many and highly frequent pseudo-prefixes (Schreuder & Baayen, 1994).

2.2 *The Full-Listing Model*

The full-listing model (Butterworth, 1983; Henderson, 1985) is more or less the opposite of the prefix-stripping model. Prefixes are never stripped from the word stems. A word is directly recognized as a single unit, not as a composition of smaller units; in other words, the whole word serves as an access unit to the lexicon. Errors due to incorrect stripping of pseudo-prefixes do not occur, which is a strong advantage over the previous model. A disadvantage of this model is that it requires large storage capacity. Every word form is stored separately, which obviously requires a much larger lexicon. Word representations are not as efficiently stored as in the prefix stripping model, and retrieval is possibly more elaborate and time consuming; but on the other hand, processing is more reliable.

Schreuder, Grendel, Poulisse, Roelofs & Van de Voort (1990) found evidence that, at least in Dutch, this model cannot be rejected. They found no evidence for a decomposed lexicon. However, opposite results were found in Italian (Caramazza, Laudanna & Romani, 1988; Jarvella, Job, Sandström & Schreuder, 1987). A decomposed lexicon proved to be more appropriate for that language. The appropriateness of the prefix-stripping model and the full-listing model appears to be dependent on language specific properties.

2.3 *Interactive models*

The descriptive validity of the full listing and the prefix-stripping model for a particular language is determined by the particular characteristics of all prefixes in that language. Those models treat prefixes as if they form a homogeneous class; interactive models on the other hand treat them individually. We hypothesize that the principle of minimizing the need for storage capacity while keeping retrieval as efficient as possible (Sandra, 1994) applies to all languages alike. However, if applied to different languages, it will lead to different outcomes if all prefixes are treated in the experimental design as a homogeneous class.

We will refer to interactive models that are based on morpheme and word-specific-characteristics as 'hybrid models'. Depending on the generalized properties of all morphemes in a language, a hybrid model may manifest itself as either a full listing model, a prefix stripping model or a mix of both. That is, some languages have many affixes, which makes these languages suitable for a decomposing strategy, whereas others only have a small number, which makes a full listing model more appropriate. Differences found between languages are actually particular manifestations of a hybrid model. A hybrid model may explain the conflicting findings between languages (cf. Caramazza, et al. (1988), Jarvella et al. (1987), vs., Schreuder & Baayen (1994)). Three influential interactive models must be discussed briefly here: Schreuder & Baayen's (1995) Morphological Race Model, the Augmented Addressed Morphology Model of Caramazza et al. (1988) and Taft's (1994) Interactive Activation Model. All models may be classified as hybrid, since they operate on prefix-specific characteristics.

The *Morphological Race Model* (Schreuder & Baayen, 1995) is based on a spreading activation network with three representational layers: a layer of form-based modality-specific access representations (lexemes) and a layer of integration nodes (lemmas) which in turn are linked to a third layer of semantic and syntactic representations. The direct route maps a full-form access representation onto its associated lemma node, which in turn activates its semantic and syntactic representations. In addition, the model contains a parsing route that operates in parallel with the direct route. According to Baayen and Schreuder, the most important difference between the Morphological Race Model and the Augmented Addressed Morphology Model (AAM Model, see next paragraph) is that the parsing route and the direct route are engaged in the recognition process from the very beginning of the recognition process (Baayen, Dijkstra & Schreuder, 1997, p.97).

The *Augmented Addressed Morphology (AAM) Model* (Caramazza et al., 1988) and the Interactive Activation (IA) model (Taft, 1994, see below) have several options for identification and both assume that access to the central lexicon can be strengthened or weakened depending on recurrent input. It is assumed in the AAM model that if a prefixed word is read a number of times, the whole word itself becomes to act as an access unit. Recognition in these models is based on morpheme and word specific parameters. The exact underlying mechanism is not important at the moment and is not described by its designers, but it may be a neural network as proposed by Seidenberg & McClelland (1989).

The AAM model has been characterized as a horse race model. In the AAM model, both whole word and morphemes have access representations. A complex word gets its own whole word representation after it has been processed in morpheme chunks several times. A word can always be recognized by its constituent morphemes if it does not have an opaque meaning. A still unidentified word activates morphemic representations of the stem and the affix. This is only a weak activation, because the orthographic overlap between input and representation is small. As a result, recognition is severely slowed down. The orthographic overlap is large in case of a whole word match. Whole word identification (if possible) is much faster because of the larger overlap between input and representation. Reading a non-word like *rewoman* is always realized through slower morphemic representations. Literate people usually do not have whole word representations for this kind of non-words, unless they have done research in this area. Morphemic and whole word identification work at the same time. Possible mutually facilitating or inhibiting interactions between these representations have not been made explicit.

According to the *Interactive Activation model* (Taft, 1994), there are several levels of activation. Word identification starts at the grapheme level and works its way up through a morpheme level and a word level to the concept level. The concept level contains abstract semantic and grammatical information. The morpheme level is, in contrast to the AAM model, serially organized with respect to the word level. The morpheme level also connects directly to the concept level. An important feature of this model is that it explicitly allows top-down interference between the recognition levels. The nature of this top down influence has not yet been specified. Like in the AAM model a frequently encountered word gets a full representation at the word level which grows stronger the more it is used. The IA model is thus an alternative interactive model based on word and morpheme specific aspects.

A serious drawback of the AAM model and the IA model is that it is difficult, if not impossible, to discriminate between them empirically. Levels of interaction between word and subword representation are different for both models, but these architectures have no discriminating properties that can be tested (Taft, 1994). At this level of explicitness, it may even be possible to design a third model with a different architecture that cannot be distinguished from those models either. We argue that architecture is not the most important feature of these models. It is more important to keep in mind that both the AAM model and the IA model are intrinsically hybrid. Interactions between 'routes' or 'levels' are organized with respect to morpheme and word specific characteristics. In our view, this aspect of interactive models is far more important than the architectural difference between them.

What we have to do first instead of concentrating on the architectural differences between the AAM and the IA model is to focus on the relevant processing parameters. Prefix reliability and sublexical frequency are two possibly relevant processing parameters, because these are morpheme-specific devices, which the recognition system can use to minimize storage while keeping the efficiency of word identification as high as possible.

3. PREFIX RELIABILITY

In this study, we focused on the recognition of prefixed words. Although the interactive models discussed above cannot be discriminated empirically, it is possible to evaluate the parameters involved in the processing of morphologically complex words. We hypothesize that morpheme and word-specific characteristics determine how morphologically complex words are recognized. Prefix reliability is a possibly important morpheme characteristic. Prefix reliability is defined as the ratio of sublexical frequency of true prefixes to the sublexical frequency of all orthographically identical letter clusters (prefixes and pseudo-prefixes). Prefix reliability is calculated for a single prefix; that is, it is morpheme specific, not language specific. A small ratio implies that the prefix is morphologically inconsistent. For this reason, we call this an unreliable prefix. Prefixes with a high ratio on the other hand are 'reliable' prefixes. The Dutch word *hertog* (En. *duke*) starts with a pseudo-prefix. *Her-* is unreliable, since it appears relatively frequently as a pseudo-prefix. *Ver-* is a reliable prefix in Dutch. *Verenkleed* (En. *feather skin*) is one of the very few examples in which *ver-* is a pseudo-prefix.

Schreuder and Baayen (1994) performed a statistical lexicographic investigation into this parameter. Table 1 presents a summary of their findings. Even in a language of minor morphological complexity like Dutch, prefixes do not constitute a homogeneous class. *Her-* and *on-* are clear examples of unreliable prefixes, whereas *ont-* and *ver-* represent reliable prefixes.

Table 1. Ratio type frequency true prefixes/total type frequency letter pattern. Adapted from: Schreuder & Baayen, 1994

Prefix	Reliability
Her-	57% (low)
On-	59%
Be-	82%
Ont-	92%
Ver-	96% (high)

Laudanna, Burani & Cermele (1994) investigated whether sublexical frequency and prefix reliability affect the processing of Italian words. They used non-words, consisting of a true stem and a true, non-matching prefix; for instance, *rinido*, which means *re-nest*. They used words like *panido* as a control condition. *Pa-* is a non-semantic/non-morphemic unit having an equal sublexical frequency as the prefix. The difference in response latencies between both conditions was the dependent variable in that study. They found main effects of both sublexical frequency of the prefix and of prefix reliability. They found that non-words with a reliable prefix resulted in longer response latencies. Therefore, they concluded that only reliable prefixes were stripped in non-words.

Can this finding be generalized to other languages? If this is the case, comparable results should also be found in a morphologically less complex language like Dutch. A recognition system that functions as predicted by a hybrid model can be tuned to this parameter in Dutch as well as in Italian. In the first experiment presented here, reliability and sublexical frequency of the prefix are studied for Dutch[1]. Experiment 2 focuses on prefix reliability and semantic interpretability of the non-words. Prefix reliability is also studied in Experiment 3, using a different method. Real words and non-words were used in Experiment 1 and 3. We used only non-words in the second experiment.

4. EXPERIMENT 1

In order to find evidence for functional use of prefixes as access codes in polysyllabic words in Dutch, three hypotheses are tested. The first hypothesis is that Dutch non-words containing a prefix element, like *ver-* in *vertulp* (*tulp* means *tulip* in English, *ver-* is a semantic modifier, see examples in Appendix 8.1), are predicted to show longer response latencies and higher error rates than the control non-words like *kertulp*, where the stem is preceded by a non-morphemic letter combination (*ker-*). The idea behind this hypothesis is that when a non-word contains a prefix, the access representation of the prefix is activated. No access representation is activated in case of a non-morphemic letter combination.

The second hypothesis predicts a differential effect of prefix reliability for non-words including a prefix. In congruence with the results of the Laudanna et al. (1994) experiment with Italian, it is predicted that only reliable prefixes will be stripped. This implies larger differences between reliable prefix and control non-words (comparable to the LN-HP and HN-HP conditions in the Laudanna et al. (1994) study) than between unreliable prefix and control words (the LN-LP condition). Thus, only reliable prefixes are predicted to facilitate morphological decomposition of non-word polysyllabic words.

The third hypothesis deals with the issue of reading experience. It is predicted that differences between unreliable and reliable prefixes will not manifest themselves clearly in the case of less experienced readers like children. This expectation is based on the suggestion of Laudanna et al. (1994) that the lexical system gradually develops and reflects the skill level of the reader. Children simply have less reading experience, and consequently less experience with morphologically complex words.

4.1 Method

4.2 Participants

Thirty-two students at Utrecht University (age range: 20 to 24 years) and thirty-two eighth-grade elementary school pupils (age range: 11 to 12 years) participated in the experiment. Students were paid for their efforts.

4.3 Materials

Forty experimental non-words, forty comparable control non-words and forty experimental words were selected. In addition, thirty-two filler non-words and sixty-six filler words were used. So, each individual subject was presented with a total of 218 stimuli. The order of the items was randomized. Examples of the stimuli are listed in Appendix 8.1. The forty experimental non-words were constructed by combining a real Dutch prefix with a real Dutch noun. In the forty comparable control non-words the same noun was preceded by a non-morphemic orthographic sequence, matched for letter cluster frequency. Four different prefixes and four control orthographic sequences were used. Each prefix was combined with ten different words and the control sequences were combined with the same ten words. The four prefixes are selected with the help of the types-frequency data published by Schreuder & Baayen (1994).

The non-morphemic orthographic sequences used for constructing the control non-words had the same consonant-vowel structure and bigram or trigram frequency in initial position as the prefixes they were matched with, see Table 2.

Table 2. Positional trigram frequency data of prefix and control trigrams. Trigram frequencies are taken from Rolf & Van Rijnsoever (1984)

Prefix		Non-prefix	
her-	609	ker-	601
on-	4556	an-	4342
ont-	1127	ond-	1436
ver-	7061	wer-	6987

The orthographic similarity of both types of non-words to true words was measured by means of the N-count (Coltheart, Davelaar, Jonasson, & Besner, 1977). The N-count is the total number of words that can be drawn from each non-word by changing one letter at a time to another letter, preserving letter position. The N-count of each prefixed and control non-word is zero. All prefixed and control non-words were seven or eight letters in length (Uit den Boogaart, 1975). In contrast to the procedure by Laudanna et al. (1994), the experimental list was not split into two sublists. Laudanna and his colleagues decided to split the list in order to avoid presenting the same embedded word (noun) in a prefixed and in a non-prefixed non-word to the same subject. In the present experiments we do not follow this line of thinking. Taking into consideration that from a methodological point of view within-subjects comparisons are preferable it was decided not to split the list of experimental items.

4.3.1 Apparatus

The experiment was presented to the subjects using an IBM computer 30/286 using the MEL program (Micro Experimental Laboratory, Schneider, 1988). The stimuli were presented in white lowercase letters against a black background. The participants were instructed to respond as fast and accurately as possible, by pushing a green button when they considered the item to be a word and a red button when the item was considered a non-word.

4.3.2 Procedure

Each subject was tested individually. The experiment lasted about 15 minutes. The instructions appeared on the computer monitor. The participants were given a series of 10 practice trials before the experimental trials began. Following each practice trial feedback about the correctness of the response was given. The stimuli were arranged in two blocks of 109 items separated by a 1-minute rest period. The items were presented in random order, all in the center of the monitor. Before an item appeared on the screen, a fixation point (+) was presented on the center of the screen for 140 ms. Next the stimulus was presented. If the subject did not respond within a preset time limit of 2 seconds, the stimulus disappeared automatically. In all other cases the stimulus disappeared when the subject pressed a button. After the stimulus had disappeared, a visual mask consisting of five asterisks (*****) was presented for 100 ms on the same place where the stimulus had been displayed. After 700 ms the fixation point (+) for the next trial appeared.

4.3.3 Design

Since we had no specific hypotheses about differential performance patterns in adults and children besides the expected effect of reading experience (cf. hypothesis 3), the data for the two groups were analyzed separately. In other words, we replicated the Laudanna et al. (1994) experiment with adults and with children separately. Therefore, no between subjects (grouping) factor was used in this experiment. The data were analyzed in two complementary steps: first the full three-way factorial 2 x 2 x 2 design Prefixedness (prefix/pseudo-prefix) by Reliability (unreliable/reliable) by Frequency (high/low) analysis of variance was performed. This analysis provided information about the effect of prefix in this type of decision task. For the specific testing of the functionality hypotheses, a new dependent variable was calculated, the difference score on the prefixed experimental non-words and the corresponding non-prefixed experimental non-words, i.e. the net difference scores on the prefixedness factor[2]. Thus, for the test of the functionality hypothesis a two-way 2 x 2 Reliability (unreliable/reliable) and Frequency (high/low) within-subjects factorial design was used.

4.4 Results

Dependent variables were response latencies for correct decisions and accuracy (% errors). Since surface (whole word) frequency was not controlled for in the present experiment the data on true words were not taken into consideration. Only significant effects found are reported. Two subjects, one adult student and one elementary school pupil, were removed from the data set because they were considered to be outliers. The student produced extremely high response latencies (two standard deviations or more above the group mean). The elementary school pupil made an extreme number of errors throughout the experiment. First the results of the adult students are discussed; this is followed by an analogous presentation of the children's data.

4.4.1 Adults: Non-word Data

In Table 3, mean response latencies and error percentage for the non-words are presented. Also the net differences in response latencies and errors between experimental non-words and control non-words are displayed.

Valid trials with correct responses made within a time limit of 2 seconds were included in the data analysis. Two three-way 2 x 2 x 2 Prefixedness (prefix/non-prefix) x Reliability (unreliable/reliable) x Frequency (high/low) analyses of variance were computed, one for the response latencies, and one for accuracy. For both dependent measures a significant main effect for Prefixedness was observed, for response latencies [$F_s(1,30)=47.04$, $p<0.001$ and $F_i(1,35)=8.24$, $p<.001$] and for accuracy [$F_s(1,30)=11.94$, $p<0.01$ and $F_i(1,35)=5.21$, $p<.03$]. Response latencies and error percentage were higher when the non-words included a prefix in comparison to non-words including a non-morphemic letter sequence (769 vs. 684 ms and 4.35% vs. 1.75% errors, respectively). Additional analyses of variance were performed with difference scores: the difference in response latencies and errors between non-words including a prefix and comparable non-words without a prefix. A two-way 2 x 2 Reliability (unreliable/reliable) by Frequency (high/low) analysis of variance was computed with both subject and item means as units. For the response latencies there was a significant main effect for Reliability in both the subjects analysis [$F_s(1,30)=7.49$, $p<0.04$] and the items analysis [$F_i(1,35)=5.178$, $p<0.04$] (105 ms net difference for the unreliable prefixes versus 64 ms for reliable prefixes).

Table 3. Students - non-words. Mean RT in ms. and error percentage for the prefix and control non-prefix conditions

	Experimental Non-words			Control Non-words		Differences	
	RT (sd)	Errors (sd)		RT (sd)	Errors (sd)	RT	Errors
HER-	*792 (122)*	*4.5% (6.2)*	**KER-**	*683 (90)*	*1.3% (3.4)*	*109*	*3.2%*
ON-	*762 (117)*	*4.2% (8.1)*	**AN-**	*660 (100)*	*1.9% (4.0)*	*102*	*2.3%*
ONT-	*746 (126)*	*2.9 % (5.3)*	**OND-**	*694 (116)*	*0.6% (2.5)*	*53*	*2.3%*
VER-	*776 (105)*	*5.8% (6.7)*	**WER-**	*700 (102)*	*3.2% (6.0)*	*76*	*2.6%*

4.4.2 Elementary school pupils: Non-word Data

Table 4 presents mean response latencies, error percentage and the net differences for the non-words.

Table 4. Elementary school pupils - non-words. Mean response latencies (RT) in ms. and error percentage for the prefix and control pseudo-prefix conditions

	Experimental Non-words			Control Non-words		Differences	
	RT (sd)	Errors (sd)		RT (sd)	Errors (sd)	RT	Errors
HER-	*956 (126)*	*7.4% (10.3)*	**KER-**	*929 (116)*	*4.5% (7.7)*	*27*	*2.9%*
ON-	*928 (154)*	*7.4% (9.3)*	**AN-**	*923 (151)*	*4.8% (8.5)*	*5*	*2.6%*
ONT-	*934 (121)*	*4.5% (6.8)*	**OND-**	*924 (120)*	*6.1% (8.0)*	*10*	*-1.6%*
VER-	*971 (137)*	*12.6% (12.1)*	**WER-**	*922 (125)*	*4.2% (6.2)*	*49*	*8.4%*

Table 4 demonstrates that the response latencies and error rates for elementary school pupils were substantially higher than for the skilled readers. In parallel with the adult data two series of MANOVA repeated measures analyses were performed, one for response latencies and one for accuracy, with a three-way 2 x 2 x 2 analysis of variance: Prefixedness (prefix/non-prefix) x Reliability (unreliable/reliable) x Frequency (high/low). For the response latencies there was a main effect for Prefixedness for subjects [$F_s(1,30)=4.23$, $p=0.04$] and for items [$F_i(1,35)=5.41$, $p<.02$]

respectively. Non-words including a prefix elicited higher response latencies than non-words including a non-prefix (947 ms for prefixed non-words versus 924 ms for non-prefixed trials). This effect was also found at the accuracy level, [$F_s(1,30)=10.32$, $p <0.01$] and [$F_i(1,35)=5.01$, $p <.03$]. More errors were made when the non-word contained a prefix (8% versus 4.9% for control non-words).

Analyses performed on difference scores (the difference in response latencies and errors between non-words including a prefix and comparable non-words without prefix), showed effects at the accuracy level only. There was an effect of Frequency [$F_s(1,30)=4.81$, $p <0.03$] for subjects and [$F_i(1,35)=4.82$, $p <.04$] for items. High frequency prefixes elicited higher error rates (5.5% errors versus 1.3% for low frequency prefixes). In the accuracy analysis there was also a Reliability by Frequency interaction in both subjects analysis [$F_s(1,30)=11.14$, $p <0.01$] and items analysis [$F_i(1,35)=5.178$, $p <0.04$]. In non-words with high frequency prefixes the reliable prefix items elicited the highest error rates, whereas in non-words with low frequency prefixes the reverse pattern was found.

4.5 Discussion

Three hypotheses were tested in the present experiment. The first hypothesis predicted an effect of prefixes in terms of longer response latencies and accuracies. This prediction was confirmed, both for skilled readers and for children, and effects were found on both dependent measures. This result is in agreement with the results reported in the Laudanna et al. (1994) study and may be interpreted as negative evidence for the full listing model and as support for the AAM model (Caramazza et al., 1988) and the Interactive Activation Model (Taft, 1994). The present data, however, does not allow discriminating between these models.

The second hypothesis was that in non-words prefixes would elicit differential response patterns, depending on whether the particular prefix occurred frequently as a pseudoprefix ('unreliable prefixes') or not ('reliable prefixes'). Following Laudanna et al. (1994) prefix effects (in terms of differences between prefix non-words and matched control non-words), were predicted in the case of reliable prefixes only. The present data, however, diverge in two respects from the results reported in the Laudanna et al. (1994) study. Firstly, as can be seen in Table 3, there is an inhibitory effect for all prefixes, regardless of reliability. This inhibitory effect, in terms of longer response latencies, ranges from 53 ms to 109 ms. These values are higher than the differences found in the Laudanna et al. (1994) study, where values of 29 and 39 ms were found. The second respect in which our results diverge, is that the present data show the largest effects for the unreliable prefix conditions.

The foregoing implies that the present study does not converge as to the functional use of prefix stripping reported by Laudanna et al. (1994). Our data suggest that prefixes affect processing of the non-word stimulus and that it is even more so if the prefix element often occurs as the first element of a real word, also when it occurs as a pseudo prefix. Our data suggest that semantic factors might be involved in processing this type of non-words. This point will be addressed further on in this paper.

The third hypothesis was about reader experience. It was predicted that the effects of morphological processing discussed in the two previous hypotheses would be small or non-existent. A brief inspection of the children's data makes clear that for less skilled readers the pattern only partially overlaps with the adult's data. For children there is also a clear prefix effect, both at the response latency level and at the accuracy level. The differential effect of prefix quality (reliability) is not present here. On the other hand, at the accuracy level we see a Frequency effect: non-words containing a high frequency prefix elicit higher error rates. This fits in with an explanation in terms of automaticity in visual word recognition. Another point in support of the automaticity explanation is the fact that for children the contrast between words and non-words was statistically non-significant.

The most noticeable difference between our data and the data reported in the Laudanna et al. (1994) study is that we found an overall prefix effect, and that this effect was most pronounced for prefixes with a high pseudo/total ratio ('unreliable prefixes'). A possible explanation for this outcome is that the prefixes used in our study differed in their semantic properties, and that these properties indirectly affected the decision process. In order to control for this type of semantic factors Laudanna et al. (1994) report that they pre-tested and subsequently matched their stimulus materials for semantic interpretability. A problem with this procedure is that, although it provides a general check for semantic effects, it does not provide sufficient grip on semantic factors in this type of experimental tasks.

In an attempt to explain the contradictory results between our data and the results of Laudanna et al. (1994) we designed a follow-up experiment aimed to further explore semantic factors in morphological processing. The central hypothesis in this follow up was that in non-words consisting of a prefix followed by a rest (that is, the stem or any new word element) participants will try to combine the semantic information present in the prefix with the semantic information of the remaining part of the word to be processed. Decision difficulty will depend on the strength of the semantic relationship involved.

5. EXPERIMENT 2

In Experiment 1, the status of prefix reliability (Laudanna et al., 1994) was subject of our investigation. The next question was whether our results could also be explained in terms of semantic processing. It is hypothesized that non-words composed of semantically compatible morphemes are more difficult to reject as a real word than combinations of incompatible morphemes. Some combinations between stem and prefix are semantically more meaningful than other combinations. A non-word like *rewoman* may be highly meaningful because of its conceptually close resemblance to *remarry*. A non-word like *repigeon* is conceptually more difficult to interpret. This latter class of combinations has a low semantic compatibility. It is possible that the observations in Experiment 1 are artifacts of semantic compatibility. Laudanna et al. (1994) have tried to control for this variable. Nonetheless, it should be questioned whether semantic aspects can interfere with prefix reliability.

In this experiment, the roles of semantic compatibility and prefix reliability are investigated. Preceding this experiment, a validation study with 132 high school students (16-17 years of age) was done to estimate semantic compatibility in a large set of non-words. We asked the students to evaluate 320 items consisting of a prefix attached to a word stem on a ten-point scale as to their semantic acceptability. Eighty items were combinations of a prefix and a non-matching, one or two syllable, 4-6 letter, word. Strong bigram troughs between prefix and stem were avoided. These words had a surface frequency range of 1-67 in the 42 million CELEX database (Baayen, Piepenbrock & Van Rijn, 1993). The word stems were randomly assigned to one of the four prefixes used in Experiment 1. We also created eighty non-words with control clusters matching the prefixed non-words. We also included real and non-word filler items as well as real prefixed words. Four students were removed from the analysis because they had been diagnosed as dyslexics, and five subjects were removed because they were non-native, and still not sufficiently fluent, speakers of Dutch.

Semantic compatibility was, based on the validation study, directly manipulated. Item evaluations were sorted according to semantic compatibility. We selected the five highest and five lowest compatible items from this list for each prefix used in the previous experiment, and constructed the stimulus list of this experiment from this set. This is in contrast with the method of Laudanna et al. (1994), who only tried to keep semantic compatibility constant across items.

5.1 Method

5.1.1 Participants

Twenty-two children (mean age: 12 years) and thirty paid undergraduate students at Utrecht University participated in this experiment. All children were good readers according to the test results, which were provided by their teacher. All participants were native speakers of Dutch. Three children were excluded from the analysis because of the large number of errors they made.

5.1.2 Materials

Stimuli were selected from the validation study. Five highly and five lowly compatible items were selected for each prefix. Semantic compatibility between control cluster and stem was low for these items. Since the control cluster has no meaning, semantic compatibility should be low. This set of 5 x 4 x 2 = 40 items was used in this experiment. Examples are presented in Appendix 8.2. We added 40 real prefixed words, 30 non-prefixed non-words and 70 real word filler-items to the stimulus list.

5.1.3 Apparatus

An IBM compatible personal computer (CPU: Pentium 100 MHz, PCI) with a 15" Phillips monitor was used. The screen had a resolution of 640x480 pixels (VGA-mode). The vertical refresh rate was 70 Hz; the horizontal refresh rate was 31.5 kHz (non-interlaced).

The stimuli were presented in the middle of the screen in a straight font type (lowercase). The letters were 6 mm high. The background was black, the foreground white. The participants' instruction was presented in yellow on a blue background.

5.1.4 Procedure

The participant sat at a distance of approximately 40 cm from the monitor. After a short instruction on the computer screen, the participant was given ten practice trials. Feedback was given on each practice trial, but not in the actual experiment. The participant could ask additional questions if necessary. The experiment started when the task was completely comprehended. The stimuli were presented in two blocks of 110 trials with a one-minute break between the blocks. Items were randomly distributed across the experiment.

A trial consisted of a fixation mark in the middle of the screen for 140 ms, followed by the stimulus until the participant made his response but not longer than two seconds. The participant made his response by pressing a button on the computer keyboard. A masking '*********' appeared on the screen during 100 ms immediately after the participant had made his response or when the time limit had expired. The screen remained empty for 700 ms before the fixation mark appeared again.

The participant was instructed to decide as fast and accurately as possible whether the presented stimulus was a real word or a non-word. The participant had to press the green key in case of a real word and the red one in case of a non-word. Both keys were situated next to each other on the keyboard and were pressed with the index finger of the preferred hand.

5.1.5 Design

Three within-subjects factors and one between-subjects factor were manipulated in this experiment. The first within-subjects factor was Prefixedness (prefix/control cluster). Each prefix used in this design had a control cluster with approximately equal sublexical frequency, like in the first experiment. In the analysis the difference in response latency and accuracy between the control- and prefix condition for every item was used. The second factor was Reliability (unreliable/reliable). The four prefixes used in this study were classified as being either reliable (*her* and *on*) or unreliable (*ver* and *ont*). The third factor was Compatibility, which also had two levels: high and low. The between-subjects factor was Reading skill. Beginning readers (elementary school pupils, 12 years of age) and experienced readers (university undergraduate students) participated in this experiment.

5.2 *Results*

5.2.1 Accuracy Data

Accuracy scores are summarized in Table 5. Skilled readers made fewer errors than beginners did, [t(47)=10.20, p <.001]. However, if we look at the difference scores, we see little difference between students and elementary school pupils, [F(1,47)=.444, p=.508]. There was a main effect of Compatibility, [F(1,47)=22.26, p <.001]. That is, the difference scores between highly compatible items and controls were larger than the difference scores between lowly compatible items and control items.

Table 5. Accuracy scores (error percentages) with standard deviation in parentheses, C+ = high semantic compatibility, C- = low semantic compatibility, R+ = reliable, R- = unreliable

	Students			Elementary school pupils		
	prefix	control cluster	difference	prefix	control cluster	difference
C+, R-	*12 (14)*	*2 (4)*	*11*	*22 (18)*	*14 (13)*	*8*
C+, R+	*13 (11)*	*1 (4)*	*12*	*28 (14)*	*16 (12)*	*12*
C-, R-	*2 (4)*	*2 (6)*	*0*	*14 (15)*	*13 (12)*	*1*
C-, R+	*5 (8)*	*4 (6)*	*1*	*22 (15)*	*12 (10)*	*10*

In the following analysis only correctly answered items were used. Means and standard deviations are presented in Table 6. Difference scores between prefix and control items were also calculated. The difference scores were calculated only if both prefix and control item had been correctly responded to.

An overall 2 x 2 x 2 Reading skill (students/beginners) x Compatibility (high/low) x Reliability (high/low) *MANOVA* with a repeated measures design on the difference scores revealed a significant main effect for Reading skill [F(1,47) = 9.48, p <.003]. The difference scores were about twice as high in the student group than in the beginners. It is also evident from the data that skilled readers reacted more promptly to non-words than beginning readers (see Table 6), [t(47)=5.64, p <.001]. There were no significant main effects of Compatibility or Reliability. The first-order interaction between Reading skill and Compatibility was significant at the 5% level. The interaction was further analyzed by single-df comparisons (Keppel, 1982, p. 213). This analysis showed that for students the differences were larger for the highly compatible items than for the lowly compatible in the non-word condition (133 vs. 64 ms); in contrast, there was no difference for the children (24 vs. 37 ms). These effects were also found in an item analysis. Additional interactions were not found.

Table 6. Response latencies (milliseconds) with standard deviation in parentheses. C+ = high semantic compatibility, C- = low semantic compatibility, R+ = reliable, R- = unreliable

	Students			Elementary school pupils		
	prefix	control cluster	difference	Prefix	control cluster	difference
C+, R-	*959 (171)*	*818 (136)*	*142*	*1128 (185)*	*1086 (189)*	*56*
C+, R+	*997 (168)*	*875 (160)*	*123*	*1181 (152)*	*1183 (228)*	*-9*
C-, R-	*873 (132)*	*764 (134)*	*76*	*1095 (188)*	*1070 (168)*	*36*
C-, R+	*886 (138)*	*837 (158)*	*48*	*1131 (179)*	*1086 (193)*	*37*

5.3 *Discussion*

The results indicate that high semantic compatibility causes larger experimental effects in students. Reliability of the prefix does not seem to be an important parameter for both students and elementary school pupils in this task. Our hypothesis that the prefix reliability effects observed by Laudanna et al. (1994) and by us in Experiment 1, are susceptible to confounding semantic aspects of the stimuli; that is, in skilled readers. Semantic compatibility between stem and prefix is an important parameter in non-word identification for skilled readers.

Post-lexical effects may thus have strongly affected performance in this task. One cannot conclude from this, however, that prefix reliability is not involved in the identification of complex words. Because of the apparently strong dependence on semantics in this task, the task used here may not be optimal to reveal the importance of prefix reliability. Semantic/post-lexical effects may have overruled all pre-lexical effects.

The interaction between semantic compatibility and reading skill showed that skilled readers are susceptible to semantic factors, whereas beginning readers do not turn out to be hindered by semantics. This is a very interesting finding, because it implies that skilled readers use semantically driven processes in their word recognition strategy. Semantic compatibility interferes with the orthographic processing of the word. Moreover, skilled readers are perhaps able to generate orthographic candidates on a (partly) recognized morpheme for the complementary parts of the words on a semantic basis. On the other hand, it is also possible that the effect is strictly post-lexical and has little to do with true word recognition.

A question that can be raised is whether semantic compatibility may exert its influence even before lexical recognition is complete. In other words, is there a top-down influence on orthographic recognition from a semantic level? The interactive morphology models are not explicit about this matter. However, it might be concluded that it is legitimate to expect a top-down influence from the semantic level in interactive models, as proposed by Seidenberg & McClelland (1989).

6. EXPERIMENT 3

It was concluded from Experiment 2 that the task used was probably not sensitive enough to uncover prelexical aspects of the word recognition process. Postlexical effects may have overshadowed the prefix reliability effect. It was also not clear whether semantic compatibility effects in skilled readers were in fact due to post-lexical processes or also had a prelexical component.

In Experiment 3 we used a different paradigm, the 'progressive demasking technique', originally developed by Grainger and Jacob (1996). This method is more suitable for investigating prelexical processes and is more robust to post-lexical interference. In this technique, the stimulus is not immediately recognizable. The stimulus is fully masked at the start. However, the visual image becomes gradually available. This technique is very suitable to investigate pre-lexical effects, because the first phase of the word recognition process is enlarged. It is like using a magnifying glass to look at prelexical processes.

A second modification to the previous two experiments is that we used a letter cluster search instead of a lexical decision task. This task does not require a full semantic evaluation, which makes it more immune to post-lexical interference. We expected to find effects of prefix reliability and sub-lexical semantic interference at the morpheme level.

6.1 Method

6.1.1 Participants

The same participants were used as in Experiment 2. No participants were excluded from the analysis because of too many errors. A short break between Experiment 2 and this experiment was given to the students. Elementary school pupils completed the experiment in two sessions, separated by an interval of one week.

6.1.2 Materials

Items with intermediate semantic compatibility between stem and prefix, according to the pilot study, and their control counterparts were used in this experiment. Semantic compatibility of the control items had a low value, since they should have no assembled meaning. There was no significant difference between the reliable and unreliable prefix conditions. No items from the previous experiment were used. Examples are presented in Appendix 8.3. All stimuli were presented twice, once for a "yes" decision and once for a "no" decision.

6.1.3 Procedure

Participants sat at a distance of 40 cm in front of a computer screen. The items were presented in two blocks with a short 1-minute break between the two blocks. The items were randomly distributed across the experiment.

A short instruction on the computer screen and eight test trials were given to the participants prior to the experiment. The participants received feedback in the test trials. No feedback was given in the actual experiment. The subject was asked to decide whether a pre-specified letter cluster was present in a stimulus and to react as fast and as accurately as possible. The letter cluster was presented visually prior to the presentation of the stimulus.

First, the letter cluster was presented for 1000 ms on the screen in a color different from the stimulus. The screen was erased and remained black for 14 ms. The stimulus was then presented in the middle of the screen. The presentation of the stimulus was masked by an array of '########' signs. After a 14 ms presentation of the stimulus the masking was presented for 300 ms. This procedure was reiterated, stimulus presentation time being increased on each run by 14 ms and masking time decreased by 14 milliseconds. Thus, the stimulus was gradually demasked. The 14 ms interval was chosen because of the vertical refresh rate of the monitor. After this, the screen remained empty for 500 ms; the next trial was subsequently initiated. This method was originally developed by Grainger & Jacob (1996).

6.1.4 Design

The overall design of this experiment can be split up into two separate designs. The first design is a 2 x 2 x 2 Reading skill (students/elementary school) x Word (true/non-word) x Reliability (high/low) design. The second design is a 2 x 2 x 2 Reading skill (student/pupils) x Prefix (prefix/control cluster) x Reliability (high/low) design. Design 2 deals with non-words only. It is evident that prefix reliability does not apply to control clusters. These control clusters are denoted reliable or unreliable because of their prefix counterparts. There is no difference score like in Experiment 1, because the control cluster levels are directly tested against the prefix levels.

The relationship between design 1 and 2 is presented in Figure 1. The four cells at the top of Figure 1 form design 1; the four cells on the right form design 2. Two cells in the design could not be filled because of the fact that they refer to impossible combinations in Dutch. Designs 1 and 2 are dealt with separately in the analysis.

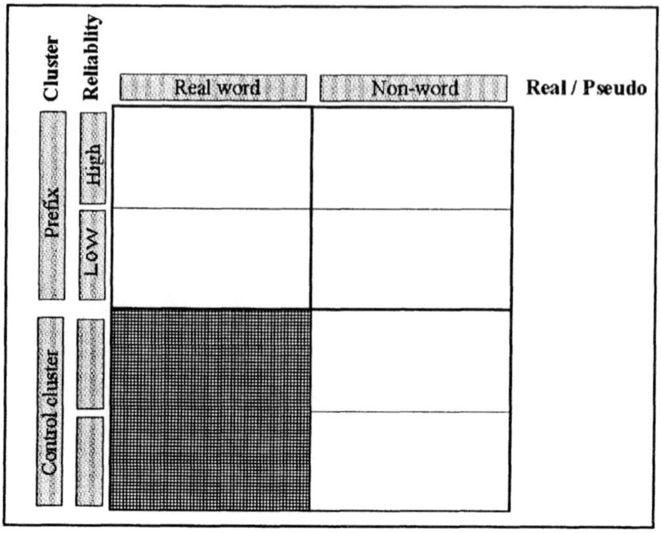

Figure 1. Design of Experiment 3. Design 1 (Reading skill x Word x Reliability) is formed by the four cells at the top, design 2 (Reading skill x Prefix x Reliability) is formed by the four cells at the right

6.2 *Results*

6.2.1 Accuracy Data

Overall error rate was lower than in Experiment 2. As expected, beginners made more errors than skilled readers. Accuracy data are presented in Table 7. All participants were included in the analysis. The first analysis was a 2 x 2 x 2 Reading Skill (students/pupils) x Word (true/non-word) x Reliability (high/low) design. There was a main effect of Reading Skill, [$F(1,50)=5.45$, $p=.024$]. Pupils produced more errors.

Table 7. Accuracy scores (error percentages), standard deviations in parentheses

			Students	Elementary school pupils
Word	Prefix	Reliable	*1.3 (3.8)*	*3.4 (6.9)*
		Unreliable	*1.7 (4.3)*	*4.5 (7.3)*
	Control cluster	Reliable	-	-
		Unreliable	-	-
Non-word	Prefix	Reliable	*3.8 (6.7)*	*6.8 (8.4)*
		Unreliable	*1.7 (4.3)*	*1.7 (5.8)*
	Control cluster	Reliable	*4.6 (8.4)*	*5.1 (8.3)*
		Unreliable	*2.5 (6.1)*	*1.7 (4.4)*

There was an effect of Reliability, [F(1,50)=4.28, p=.044]. Reliable prefixes elicited more errors. Finally, there was a Word by Reliability interaction, [F(1,50)=8.12, p=.006]. There was a significant effect of Reliability in the non-words, [t(51)=2.94, p=.005], and there was a significant effect of Word in the reliable prefix condition, [t(51)=2.13, p=.038].

The second analysis was a 2 x 2 x 2 Reading Skill (students/beginners) x Prefix (true/control cluster) x Reliability (high/low) design; that is, non-word data only. There was a significant effect of Reliability, [F(1,50)=10.65, p=.002].

6.2.2 Reaction time Data

Response latencies are given in Table 8. Even a quick inspection of the results shows that beginning readers are slower than skilled readers, but the pattern does not seem to be different for beginning and skilled readers.

The analysis of the response latency data was split into two separate orthogonal *MANOVAs* for both subjects and items. The first analysis was a 2 x 2 x 2 Reading skill (students/pupils) x Word (true/non-word) x Reliability (high/low) design. A significant main effect was found for Reliability [$F_s(1,50)=26.98$, $p<.001$ and $F_i(1,28)=11.97$, $p<.002$]. Reliable prefixes were more difficult to identify than unreliable prefixes (1424 vs. 1289 ms for the students, and 1774 vs. 1593 ms for the elementary school pupils). The effect for Word was also significant [$F_s(1,50)=32.62$, $p<.001$ and $F_i(1,28)=17.18$, $p<.001$]. That is, prefixes were more difficult to spot in non-words than in real words (1443 vs. 1270 ms for the students, and 1865 and 1603 vs. 1683 and 1582 ms for the children). In addition, there was a significant main effect of Reading skill [$F_s(1,50)=9.24$, $p<.004$] and [$F_i(1,28)=5.97$, $p<.021$]. Skilled readers were faster than beginning readers.

Interestingly, there was a significant first order interaction between Reliability and Word condition [$F_s(1,50)=9.88$, $p<.003$ and $F_i(1,28)=67.64$, $p<.001$]. The difference between reliable and unreliable prefixes is much stronger in the non-words than in the real word condition. Single df comparisons of the interaction revealed two significant differences. Firstly, response latencies on real words with highly reliable prefixes differed from the latencies on the corresponding non-words [$F_s(1,51)=32.41$, $p<.001$]. Secondly, reliable and unreliable prefix conditions differed significantly [$F_s(1,51)=40.56$, $p<.001$] for non-words. The other two tests did not reach significance. There were no additional first or higher-level interactions. The interaction showed the same pattern in the item-analysis as in the subject analysis.

The second analysis was a 2 x 2 x 2 Reading skill (students/beginners) x Prefix (true/control cluster) x Reliability (high/low) design; that is, non-word data only. First, a significant main effect was found for Reliability [$F_s(1,50)=52.81$, $p<.001$ and $F_i(1,28)=48.51$, $p<.001$]. Reliable prefixes or their matching control clusters were not spotted as fast as unreliable clusters (1650 vs. 1415 ms for the students, and 1981 vs. 1695 ms for the elementary school pupils). The second factor, Prefix, was also found to yield significant differences [$F_s(1,50)=49.85$, $p<.001$ and $F_i(1,28)=24.45$, $p<.001$]. Prefixes were recognized faster than control clusters (1443 vs 1622 ms for the students, and 1734 vs. 1941 ms for the beginners). Finally, Reading skill was significant [$F_s(1,50)=6.31$, $p <.015$ and $F_i(1,14)=63.07$, $p <.001$]. Skilled readers were again faster than beginning readers. No first or higher order interactions could be established.

Table 8. Response latencies (milliseconds), standard deviations in parentheses

			Students	Elementary school pupils
Word	Prefix	Reliable	*1283 (418)*	*1683 (438)*
		Unreliable	*1257 (408)*	*1582 (348)*
	Control cluster	Reliable	-	-
		Unreliable	-	-
Non Word	Prefix	Reliable	*1564 (416)*	*1865 (549)*
		Unreliable	*1321 (411)*	*1603 (357)*
	Control cluster	Reliable	*1735 (450)*	*2096 (671)*
		Unreliable	*1508 (451)*	*1786 (469)*

6.3 Discussion

In agreement with Experiment 2, the data of Experiment 3 demonstrated once again that prefixes are processed differently from other letter clusters in the recognition process. That is, prefixes are detected faster than comparable control clusters in non-words. An effect of prefix reliability was found in the non-word conditions, but there was no interaction with the factor Prefix. In other words, the effect of reliability is present in both prefixed non-words and their matching control non-words. Therefore, it must be concluded that prefix reliability as defined in Laudanna et al. (1994) was *not* a discriminating factor in our letter cluster detection task. The established effects can entirely be accounted for by the orthographic properties of the stimuli in this task. The source of this difference should thus be sought in other factors, such as word shape and letter cluster frequency.

An interesting finding is that the letter clusters were more easily recognized in real words than in non-words. Moreover, the first analysis showed that prefix reliability was found to interact with the factor 'real/non-words'. When letter clusters are part of non-words, prefix reliability does matter. But, if they are, on the other hand, a part of real words, the effect disappears. This allows us to conclude that this effect is the result of a top-down effect from the 'whole word' level. Apparently, in the case of non-words insufficient contact can be made to suppress bottom-up orthographic effects. On the other hand, in real words enough contact can be made, since the prefix is part of a real word. Top down facilitation causes reliable prefixes to be recognized faster. Unreliable prefixes, however, do not benefit as much from this facilitation as reliable ones. This word superiority effect manifests itself even in a letter cluster detection task with a progressive demasking technique. Apparently it is strong enough to by-pass orthographic differences in early reading stages.

Beginning readers are slower and make more errors than skilled readers, but no interaction effects with reading skill were observed. That is, their performances did not qualitatively differ from those of skilled readers, which indicates that the strategies needed for complex word reading had already been acquired by them. Apparently, they constitute a relatively basic reading skill, which is acquired early in the process of learning to read.

7. GENERAL DISCUSSION

This discussion starts with an overview of the main findings of the three experiments presented in this chapter. After this we will present a discussion of our results in terms of an update of current issues in the domain of decoding morphologically complex words. The models presented in the introductory part of this chapter will be addressed and our goal is to find the model that fits best with our data.

Experiment 1 confirmed earlier research by Laudanna et al. (1994), demonstrating a special status for prefixes as access units in visual word recognition. Laudanna et al. found that non-words containing a prefix took longer decision times than non-words with an orthographically comparable initial syllable. However, contrary to the Laudanna et al. results, we found this prefix effect both with reliable and unreliable prefixes. It turned out that unreliable prefixes even elicited stronger effects, which was exactly the opposite of the result found in the Laudanna et al. experiment.

Experiment 2 was designed to further investigate these effects. It was hypothesized that the established effects were not the result of "pure" prefix reliability, but the outcome of a semantic integration mechanism of prefix and following stem morpheme. More specifically, it was hypothesized that subjects try to integrate semantic information available in the novel prefix+stem combination during the process of assessing the status, word or non-word, of the presented stimulus. It was found that highly compatible prefix-stem combinations took longer decision times and elicited more errors. This effect was found in skilled readers only.

Experiment 3 focused on prefix processing in an early stage of word recognition. A progressive demasking paradigm was used. The stimulus materials used in this study enabled us to analyze the data in two distinct factorial designs. Design 1 compared words and non-words containing a prefix. There were two prefix conditions: reliable and unreliable. As expected, real words were processed faster. There was also a reliability effect: unreliable prefixes took shorter decision times. In addition to these relatively uninformative main effects there was a Reliability by Word Type interaction. Further analysis of this interaction showed that the reliability effect manifested itself most prominently in the *non-word* condition: unreliable prefix items took shorter response latencies.

Design 2 dealt exclusively with the non-words. In this design prefixed non-words were compared with their corresponding controls, containing the same stem, but preceded by an orthographically matched control cluster. In this 2 (prefix/control) by 2 (reliability) design two main effects were found. Prefixed non-words were processed faster and the same was true for unreliable prefixes and their control counterparts. Interestingly, there was no interaction in this design.

If we reconsider the four prefix processing models discussed in the introduction this pattern of results fits best with Caramazza et al.'s (1988) AAM model. A prefix effect was found in Experiment 1 (non-words) and in Experiment 3 (design 2).

However, the AAM model cannot account for the results of Experiment 1 completely. The finding that unreliable prefixes elicited even a larger effect is in contrast with predictions of the AAM model. The same holds true for Taft's (1994) Interactive Model.

Our preliminary conclusion is that the prefix models discussed in the introduction fall short of explaining the data collected in Experiments 1 and 3. In our view, the reason for this is that the AAM and Interactive models are too implicit on the point of specifying the obligatory semantic integration process occurring during reading polymorphemic words. The subject automatically relates the semantic content of the first element (prefix or not) to the following stem morpheme.

Prefixed words are a specific class of compound words and it is appropriate to presume that this class of words is dealt with by the reader in a way similar to the general class of compound words. Therefore, at this point we think that a more general model for complex word decoding like the Morphological Race Model of Schreuder & Baayen (1995), as described in the present chapter, is more appropriate.

Let us explain in terms of the Schreuder & Baayen (1995) model what happens if a reader is confronted with a prefixed word and has to decide if the presented item is a word or not. We can describe this process in a series of successive decision steps. These steps may be summarized as follows.

First check if the stimulus is a familiar word or not. If positive, the decision process stops. If the check is negative the second check is activated; i.e., the subject follows the parsing route (Schreuder & Baayen, 1995). In this second phase of the process a check for the presence of a prefix follows. If this leads to a positive result, a check of the second element in the compound word follows. The frequency of the stem element determines the amount of time needed. At this moment the process of semantic integration is initiated. In terms of the Schreuder & Baayen model, integration nodes mediate in the integration process. If no prefix is detected stage three of the decision process starts. It is important to notice here that according to the Schreuder & Baayen model there are dichotomous decision options (the "morphological race" options), which have to be solved by the morphological processing system.

If both checks are negative the subject proceeds by parsing the non-word stimulus. The first syllabic element encountered is scanned for orthographic properties. Orthographic properties of the first element determine the amount of time needed. This is demonstrated by our data in Experiment 3, design 2. In this design non-words containing a prefix were compared with non-words containing a control cluster, matched for orthographic properties in terms of positional bigram frequency. In this design two main effects of affix status (prefix vs. control) and reliability (reliable vs. unreliable) were found. It should be noted that reliability in the non-prefix condition refers to sublexical frequency distribution properties of the letter clusters involved. It turned out that these effects work in prefixes and control clusters in a similar way, which is demonstrated by the absence of an interaction effect in this design.

The previous observations become interesting if combined with the results of design 1 of Experiment 3. Here a complementary picture emerges.

We also have a main effect of reliability, but now in combination with an additional interaction with word type. The reliability effect was present in the non-word condition, and non-significant for real words. This strongly suggests that the sublexical effect of reliability is overruled by surface frequency in the real word condition. This combination of effects in design 1 and design 2 of Experiment 3 clearly demonstrates that sublexical processing mechanisms only become manifest if conditions are favorable; i.e., in non-words or comparable very low frequency or novel compounds.

Taken together, our data allow us to draw two major conclusions. First, present models for decoding prefixed words are incomplete in terms of the semantic integration process, which plays a crucial role during word recognition. Current models are too narrowly focused on the isolated properties of the affix involved. More focus on the semantic relationship with the stem is necessary. The second conclusion is that sublexical processing mechanisms contribute to the identification process mainly under conditions where relatively new or unknown words are involved. This does not imply that these mechanisms can easily be discarded. Our data suggest that sublexical word identification units become important when the reader cannot rely on his normally used default decoding routines.

8. NOTES

[1] Experiment 1 was previously published in Assink, Vooijs & Knuijt (2000).

[2] Experiment 1 was designed as a replication study of the second experiment described in Laudanna et al. (1994), including their use of difference scores as a dependent measure for testing the experimental effects. Therefore we adopted this method in the present Experiment 1. This also holds for Experiment 2 in this chapter, which further investigates the outcomes of Experiment 1. In Experiment 3, however, a different technique of stimulus presentation, referred to as 'progressive demasking' (Grainger & Jacob, 1996) is used. This technique enables the experimenter to project a letter array on a computer screen gradually. For that reason we decided to drop the method of difference scores in Experiment 3 and adopted the method of direct comparisons of experimental conditions in the data analysis.

9. APPENDIX

11.1 Examples experiment 1

Non-words				
	Reliable		Unreliable	
	High frequency	Low frequency	High frequency	Low frequency
Prefix	*vervogel* *verbaby* *vertrui* *vervlek*	*ontezel* *ontaula* *ontappel* *ontauto*	*onbroer* *onknecht* *onbloed* *onbalkon*	*herraam* *hervrouw* *herpoes* *herhand*
Control cluster	*wervogel* *werbaby* *wertrui* *wervlek*	*ondezel* *ondaula* *ondappel* *ondauto*	*anbroer* *anknecht* *anbloed* *anbalkon*	*kerraam* *kervrouw* *kerpoes* *kerhand*

Real words			
Reliable		Unreliable	
High frequency	Low frequency	High frequency	Low frequency
verslaan	*ontwijken*	*onjuist*	*herbouwen*
verval	*ontploffen*	*onlust*	*herdenking*
verdringen	*ontbreken*	*onaangenaam*	*herhalen*
verweven	*ontwerpen*	*onnozel*	*herkennen*

11.2 Examples experiment 2

	Reliable		Unreliable	
	Highly compatible	Lowly compatible	Highly compatible	Lowly compatible
Prefix	*ontoogst* *ontijver* *vernaald* *verboete*	*ontivoor* *ontadres* *verbraam* *verhavik*	*hergloed* *herwraak* *onkerel* *onbende*	*herzwijn* *herblaar* *onbarak* *onboter*
Control cluster	*ondoogst* *ondijver* *wernaald* *werboete*	*ondivoor* *ondadres* *werbraam* *werhavik*	*kergloed* *kerwraak* *ankerel* *anbende*	*kerzwijn* *kerblaar* *anbarak* *anboter*

11.3 Examples experiment 3

	Real word		Non-word	
	Prefix	Control cluster	Prefix	Control cluster
Reliable	*ontstemd* *ontharen* *verlicht* *verroest*	--	*ontadder* *onterker* *verzenuw* *verwezel*	*ondadder* *onderker* *werzenuw* *werwezel*
Unreliable	*herdruk* *herstel* *onrust* *onrecht*	--	*herprooi* *herzweet* *onlever* *onspier*	*kerprooi* *kerzweet* *anlever* *anspier*

10. REFERENCES

Assink, E.M.H., Vooijs, C. & Knuijt, P.P.N.A. (2000). Prefixes as Access Units in Visual Word Recognition: a Comparison of Italian and Dutch Data. *Reading and Writing, 12, 149-168.*

Baayen, R.H., Piepenbrock, R. & Van Rijn, H. (1993). *The CELEX lexical database.* (CD-ROM). Philadelphia, PA: Linguistic Data Consortium, University of Pennsylvania.

Bergman, W.M. (1988). *The visual recognition of word structure: Left to right processing of derivational morphology.* Doctoral thesis Katholieke Universiteit Nijmegen. Enschede: sneldruk Enschede.

Butterworth, B. (1983). Lexical Representation. In Butterworth, B. (Ed.). *Language Production, vol II.* London, etc: Academic Press.

Caramazza, A., Laudanna, A. & Romani, C. (1988). Lexical access and inflectional morphology. *Cognition, 28, 297-332.*

Coltheart, M. , Davelaar, C., Jonasson, J. & Besner, D. (1977). Access to the internal lexicon. In S. Dornic (Ed.), *Attention and Performance VI* (pp. 535-556). New York: Academic Press.

Ehri, L.C. (1992). Reconceptualizing the development of sight word reading and its relationship to recoding. In Gough, P., Ehri, L. & Treiman (Eds.) *Reading acquisition, 107-143.* Hillsdale, NJ: Erlbaum.

Grainger, J. & Jacob, A.M. (1996). Orthographic processing in visual word recognition: A multiple read-out model. *Psychological review, 103(3), 518-565.*

Grainger, J., Colt, J, P. & Segui, J. (1991). Masked morphological priming in visual word recognition. *Journal of memory and language, 30, 370-384.*

Henderson, L. (1985). Toward a psychology of morphemes. In Ellis, A.W. (Ed.) *Progress in the psychology of language (vol. 1. pp 15-72).* London: Lawrence Erlbaum Associates.

Jarvella, R.J., Job, R., Sandstrom, G. & Schreuder, R. (1987). Morphological constraints on word recognition. In: A. Allport, D.G. MacKay, W. Prinz & E. Schreerer (Eds). *Language perception and production: Relationships between listening, speaking, reading, and writing* (pp. 245-265). London: Academic Press.

Keppel, G. (1982). *Design and Analysis. A Researcher's Handbook.* Englewood Cliffs, NJ: Prentice Hall.

Laudanna, A., Burani, C. & Cermele, A. (1994). Prefixes as processing units. *Language and cognitive processes, 9 (3), 295-316.*

Orden, G.C. van & Goldfinger, S.D.(1994). Interdependence of form and function in cognitive systems explains perception of printed words. *Journal of experimental psychology: Human perception and performance, 20 (6), 1269-1291.*

Reitsma, P. (1983). *Phonemic and Graphemic codes in learning to read.* Doctoral thesis. Vrije Universiteit Amsterdam. Utrecht: Elinkwijk bv.

Rolf, P.C. & van Rijnsoever, R.J. (1984). Positionele letterfrekwenties van het Nederlands. Lisse: Swets & Zeitlinger.

Sandra, D. (1994). The morphology of the mental lexicon: internal word structure viewed from a psycholinguistic perspective. *Language and cognition, 9 (3), 227-269.*

Schreuder, R. (1991). Woordherkenning en morfologie. In Thomassen, A.J.W.M., Noordman, L. & Eling, P. (1991). *Lezen en Begrijpen: De psychologie van het leesproces. pp. 69-83.* Amsterdam/Lisse. Swets & Zeitlinger bv.

Schreuder, R. & Baayen, R.H. (1994). Prefix stripping Re-revisited. *Journal of memory and language, 33, 357-375.*

Schreuder, R. & Baayen, H.R. (1995). Modeling morphological processing. In L.B. Feldman (Ed.) Morphological aspects in language processing (pp. 131-154). Hillsdale, NJ: Erlbaum.

Schreuder, R., Grendel, M., Poulisse, N., Roelofs, A. & Voort, M. van de (1990). Lexical processing, morphological complexity and reading. In Balota, D.A., Flores d'Arcais, G.B. & Rayner, K. (Eds.)(1990). *Comprehension processes in reading. (pp. 125-141).* Hove, London: Lawrence - Erlbaum Associates.

Seidenberg, M.S. & McClelland (1989). A distributed, developmental model of word recognition and naming. *Psychological Review, 96(4), 523-568.*

Segui, J. & Grainger, J. (1990). Priming word recognition with orthographic neighbors: Effects of relative prime-target frequency. *Journal of experimental psychology: human perception and performance, 16 (1), 65-76.*

Schneider, W. (1988). *Micro Experimental Laboratory User's Guide: Computer Techniques for Real Time Psychological Experimentation.* Pittsburgh: Psychology Software Tools, Inc.

Taft, M. (1994). Interactive-activation as a framework for understanding morphological processing. *Language and cognition, 9 (3), 271-294.*

Taft, M & Forster, K.I.(1975). Lexical storage and retrieval of prefixed words. *Journal of verbal learning and verbal behavior 14, 638-647.*

Uit den Boogaart, P. (1975). *Woordfrequenties* (word frequencies). Utrecht: Oosthoek, Scheltema & Holkema.

Zwitserlood, P. (1994). The role of semantic transparency in the processing and representation of dutch compounds. *Language and cognitive processes, 9 (3), 341-368.*

Thomassen, A.J.W.M., Noordman, L.G.M. & Eling, P.A.T.M. (Eds.). (1991). *Lezen en begrijpen: De psychologie van het leesproces.* Amsterdam, Lisse: Swets & Zeitlinger B.V.

13. ACKNOWLEDGEMENT

Experiment 1 was previously published in Assink, Vooijs & Knuijt (2000).

14. ADDRESS FOR CORRESPONDENCE

Harold T. Nefs, Egbert M.H. Assink and Paul P.N.A. Knuijt
Utrecht University
Psychology Department
Heidelberglaan 2
3584 CS Utrecht
The Netherlands
Phone: +31-30.253.30.43
Fax: +31-30.253.45.11
email e.assink@fss.uu.nl

GARY LIBBEN

MORPHOLOGICAL PARSING AND MORPHOLOGICAL STRUCTURE

1. INTRODUCTION AND OVERVIEW

A language's ability to create new word forms by recombining morphemes has obvious advantages for both language comprehension and production. It allows a relatively large whole-word vocabulary to develop from a considerably smaller set of morphemes, it allows novel forms to be immediately comprehensible in terms of their constituent morphemes, and it allows the semantic relationships among words to be coded through shared morphological elements. For these advantages to be realized, however, the constituent morphemes of complex and compound words must be available to the language user during on-line processing, so that novel forms such as *fruitpepper* or *reflocking* can be easily understood. What is less than clear, however, is the role that such constituent extraction plays in the comprehension of existing words of the language.

Existing words present a more complex problem, quite simply because they are existing. For novel words, the only path to comprehension is through morphological decomposition. However, in the case of existing words, purely constituent-based interpretation is not always possible. Thus, the exact meaning of *rewire* cannot be easily derived from *re-* and *wire* and the meaning of *professor* cannot be easily derived from the meanings of *profess* and *-or*.

In response to these observations, we are forced to conclude that the mental lexicon contains both multimorphemic and monomorphemic representations. This conclusion has led to the rather difficult problem of understanding how whole-word and constituent activation interact during word recognition. The problem has turned out to be difficult, primarily due to the fact that the would-be elegant answer, namely that they do not interact, appears to be incorrect. The early literature on morphological processing was dominated by two strong non-interactionist positions. Taft and Forster's (1976) morphological processing hypothesis (see also Taft 1981) contained within it the claim that whole-word activation is driven by constituent-based access in visual word recognition. The contrary position, attributed primarily to Butterworth (1983), claimed that the recognition of multimorphemic forms is based on whole-word activation. As has been repeatedly noted in the more recent literature (e.g., McQueen and Cutler 1998), neither of these strong positions appears to be correct. Rather it seems to be the case that whole-word and constituent activation are obligatory components of word recognition and that the mental lexicon contains both multimorphemic and monomorphemic forms. The question then becomes: How are these forms related?

My goal in this paper is to address this question by focusing on English trimorphemic words such as *unfillable*. These prefixed and suffixed words possess the minimum complexity required to address the question of whether multimorphemic forms in the mental lexicon show evidence of hierarchical structure.

The notion of hierarchical structure has been one of the cornerstones of generative approaches to language in general and to generative approaches to morphology in particular. This approach, perhaps most clearly represented in Lieber (1980) and Selkirk (1982), captures the arrangement of morphemes within multimorphemic words as hierarchical tree structures such as those shown in Figure 1.

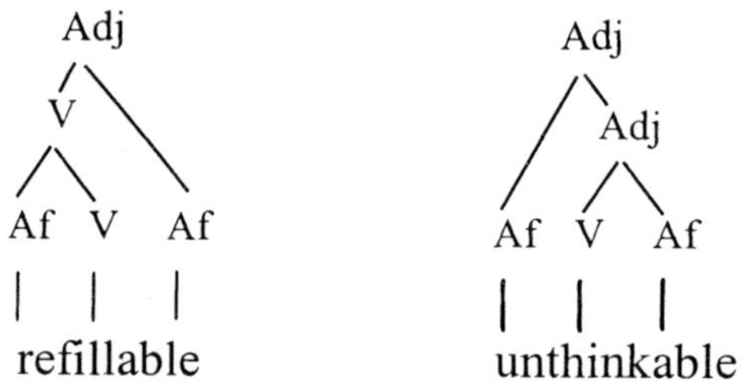

Figure 1. The arrangement of morphemes within hierarchical morphological structures.

These trees represent the claim that multimorphemic words possess internal substructures formed by binary trees in which one branch is the head and in which properties of that head percolate to the node above it. In many cases, the exact arrangement of trees is determined by the selectional restrictions of affixes. The concept of selectional restriction, (see for example Pesetsky, 1985; Sproat, 1988; Zwicky, 1988) captures the fact that some morphemes can only combine with other morphemes of a particular class. English has many suffixes that display this property, but only one prefix. The prefix *re-* is unique because it can only combine with verbs. Thus, although words such as *pencil, chair,* and *wheel* are typically interpreted as nouns in isolation, words such as *re-pencil, re-chair,* and *re-wheel* are immediately interpreted as verbs as a result of the presence of the *re-* prefix.

The importance of selectional restrictions in morphological hierarchies is well established in the theoretical literature. However, it is not at all clear whether such restrictions and hierarchies relate primarily to word formation processes or whether they might also relate to the manner in which the representations for complex words are structured in the mind and the manner in which complex words are related to other elements within the mental lexicon. This issue is essential to address because it moves us beyond the relatively simple question of what units may be represented in the mental lexicon and toward the much more complex question of how such units are organized and related to one another.

That morphemes must be organized, seems uncontroversial. Compounds such as *fiberglass-boat house* and *fiberglass boathouse* have different meanings. A word such as *undoable* can mean both "not able to be done" and "able to be undone". In all these cases, the key to interpretation must lie in the relation of individual morphemes to the complex construction because, in each pair, the morphemes are identical.

This study explores how these relations are instantiated in the mental lexicon. I first review two experiments that have been conducted in our laboratory that investigate whether hierarchical structure is computed for novel words and the extent to which hierarchical structure plays a role in the recognition of existing trimorphemic words. The evidence thus far suggests that native speakers of English are sensitive to some aspects of morphological structure, but that lexical access is not constrained by morphological hierarchy. The straight-forward hypothesis that representations in the mental lexicon reflect the "syntax of words" as formulated for example by Selkirk (1982) is not supported by the data. As a more psychologically plausible alternative, I propose an underspecified network representation for trimorphemic words and test the predictions of this network approach in a lexical decision experiment in which participants are presented with "preparsed" stimuli.

2. MORPHOLOGICAL STRUCTURE IN TRIMORPHEMIC NONSENSE WORDS

If indeed morphemes with trimorphemic words are grouped in the manner suggested by word syntax theories, then this grouping should in principle be evident in on-line lexical processing. Libben (1993) reasoned that even if hierarchical morphological structure did play a role in lexical processing, its effects would be extremely difficult to detect in experiments with real words because the role of this structure would be very subtle in comparison with other real-word effects such as frequency and abstractness. It was proposed, however, that the effects of morphological structure might indeed be detectable in a non-word paradigm in which by definition, real-word effects could not play a role.

The key feature of the Libben (1993) approach was the creation of trimorphemic nonsense words that could be argued to have left-branching, right-branching, or illegal morphological structure. In all cases, this morphological structure was determined by the interplay between the selectional restrictions of the English prefix *re-* and a set of derivational suffixes with specific selectional restrictions. Thus all trimorphemic stimuli employed in the study contained the prefix *re-*, a nonsense root, and a suffix. This resulted in the three categories of trimorphemic nonsense words shown in Figure 2. As can be seen in Figure 2, the first category shows a left-branching structure. This structure derives from the claim that the prefix *re-* and the suffix *-able* can only attach to verbs. Furthermore, because the result of *–able* affixation is an adjective, the root+suffix form would not be available for *re-* prefixation. Thus, although the full form *re-ponkable* is meaningless, it can only have the left-branching structure shown in category 1 of Figure 2. The same reasoning was employed to motivate the right-branching structure for the category 2 stimulus *reponkize*. Here, because *-ize* can only attach to adjectives to form verbs, the prefix *re-*, which must attach to verbs, obligatorily creates a right-branching structure for the trimorphemic nonsense word.

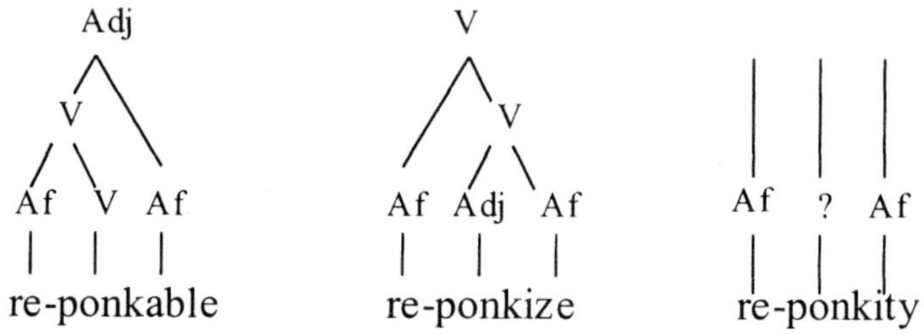

Figure 2. Left-branching, right-branching and illegal nonsense stimuli employed in Libben (1993).

The final crucial stimulus category in this experiment is represented by the word *re-ponkity* in Figure 2. Although this word is no more or less meaningful than the other two stimulus categories, it differs from these in that it can be described as being morphologically illegal. The source of the illegality is that the nonsense root *ponk* cannot simultaneously fulfill the requirements of both the prefix *re-* and the suffix *-ity*. Whereas the prefix requires *ponk* to be a verb, the suffix requires it to be an adjective. This leads to the morphologically illegal structure represented in category 3 of Figure 2.

In the study, participants were presented with all categories of *re-* prefixed stimuli and were required to read them aloud as quickly as possible. The morphologically illegal forms were read significantly slower than the legal ones. No difference was found between left-branching and right-branching legal structures.

The Libben (1993) study offers evidence that the selectional restrictions of affixes play a role in on-line lexical processing. It is important to note, however, that the study does not provide direct evidence for the presence of morphological hierarchies. Rather, it simply reveals that the non-satisfaction of affixes' selectional restrictions leads to elevated response times. In other words, the finding that *reponkity* is more difficult to process than *re-ponkable* and *re-ponkize* does not necessarily lead to the conclusion that real words such as *re-fillable* and *re-formalize* have left and right branching structures respectively. It is also conceivable that the findings in Libben (1993) could reflect analogical effects. The same selectional restrictions that disallow *re-ponkity* also disallow the presence of any English word having the structure *re-X-ity*. Thus naming latency for the legal forms might have been accelerated by the presence of structurally similar real words in the language and the naming latency for illegal forms may have been decelerated by the absence of *re-X-ity* real words.

3. HIERARCHICAL STRUCTURE IN EXISTING WORDS

The considerations above force us to re-visit the feasibility of investigating hierarchical morphological structure psycholinguistically with existing words. In Libben (in press) I reasoned that some of the inter-stimulus effects with real words might be attenuated if we were to employ experimental paradigms in which existing words function as their own experimental controls in a task that targeted the manner in which morphemes are arranged in a multimorphemic word. The resulting study employed a lexical decision paradigm with masked morphological priming. It was argued that if indeed a left-branching word such as *refillable* is represented in the mental lexicon in a manner analogous to *[[re-fill]-able]* and a right-branching word such as *unsinkable* is represented in a manner analogous to *[un-[sink-able]]* then there should be observable differences in the extent to which the word categories are primed by their respective root+suffix substrings (e.g., *fillable* or *sinkable*). The reasoning behind this prediction is that although *fillable* and *sinkable* are both real-word final substrings of their respective trimorphemic words, *sinkable* is a morphological constituent of *unsinkable*, whereas *fillable* is not a morphological constituent of *refillable*. Thus, if morphological constituency counts, right-branching trimorphemic words should show greater root+suffix priming effects.

This prediction was not supported by the data. As can be seen in Table 1, both the left-branching and right-branching stimuli showed significant final substring priming effects. In fact, the priming effect for the left branching stimuli was more than double the magnitude of the effect for the right-branching stimuli — but in the opposite direction to that predicted.

Table 1. Morphological substring priming effects obtained by Libben (in press) with left-branching and right-branching stimuli

Category	*Prime*	*Target*	*Neutral RT*	*Primed RT*	*Priming Effect*
Left-branching	fillable	refillable	887	752	135
Right-branching	sinkable	unsinkable	832	778	54

There are two ways in which these data might initially be interpreted. The first line of interpretation would claim that the experiment offers straightforward evidence against the view that trimorphemic English words are hierarchically structured. The second line of interpretation might claim that the experiment targets surface characteristics of the stimuli rather than the deeper levels of lexical may representation at which we are likely to find morphological effects. Thus, the results reveal that both left-branching and right-branching stimuli show root + suffix priming effects simply because those two morphemes are substrings of the entire unit.

It was reasoned that if surface stimulus characteristics of words are the only things at work in this experiment, the same final-substring priming effects would be obtained for pseudoprefixed words such as *recoverable* and for words with bound roots such as *refutable.* As can be seen in Table 2, however, these stimulus categories showed no priming effects (p >.19).

Table 2. Morphological substring priming effects obtained by Libben (in press) with pseudoprefixed and bound/fused left-branching stimuli

Category	*Prime*	*Target*	*Neutral RT*	*Primed RT*	*Priming Effect*
left-pseudoprefixed	coverable	recoverable	805	796	9
left-bound/fused	futable	refutable	827	808	19

Now, how can these results be accounted for? It seems that morphological hierarchies do not predict the correct results. Yet, the data support the view that the manner in which constituents are represented within multimorphemic strings affects priming patterns. The observation of no priming effects for words such as *recoverable* accords well with native speaker intuitions that the units *cover*, *fund,* and *mark* are not fully represented in the words *recoverable, refundable,* and *remarkable.* Thus, if they were to be considered trimorphemic at all, they would possess extremely strong left-branching structure.

Similarly, words such as *receivable*, *remittable,* and *retractable* must be viewed as having extremely strong left-branching structure. Although a word such as *receivable* may be said to be composed of *prefix + bound root + suffix*, the fact that the substring *receive* is a word but the substring *ceivable* is not, clearly has consequences for the manner in which the multimorphemic string may be linked to other entries in the mental lexicon.

In the following section, I explore how the priming effects discussed above may be captured with relatively simple assumptions about associations within the mental lexicon and no assumptions about the internal structure of lexical entries. This is followed by a report of an "artificial morpheme boundary" experiment that further targets the relationship between trimorphemic English words and their morphological constituents.

4. TRIMORPHEMIC WORDS AS LEXICAL NETWORKS

Virtually all approaches to the organization of words in the mind assume that the mental lexicon is best seen as a network. Individual proposals within this domain differ with respect to the organization of the network, the question of whether it contains subdivisions, and finally the question of whether lexical entries are themselves distributed networks. For the purposes of this discussion, I assume that individual morphemes as well as multimorphemic representations can be considered as individual nodes. Within this framework, the specific proposal that I advance is that hierarchical structure need not be directly represented as a property of multimorphemic entries. Rather, I claim that morphological structure essentially boils down to whether individual constituents of a multimorphemic string have their own representations in the mental lexicon and how those constituents are linked to multimorphemic forms. In Figure 3 below, the left branching, right-branching, pseudoprefixed, and bound-root words discussed in Section 2 are represented. The distinction between thick and thin lines connecting elements reflects the claim that connections between free forms are stronger than those involving bound morphemes (i.e., bound roots and affixes).

As can be seen in Figure 3, the differences posited between left-branching and right-branching structures is simply that in the latter case the prefix + root substring does not exist as a free form, or has a different meaning (as in *unlike* vs. *unlikable*). In the case of a word such as *recoverable*, the representation in the figure claims that its critical characteristic is that the full form is neither linked to the monomorphemic entry for *cover* nor to the *root + suffix* form *coverable,* which both have different meanings. Finally, in the case of *receivable*, no free *root + suffix* form exists, and the link to the bound morpheme *ceive* is weak.

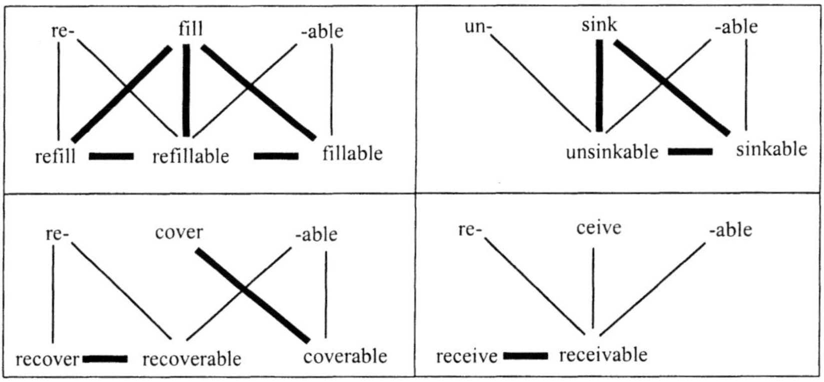

Figure 3. Network configurations for left branching structures (refillable), right-branching structures (unsinkable), pseudoprefixed structures (recoverable) and bound morpheme structures (receivable).

Let us now consider how these representations account for the morphological priming patterns reported in Libben (in press). In the first three representations, the root+suffix prime would activate a representation in the bottom right-hand corner of each frame. It is assumed that the effectiveness of the prime is simply a result of whether a strong line of association exists between the representation in the bottom right-hand corner and the multimorphemic target stimulus, which is represented in the bottom center of all four frames. As is evident in the figure, the left-branching and right branching structures both show strong lines of association, which according to this account, generate priming effects in both cases. The pseudoprefixed items, however, are quite different: In this case, the prime *coverable,* is not directly connected to the target *recoverable* and is therefore unable to facilitate its recognition. The direct strong line of association to the root *cover* does not aid priming, because *cover* is also not associated to the trimorphemic target (in other words, it is not really a root).

Finally, the network associations in Figure 3 also provide an account of the absence of priming effects for words with bound roots. Because the prime *ceivable* does not have an independent entry in the mental lexicon, priming effects can only be obtained through the bound root *ceive* and the suffix -able. These bound roots, however, have only weak lines of association to the target.

It is important to note that the representations in Figure 3 account for the priming effects reported in Libben (in press) without any special mechanisms designed specifically for that purpose. The network configurations simply represent the "facts" of the semantic relations between multimorphemic forms and their morphological substrings.

Is it the case then that morphological hierarchies are not computed at all? The network representations in Figure 3 seem not to require any hypothesis of substructure within multimorphemic entries. The claim in these networks is that morphological constituency is a matter of linkages. While the results of Libben (in press) are consistent with this approach, the morphological priming experiment was not designed to be a test of it. Because the *root + suffix* priming paradigm probes only the bottom-right quadrant of each frame in Figure 3, it does not yield data concerning other aspects of the hypothesized networks and the extent to which they map onto morphological constituency. The experiment reported in the following sections was designed for this purpose.

5. THE ARTIFICIAL MORPHEME BOUNDARY EXPERIMENT

The "Artificial Morpheme Boundary" experiment directly probes whether the processing of trimorphemic words such as *refillable* reflects the representation [[re-fill]-able] that is posited on the basis of affixes' selectional restrictions and, similarly, whether the processing of *unsinkable* reflects the right-branching structure [un-[sink-able]].

In this experimental paradigm, participants were presented with trimorphemic words under one of three conditions:

(a) *The no-break condition*: In this baseline condition, stimuli are presented in an undisrupted manner in the center of the screen.

(b) *The first-break condition*: In this case, three dashes (---) were inserted immediately following the prefix, so that a word such as *refillable* appeared as "re---fillable".

(c) *The second-break condition*: In this case, three dashes (---) were inserted immediately following the root, so that a word such as *refillable* appeared as "refill---able".

If hierarchical structure plays a role in a lexical decision task such as this, lexical processing should be easier when the artificial morpheme boundary (---) occurs at a major constituent boundary. In other words, for left-branching words such as *refillable*, it should be more difficult to process *refill---able* than *re---fillable.* The opposite pattern would be expected for right branching structures: it should be more difficult to process *unsink---able* than *un---sinkable.*

In addition to providing a test of the morphological hierarchy hypothesis, the artificial morphemic boundary experiment offers a test of whether the network approach better predicts the data. Under the network approach, stimuli such as *re---fillable* are not seen as pre-parsed. Rather the artificial morpheme boundary experiment is interpreted as highlighting particular substrings of a multimorphemic word. So, when *refillable* is presented as *re---fillable*, both the whole word and the substring *fillable* are activated. However, when it is presented as *refill--- able*, the whole word and the substring *refill* are activated.

This line of reasoning generates predictions that differ from those presented under the morphological hierarchy hypothesis. If the network representations in Figure 3 are appropriate, and if the artificial morpheme boundary experiment indeed highlights individual substrings, then there should be no difference in processing difficulty for *refillable* presented as *re---fillable* or *refill--- able*. The reason for this is that in both cases access to the whole word representation *refillable* is facilitated by a single strong connection within the network. It makes no difference whether this association to the bottom center unit comes from the left substring or the right substring.

In contrast, substantial differences would be expected for the manner in which right-branching stimuli are presented. The reason for this is that when a word such as *unsinkable* is presented as *un---sinkable,* a direct line of strong association exists between the highlighted substring and the multimorphemic word. This is not the case when the word is presented as *unsink-able*. Because the word *unsink* does not exist, processing is slowed. In other right-branching cases such as *unlikable*, processing is also slowed because the left substring activates a different sense of the root. The source of these predictions in terms of network representations is presented graphically in Figure 4 below.

5.1 Participants

Seventy undergraduate students in linguistics participated as volunteers in the experiment. All were native speakers of English and none had taken part in the Libben (in press) study.

5.2 Stimuli

The full stimulus set consisted of 225 prefixed and suffixed forms based on the stimuli employed by Libben (in press). In total, nine categories of 21-25 words each were constructed. Of these, 125 were existing words of English and 100 were either novel constructions or trimorphemic constructions based on nonsense roots. The five categories of real word stimuli are presented below:

(a) *Left-branching words.* Twenty-five dictionary listings prefixed by *re-* and suffixed by *-able* were selected from the Random House Dictionary of the English Language and Webster's New World English Dictionary. In each case, the root was a verb and the words were thus considered to be left branching (because of the selectional restriction associated with the prefix *re-*). The final two morphemes of these words also formed real words with meanings related to the trimorphemic stimuli.

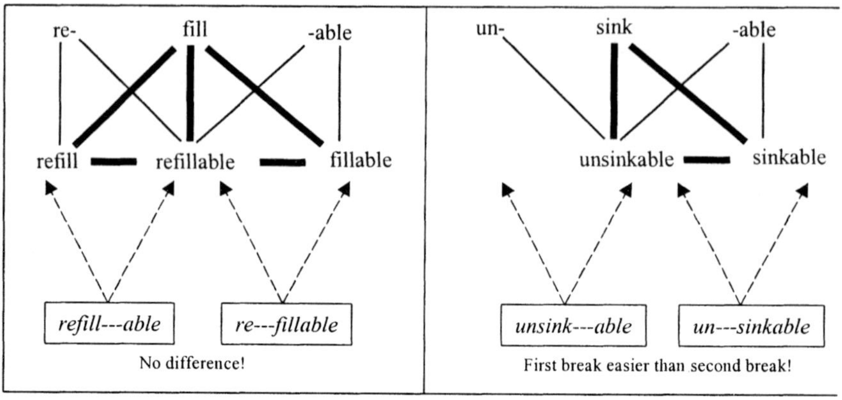

Figure 4. The hypothesised effect of 'first-break' and 'second-break' presentations in terms of network representations for trimorphemic words.

(b) *Right-branching words.* This set was constructed to be the right-branching counterpart of the left-branching stimuli. All 25 words in this set were dictionary entries prefixed by *un-* that were uninterpretable as simple prefixed forms (e.g., **unthink*). Thus they could only be interpreted under a right-branching structure.

(c) *Structurally ambiguous words.* These were 21 dictionary entries that had the form *un-X-able* (e.g., *unfoldable*) but were structurally ambiguous. Thus although these items possessed the same surface form as the true right-branching stimuli, they could be interpreted as also having a morphological tree structure identical to that of the left-branching stimuli. In an off-line segmentation experiment conducted by Libben (in press), participants showed an equal preference (53%) for left segmentations (e.g., *un/foldable*) and right segmentations (e.g., *unfold/able*) of these stimuli. Similarly, de Almeida and Libben (2000) found that both interpretations of these ambiguous stimuli were available in both neutral and biasing sentence contexts.

(d) *Pseudoprefixed stimuli.* This set of 22 stimuli had the form *re-X-able.* However, their final bimorphemic substrings were semantically unrelated to the full trimorphemic string (e.g., *recoverable*).

(e) *Left-branching words with bound/fused roots.* These 25 stimuli also had the form *re-X-able* (e.g., *refutable*, *regrettable*). Although these items share surface characteristics with re-prefixed left-branching stimuli, the status of the root as either a bound or a pseudo-morpheme makes it unclear whether indeed the full forms are treated as trimorphemic stimuli by native speakers of English.

The four categories for which the correct lexical decision response is "no" are presented below. In all cases, the stimuli in these groups begin with prefix *re-* or *un-* and end with the suffix *–able.*

f) *Left-branching novel stimuli*. The 25 items in this category were interpretable English trimorphemic strings (e.g., *refloodable*) that were, however, not listed in standard English dictionaries. It was assumed, therefore, that these left-branching structures would have to be processed in terms of their constituent morphemes.

(g) *Right-branching novel stimuli*. These 25 items were constructed around the same root verbs used for the novel *re*-prefixed stimuli and differed only in that they were prefixed by *un-* rather than by *re-*.

(h) *Nonsense words prefixed by re-*. The 25 words in this category were constructed from the prefix *re-*, a nonsense root such as *ponk*, and the suffix *–ity*.

(i) *Nonsense words prefixed by un-*. The 25 words in this category were constructed from the same nonsense roots employed in (*h*) above. In this case, however, the roots were prefixed by *un-*, rather than *re-*, creating stimuli such as *unponkity*.

5.3 *Procedure*

The participant's task was to decide as quickly as possible whether the words presented on the screen were "real" English words (i.e., words they had seen before). Participants were also warned that "dashes" might appear within the words but to ignore these completely when they occurred and to base their lexical decision on whether the words as wholes were real English words.

Each participant in the experiment was presented with all 225 stimuli. Each stimulus was presented in either the *no-break*, *first-break*, or *no-break* conditions. Participants were assigned to one of three groups such that each stimulus word was presented in all three conditions across groups and each participant saw one-third of the stimuli in each category under each of the presentation conditions.

The experiment was conducted in a single block of trials. In each trial, participants saw a fixation point for 500 milliseconds after which the screen went blank for 250 milliseconds. The target stimulus then appeared in 24 point and remained on the screen until the participants responded by pressing either a key labeled "yes" or a key labeled "no". The "yes" response was provided with the index finger of the preferred hand and the "no" response was provided with the middle finger of the same hand. As soon as the response key was pressed, the screen went blank for 350 milliseconds, which completed the trial.

5.4 *Results and conclusions*

Response times above 2000 milliseconds (3%) and errors were removed from the data set. As a result, the data obtained for the novel stimuli were not analyzed because of the high variability in the manner in which participants classified them. Thus, in the sections below, the data for existing words are reported followed by the data for words with nonsense roots.

5.4.1 Real word stimuli

The analysis of the response times for the three stimulus presentation categories began with the basic assumption that introducing the artificial morpheme boundary (---) into a visually presented stimulus disrupts the stimulus presentation and should therefore elevate lexical decision response times. Thus, in general, there should be a "break cost" associated with both the *first-break* and *second-break* conditions. This prediction was evident in the results. The initial two-way ANOVA showed a significant effect of stimulus presentation type in both the participants analysis (F_{partic} (2,130) = 18.9, p< .0001) and the items analysis (F_{items}(2,236)= 4.7, p=.01). As is shown, in Table 3, the unbroken conditions showed higher response times than the first-break condition (F_{partic} (1,130) = 32.5, p< .0001; F_{items}(1,236)= 7.8, p<.01) and higher response times than the second-break condition (F_{partic} (1,130) = 23.5, p< .0001; F_{items}(1,236)= 6.2, p=.01). There was no overall difference between the first-break and second-break conditions (F_{partic} (1,130) = 0.7=.40; F_{items}(1,236)= 0.1, p=.75).

Table 3. Response times (RT) in milliseconds and standard deviations (SD) by participants for the three stimulus presentation conditions across all real-word stimuli

Category	*RT*	*SD*
No-break	979	254
First-break	1036	266
Second break	1020	255

The next step in the analysis was to calculate, for each stimulus category, the cost of the first break and the cost of the second break in milliseconds. This was done by subtracting the no-break response times from the response times for the first-break and second-break conditions. The resulting *break costs* are presented in Table 4.

As can be seen in Table 4, the data do not support the hierarchical structure approach, which predicted a *cross-over effect* between the left-branching and right branching stimuli. If morphological constituency played a role in this task, the left-branching stimuli would have shown lower cost for the second-break condition. In other words, the last column of Table 4 should have shown a positive rather than the negative value that was obtained.

The network approach predicted no difference between the first-break condition and the second-break condition for the left-branching stimuli. A 50 millisecond difference was found between the first-break and second-break conditions. This difference was significant in the participants analysis, but not in the items analysis. Thus, although neither the hierarchical approach nor the network approach predicts the data fully, the prediction of the hierarchical approach is clearly in the opposite direction to the results obtained.

Table 4. No-break response times in milliseconds and break costs by items for the five categories of real word stimuli

Category	*No break RT*	*1st break (cost)*	*2nd break (cost)*	*1st minus 2nd*
Left-branching *(refillable)*	927	960 (33)	1010 (83)	-50 *P
Right-branching *(unsinkable)*	985	1014 (19)	1059 (74)	-55 *P
Ambiguous *(unfoldable)*	951	1014 (63)	1000 (49)	14
Pseudoprefixed *(recoverable)*	874	988 (114)	935 (61)	53*IP
Bound/fused *(receivable)*	934	1027 (93)	950 (16)	77*IP

*Note. Significance at the .05 level in the participants planned comparisons between first break cost and second break cost is denoted by "*P". Significance in both participants and items analyses is denoted by "*IP"*

The right-branching stimuli also showed a clear preference for the break occurring before the root, resulting in an almost identical pattern (1st minus 2nd = -55 ms) to that shown for the left-branching stimuli.

We are left then with the question of why the right branching and left branching stimuli show essentially the same pattern — namely that the first-break condition was less problematic than the second break condition. This was predicted by neither the hierarchical or network approaches and suggests that perhaps another factor may be playing a role in the determination of the data pattern. As will be more fully discussed below, automatic prefix-stripping, along the lines originally proposed by Taft and Forster (1975), may create a strong overall advantage for the first-break condition over the second-break condition.

The ambiguous stimuli show a balance between the cost associated with the first-break and second-break conditions. This balance in contrast with the bias shown for the right-branching stimuli is important because it points to the conclusion that the experimental paradigm indeed targets deeper levels of lexical association. If surface characteristics were only at work, then there should have been no difference in the patterns shown for the right-branching and ambiguous stimuli.

A similar line of reasoning applies to the data obtained for the pseudoprefixed and bound-root stimuli. In both these cases, the first break was significantly more disruptive than the second break. This is not the pattern shown by the left-branching stimuli. We are forced to conclude then that the experimental paradigm taps deeper levels of lexical representation in the mental lexicon. The fact that the pseudoprefixed and bound-root stimuli show a pattern that is opposite to that of the left-branching stimuli offers evidence in favor of the network hypothesis and against the hierarchical structure hypothesis.

The hierarchical structure hypothesis claims that the left-branching stimuli and the bound root stimuli are essentially two versions of the same thing. In contrast, they are assumed to be entirely different in terms of the network representations in Figure 3. The pattern of results thus supports the network view.

5.4.2 Nonsense word stimuli

For both the *re*-prefixed and *un*-prefixed nonsense stimuli, there was a tendency for participants to find the first-break position less disruptive than the second break position (see Table 5). This tendency reached significance in the participants analysis for *un*-prefixed stimuli. It should be noted that the network hypothesis has no predictions regarding these stimuli because they involve nonsense roots. The hierarchical hypothesis predicts, however, that for the *re*-prefixed stimuli, the first-break condition should be more disruptive than the second break condition. This is not what was observed. Instead, we again see a pattern that seems consistent with the view that participants prefer prefixed-stripped presentations.

Table 5. No-break response times in milliseconds and break costs by items for the two categories of nonsense word stimuli

Category	*No break RT*	*1st break (cost)*	*2nd break (cost)*	*1st minus 2nd*
Left-branching *(reponkable)*	1001	1028 (27)	1054 (53)	-26
Right-branching *(unponkable)*	985	996 (11)	1038 (53)	-42*P

*Note. The symbol "*P" denotes significance at the .05 level in the participants planned comparisons between first break cost and second break cost*

6. DISCUSSION

The results from the artificial morpheme boundary experiment are consonant with those obtained by Libben (in press) and provide converging evidence that positing internal hierarchical structure for existing trimorphemic words does not enhance our ability to account for patterns of lexical processing performance in these experiments. It seems that the pattern of results is not related to an internal structuring of a lexical entry taken in isolation. Rather, the dominant factor is the extent to which complex words are linked to other representations in the mental lexicon that correspond to subunits of the complex word.

We might call the influence of these links on performance in the priming and artificial morpheme boundary experiments, the *morphological network effect*. This effect is, however, only one component of the performance pattern. Another component is evident from the pattern of results obtained for words with nonsense roots. As has been noted above, nonsense word stimuli do not activate any roots or whole words in the mental lexicon and therefore may be seen as revealing general parsing tendencies. The finding of a greater cost associated with breaks after the root is consistent with the view that prelexical morphological parsing operates in a left-to-right manner as has been claimed by Hudson & Buis (1995) and Libben (1994). It seems reasonable to suppose that this parsing directionality results in a bias that favors prefix-stripping over suffix-stripping and thus creates the increased costs associated with the second break position for the nonsense word stimuli in the artificial morpheme boundary experiment.

If indeed left-to-right prelexical parsing and the morphological network effect interact in influencing the lexical decision response times in this experiment, then the results for the left-branching stimuli may be seen as a combination of (a) the tendency to isolate prefixes first and (b) the balanced configuration of the morphological network for these stimuli. For the right branching stimuli, this interaction may have also reduced the cost associated with the first break condition by, for example, making the root *sink* available even in a presentation such as *unsink-able*. In this case, the network would indeed be activated through the root representation, yielding similar profiles for the left-branching and right-branching stimuli.

It is important to note that although left-to-right parsing may play a role in the pattern of results, it cannot wholly predict them. If parsing direction were the only factor at work in this experiment, the ambiguous items (e.g., *unfoldable*) would have also shown a lower cost in the first break condition, resulting in a negative number in the last column of Table 4. In fact, these stimuli showed a significant first break cost (63 ms) and a slightly positive difference (14 ms) between the first break and second break conditions. It appears then that in addition to factors associated with morphological parsing, the data reflect the fact that a first-break is inconsistent with one of the possible interpretations for the ambiguous stimuli. This may account for the increase in first-break cost.

Thus the results of this study offer support for Taft and Forster's (1975) original (and somewhat embattled) proposal that multimorphemic word recognition in English involves a mechanism by which prefixes are stripped from their morphological stems. The effect of this prelexical parsing is then dependent on the nature of the morphological network that it activates.

Returning to the notion of hierarchical structure, we do not see any evidence that the description of words such as *refillable* as left-branching and *unsinkable* as right-branching have any applicability in tasks such as these. It may be the case that the network links that have been posited here may themselves be seen as representing subgroup hierarchies. Nevertheless, there is an important distinction: the hypothesis of morphological networks presented here claims that hierarchical structure is related to the organization among words in the mental lexicon, not within them.

7. APPENDIX

The Core Trimorphemic Stimuli

	LEFT-BRANCHING	RIGHT-BRANCHING	PSEUDOPREFIXED	BOUND/FUSED
1	rearmable	unacceptable	recommendable	rebukable
2	rebuildable	unapproachable	recoverable	receivable
3	recallable	unbelieveable	refinable	reclinable
4	rechargeable	undesirable	reformable	recordable
5	reclaimable	unjoinable	refundable	recoupable
6	refillable	unlikable	refusable	redeemable
7	refoldable	unmeltable	regardable	reducable
8	refreezable	unmovable	relapsable	referable
9	regrowable	unpaintable	releasable	refractable
10	reheatable	unpleasable	remarkable	refutable
11	relinkable	unprintable	remindable	regretable
12	reloadable	unreasonable	removable	rehearsable
13	remixable	unshapable	renewable	relatable
14	remoldable	unshipable	repairable	remittable
15	renameable	unsinkable	replaceable	renounceable
16	repackable	unsolvable	reportable	repeatable
17	repayable	unstoppable	reservable	reproachable
18	replantable	unsweepable	resolvable	respectable
19	rereadable	untamable	restorable	retainable
20	rerollable	unthankable	restrainable	retractable
21	resealable	unthinkable	returnable	retrievable
22	retellable	untouchable	reviewable	reversable
23	retwistable	untrickable		revivable
24	reuseable	unutterable		revokable
25	rewirable	unwatchable		rewardable

	AMBIGUOUS	RIGHT-BRANCHING	UN-NOVEL	RE-NOVEL
1	unarmable	unacceptable	unburnable	reburnable
2	unbendable	unapproachable	unchewable	rechewable
3	unbuttonable	unbelieveable	unchopable	rechopable
4	uncapable	undesirable	uncookable	recookable
5	undoable	unjoinable	undrinkable	redrinkable
6	undressable	unlikable	unfarmable	refarmable
7	unfoldable	unmeltable	unfloodable	refloodable
8	unfoldable	unmovable	ungraspable	regraspable
9	unglueable	unpaintable	unhitchable	rehitchable
10	unhookable	unpleasable	unjoinable	rejoinable
11	unlockable	unprintable	unjumpable	rejumpable
12	unmaskable	unreasonable	unkillable	rekillable
13	unpackable	unshapable	unknockable	reknockable
14	unpavable	unshipable	unlightable	relightable
15	unrollable	unsinkable	unloanable	reloanable
16	unscrewable	unsolvable	unscratchable	rescratchable
17	untieable	unstoppable	unshellable	reshellable
18	untwistable	Unsweepable	unshelvable	reshelvable

19	unwindable	Untamable	unshoutable	reshoutable
20	unwrapable	Unthankable	unspankable	respankable
21	unzipable	Unthinkable	unstompable	restompable
22		Untouchable	unsweepable	resweepable
23		Untrickable	unswimable	reswimable
24		Unutterable	untipable	retipable
25		Unwatchable	unwalkable	rewalkable

8. REFERENCES

Butterworth, B. (1983). Lexical representation. In B. Butterworth (ed.) *Language Production* 2. New York, Academic Press, 257-294.

Hudson, P. T. W. & Buis, D. (1995). Left-to-right processing of derivational morphology. In: L. B. Feldman (ed.), *Morphological aspects of language processing*. Hillsdale, NJ: Lawrence Erlbaum,

Libben, G. (in press). Getting at psychological reality: On- and off-line tasks in the investigation of hierarchical morphological structure. In R. Smyth (Ed.) *Festschrift for Bruce Derwing*.

Libben, G. (1993). Are morphological structures computed during word recognition?. *Journal of Psycholinguistic Research, 22(5)*, 535-544.

Libben, G. (1994). How is morphological decomposition achieved? *Language and Cognitive Processes, 9*, 369-391.

Lieber, R. (1980). *The organization of the lexicon*. PhD Dissertation MIT. [Distributed by IULC 1981a].

McQueen, J. & Cutler, A. (1998). Morphology in word recognition. In: A. Spencer & A. Zwicky (eds.), *The handbook of morphology*. Oxford: Blackwell.

Pesetsky, D. (1985). Morphology and logical form. *Linguistic Inquiry 16*, 193-246.

Selkirk, E. O. (1982). *The syntax of Words*. Linguistic Inquiry Monograph I, Cambridge Mass: MIT Press.

Sproat, R. (1988). Bracketing paradoxes, cliticization and other topics: the mapping between syntax and phonological structure. In M. Everaert, A. Evers, R. Huybregts & M. Trommelen (eds.) and *Morphology Modularity*. Dordrecht: Foris.

Taft, M. (1981). Prefix Stripping Revisited. *Journal of Verbal Learning and Verbal Behavior, 20*, 289-297.

Taft M. & Forster, K.I. (1975). Lexical storage and the retrieval of prefixed words. *Journal of Verbal Learning and Verbal Behavior, 14*, 630-647.

Taft, M. & Forster, K.I. (1976). Lexical storage and retrieval of polymorphemic and polysyllabic words. *Journal of Verbal Learning and Verbal Behavior, 15*, 607-620.

Zwicky, A. (1988). Morphological rules, operations and operation types. *Proceedings of the Fourth Annual Meeting of the East States Society for Computational Linguistics*. 318-334.

9. ACKNOWLEDGEMENT

This research was supported by a Major Collaborative Research Initiative Grant from the Social Sciences and Humanities Research Council of Canada awarded to Gonia Jarema (Co-Principal Investigator and Director), Eva Kehayia, (Co-principal Investigator), and Gary Libben, (Co-Principal Investigator).

10. ADDRESS FOR CORRESPONDENCE

Gary Libben
Department of Linguistics
University of Alberta
4-36 Assiniboia Hall
Edmonton, Alberta
Canada T6G 2E7
Email: gary.libben@ualberta.ca

CRISTINA BURANI AND ALESSANDRO LAUDANNA

MORPHEME-BASED LEXICAL READING: EVIDENCE FROM PSEUDOWORD NAMING

1. INTRODUCTION

A large number of current models of word naming distinguish between a lexical routine, and a non-lexical (either extralexical or prelexical) routine for reading aloud (see, e.g., Coltheart & Rastle, 1994). According to these models, when the lexical pathway is involved, naming is based on whole-word processing and is obtained through a lexical lookup procedure. By contrast, when the non-lexical routine is activated, spoken output is the product of grapheme-to-phoneme conversion which is based on sublexical units, i.e. single graphemes or syllables, and is largely independent of lexical knowledge.

Models of word naming usually do not incorporate one possible source of lexical processing which is constituted by a word's morphological structure. Processing and representation of morphological structure is taken into account by recent models of word recognition (see, e.g., Taft, 1994; Schreuder & Baayen, 1995) but not yet by models of word naming. Several reasons could be responsible for this discrepancy. One is that naming involves more clearly both recognition and production processes and this renders more difficult to articulate hypotheses about how the same type of information is first used for activating orthographic representations in the input lexicon and then for selecting semantic entries and phonological forms for production. Another reason might be that, while in word recognition experiments the morphological structure can be manipulated and contrasted with other types of information, one of he main sources of evidence used for constraining models of naming – errors – cannot be always interpreted unambiguously as morphological errors rather than semantic and/or orthographic/phonological errors.

However, there is increasing evidence that naming may take advantage of morphological constituents, and can be attained by exploiting morpheme-based lexical processing. Evidence comes largely, although not exclusively, from a language (i.e.

Italian) which is rich in morphology while being transparent for orthography-to-phonology conversion. This might pose a challenge to two-routes models of reading. On the one hand, Italian apparently is a good candidate for efficient non-lexical naming: in most cases, no lexical lookup is needed for correctly translating orthography to phonology (even though word stress is assigned lexically). On the other hand, the wide-spread involvement of morphological processing in lexical access to Italian words (see Burani & Laudanna, 1992; Chialant & Caramazza, 1995, for reviews) makes it quite probable that the same sort of processing is involved in reading aloud.

Thus, the issue is to assess whether and how far morpheme-based lexical reading is involved in Italian, how effective it is, and which are the conditions and constraints that might operate on its activation. In this chapter, we will review current evidence for morpheme-based lexical reading. A peculiarity of this evidence is that it was obtained by investigating *morphological* pseudowords, i.e. new combinations made up of different morphemes (for the rationale underlying the use of morphological pseudowords, see Burani, Thornton, Iacobini, & Laudanna, 1995). We will focus specifically, but not exclusively, on studies conducted from our research group, and will suggest how a model of reading aloud might incorporate a morpho-lexical routine. Evidence will be given for factors constraining the activation of morpho-lexical processing. Considerations will be suggested that pertain mainly to Italian but may be extended to the process of reading aloud in other languages.

The chapter is organized as follows. After summarizing some evidence from acquired disturbances of reading, which pioneered research on this topic (1.), evidence from naming experiments will be reviewed. Results will be reported from published studies and from a new experiment. In these studies, naming of pseudowords involving different sorts of affixes (inflections (2.), derivational suffixes and prefixes) was investigated. Results that showed the role of quantitative statistical properties of derivational affixes in constraining morpho-lexical reading, with possible differences for suffixes (3.) and prefixes (4.) will be outlined. Studies that investigated whether different sorts of morpheme combinations may activate different grammatical structures (5.) or different interpretations (6.) in the inner lexicon, and whether the activation of these syntactical and/or semantic representations affects reading performance will be reviewed. Finally, a study that investigated whether different list contexts affected the probability of activating differentially the morpho-lexical and the non-lexical pathways will be reviewed (7.). It will be concluded (8.) that morpheme-based lexical reading is in Italian quite an efficient and strong routine.

2. PRESERVED MORPHO-LEXICAL READING IN PHONOLOGICAL DYSLEXIA

In the eighties' literature on acquired disturbances of reading, some cases were described which provided the first observations on the existence of a morpheme-based lexical pathway for reading aloud.

Two Italian patients were described who, while reading aloud words almost flawlessly, were severely impaired in reading non-words, i.e. orthographically legal linguistic stimuli that did not correspond to existing words. These patients (Job & Sartori, 1984; Caramazza, Miceli, Silveri, & Laudanna, 1985), like other so called phonological dyslexics, were interpreted as suffering of the selective disruption of the mechanism for reading aloud new sequences of letters which are not present in the lexicon (for a recent review, see Coltheart, 1996). In other words, this disturbance of reading seems to result from a disturbance to the non-lexical routine for reading, by which a printed stimulus, although never encountered before, could be read aloud by exploiting sublexical units smaller than the entire word, (i.e., single graphemes, graphemic clusters, syllables), and by converting them in the corresponding phonological units. By contrast, lexical reading of known stimuli, obtained through activation of orthographic, semantic and phonological lexical representations, would be intact in these patients.

However, the two Italian patients reported by Job & Sartori (1984), and by Caramazza et al. (1985), showed quite a better performance when submitted to pseudowords made up of morphological constituents (roots and affixes), although not in the correct combinations. For example, the patient described by Job & Sartori (1984) read much better, with respect to other pseudowords, stimuli like *rileone* (relion), *presedia* (prechair), *aranciando* (oranging) in which either a prefix or a suffix were combined with a word or a root that were not appropriate to the affix.

Analogously, the patient L.B. reported by Caramazza et al. (1985) read much better a pseudoword like *chiediva* (formed by the root *chied-* of the verb *chiedere* (to ask), and by the verb inflectional suffix *-iva* not appropriate to the verb conjugation), than a pseudoword like *chiadova,* that was matched for length, visual and word similarity, but was not parsable in morphemes (neither *chiad* nor *ova* are Italian morphemes). When pseudowords with only one morphological constituent in combination with a non-morpheme were tested, a main role for the root with respect to the suffix was apparent. The patient showed an advantage in reading stimuli formed by real root+not real inflection (e.g., *chiedova*, made up of the real root *chied-* plus the orthographic string *ova*), but no advantage, with respect to non-morphological pseudowords, when the pseudoword included a real inflectional suffix in combination with a non-root (e.g., *chiadiva*, where *chiad* is not a root while *-iva* is a real verb inflection).

The authors drew additional evidence for morpho-lexical reading from the qualitative analysis of the patient's reading errors. The patient made more lexicalizations (namely, substitutions of either an appropriate root or an appropriate suffix) when reading pseudowords with morphological structure than when reading nonmorphological pseudowords.

This pattern of errors is consistent with the frequently described tendency in patients of this type to make lexicalizations in their attempts to read aloud non-words (see, e.g., De Bastiani, Barry, & Carreras, 1987; Patterson & Marcel, 1992). Additionally, the high proportion of morpheme-based lexicalizations is further evidence for reliance, in reading, on morphemically structured lexical representations.

Recently, Laine & Niemi (1997), relying on the assumption that inflected Finnish nouns are recognized (and retrieved) through their roots and suffix representations, tested a Finnish deep dyslexic patient for reading morphologically structured pseudowords. Like in the Italian case reported by Caramazza et al. (1985), only bound roots and inflectional suffixes were considered. There were four types of pseudowords. These could include either two or one (either the root or the inflection) or no morphological constituents.

All the pseudowords were read worse than real morphologically complex words. Pseudowords with morphemic structure were not read better than other pseudowords, because of floor effects due to the severity of the patient's reading disorder (deep dyslexia). However, interesting evidence came from the qualitative analysis of the patient's responses. When the number of correctly read constituents was scored, there was a facilitation effect due to the presence in the stimulus of a morpheme. However, the facilitation was asymmetrical in the sense that the existence of real suffixes facilitated root reading, but suffix reading was equally poor for root+suffix and non-root+suffix combinations. In other words, while inflectional suffixes were read poorly in all conditions, the probability of correct root reading reflected pseudoword structure: roots occurring with suffixes were read better than the same roots occurring with a non-suffix. This root facilitation effect was taken as evidence, like in Caramazza et al.'s (1985) study, for differential roles of roots with respect to inflectional suffixes.

Furthermore, when neologistic responses carrying one or more morphemes were analyzed, it was found that they were significantly more numerous in response to a morphologically complex pseudoword than to morphologically simple pseudowords. Like lexicalizations of morphologically complex pseudowords described by Caramazza et al. (1985), these neologistic morphologically complex responses were evidence for activation of morphemic lexical representations.

In synthesis, the reviewed cases demonstrate the possibility of segmenting and accessing orthographic lexical units that are smaller than the whole-word and correspond to single morphemic constituents. The morphological units in the input lexicon (roots and affixes) would activate the lexical pathway, which is intact in the patients, and would allow reading aloud by activating corresponding phonological units in the output lexicon, thus bypassing the patients' impairment in reading nonce stimuli.

For patients characterized by a disturbance of non-lexical reading, the possibility of relying on morphological lexical units when reading new stimuli is advantageous, also because the morphemic units are available as preassembled units not only in the input lexicon but also in the output components which are involved in spoken production. The possibility of relying on preassembled units would thus obviate the difficulties encountered by these patients in tasks in which phonological abilities like phonological segmentation or specifically phonological assembly are involved (Patterson & Marcel, 1992).

By showing the involvement of a morpheme-based lexical reading pathway, these cases provide evidence that the inner lexicon, and specifically the phonological output lexicon, is structured morphologically (for additional evidence from studies of patients with different disturbances in different languages, see also Panzeri, Semenza, Ferreri, & Butterworth, 1990; Badecker & Caramazza, 1991; Niemi, Laine, & Tuominen, 1994; Laine, Niemi, Koivuselkä-Sallinen, & Hyönä, 1995).

The study of patients with selective disturbances to pseudoword reading is quite useful for investigating the morpho-lexical reading process, as well as the morphological organization of the inner lexicon. However, evidence from patients is usually based on the quantitative and qualitative analysis of errors. While being inspiring for the study of the normal process of reading aloud and while providing interesting data for a model of morpho-lexical processing, neuropsychological evidence should be usefully integrated with on line studies in which reading components and processes are further detailed by inspecting naming latencies under different conditions and with different sorts of stimuli.

3. READING ALOUD INFLECTED PSEUDOWORDS

In a follow-up of Caramazza et al.'s (1985) neuropsychological study, Laudanna, Cermele, & Caramazza (1997) ran two experiments with unimpaired adult participants. Participants named aloud as quickly and as accurately as possible pseudowords with differing constituencies. The four sets of pseudowords that were submitted to naming were of the same types that were employed by Caramazza et al. (1985) for testing their patient's reading, and partly by Caramazza, Laudanna, & Romani (1988, Experiments 1 and 2) for a broader lexical decision study with unimpaired adults.

One set consisted of fully morphologically decomposable pseudowords (e.g., *duriva*, formed by the verbal root *dur-* of the verb *durare* (to last) and by the verb inflectional suffix *-iva*, not appropriate to the root's verbal conjugation). The control set was constituted of morphologically non-decomposable pseudowords including neither a root nor a suffix (e.g., *deliso*, where neither *del* nor *iso* are morphemes). There were then two intermediate sets, which were formed by a root plus a non-inflection (e.g., *donaca*, including the verbal root *don-* of the verb *donare* (to donate) and the non-morphological string *aca*), and by a non-root plus a real inflection (e.g., *dediva*, where the non-root *ded* is combined with the verbal inflection *-iva*), respectively.

The experimental list was intended to favor lexical processing of pseudowords. Accordingly, the experimental pseudowords were presented in a list which included 67% words and 33% pseudowords, both experimental and fillers. The assumption was that, if morpheme-based reading was elicited in this context, and if morpho-lexical reading via preassembled morphemic constituents was more efficient than non-lexical reading, morphologically complex pseudowords would be named more quickly and more accurately than pseudowords with no or partial morphological constituency. The facilitatory effect of morpheme-based reading should arise from the possibility of exploiting, for pronunciation, the combination of preassembled morphemic units, whereas pronunciation of non-decomposable pseudowords, which cannot access the lexicon, must necessarily be accomplished through the non-lexical procedure by segmenting, converting and assembling more and smaller units (letters, letter clusters and/or syllables).

Results were expected to complement the opposite pattern found in lexical decision (Caramazza et al., 1988), where decisions to pseudowords with morphological constituencies showed lexical interference. In lexical decision, pseudowords which included two morphemes were rejected more slowly and less accurately than pseudowords which included only one morpheme (either a root or an inflection), and all of them were rejected with longer latencies and higher error rates than non-morphological controls.

For reading, the additional hypothesis was made that partial morphological structure, as present in root+non-inflection stimuli and in non-root+inflection stimuli, should not be sufficient to involve the lexical system for pronouncing pseudowords. According to the hypothesis, the likelihood that the morpho-lexical routine is engaged in pseudoword reading is higher for the stimuli that meet all the conditions for the lexical status, that is stimuli which are exhaustively parsable in morphemes, like any word of the language. Furthermore, pseudowords entirely parsable in morphemes may be read through one pathway (the lexical pathway), while pseudowords with partial morphological structure would require the additional operation of combining the outputs of two different pathways.

Results of Laudanna et al.'s (1997) Experiment 2 supported the latter prediction: only root+inflection pseudowords were named more quickly and more accurately than all the other pseudowords. No advantage was found for stimuli including only one morpheme. Consequently, it was concluded that morpho-lexical reading is exploitable in Italian, at least under appropriate list conditions and at the additional condition that both the constituents of the stimulus have lexical representations corresponding to a morpheme.

4. IS MORPHO-LEXICAL READING CONSTRAINED BY QUANTITATIVE PROPERTIES OF AFFIXES? EVIDENCE FROM DERIVATIONAL SUFFIXES

The studies reviewed so far took in consideration pseudowords including inflectional suffixes. In principle, there should be no reasons for not expecting that derivational affixes may function as access units as well and may lead to activation of the lexical pathway for reading. There is large evidence that, in different languages, affixed derived stimuli are decomposed in root+derivational affix during lexical access (see, e.g., Taft & Forster, 1975; Taft, 1979; Burani & Caramazza, 1987; Colé, Beauvillain, & Segui, 1989; but see, for a different view, Feldman, 1994; see also, for reviews, Burani & Laudanna, 1992; Sandra, 1994).

However, more recently both Laudanna & Burani (1995), and Schreuder & Baayen (1994) made detailed arguments and provided data showing why derivational affixes should not be considered a homogeneous class. Specifically, these authors suggest that various characteristics of derivational affixes may affect the probability that an affixed derived stimulus is processed and represented in terms of its constituent root and affix.

Among the characteristics of derivational affixes that constrain processing and representation, quantitative properties have a specific role. The most obvious quantitative property that may affect processing is frequency. If it is assumed that words including more frequent morphemes are more likely to be accessed via morphological parsing, a role for affix frequency could also be assumed.

While the role of root frequency in affecting morphological parsing of affixed words has been object of investigation (see, e.g., Taft, 1979; Burani, Salmaso, &

Caramazza, 1984; Burani & Caramazza, 1987; Colé et al., 1989; Beauvillain, 1996; Laudanna & Caramazza, 1997; see also Funnell, 1987 for extensions to the performance of dyslexic patients), surprisingly frequency of affixes (perhaps for the difficulty of measuring it) has been quite rarely taken into account.

There could be two different characterizations of affix (and more generally morpheme) frequency. One quantitative characterization is in terms of the number of word types (or lemmas) in which a given affix occurs in a given language. This factor might also be called "numerosity" (of the affix): the higher the number of word types in which a given affix occurs, the more "numerous" the affix is. This measure might play a crucial role in favoring morphological parsing (Frauenfelder & Schreuder, 1992), being strictly connected to the quantitative characterization of affix productivity (see Baayen, 1992; Bybee, 1995).

A different quantitative measure of affix frequency (usually referred to as "frequency") is in terms of the cumulative frequency of all the occurrences of the words (i.e., word tokens) in which a given affix occurs.

Both frequency measures might affect morphological decomposition, with words which include affixes that occur in a greater number of word types and word tokens being more likely to be accessed quickly and effectively via their constituent morphemes than words that include less numerous and less frequent affixes.

For most affixes the two frequency measures tend to be highly correlated. Thus, in a first study on the effects of affix frequency in reading, Burani, Dovetto, Thornton, & Laudanna (1997) did not disentangle the two measures, and compared two sets of affixes differing for both the frequency measures. Burani et al. (1997) aimed at showing not only that derivational suffixes could function as lexical units in activating the morpho-lexical reading pathway, but also that the probability of morpho-lexical reading is constrained by the suffix' frequency properties.

Fully morphologically decomposable pseudowords were used. These stimuli seemed particularly appropriate in the light of the following consideration. When considering the role of frequency factors in determining the probability for a word to be accessed through its morphemic constituents, not only frequency of the included morphemes, but also the balance between morpheme frequencies and whole-word frequency (i.e., the frequency of that specific root-affix combination) should be relevant for processing.

Low frequency morphologically complex words that include high frequency constituent morphemes should be the best candidates to be accessed through morphological decomposition (see Burani & Laudanna, 1992; Frauenfelder & Schreuder, 1992; Schreuder & Baayen, 1995; Burani & Thornton, in press). In this respect, morphological pseudowords are interesting cases. In a sense, they are cases of zero whole-word frequency (the specific combination being not existing in the language), with morphemic constituents of varying frequencies. While not activating whole-word access units, pseudowords of this type are nevertheless candidates for activating morphemic access units and, consequently, they might show effects of differing frequencies of morphemic constituents.

Burani et al. (1997) ran both a lexical decision and a naming experiment. In lexical decision, the differential probability of activating morphemic access units resulted in great interference for pseudowords which included suffixes that occur in many word types and word tokens (i.e. suffixes with "high" quantitative values, hereafter H) with respect to non-suffixed control pseudowords, and in a null interference for pseudowords including suffixes that occur in fewer word types and tokens (i.e. suffixes with "low" quantitative values, hereafter L) with respect to control pseudowords.

By contrast, in the naming task the opposite pattern of results was expected: pseudowords including frequent suffixes which are more likely to be activated would be named more quickly and more accurately (with respect to control pseudowords) than pseudowords including infrequent suffixes that are less likely to be activated.

This pattern should result from the fact that pseudowords of the first kind, although not susceptible to be read lexically as whole strings (being non-existing root-suffix combinations), would nevertheless benefit of lexical reading by accessing the lexicon through both the root and the suffix. By contrast, suffixed pseudowords which include suffixes with "low" quantitative values, being less likely to gain access to the lexicon via root and suffix parsing, would also be less likely to take advantage of lexical naming. Suffixed pseudowords of the latter kind would be preferentially read through the non-lexical route, not differently from their unsuffixed controls. Accordingly, suffixed pseudowords of this latter type should not be named faster than non-suffixed controls.

Burani et al. (1997) selected two groups of nominal and adjectival derivational suffixes which had extremely different frequency values. There were four suffixes in each set (*-ario,-ezza,-ismo,-ista* in set H; *- ardo,-igia,-igno,-ingo* in set L).

The selected suffixes were combined with unambiguous verbal roots of medium-high frequency that were inappropriate to the suffixes by violating restrictions on the syntactic category of the base (the selected suffixes combine only with nominal or adjectival roots).

Each suffixed pseudoword was matched with a control pseudoword. This included the same root in combination with a non-suffix which had the same phonological and syllabic structure as the suffix. The sequences corresponding to a suffix and the control sequences were matched for frequency calculated on word tokens.

Thus pseudowords in each suffixed-control pair had the same length, the same syllabic structure, analogous orthographical/phonological structure, the same bigram frequency, the same frequency of the initial string (the root), and the same orthographic frequency of the final part, either corresponding to a suffix or to a non-suffix. Pseudowords in the four sets were also matched for their overall degree of similarity to a real word.

In synthesis, there were four sets of pseudowords, arranged in a 2x2 design, in which the main factors were the presence vs. absence of a Suffix, and the High vs. Low Frequency of the orthographic string corresponding either to a possible suffix or to a non-suffix.

Examples were: *guardismo* (formed by *guard-* and *-ismo*) for the suffixed set including High frequency Suffixes, *guardosta* (formed by *guard-* and *osta*) for its control set including High frequency Control sequences; *nutrigno* (formed by *nutr-* and *-igno*) for the suffixed set including Low frequency Suffixes, *nutregna* (formed by *nutr-* and *egna*) for its control set including Low frequency Control sequences.

The experimental list included 50% words and 50% pseudowords.

With respect to previous studies in which naming of morphological pseudowords was investigated (Taft, Hambly, & Kinoshita, 1986; Laudanna et al., 1997), this experiment not only extended investigation to affixes characterized by varying quantitative properties, but it had also the advantage of contrasting suffixed and control pseudowords which had exactly the same initial sequence of letters. In this way, possible asymmetries between suffixed and control stimuli could not be attributed to different orthographical/phonological characteristics of the onset of the stimulus to be named.

Table 1 shows the mean reaction times and error scores for the different sets of pseudowords.

Table 1. Naming times, percent errors and differences in reaction times and errors between suffixed and control pseudowords (Adapted from Burani et al., 1997)

	Suffixed Pseudowords		Unsuffixed Pseudowords		Effect size	
	RT	ERR (%)	RT	ERR (%)	RT	ERR (%)
HF	635	9	669	13	-34	-4
LF	635	12	648	10	-13	+2

Note. HF: High-frequency final sequence; LF: Low-frequency final sequence

Results on reaction times showed that suffix type affected naming of pseudowords: the presence of a suffix in combination with a root facilitated pseudoword naming when the suffix was very frequent and numerous. In this case, significantly shorter naming times and lower error scores were found for suffixed pseudowords with respect to control pseudowords. By contrast, the tendency to faster naming for pseudowords which included suffixes with "low" quantitative values with respect to their controls, only approached significance. This tendency was further weakened by the trade off between the differences on reaction times and on error scores. In synthesis, there was no evidence for facilitation in the case of pseudowords that included suffixes with "low" values.

These results show that the probability that a suffix allows for lexically mediated reading could be constrained by the quantitative properties of the affix itself, like its numerosity (i.e. the number of word types in which it occurs), and its frequency (i.e. the number of word tokens in which it is included in a corpus). Specifically, suffixes characterized by high quantitative values activate units of processing/representation in the lexical reading route, while suffixes with extremely low quantitative values do not seem to activate corresponding lexical units, at least not for the purpose of naming morphologically complex stimuli.

The results obtained by Burani et al. (1997) provide further evidence for a class of models of lexical access (Burani & Laudanna, 1992; Frauenfelder & Schreuder, 1992; Chialant & Caramazza, 1995; Laudanna & Burani, 1995; Schreuder & Baayen, 1995), in which activation of morphemic units (morphological decomposition) in processing morphologically complex stimuli is not mandatory, as it is assumed by models like Taft's (1991, 1994), but is conditioned by the characteristics of both the derived form (for contrasting results in different languages on the role of semantic transparency of derived words, see Marslen-Wilson, Tyler, Waksler, & Older, 1994 for English; Bentin & Feldman, 1990; Frost, Forster, & Deutsch, 1997, Exp.5, for Hebrew), and of its constituent morphemes.

Burani et al. (1997) showed that the differential probability for morphemic units of being activated may be constrained by their quantitative characteristics, and this has consequences for morpho-lexical reading. The facilitation consequent from the availability of preassembled affix units would be obtained only when affixes are frequent and numerous. By contrast, for affixes characterized by extremely low values in terms of frequency and numerosity, preassembled morpho-lexical units would not be available.

5. NO ROLE OF QUANTITATIVE PROPERTIES IN READING PREFIXED PSEUDOWORDS? NEW FINDINGS

The data presented in the preceding section concur to show that units which could equally well be considered derivational affixes, are not equally likely activated as processing units. The quantitative properties that affected, for suffixes, the probability of relying on corresponding lexical units for reading, should in principle affect the probability of activating units corresponding to prefixes as well.

Prefixed pseudowords were investigated, for lexical decision, by Laudanna, Burani, & Cermele (1994). Among the quantitative properties that could contribute to the "salience" of the orthographical string corresponding to an affix, thus enhancing the availability of its corresponding access unit, Laudanna et al. (1994) included the rate of orthographic ambiguity (or confusability) of a prefix with existent homographic pseudoprefixes in a given language. This measure is derived by rating, on either word types or word tokens, the number of strings corresponding to real prefixes (e.g., *re-* in *reload*) to the number of cases in which the same string corresponds to a merely orthographic non-morphemic sequence (a pseudoprefix) (e.g., *re* in *religion*).

Laudanna et al. (1994) assumed that, when the number of truly prefixed word types beginning with a given prefix (or the number of their occurrences) is high relative to the number of word types (or to the number of word occurrences) in which the same orthographic sequence is present as a pseudoprefix, the probability that the prefix activates a lexical representation is higher. This measure was found to be the better predictor of the probability for the prefix to be accessed as a morphemic processing unit.

In a new study, that will be described below, we submitted to speeded naming stimuli of the same type considered in Laudanna et al.'s (1994) Experiment 2 of lexical decision, to evaluate the impact on prefix processing of two variables, namely the number of prefixed word types and the proportion of really prefixed word types.

We used prefixes as Laudanna et al. (1994), divided in three experimental categories which significantly diverged among each other for the values of one or both variables. The experimental categories included:

1) Prefixes (e.g., *co-*) which had low values for both variables (they occurred in a low number (LN) of prefixed word types and in a low proportion (LP) of truly prefixed word types with respect to pseudoprefixed words, LN-LP).
2) Prefixes (e.g., *sub-*) which also occurred in a low number of prefixed word types in the language. However, in this case, the small number corresponded to a high proportion (HP) of truly prefixed word types beginning with that sequence (LN-HP).
3) Prefixes (e.g., *dis-*) occurring in a high number (HN) of prefixed word types, this high number also representing a high proportion of word types beginning with that sequence (HN-HP).

If the absolute number of prefixed words in the language is the main factor affecting the probability that a given prefix acts as a morphemic lexical unit in reading, then we would expect quicker naming latencies for pseudowords containing prefixes of the third category (prefixes occurring in many words) with respect to control pseudowords. If, as shown by Laudanna et al. (1994) for lexical decision, the relevant dimension in predicting the activation of a prefix processing unit is the proportion of prefixed vs. pseudoprefixed words in the language, we would expect significant effects of prefixed pseudowords, with respect to controls, in the third as well as in the second category, where prefixes had an equally high proportion of truly prefixed words in the language. If both parameters are important in affecting the likelihood that a prefix is activated in the mental lexicon, then we would expect effects ordered by the decreasing values of both variables from the third category to the first.

The nine selected prefixes, three for each category, were the same as in Laudanna et al. (1994). The three prefixes included in the first category (LN-LP), were *sin-*, *dia-* and *co-*. In Italian, these prefixes appear in a low number of prefixed words, which represents a low percentage over the total number of words (prefixed and pseudoprefixed) beginning with the same orthographic sequences. In the second category (LN-HP), the three prefixes were *sur-*, *sub-* and *ir-*. They appear in a low number of prefixed words, but the percentage of prefixed words over the number of prefixed plus pseudoprefixed words is high. In the third category (HN-HP), the three selected prefixes, *dis-*, *ri-* and *im-*, are present in a much higher number of prefixed words, which also represents a high percentage over the total number of prefixed plus pseudoprefixed words.

Each of the nine prefixes was combined with four different nouns of Italian (different from those used by Laudanna et al., 1994), in order to form 36 prefixed pseudowords, 12 for each experimental category. An equal number of control pseudowords were created, in which the same nouns were combined with nine different non-morphemic orthographic sequences. These sequences had the same bigram or trigram frequency in initial position, the same CV structure and the same initial phoneme as the prefixes they were matched with.

The control sequences were the following (in parentheses we report the prefix with which they were paired). Cat. 1 (LN-LP): *sil* (sin-), *die* (dia-), *ca* (co-). Cat. 2 (LN-HP): *sir* (sur-), *suc* (sub-), *ur* (ir-). Cat. 3 (HN-HP): *des* (dis-), *ra* (ri-), *er* (im-).

Each category of prefixed pseudowords was exactly matched with its own control category for length (mean length = 7.5; range = 7-8) and for word similarity, measured by means of the N count (Coltheart, Davelaar, Jonasson, & Besner, 1977). Across categories, prefixed pseudowords were matched for semantic interpretability, assessed by empirical ratings on a seven-point rating scale. The mean values of interpretability were 3.64, 3,49 and 3.62 for categories 1 through 3. These differences were not significant in the ANOVAs by participants and by items ($p>.1$ in both cases).

Examples of stimuli pairs (prefixed and non-prefixed pseudowords, respectively) in each category are the following. Cat. 1: *sintorre-siltorre*. Cat. 2: *surmassa-sirmassa*. Cat. 3: *disbeffa-desbeffa*.

Sixty-two participants were asked to name as quickly and as accurately as possible, a list composed of three hundred and fifty stimuli, half words and half pseudowords. Each participant saw thirty-six members of experimental-control pseudoword pairs, in order not to see the same embedded word twice. For each experimental-control pseudoword pair, the entire set of single scores was provided by two participants presented with two complementary sublists.

In the analysis of results, four pairs of prefixed-control pseudowords in Category 2 (pseudowords including the prefix-control pair *sub-/suc-*) were excluded from the analyses because of high error rates due to articulatory difficulties associated with the phonemic sequences *subr*, *subl*, *sucr*, *sucl* included in the pseudowords (e.g., *sublatta* and *suclatta*). After excluding these items, the three experimental groups were still matched for the relevant variables.

Table 2. Naming times, percent errors and differences in reaction times and errors between prefixed and control pseudowords

	Prefixed Pseudowords		Unprefixed Pseudowords		Effect size	
	RT	ERR (%)	RT	ERR (%)	RT	ERR (%)
LN/LP	605	11	631	16	-26	-5
LN/HP	588	10	620	16	-32	-6
HN/HP	569	6	591	13	-22	-7
Mean	587	9	614	15	-27	-6

Note. LN: Low number of prefixed words; HN: High number of prefixed words
LP: Low percentage of prefixed words; HP: High percentage of prefixed words

Mean reaction times and percentage errors for the three experimental conditions and their respective controls are reported in Table 2. Taken as a whole, the prefixed pseudowords were read 27 milliseconds faster and induced about 6% fewer errors than non-prefixed pseudowords. Two-way Anovas by participants and by items were performed on both reaction times and error data and showed the following pattern of results. A significant main effect of prefixedness for reaction times was obtained in the analysis by participants ($F(1,30) = 35.7$, $p <.001$), while in the analysis by items it was only marginally significant ($F(1,58) = 3.32$, $p <.08$). The interaction between prefixedness and prefix type for reaction times was very far from significance ($F<1$), both by participants and by items. A significant difference between experimental and control condition was obtained for error data in the analyses by participants ($F(1, 30) = 17.23$, $p <.001$) and by items ($F(1,58) = 8.1$, $p <.008$). Even in this case, the interaction between prefixedness and prefix type was not significant by participants ($F(2,60) = .32$) and by items ($F(2,58) = .17$).

Additional comparisons based on Duncan's test were carried out in order to detail the pattern of single comparisons between prefixed pseudowords and the respective control categories. The results of these comparisons revealed significant differences on both reaction times and errors for all the possible comparisons, with a protection level that was always below .01. In sum, the results show that pseudowords including prefixes are named significantly more quickly and more accurately than corresponding non-prefixed pseudowords, irrespectively of differences among prefixes in the two quantitative measures considered (number of word types in which the prefix occurred, and proportion of truly prefixed words over the total number of prefixed plus pseudoprefixed words).

Results from naming prefixed stimuli are at variance with those obtained on naming stimuli with derivational suffixes. Empirical evidence is at the moment scarce to draw strong conclusions. However, among possible reasons for explaining the different pattern of results between suffixes and prefixes, the following two arguments may have some interest.

First, in prefixed pseudowords prefixes are combined with whole words, while in suffixed pseudowords suffixes attach to roots that, in Italian, never coincide with a possible word (i.e., they are always bound). Even though one could argue that the recurrence of a root across many word forms contributes to its saliency, another reasonable hypothesis might be that, when an affix has a low frequency and consequently is less easily activated in the lexicon, the presence in the affixed stimulus of an entire word might help the segmentation of the stimulus and its parsing in constituent morphemes, thus favoring the identification of the (weakly available) prefix. By contrast, the absence of an entire word in the suffixed stimulus would not equally favor the segmentation of the (analogously weakly available) suffix.

The second possible reason for the different pattern of results between suffixes and prefixes is related to the first, but it involves other mechanisms. In most Italian prefixed words – as well as in our prefixed pseudowords which tried to mimic real words – the morphemic boundary between prefix and word tends to coincide with the syllabic boundary. The same does not hold for the majority of suffixes, and did not hold for our specific experimental set of suffixes. For most derivational suffixes, the initial vowel tends to be split from the remaining part of the suffix, becoming part of the last syllable of the base. For the purposes of the naming task, which probably implies the activation of both morpho-lexical and non-lexical pathways (see Conclusions, for further considerations), the congruence of syllabic and morphemic composition may be of some importance. This congruence could have some role in favoring morpho-lexical naming also for prefixes with "low" quantitative parameters. Even in case the syllable-based non-lexical pathway is quicker in giving an output with respect to the morpho-lexical pathway, nevertheless its phonological output (specifically, the output of the initial syllable) would be congruent with that provided by the slowly activated morpho-lexical pathway.

By contrast, the lack of coincidence between morphemic and syllabic information in suffixed pseudowords could be disadvantageous for *low* suffixes. These suffixes, which already do not benefit from sufficiently strong morpho-lexical activation, could be further interfered by the non-congruent syllabic unit which would be activated in the non-lexical route. This hypothesis, however, should be explicitly addressed through more direct empirical tests.

6. ANY ROLE FOR AFFIXES' SELECTIONAL RESTRICTIONS IN MORPHO-LEXICAL READING?

In our studies reviewed so far, derivationally affixed pseudowords in the different experimental groups were controlled for syntactical/semantic characteristics of the combination. This constraint was adopted because, when testing items for possible differences due to quantitative properties of the affixes, we aimed at excluding that the differences could be attributable to syntactical or semantic differences in the pseudowords resulting from the combination.

Possible structural differences in the pseudowords were controlled by equally violating, in the groups that were compared, the selectional restrictions of the affix on the grammatical category of the base. The suffixed pseudowords used by Burani et al. (1997) all involved nominal or adjectival suffixes that did not attach to verbal roots. Thus they were combined with verbal roots, categorically inappropriate to the suffix. Conversely, prefixes selected by Laudanna et al. (1994), and used also for the naming experiment reported in the preceding section, all should attach to verbs. Therefore, in the pseudowords they were combined with nouns, that are categorically inappropriate to the prefix.

Furthermore, in order to match the experimental items for possible differences in semantic plausibility, the items were submitted, before selection, to ratings for interpretability. Participants rated each item on a 7-point scale, from "not interpretable" to "fully interpretable". Items were selected that, in the different groups, were matched for the degree of interpretability.

Because of their relevance in licensing a new combination, syntactic and semantic properties of new root-affix combinations should play a more central role in tasks like lexical decision. However, syntactic and semantic characteristics of new root-affix combinations could be systematically investigated in order to assess whether they are involved in morpho-lexical reading as well.

The only study, to our knowledge, that addressed the issue whether computation of hierarchical morphological structures is involved in reading aloud, took in consideration, for English, pseudowords made up of nonsense roots which were simultaneously both prefixed and suffixed (Libben, 1993). The author adopted stimuli of this type in order to vary systematically structural configurations without involving effects of lexical frequency, semantic plausibility, or lexical transparency.

Pseudowords of the three following types, i.e.(i) *re-birmable*, (ii) *re-birmize*, and (iii) *re-birmity* were constructed. Pseudowords of the third type were morphologically illegal, because they included illegally affixed nonsense roots: the nonsense root *birm* cannot simultaneously satisfy the selectional restrictions of the two affixes (i.e., it cannot be both a verb and an adjective, as required by the prefix *re-*, which can only attach to verbs, and by the suffix *-ity*, which creates nouns by only attaching to adjectives). Thus, differently from pseudowords in (i) and in (ii), pseudowords in (iii) cannot be assigned a morphological structure.

Naming latencies were significantly longer to morphologically "illegal" pseudowords of the third (*rebirmity*) type. However, the structural differences between left branching pseudowords of the (i) *re-birmable* type, and right branching pseudowords of the (ii) *re-birmize* type, did not result in different naming latencies.

From these results, Libben (1993) concluded that, although morphological computation is not sensitive to the hierarchical ordering of morphemes (no differences were found between legal left branching and right branching structures), nevertheless it plays a role in lexical processing. Participants would compute morphological representations (as shown by longer latencies to illegal structures that violate the selectional restrictions of affixes) as part of the normal word recognition process, mainly because of the role played by selectional restrictions in the creation of interpretable structures.

7. MORPHO-LEXICAL NON-SEMANTIC READING

New or not lexicalized structures can be more or less interpretable as a result of combining the meanings of constituent morphemes. Thus new combinations of morphemes which equally do not violate selectional restrictions on the grammatical category of the base can be assigned meanings in different degrees. In other words, although structurally equal, new morphological combinations can be more or less semantically interpretable.

That the assignment of meaning may affect the process of accepting a word (especially when it is low-frequency), as an existent one, is not a recent result (see James, 1975). More recently, it was shown that meaning assignment may affect lexical decision to new combinations of morphemes. Both Coolen, Van Jaarsveld, & Schreuder (1991) for new Dutch compounds, and Burani, Dovetto, Spuntarelli, & Thornton (1999) for Italian new root-suffix combinations, showed that lexical decision was strongly affected by semantic interpretability of the new combinations. With other factors controlled for, participants were slower and made more errors in deciding that the new combinations were non-existent when they were highly interpretable.

Investigating whether semantic interpretability of new morphemic combinations may also affect morpheme-based lexical reading implies assuming that the lexical process of reading aloud may involve deeper components of processing in which not only the stored forms corresponding to morphemes, but also the combination of their meanings, are activated. It is controversial whether naming aloud involves activation of semantics. The activation of semantics is assumed to depend on several characteristics of the language under investigation, of the context and of the words themselves (see, e.g., Strain, Patterson & Seidenberg, 1995, for naming of English low-frequency words being affected by concreteness).

However, the possibility could be considered that, in reading aloud, (morpho-) lexical representations are exploited, with no necessary involvement of the semantic component. This possibility would assume activation of the components in which lexical representations corresponding to morphemes are stored as formal units, with no involvement of their semantic counterpart.

Evidence for lexical non-semantically mediated oral reading (the "third reading route") comes almost exclusively from the neuropsychological literature on acquired reading disorders, in which patients have been described who could read aloud English words with irregular spelling-sound correspondences without understanding their meanings (see, e.g., Coslett, 1991; Schwartz, Saffran, & Marin, 1980). This evidence, if taken alone, is problematic as convincing demonstration of a non-semantic, frequency sensitive lexical route in speeded oral reading (for reservations concerning this sort of evidence, see e.g., Besner & Smith, 1992, footnote 9). At the same time, evidence for a frequency-sensitive non-semantic reading pathway is absent in the experimental literature on unimpaired readers, perhaps for the difficulty of devising relevant experiments. To the best of our knowledge, only a study by Buchanan & Besner (1993) on reading Japanese Kana words addressed directly the issue, and concluded that normal readers of a shallow orthography can use a lexical non-semantic routine to read aloud, at least under some specific circumstances.

By using morphological pseudowords, we already demonstrated the existence of morpheme-based lexical reading, and also demonstrated how this could be frequency-sensitive, at least as far as sensitivity to suffix frequency is concerned (Burani et al., 1997). Thus naming morphological pseudowords might add some evidence for the dissociability, under specific circumstances, of the lexical and the semantic routes.

Burani et al. (in press) submitted to speeded naming two sets of root-suffix pseudowords which, matched on all dimensions, only differed for interpretability. An example of highly interpretable pseudoword is *divanaio*, in which the root *divan-* of *divano* ('sofa, divan') is combined with the agentive suffix *-aio* thus resulting in the meaning of 'sofa seller or maker'. By contrast, a less interpretable pseudoword is *terroraio* derived by combining the same suffix *-aio* with the root *terror-* of *terrore* ('terror'), thus producing 'terror seller, terror maker'.

The two sets included pseudowords which had exhibited large differences in lexical decision, with items judged highly interpretable on the 7-point scale (mean interpretability = 5.37) being more subject to be accepted as a word than less interpretable (mean interpretability = 3.43) combinations. The two sets were compared with a third set of control pseudowords that, although matched for all the relevant aspects, did not include either a root or a suffix.

On the basis of our previous results we expected that both sets of morphological pseudowords, made up of common roots and frequent suffixes, would be read aloud more quickly and accurately than control non-morphological pseudowords. With regard to differences in interpretability between the two morphological sets, two possible outcomes were predicted.

If morpho-lexical naming is sensitive to the activation of semantic information, for highly interpretable pseudo-words the activation of morphemic representations in the output lexicon might not only be function of the direct match of morphemes in the input and in the output lexicon, but might benefit also of the activation of some newly created concept in a semantic component (e.g., for a highly interpretable pseudoword like *divanaio*, the concept of a person who sells or makes only sofas). Consequently, if semantic information contributes to the activation of units in the morphologically decomposed output lexicon, the prediction could be made that highly interpretable pseudowords are named faster and more accurately than less interpretable pseudowords.

By contrast, if morpho-lexical naming could be obtained by direct match of input and output morphemic representations, with no involvement of the semantic system, morphological pseudowords differing for interpretability should not also differ in naming performance.

Results confirmed the latter prediction. Interpretability did not affect naming performance. While both sets of morphological pseudowords were named more quickly and more accurately than control pseudowords, they did not differ from each other either on reaction times or in accuracy. Thus, at least for new root-suffix combinations, morpheme-based lexical naming does not necessitate to be semantically mediated (analogously, no differences in naming times were found by Coolen et al., 1991 with compound pseudowords differing in interpretability, which, by contrast, largely differed in lexical decision performance).

The strong lexicality effects found by Burani et al. (in press) in absence of differential effects of differing degrees of interpretability, contribute to the hypothesis of a lexical non-semantic pathway for reading. Morpho-lexical non-semantic pseudoword naming would be obtained by direct match of morphemic input units with homologous output units, with no involvement of the semantic component.

8. IS MORPHO-LEXICAL READING AFFECTED BY LIST CONTEXT?

The last issue that will be addressed deals with the hypothesis that lexical reading is driven by the linguistic context in which stimuli to be named occur. The hypothesis that list composition influences recourse to lexical naming pertains specifically, although not exclusively, to languages like Italian, which are characterized by so called shallow orthographies. In these languages, the non-lexical pathway would be quite often successful and efficient, for purposes of speeded naming, because of the high regularity, or transparency, of grapheme-to-phoneme correspondences. Thus, according to some views, involvement of the lexical routine would be apparent only in cases in which the list context includes items that necessitate lexical lookup to be named correctly. Tabossi & Laghi (1992) argued that recourse to lexical naming would occur, in Italian, when the experimental list included, along with non-words, a proportion of words that could be assigned stress only by lexical lookup. By contrast, according to Tabossi & Laghi (1992), no lexical reading, as demonstrated by the absence of semantic priming effects, would be involved when word reading occurs in the context of regularly stressed words and pseudowords mixed together (but see also, for different data from another shallow orthography, i.e. Spanish, Sebastian-Gallés, 1991).

The data that were presented in the preceding sessions in favor of morpheme-based lexical reading were obtained in lists that included either 50% words (of different sorts, including words with unpredictable lexical stress) along with 50% pseudowords, or that included an even higher proportion of words of different types, up to a 75% of words in the last experiment by Burani et al. (in press), in which the highly lexically dense list aimed at favoring to the highest extent (although unsuccessfully) recourse to semantic processing.

Thus it might be argued that the dense lexical lists that were used did favor, if not induced, recourse to lexical processing which could disappear in lists fully composed of non-lexical items. Would morpheme-based lexical reading be reduced up to disappear with massive presence of non-lexical items, or would it be strong enough to survive in highly non-lexical contexts?

To provide some answer to the latter question, Burani, Spuntarelli, & Arduino (in preparation) inserted the same pseudowords (highly interpretable root-suffix *vs* low interpretable root-suffix *vs* control non-morphological pseudowords) in two different list contexts, which aimed at favoring to the highest degree either lexical or non-lexical processing, respectively. In contrast to the lexically dense list including only 25% pseudowords in the context of 75% words, the non-lexical list included only pseudowords, the large majority of which (63%) had no morphological constituency at all, although being orthographically legal.

Results were clear-cut. The same patterns on both reaction times and accuracy were obtained in the two list contexts, with morphologically complex pseudowords being named more quickly and more accurately than non-morphological ones in both contexts, with some evidence for quicker naming latencies and stronger morphological effects in lexically dense list contexts. By contrast, no evidence for differential effects of interpretability were found in any list context.

These results are evidence for the automaticity (and the efficiency for naming purposes) of recourse to morphemic representations, when available, even in contexts that would highly disfavor activation of lexical information. In a language orthographically simple but morphologically rich like Italian, for which morphological parsing of lexical items is largely used, the activation of morphemic units is in most cases (except when morphemic units do not have sufficiently high frequency) the favored procedure. With respect to the process of speeded reading aloud, the efficiency of the morpheme-based routine would arise from being less time consuming and less subject to assembly errors than the non-lexical reading routine, which by contrast will involve a larger number of not assembled processing units.

9. CONCLUSIONS

The results discussed in this chapter strongly support the existence of a reading pathway which is not assumed in current models of reading aloud, namely the morpho-lexical pathway by which pronunciation is obtained through activation of morphemic units both in the input and in the output lexical components.

The morpho-lexical reading routine was shown to be highly efficient due to quicker processing (segmentation and activation) of morphemic units and to greater accuracy in assembling, with respect to the orthography-to-phonology non-lexical routine.

The processing advantages of the morpho-lexical routine were shown to hold for different root-affix combinations, i.e. for stimuli including verbal inflections, derivational suffixes and derivational prefixes.

The activation of morphemic units corresponding to affixes in the reading routine was shown to be sensitive to the frequency characteristics of the affixes themselves, with low-frequency derivational suffixes being less subject to result in processing advantages than suffixes of higher frequency.

The possibility that the morpho-lexical reading routine involves activation of input and output components in which the formal representations of morphemes are stored, with no necessary involvement of a semantic component as well, was suggested.

Finally, the insensitivity of the morpho-lexical procedure to different list compositions (with comparable lexicality effects due to activation of morphemic units both in lexically dense and in totally non-lexical list contexts) was shown.

Some of these results, specifically the presence of frequency effects for suffixes and the activation of morphemic units in both highly lexical and highly non-lexical list contexts, point to the genuinely "lexical" character of the morpheme-based reading pathway. This lexicality would result specifically from the fact that, differently from the units included in other sorts of pseudowords which could be differentially affected by lexical interference, morphemic units included in morphological pseudowords already have a representation at the orthographical input stage.

For some models, strategies induced by list composition would affect the nonlexical routine specifically (see, e.g., Monsell, Patterson, Graham, Hughes, & Milroy, 1992; Paap & Noel, 1991). And indeed, for Italian, lexically mediated consistency effects in naming non-morphological pseudowords were shown when pseudowords were mixed with words, while no effects occurred when only pseudowords were presented (Job, Peressotti, & Cusinato, 1998).

While pointing to the peculiarity of processing allowed by morphologically complex pseudowords (which involve activation of morphemic units at the orthographic input lexicon stage), present findings still need two main developments among many others.

First, as mentioned when discussing results for prefixes, if it is assumed, as some current models do (see, e.g., Coltheart & Rastle, 1994), that both routes, the (morpho-)lexical and the non-lexical, are simultaneously activated, then the complex interplay at different processing stages of the two reading routes due to different time courses should be further detailed. Specifically, how the reading system deals with either converging or conflicting results from the two reading routines at the phonological output stages, including the phoneme system (or buffer) where phonological units are stored for planning articulatory execution, should be further investigated and modeled.

Finally, in this chapter we did not mention the role of the whole-word lexical processing route, which should exist even for orthographically shallow Italian (for evidence of whole-word processing from lexical decision to Italian inflected nouns, see Baayen, Burani, & Schreuder, 1997). Which should be the relative roles of whole-word and morpheme-based routines when reading aloud real words? Which should be their relative time courses? When should one of the routes be more effective than the other? At the moment, we do not have any experimental evidence from word naming. However, our prediction is that morpheme-based lexical naming should be highly efficient for low-frequency derived words with high frequency constituents. For these morphologically complex words, evidence of advantageous morphological parsing already exists from lexical decision (Burani & Thornton, in press).

10. REFERENCES

Baayen, R.H. (1992). Quantitative aspects of morphological productivity. In G.E. Booij & J. van Marle (Eds.), *Yearbook of Morphology 1991*. Dordrecht: Kluwer, pp. 109-149.

Baayen, H., Burani, C., & Schreuder, R. (1997). Effects of semantic markedness in the processing of regular nominal singulars and plurals in Italian. In G.E. Booij & J. van Marle (Eds.), *Yearbook of Morphology 1996*. Dordrecht: Kluwer Academic Publishers, 13-33.

Badecker, W., & Caramazza, A. (1991). Morphological composition in the lexical output system. *Cognitive Neuropsychology*, *8*, 335-367.

Beauvillain, C. (1996). The integration of morphological and whole-word form information during eye-fixations on prefixed and suffixed words. *Journal of Memory and Language*, *35*, 801-820.

Bentin, S. & Feldman, L.B. (1990). The contribution of morphological and semantic relatedness to the repetition effect at long and short lags: Evidence from Hebrew. *Quarterly Journal of Experimental Psychology*, *42(A)*, 693-711.

Besner, D. & Smith, M.C. (1992). Models of visual word recognition: When obscuring the stimulus yields a clearer view. *Journal of Experimental Psychology: Learning, Memory, and Cognition*, *18*, 468-82.

Buchanan, L. & Besner, D. (1993). Reading aloud: Evidence for the use of a whole word non-semantic pathway. *Canadian Journal of Experimental Psychology*, *47*, 133-152.

Burani, C., Spuntarelli, A., & Arduino, L.S. (in preparation). How strong is morpheme-based access and naming: Evidence from pseudowords.

Burani, C. & Caramazza, A. (1987). Representation and processing of derived words. *Language and Cognitive Processes, 2*, 217-227.

Burani, C., Dovetto, F.M., Spuntarelli, A., & Thornton, A.M. (1999). Morpho-lexical access and naming: The semantic interpretability of new root-suffix combinations. *Brain and Language, 68*, 333-339.

Burani, C., Dovetto, F.M., Thornton, A.M., & Laudanna, A. (1997). Accessing and naming suffixed pseudo-words. In G.E. Booij & J. van Marle (Eds.), *Yearbook of Morphology 1996*. Dordrecht: Kluwer Academic Publishers, 55-72.

Burani, C. & Laudanna, A. (1992). Units of representation of derived words in the lexicon. In R. Frost & L. Katz (Eds.), *Orthography, Phonology, Morphology, and Meaning*. Amsterdam: North-Holland, pp. 361-376.

Burani, C., Salmaso, D., & Caramazza, A. (1984). Morphological structure and lexical access. *Visible Language, 4*, 348-358.

Burani, C. & Thornton, A.M. (in press). The interplay of root, suffix and whole-word properties in processing derived words. *Linguistics*

Burani, C., Thornton, A.M., Iacobini, C., & Laudanna, A. (1995). Investigating morphological non-words. In W.U. Dressler & C. Burani (Eds.), *Crossdisciplinary approaches to morphology*. Wien: Verlag der Österreichischen Akademie der Wissenschaften, pp. 37-53.

Bybee, (1995). Regular morphology and the lexicon. *Language and cognitive processes*, *10*, 425-455.

Caramazza, A., Laudanna, A., & Romani, C. (1988). Lexical access and inflectional morphology. *Cognition*, *28*, 297-332.

Caramazza, A., Miceli, G., Silveri, M.C., & Laudanna, A. (1985). Reading mechanisms and the organization of the lexicon: Evidence from acquired dyslexia. *Cognitive Neuropsychology*, *2*, 81-114.

Chialant, D. & Caramazza, A. (1995). Where is morphology and how is it processed? The case of written word recognition. In: L. B. Feldman (Ed.), *Morphological Aspects of Language Processing*. Hove: Erlbaum, pp. 55-76.

Colé, P., Beauvillain, C., & Segui, J. (1989). On the representation and processing of prefixed and suffixed derived words: A differential frequency effect. *Journal of Memory and Language*, *28*: 1-13.

Coltheart, M. (1996). Phonological Dyslexia: Past and future issues. *Cognitive Neuropsychology*, *13*, 749-762.

Coltheart, M., Davelaar, C., Jonasson, J., & Besner, D. (1977). Access to the internal lexicon. In S. Dornic (Ed.), *Attention and Performance II*. New York: Academic, pp. 335-355.

Coltheart, M. & Rastle, K. (1994). Serial processing in reading aloud: Evidence for dual-route models of reading aloud. *Journal of Experimental Psychology: Human Perception and Performance*, *20*, 1197-1211.

Coolen, R., Van Jaarsveld, H.J., & Schreuder, R.(1991). The interpretation of isolated novel nominal compounds. *Memory & Cognition*, *19*, 341-352.

Coslett, H.B. (1991). Read but not write "Idea": Evidence for a third reading mechanism. *Brain & Language*, *40*, 425-443.

De Bastiani, P., Barry, C., & Carreras, M. (1987). Mechanisms for reading non-words: Evidence from a case of phonological dyslexia in an Italian reader. In: G. Denes, C. Semenza, & Bisiacchi, P. (Eds.), *Perspectives on Cognitive Neuropsychology*. Hove: Lawrence Erlbaum, pp. 253-267.

Feldman, L.B. (1994). Beyond orthography and phonology: Differences between inflections and derivations. *Journal of Memory and Language*, *33*, 442-470.

Frauenfelder, U.H. & Schreuder, R. (1992). Constraining psycholinguistic models of morphological processing and representation: the role of productivity. In G.E. Booij & J. van Marle (Eds.), *Yearbook of Morphology 1991*. Dordrecht: Foris, pp. 165-183.

Frost, R., Forster, K.I., & Deutsch, A. (1997). What can we learn from the morphology of Hebrew? A masked-priming investigation of morphological representation. *Journal of Experimental Psychology: Learning, Memory and Cognition*, *23*, 829-856.

Funnell, E. (1987). Morphological errors in acquired dyslexia: A case of mistaken identity. *The Quarterly Journal of Experimental Psychology*, *39A*, 497-539.

James, C.T. (1975). The role of semantic information in lexical decisions. *Journal of Experimental Psychology: Human Perception and Performance*, *1*, 130-136.

Job, R., Peressotti, & Cusinato, A. (1998). Lexical effects in naming pseudowords in shallow orthographies: Further empirical data. *Journal of Experimental Psychology: Human Perception and Performance*, *24*, 622-630.

Job, R., & Sartori, G. (1984). Morphological decomposition: Evidence from crossed phonological dyslexia. *The Quarterly Journal of Experimental Psychology*, *36A*, 435-458.

Laine, M. & Niemi, J. (1997). Reading morphemes. *Aphasiology*, *11*, *9*, 913-926.

Laine, M., Niemi, J., Koivuselkä-Sallinen, P., & Hyönä, J. (1995). Morphological processing of polymorphemic nouns in a highly inflected language. *Cognitive Neuropsychology*, *12*, 457-502.

Laudanna, A. & Burani, C. (1995). Distributional properties of derivational affixes: implications for processing. In L. B. Feldman (Ed.), *Morphological Aspects of Language Processing*. Hove: Erlbaum, pp. 345-364.

Laudanna, A., Burani, C., & Cermele, A. (1994). Prefixes as processing units. *Language and Cognitive Processes*, *9*, 295-316.

Laudanna, A. & Caramazza, A. (1997). Orthographic and morphemic priming in written word recognition. Paper presented at the Joint Meeting AIP (Associazione Italiana di Psicologia)-EPS (Experimental Psychology Society), Cardiff, June.

Laudanna, A., Cermele, A., & Caramazza, A. (1997). Morpho-lexical representations in naming. *Language and Cognitive Processes*, *12*, 49-66.

Libben, G. (1993). Are morphological structures computed during word recognition? *Journal of Psycholinguistic Research*, *22*, 535-544.

Marslen-Wilson, W., Tyler K.L., Waksler. R., & Older, L. (1994). Morphology and meaning in the mental lexicon. *Psychological Review*, *101*, 3-33.

Monsell, S., Patterson, K. E., Graham, A., Hughes, C.H., & Milroy, R. (1992). Lexical and sublexical translation of spelling to sound: Strategic anticipation of lexical status. *Journal of Experimental Psychology: Learning, Memory and Cognition*, *18*, 452-467.

Niemi, J., Laine, M., & Tuominen, J. (1994). Cognitive morphology in Finnish: Foundations of a new model. *Language and Cognitive Processes*, *9*, 423-446.

Paap, K.R. & Noel, R.W. (1991). Dual-route models of print to sound: Still a good horse race. *Psychological Research*, *53*, 13-24.

Panzeri, M., Semenza, C., Ferreri, T., & Butterworth, B. (1990). Free use of derivational morphology in an Italian jargonaphasic. In: J-L. Nespoulous & P. Villiard (Eds.), *Morphology, Phonology, and Aphasia*. New York: Springer, pp. 72-94.

Patterson, K. & Marcel, A. (1992). Phonological ALEXIA or PHONOLOGICAL alexia? In: J. Alegria, D. Holender, J. Junca de Morais & M. Radeau (Eds.), *Analytic Approaches to Human Cognition*. Amsterdam: Elsevier, pp. 259-274.

Sandra, D. (1994). *Morphology in the reader's mental lexicon*. Frankfurt am Main: Peter Lang.

Schreuder, R. & Baayen, R.H. (1994). Prefix stripping re-revisited. *Journal of Memory and Language*, *33*, 357-375.

Schreuder, R. & Baayen, R.H. (1995). Modeling morphological processing. In L. B. Feldman (Ed.), *Morphological Aspects of Language Processing*. Hove: Erlbaum, pp. 131-154.
Schwartz, M.F., Saffran, E.M., & Marin, O.S.M. (1980). Fractionating the reading process in dementia: Evidence for word-specific print-to-sound associations. In: M. Coltheart, K. Patterson, & J.C. Marshall (Eds.), *Deep Dyslexia*. London: Routledge & Kegan Paul, pp. 259-269.
Sebastian-Gallés, N. (1991). Reading by analogy in a shallow orthography. *Journal of Experimental Psychology: Human Perception and Performance*, *17*, 471-477.
Strain, E., Patterson, K., & Seidenberg, M.S. (1995). Semantic effects in single word-naming. *Journal of Experimental Psychology: Learning, Memory and Cognition*, *21*, 1140-1154.
Tabossi, P. & Laghi, L. (1992). Semantic priming in the pronunciation of words in two writing systems: Italian and English. *Memory and Cognition*, *20*, 303-313.
Taft, M. (1979). Recognition of affixed words and the word frequency effect. *Memory and Cognition*, *7*, *263-272*.
Taft, M. (1991). *Reading and the Mental Lexicon*. Hove: Lawrence Erlbaum.
Taft, M. (1994). Interactive-activation as a framework for understanding morphological processing. *Language and Cognitive Processes*, *9*, 271-294.
Taft, M. & Forster, K. (1975). Lexical storage and retrieval of prefixed words. *Journal of Verbal Learning and Verbal Behavior*, *14*, 637-647.
Taft, M., Hambly, G., & Kinoshita, S. (1986). Visual and auditory recognition of prefixed words. *Quarterly Journal of Experimental Psychology*, *38A*, 351-366.

11. ADDRESS FOR CORRESPONDENCE

Cristina Burani or Alessandro Laudanna
Istituto di Scienze e Tecnologie della Cognizione
Consiglio Nazionale delle Ricerche (CNR)
viale Marx 15
00137 Roma
Italy
Phone: (+39) 06-8609-0386
Fax : (+39) 06-824737
Email: burani@ip.rm.cnr.it
allaudan@ip.rm.cnr.it

JOHN P. SABATINI

WORD READING PROCESSES IN ADULT LEARNERS

1. INTRODUCTION

The National Adult Literacy Survey (Kirsch, Jungblut, Jenkins & Kolstad, 1993) reported estimates of 40 to 44 million Americans with literacy scores in the lowest proficiency level and another 50 millions in the second lowest level of prose literacy skills. Some 4 million of these adults participate in adult literacy and education programs to improve their basic reading skills and further their educational prospects. The adult literacy gap has significant implications for social and economic equity in the U.S. Despite the scope of the problem, our understanding of the reading processes of low literate adults is incomplete, especially when compared with the research base on reading in children.

Understanding the nature of word reading processes in low literate adults has practical as well as theoretical importance. It has practical importance for the design of literacy programs. Early reading difficulties are now more readily diagnosed in the U.S schools and empirically tested instructional interventions are available for remediation. However, most adult learners completed their schooling before the ready availability of such measures and methods and most adult educators who serve low literate adults scoring above the 3rd or 4th grade level on standardized tests typically apply either a vocabulary/comprehension basic skills or functional literacy instructional approach. Only a small percentage of adults are diagnosed as having specific reading disabilities or participate in instructional programs targeted specifically at developing word reading processes (e.g., Fowler & Scarborough, 1993; Ross-Gordon, 1998; Wilson, 1998). As yet, no studies have convincingly demonstrated that reading interventions designed for children will generalize to this broad population of adults with word reading difficulties.

The theoretical value of studying low literate adults stems from the characteristics that differentiate them from children and from the typically studied reading-disabled adult. First, in comparison to children, adults are undergoing minimal or more slowly evolving developmental and maturational changes. Basic cognitive processes such as general speed of processing, working memory, and attention are relatively stable from young adulthood through middle age, declining only slowly with age (Kail & Salthouse, 1994; Salthouse, 1991, 1992). Second, in comparison to typical reading-disabled learners, cognitive and neural substrates underlying reading difficulties cannot be assumed. The low proficiency adult learners who attend programs are a mix of undiagnosed disabled readers, as well as individuals who may have experienced inadequate schooling opportunities. They are also less likely to have received extensive compensatory educational opportunities. Most studies of diagnosed reading-disabled adults are of individuals with normal to high verbal IQ, normal math achievement, mainstream social and educational background, and often a history of formal and informal attempts at compensating for their specific reading disability (Fowler & Scarborough, 1993). As a consequence, many of the reading-disabled adults studied have achieved a relatively high level of educational achievement such as reading comprehension at the college level (Bruck, 1990). Repeated attempts at compensations influence certain variables - for example, a relative advantage in orthographic processing, wider exposure to texts, and growth or maintenance of age appropriate verbal IQ. Because of the absence of these compensatory experiences, studying low literate adults provides a broader perspective for understanding the acquisition of word reading processes.

1.1 Word reading processes and comprehension in adult dyslexics and low literate adults

There is a considerable research base on adults with specific reading disabilities (e.g., Bell & Perfetti, 1994; Booth, Perfetti, MacWhinney, & Hunt, 2000; Bruck, 1990, 1992, 1993; Byrne & Ledez, 1983; Pennington et al., 1990). There have also been a few studies of low reading ability adults in literacy classes (Greenberg, Ehri, & Perin, 1997; Pratt & Brady, 1988; Read & Ruyter, 1985). These studies of adults consistently report deficiencies, like in children, in decoding and word recognition skills, though reading comprehension performance is more variable. Deficiencies were found in phonemic awareness, decoding non-words, and knowledge of sight to sound correspondences. The literature on relatively successful disabled adult readers also shows persistent deficits in processing speed on a variety of reading tasks (e.g., Abadzi, 1996; Fowler & Scarborough, 1993). This latter finding is consistent with the literature on reading disability in children from countries with transparent orthographies in which symptoms most often manifest themselves in processing speed, rather than word recognition errors (Wimmer, Mayringer, & Landerl, 1998; Wolf, Bowers, & Biddle, 2000).

For example, Bruck (1990) compared college level dyslexics to normally reading college students and Grade-6 control groups. With respect to word recognition skills, the adult dyslexics showed the same accuracy as Grade-6 children in reading words, but had greater difficulty in reading non-words and were slower to read both words and non-words than were both control groups. The adult dyslexics could use orthographic properties, that is, segments that assist in parsing words into syllables. Also, reading words in meaningful contexts facilitated more accurate, quicker word recognition, though reaction times were still considerably longer for even high frequency words than for the control groups.

With respect to the relationship between comprehension and word recognition, Bruck (1990) noted that many models predict that lower level word-recognition skills must be accurate and fast in order for higher level comprehension skills to proceed efficiently, but found that many of her college-level dyslexics achieved high levels of comprehension despite poor levels of word-recognition. Bruck provided two possible explanations. First, there may be a threshold level for word recognition, above which there is minimal contribution of variance to predicting comprehension (Grade-6 in her study). Alternatively, it may be that standardized, academic reading comprehension tests are biased in favor of the high IQ, high language ability subjects selected for her study, with scores potentially dropping under more naturalistic, less structured formats.

One study has addressed directly the degree to which adults in literacy classes apply similar or different reading processes than children. Greenberg et al. (1997) compared word reading processes in adults to children with reading comprehension scores between 3-5th grade level. They found that adults' performances on phonologically complex tasks were significantly poorer than children, but show a mixture of strengths and weaknesses on orthographically complex tasks. They concluded that adult literacy students and children used similar processes to read sight words, real words, and non-words. They further concluded that orthographic and phonological processes were less closely integrated in adults based on weaker correlations across these measures in the adult literacy students as compared to the children. The implication is that some adults may use orthographic knowledge to help compensate for poor basic decoding or a core phonological deficit (Stanovich, 1990; Stanovich, West, & Cunningham, 1991).

Because Bruck (1990) and Greenberg et al. (1997) restricted the range of adults studied to those scoring in the 3rd to 6th grade level in reading, their research does not fully address whether or to what degree there are adults with discrepant profiles in comprehension, decoding, or word recognition and how patterns may change across ability levels.

The relationship between word recognition and comprehension in adult literacy learners as compared to college-level reading-disabled populations is one issue that needs to be clarified. Poor readers might compensate for poor word reading skills with top-down skills. Analogously, some poor readers may have strong word reading skills, but poor comprehension skills. Research with college level readers with specific reading disabilities suggests a pattern of poor non-word decoding and word recognition, but higher than expected comprehension to be more prevalent (e.g., Bruck, 1990; Pennington et al., 1990). When Shankweiler et al. (1999) explored this issue in children, they found a small proportion of readers with appreciable discrepancies between decoding and comprehension in a study of 361 7.5 to 9.5 year olds. Thirty-two were better comprehenders than decoders and 17 were better decoders than comprehenders. Both of these groups were only discrepant relative to each other. Overall, they were in the middle of the distributions of comprehension and decoding ability relative to their poor reading peers in the sample. Another issue in need of further study concerns the relationship between component skills to the overall word recognition achievement levels in adults, as discussed next.

1.2 The acquisition and nature of expert word recognition ability

Novice word recognizers, whether children or adults, apply a mix of strategies or heuristics (e.g., decoding, analogy, context clues, morphological knowledge, syntax) to recognizing an unknown or uncertainly known word (Ehri, 1991, 1992; Goswami & Bryant, 1992; Moustafa, 1995; Share, 1995). No single strategy is sufficient or algorithmically guaranteed to ensure a correct result in any given case. Decoding may be the *sine qua non* (Share, 1995) of reading acquisition, but the learning and application of basic decoding procedures to each new word is an effortful task with uncertain outcomes. By contrast, skilled word recognition performance draws on implicit, proceduralized code knowledge, evident in any word level componential task - naming frequent English words, pronouncing pseudowords, or deciding whether a pseudoword sounds like a real English word. Even at the high end of difficulty, i.e., recognizing multi-syllabic, complex words, domain-specific knowledge (including recall of having seen or heard the word before) will dominate over basic decoding strategies. This novice-expert word reading distinction is observable both in performance (accuracy) and in processing speed differences.

A number of researchers have put forward models of how phonological analysis and recoding skills in early reading acquisition lead to the growth of higher order orthographic and phonological code knowledge, enroute to rapid, skilled word recognition skills (Bowers, Sunseth, & Golden, 1999; Ehri, 1992; Perfetti, 1992; Share, 1995). In each, development is considered to be better described as item-based rather than stage-based (Logan, 1988). That is, high frequency words in the spoken lexicon are becoming sight words in the sense that there is a strong set of memory connections for specific words. Perhaps because of the debate and controversy regarding whether dual-route versus connectionist network theories best describe the underlying cognitive processes (e.g., Coltheart, Curtis, Atkins, & Haller, 1993; Harm & Seidenberg, 1999), these models are largely silent on this specific issue. In Ehri's (1992) amalgamation theory, emphasis is placed on the binding among code systems - orthographic, phonological, morphological, syntactic, and semantic. The mechanism of word learning in amalgamation theory can be characterized as more explicit than implicit, favoring declarative over procedural knowledge learning, and leading to a lexical item knowledge-base. However, there is also posited a growing knowledge base of sublexical orthographic patterns available for procedural analysis of novel words.

Share's (1995) self-teaching hypothesis is more explicit about the mechanism for acquiring higher order code knowledge via the notion that phonological recoding becomes increasingly "lexicalized" in the course of reading development. One primary function of phonological recoding, Share notes, is to generate pronunciations to match against one's listening lexicon (self-teaching) - the means-end analysis of word recognition problem solving. However, a second function emerges with extensive practice of this analytic activity. Higher order generalizations of phonological and visual-orthographic patterns and knowledge accumulate (lexicalization), conserving attentional resources and speeding up the process of recognizing novel as well as overlearned words. High levels of lexicalization make the performance of sublexical analyses indistinguishable from a whole word lexicon (Share, 1995).

Lexicalization, as used by Share, may be characterized as implicit learning of procedural knowledge (Underwood, 1996). Underwood describes the two related constructs that implicit cognition embraces: implicit learning and implicit memory. Implicit learning is said to occur when there is an increase in task performance without an accompanying increase in verbal knowledge about how to carry out the task, that is, procedural knowledge in the absence of declarative knowledge. Implicit memory is characterized as the influence of a previously memorized piece of information on a task without the explicit or deliberate attempt to recall the memory. Underwood describes studies in which tasks are learned faster on a subsequent occasion due to the influence of previously learned material. Venezky (1999) also suggests an implicit learning correlate to explicit teaching of phonics. The function

> is to focus the reader on the letters and letter strings of a word, so that visual word recognition can develop properly for that word...That is, through learning to decode, readers develop a familiarity with letters, functional units, and other familiar sequences of letters, and these help speed word recognition.

Venezky goes on to speculate that the extra effort required to determine pronunciations in learning a complex orthography like English may lead to faster word recognition than does learning a transparent orthography using a single letter, left-to-right scanning strategy without considering larger units.

A study by Oney, Peter, and Katz (1997) supports this expectation. They hypothesized that readers of transparent orthographies, such as Turkish, would be slower to develop visual-orthographic representations in memory. They reasoned that because there is little processing cost associated with obtaining a phonological representation in the first place, there is less need to develop visual-orthographic representations. On the other hand, readers of highly opaque orthographies (e.g., Hebrew) or moderately opaque orthographies (e.g., English) will show more evidence of visual-orthographic representations in memory at an earlier age, with the strongest effects for older, more experienced readers, because of the ambiguity of lexical identification stemming from strictly phonological processing. Their hypothesis was confirmed with English readers showing large error and naming latency decreases between 2nd to 5th grades to adult using high frequency words in a rhyme-priming paradigm.

Thus, all of these models of word reading emphasize the acquisition of higher order, implicit, procedural knowledge of sublexical phonological and visual-orthographic information. Whatever the precise cognitive structure of this knowledge, the consequence for individuals possessing such knowledge should be not only a mechanism for self-teaching, but also the simplifying of the apparent processing complexity of multi-letter, multi-syllable words resulting in speedier, more efficient word recognition and learning at all levels of processing. Phonological recoding in the advanced word reader consists of procedural processing of visual stimuli through a rich visual-orthographic knowledge-base, which has the side consequence of facilitating more rapid and efficient learning, then overlearning (committing to memory or becoming familiar with) individual words. Generating plausible pronunciations of complex items, an explicit process forming a declarative knowledge memory, is an occasional and less central learning function. Declarative knowledge memory formation may be more primarily used for acquiring conceptual knowledge relating word forms to meaning, that is, binding or amalgamating semantic (and perhaps morphological) codes. The growth of procedural skill knowledge predicts speed, efficiency improvements across a range of lexical tasks, as a consequence of improved sublexical perceptual processing, not merely rapid recognition of familiar, high frequency words.

The discussion up to this point treats speed of processing solely as a function of the normal acquisition of word recognition expertise. However, speed of processing, specifically rapid automatized naming (RAN) rate has also been identified as a potential individual difference variable for identifying dylexic readers (Wolf, 1991; 1997; Wolf et al., 2000). The double-deficit hypothesis suggests that naming speed deficits interfere with the growth of word recognition in children and, when combined with a core phonological deficit (Stanovich, 1990), results in a more severe type of reading disability (Wolf, 1991). The focus of recent research has been on confirming that rapid automatic naming (RAN) is unique and predicts variance in reading difficulties over and above the variance predicted by phonemic awareness or other phonological tasks. The cumulative results so far suggest that RAN deficits exist independent of a core phonological deficit, and differentiate dyslexic readers from average readers, nondiscrepancy or 'garden variety' poor readers, and readers with other learning disabilities (Wolf & Bowers, 2000; Wolf et al., 2000). However, alternate viewpoints are still being vigorously researched (Manis, Seidenberg, & Doi, 1999; Wagner, et al., 1993) .

Whether it turns out that there are distinct naming-speed and double-deficit subtype or not, it is important to understand the influence of processing speed in the acquisition and performance of word reading in adults (and children). Efficiency of word reading, that is, word recognition that is rapid and fluent, is essential to skilled reading. Speed of processing could play an important role in implicit learning and memory via the acquisition of "lexicalized" procedural skills, as it does in other procedural skill learning domains (Ackerman, 1989). For example, training studies that have demonstrated that practice in speeded recognition of orthographic patterns can lead to improved decoding ability (Das-Smaal, Klapwijk & van der Leij, 1996; Fredriksen, Warren, & Rosebery, 1985). Other studies using speeded practice as part of an intervention have also shown positive results (Breznitz, 1997; Gilbert, 1996; Tressoldi, Lonciari & Vio, 2000).

1.3 Specific research questions

1. One aim of this study is to examine the relationship between word recognition and comprehension. Specific questions addressed include:

(a) Are there threshold levels of either ability above or below which no further variance in the other is evident?

(b) Are there poor decoders who are good comprehenders and are there good decoders who are poor comprehenders?

(c) Are there a subtype of poor/good decoders, good/poor comprehenders and if so, which pattern is more prevalent?

2. A second aim is to explore the relationship of measures of speed/rate of processing and accuracy in component reading skills to overall word recognition ability using hierarchical regression. Specifically:

(a) Is there significant variance in word recognition ability accounted for by basic speed of processing after accounting for age?
(b) How much variance in word recognition ability is accounted for by decoding skill accuracy?
(c) Is there significant variance in word recognition ability accounted for by speed of response in reading skill tasks (e.g., word naming) and is this the same as the basic speed measures (e.g., digit naming)?
(d) What is the best fitting model of component skills for predicting word recognition ability?
(e) Is there significant variance in word recognition ability accounted for by the sentence level and comprehension measures after the variance accounted for by the best set of lexical level variables is removed?

2. METHOD

2.1 Participants

Ninety-five participants [ages 16-52] were recruited for the study. Fifty-two adult literacy (AL) learners [ages 18 - 54] were recruited from adult education programs in the mid-Atlantic region, including correctional institution educational classes, community-based programs, adult basic education classes, general educational development (GED) classes, public assistance job programs, and tutoring services.[11] Participants were recruited by project staff with the support of instructors and were paid up to $50 for participating in the study. Participants were judged by teachers and staff to be in the normal range of IQ, but no intelligence tests were administered. All testing was done at instructional sites by project staff and the author.

A total of 43 college level (CL) learners [ages 18 - 60] were recruited. Twenty-nine were volunteers taking an undergraduate study skills class. Another 13 were continuing education students who responded to study recruitment announcements. Twelve reported that they received help for a learning problem while in school; one was undergoing testing at the time of the study. Some self-identified themselves as struggling readers and were subsequently identified as outlying cases based on the distance of some of their component reading scores from the distribution plots of the other skilled readers, however, they were not outliers with respect to the full sample.

2.2 Instruments

2.2.1 Standardized measures of reading achievement.

Wechsler Individual Achievement Test (WIAT). The WIAT (Psychological Corporation, 1990) is a reading comprehension test that consists of short passages followed by free response questions. The learner reads a passage at his or her own rate and answers a single question read aloud by a trained administrator. Responses are given orally. The 38-item test takes between 10 and 20 minutes to administer. The test is not administered under any time pressure; respondents have as much time as they need to answer each item.

Wide Range Achievement Test-Reading (WRAT-R). The WRAT-R (Jastak & Associates, 1993) is a word recognition test that consists of naming 15 letters and 38 words. Scoring is based on accurate pronunciations, including unusual pronunciations due to colloquialisms, foreign accents, or defective articulation. The test is not administered under any time pressure; respondents have as much time as they need to answer each item.

2.2.2 *Basic Speed Measures*

Digit and picture naming. DIGIT naming consists of 10 single digit Arabic numerals repeated twice in random order. PICTURE naming consists of 11 line drawings of well-known objects (e.g., pencil, elephant) repeated twice in random orders. Items are presented individually and voice onset for response is the main measure. Responses were also audio recorded to check accuracy.

Perceptual-Motor (PERC -RT) Reaction Time. The tasks just described use voice onset time as the primary measure of response rate. To test whether slow response time was a general characteristic of the individual (evidenced by slow voice onset time and slow motor reaction time), a composite variable was constructed. The variable consists of the average response time of correct practice trials used to acclimate the participant to the key pad choices in the decision-style tasks (described below). Participants had 10 practice trials for each of the three decision tasks described below.

2.2.3 *Decoding Tasks*

Word and pseudoword naming. WORD naming consisted of thirty 1-, 2-, or 3-syllable words covering a span of printed word frequency bands based on Kucera and Frances (1967). PSEUDOWORD naming consisted of twenty-four 3 to 5- letter pseudowords. Items were presented individually. Accuracy and voice onset for response are the main measures. Responses were audio recorded to score for accuracy.

Lexical decision decoding tasks. In addition to pseudoword naming, two lexical decision style decoding tasks were administered. In the PAIRED-WORD task, participants see pairs of made up words. One is a pronounceable pseudoword, the other a pseudohomophone. They must choose the word that sounds most like an English word by pressing a key pad with their index finger (left-index for left side word or right-index for right side word). The test consists of 30 items. Participants were randomly assigned to one of two parallel forms. In the SINGLE-WORD Task, participants see a single made up word (half pronounceable pseudowords; half pseudohomophones) and are asked to decide yes or no whether it sounds like an English word by pressing a key pad with their index finger ("Y" for yes; "N" for no). The test consists of 3 blocks of 40 items each. The 3 blocks are random reordering of the 40 items, thus each item is seen three times by each participant. Participants were randomly assigned to one of two parallel forms. Measures of both accuracy and response time were collected.

Sentence Processing. A SENTENCE level processing tasks was also administered. Participants see a simple line picture (e.g., a triangle over a square), then two seconds later see a sentence centered below the picture. Thirty-two picture/sentence pairs were constructed that differed systematically on two dichotomous dimensions: affirmative/negative sentence form (e.g., The square is in the triangle./The square is not in the triangle.) and true/false relationship between sentence and picture. There are various relationships described (e.g., over, under, inside of, between) in random orders with half true, half false, half affirmative, half negations. Measures of both accuracy and response time were collected. (See Clark & Chase, 1972) for review of this paradigm in the psychological literature.)

2.3 Procedure

All Tests were programmed for use on Macintosh LC 575's with 12" screens. In general, all instructions, demonstration trials, practice trials, and test items were delivered by the computer. The administrator observed and answered participant questions as necessary.

Test score accuracy was calculated in percentage correct. The items used in the component skill tasks were designed to be of low difficulty for skilled readers, so as to more reliably estimate mean response rates. This decision led to ceiling effects on several tests. Ceiling effects are reported and interpreted in the relevant analyses. The effects of guessing was handled by dropping mean response rate for the 10 AL participants scoring at chance on forced choice tests.

Reaction time was calculated using mean response rate for items answered correctly. Items more than two standard deviations from an individual's mean response rate were eliminated. An inverse transformation was applied to reaction time variables to improve normality and the linear relationship in regression models. The inverse functions can be interpreted to mean that smaller differences at higher rates are similar to larger differences at slower rates. Millisecond differences between 455 to 500 (45), 555 to 625 (70), 625 to 714 (89), 714 to 833 (119), and 833 to 1000 (167) are all equivalent intervals. Thus, rate (items/msec) in contrast with speed (msec/item) is the measure used in analyses.

3. RESULTS

3.1 Comparisons between adult literacy learners (AL) and college-level (CL) readers

Tables 1 shows summary statistics for the adult literacy learners (AL) (n=52), College-level (CL) (n=43), and the Combined (N=95) groups. The variables are grouped into three categories: a) scores on reading comprehension (WIAT) and word recognition (WRAT) tests based on the publishers' norm-referenced tables, b) percentage correct on component skill tasks, and c) mean response time for correct items only on component skill tasks. Age (AGE) is also presented.

3.1.1 Performance on standardized measures of word recognition and reading comprehension

Figure 1 shows a cross-plot for the WIAT and WRAT for the combined group, coded by group (ALL=0, CL=1). Standardized scores based on 17 to 20 year olds were used as the reference scale. Note that the two groups overlap near the center of the distributions such that combining the two groups creates a normal distribution of scores with mean and standard deviation values close to the norming population for each test (m=100, sd =15). The combined group means range from a third of a standard deviation lower for the WIAT mean to very close to the mean for the WRAT. Visual examination of the WIAT by WRAT cross-plot shows a linear relationship across the entire group. Splitting the group into subgroups weakens the linear relationship, with more spread in scores apparent in the top quadrant of the figure.

Table 1. Summary statistics and T Tests for adult literacy (AL), college and combined groups

	AL		CL		Combined		
	M	SD	M	SD	M	SD	t test
AGE	29	9.18	23.95	8.7	26.7	9.3	*
		Published Tests (standard scores)					
WIAT	84.4	11.8	104.3	12.4	93.4	15.6	*
WRAT	87	12.5	108.1	11.4	96.6	15.9	*
		Percentage Correct					
Word	0.88	0.15	0.99	0.01	0.93	0.13	*
Pseudoword	0.73	0.24	0.9	0.1	0.81	0.21	*
Paired-Word	0.77	0.18	0.94	0.09	0.85	0.17	*
Single-Word	0.75	0.16	0.89	0.09	0.81	0.15	*
Sentence	0.81	0.17	0.94	0.05	0.87	0.15	*
		Mean Response Rates (msec)					
Perc-RT	533	203	422	95	482	172	*
Digit	570	97	484	74	531	97	*
Picture	731	179	641	94	690	153	*
Word	885	412	570	170	742	360	*
Pseudoword	1046	566	637	185	861	480	*
Single-Word[a]	1133	315	986	285	1062	308	*
Paired-Word[ab]	3470	1641	2040	835	2747	1476	*
Sentence	3618	972	2453	599	3091	1007	*

Note. [a] *Response rates for participants scoring at chance levels were eliminated*
[b] *Missing data for three participants.*
** p <.05, (t test, two tailed)*

3.1.2 Relation between speed and accuracy on component task measures

The WORD, PSEUDOWORD, SINGLE-WORD, PAIRED-WORD, and SENTENCE component skill tasks were initially meant to be response time measures. An attempt was made to keep individual items relatively simple, with a modest range of difficulty. The intention was to have low error rates, but variability in response rate. It became evident early in the study that the adult literacy learners did show variability in accuracy on these tasks, consequently, accuracy became a measure. The college level learners performed near ceiling on all of these tasks.

Thus, in contrast to the variability in the standardized scores, the variance on the component skill accuracy scores tasks are significantly different ($p <.05$). The standard deviations for the AL group are twice that of the CL group due to the ceiling effect. College learners had relatively little difficulty with any but the most difficult of items. A ceiling effect is evident in the AL group for WORD naming, less so for the other component skill tasks. The College group was significantly speedier in responses on all of the measures in the study ($p <.02$, two tailed test).

There is a small but significant difference in measures that are more distally related to reading skills such as DIGIT naming or PERC-RT reaction time. The differences are of a larger magnitude in reading measures. For example, the mean difference in DIGIT naming rate is 82 ms, while the mean difference in WORD naming rate is 312 ms. This result is not a function of slowing with age. Separate regression equations predicting the three most basic processing speed measures, DIGIT, PICTURE, and PERC-RT, from age predicted from 5 to 10 percent of the variance. The difference in ages between the AL and College groups was significant ($t=2.29$, $p <.05$).

The variability in the mean response rates was greater in the AL group than in the CL group, especially on the decoding tasks. In the untransformed response variables, the variances were significantly different for response time to WORD, PSEUDOWORD, and SENTENCE. The variances were not different for DIGIT, PICTURE, or PAIRED-WORD. To illustrate, the standard deviations for the AL and College groups in DIGIT naming rate were 92 and 74 ms respectively, an 18 ms mean difference, while the standard deviations in WORD naming were 423 and 170 ms respectively, a 253 ms difference. After transformation using the inverse, the variances of all the response time variables were not significantly different between the two groups ($p >.10$), however, all the mean differences were still significant, except SINGLE-WORD decision. Eliminating the response times of the chance scorers may have contributed to this null finding or AL respondents may have attempted to respond more quickly in this task context. The generally weaker relation of lexical decision time rates in contrast to naming rates is consistent with other reading research on naming speed.

3.1.3 Summary

The results of the first set of analyses can be summarized as follows. First, the AL group had difficulty on all standardized and component skill measures both in speed and accuracy. In general, the College group was near ceiling accuracy performance on all of the component skills tasks and had speedier mean response rates to the reading and non-reading measures. Applying an inverse transformation to response rate variables increased their linearity with respect to other variables in the study. The College group also scored a little better than the fiftieth percentile of 17 to 20 year olds on the WIAT and WRAT. They can be described as good readers, but not all superior readers.

Scatterplots showed the distribution of scores on the standardized measures (WIAT and WRAT) support combining the AL and College Groups into one group. The roughly equal variances on the standardized measures within the two groups also supports this conclusion. Combining the groups yields means on the WIAT and WRAT a little below the mean of 17 to 20 year olds, but a standard deviation about the same for the norming sample of the tests. Furthermore, the scatterplots show a truncated linear relation when the two groups are split apart.

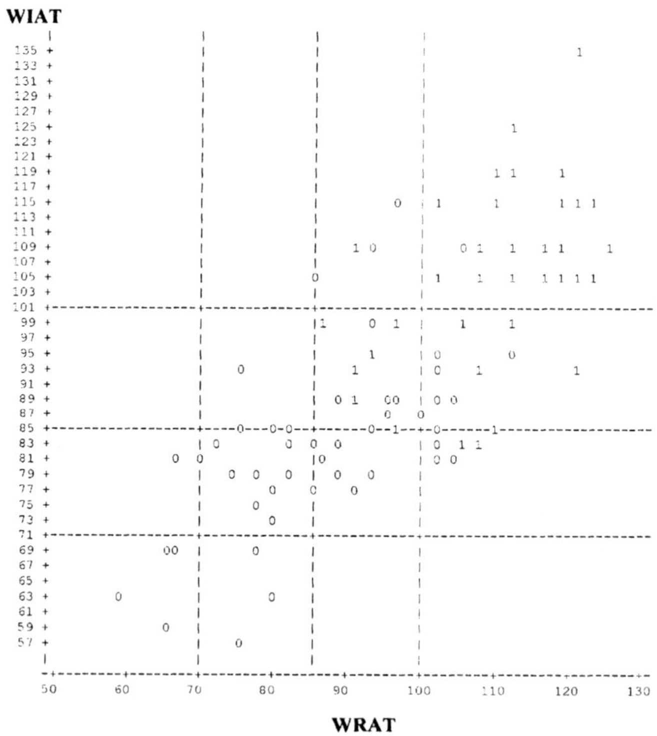

Notes: Symbol Value is Group: 0=ABE group (n=52); 1=College group (n=43)

Figure 1. PLOT OF WIAT*WRAT

3.2 Hierarchical, multiple regression analyses

A second set of analyses were conducted to extend our understanding of the nature of word recognition processes in adult learners at different levels. Hierarchical, multiple regression analyses were used to determine whether component measures accounted for additional variance after the removal of variance from other measures of different theoretical priority in predicting word recognition ability on the WRAT. To maintain a ratio of about 15 observations to each predictor variable, variables were run in sets (e.g., SINGLE-WRD accuracy, SINGLE-WRD rate). Variables with non-significant beta weights were dropped from subsequent analyses.

The model specifics include beta weights (b), standard errors (SE), standardized beta weights (bstd), semi-partial regression coefficients (sr2), the adjusted multiple correlation coefficient (adj. R2), change in R2 from the previous model (*R2), and whether the change was significant (F (*R2)).

3.2.1 The contribution of basic processing rate

The contribution of basic processing rate measures (and the background variable AGE) were assessed in an initial series of regression models. An initial model with WRAT as the dependent variable and AGE as the independent variable was significant ($F(1,93) = 5.78$, $p <.05$). AGE accounted for 5% of the adjusted variance. The subsequent model (Table 2, Model 2) with AGE and PERC-RT as independent variables was also significant ($F(2,92) = 8.66$, $p <.001$). PERC-RT added 10% unique variance; the model accounted for 14% of the adjusted variance in the WRAT.

A multiple regression model with WRAT as the dependent variable and AGE, PERC-RT, and DIGIT as the predictor variables was significant ($F(3, 90) = 11.50$, $p <.001$). DIGIT naming rate resulted in an additional 12% unique variance after AGE and PERC-RT, for a total of 25% of the variance in the WRAT measure. The beta coefficients for AGE and PERC-RT were no longer significant after the addition of DIGIT naming. This indicates that AGE and PERC-RT were not contributing any unique variance to the model, not already predicted by DIGIT. A subsequent model with DIGIT alone predicts as much variance as with AGE and PERC-RT in the model.

PICTURE naming rate has been found to be associated with reading ability in children, though most models suggest that PICTURE and DIGIT naming are essentially measures of the same underlying construct (Denckla & Rudel, 1976; Kail & Salthouse, 1994; Olson, Kliegl, Davidson, & Foltz, 1985; Wolf, 1991). In a multiple regression model with WRAT as the dependent variable and DIGIT and PICTURE as the independent variables, the model was significant ($F(2,92) = 16.00$, $p <.001$). PICTURE, however, was not a significant predictor variable in addition to DIGIT ($p >.10$), consistent with this equivalence notion.

To summarize, the DIGIT naming variable was the strongest predictor of the basic processing rate measures, accounting for 25% of the variance in predicting word recognition ability. DIGIT naming was carried forward as the first variable in subsequent models including decoding accuracy measures.

Table 2. Summary of regression analysis for variables predicting WRAT scores: age, perceptual-motor speed (PERC-RT), DIGIT and PICTURE naming, WORD naming percentage correct (PCT)

Model	Variable	*df*	*β*	*SE*	β_{std}		sr^2	*adj.* R^2	•R^2	*F* (•R^2)
1	AGE	1, 93	-0.41	0.17	-0.24	*	0.06	0.05	-	
2	AGE		-0.18	0.18	-0.11	ns	0.01			
	PERC-RT	2, 92	0.52	0.16	-0.36	**	0.10	0.14	0.09	9.70 **
3	AGE		-0.18	0.17	-0.10	ns	0.01			
	PERC-RT		0.13	0.18	0.08	ns	0.00			
	DIGIT	3, 91	2.13	0.56	0.43	***	0.12	0.25	0.11	13.13 ***
3a	DIGIT	1, 93	2.51	0.44	0.51	***	0.26	0.25	-	-
4	DIGIT		2.64	0.71	0.53	***	0.11			
	PICTURE	2, 92	-0.23	0.95	-0.03		0.00	0.24	-0.01	-1.31 ns

Note. F-values for individual models in text (all models were significant)
**p <.05 **p <.01 ***p <.001*

3.2.2 The contribution of decoding skill accuracy

A series of multiple regression model with WRAT as the dependent variable and DIGIT and a decoding accuracy variable (WORD, PSEUDOWORD, PAIRED-WRD, or SINGLE-WRD) as the independent variables were run. With DIGIT and WORD naming accuracy as the independent variables, the model was significant ($F(2, 92) = 57.85$, $p < .001$), as were both predictor variables. An additional 30% of unique variance was predicted by WORD naming accuracy after the initial 25% predicted by DIGIT, accounting for a total of 55% of the variance by the model. WORD naming captured about 19% of the variance of DIGIT as overlap. Thus, there was a small, unique contribution of number naming rate of 6% to the model. (See Table 3)

Each model was significant (DIGIT+ PSEUDOWORD: $F(2,92) = 66.56$, $p < .001$), DIGIT+PAIRED-WRD: $F(2,92) = 68.64$, $p < .001$), and DIGIT+SINGLE-WRD: $F(2,89) = 87.08$, $p < .001$).[2] PSEUDOWORD added an additional 33% of unique variance to DIGIT and captured about 20% of the variance of DIGIT as overlap, accounting for a total of 58% of the variance. The model SINGLE-WORD added the most additional, unique variance, 41%, and captured the most variance of DIGIT as overlap (24%), accounting for a total of 67% of the total variance. The beta coefficient for DIGIT was significant in each model, though the unique variance accounted for by DIGIT was minimal.

To summarize, the each of the decoding skill accuracy measures contributed significant variance in predicting word recognition ability (from 55% to 67%). Each of the decoding measures captured most of the variance attributable to DIGIT naming as well, however, a small, significant contribution of unique variance attributable to the basic speed measure remained.

Table 3. Summary of regression analysis for variables predicting WRAT scores: DIGIT naming speed and decoding accuracy. (WORD, PSEUDOWORD, SINGLE- and PAIRED-word decision percentage correct (PCT)

Model	Variable	*df*	*β*	*SE*	β_{std}	sr^2	*adj.* R^2	•*R*	*F* (•R^2)
5	DIGIT		1.36	0.37	0.28 ***	0.06			
	WORD PCT	2, 92	73.89	9.37	0.59 ***	0.30	0.55	0.30	59.08 ***
6a	DIGIT		1.25	0.36	0.25 ***	0.05			
	PSEUDO WORD PCT	2, 92	48.78	5.62	0.63 ***	0.33	0.58	0.33	125.7 ***
6b	DIGIT		1.11	0.35	0.22 **	0.04			
	WORD		36.62	12.5	0.29 **	0.04			
	PSEUDO WORD PCT	3, 91	32.21	7.84	0.42 ***	0.07	0.61	0.36	15.5 **
6c	DIGIT		0.75	0.38	0.15 *	0.02			
	PAIRED-WORD PCT	2, 92	64.98	7.35	0.68 ***	0.34	0.59	0.34	131.0 ***
6d	DIGIT		0.88	0.34	0.18 *	0.03			
	SINGLE-WORD PCT	2, 89	76.43	0.37	0.67 ***	0.41	0.65	0.40	166.3 ***
6e	DIGIT		0.65	0.35	0.13 [a]	0.01			
	PAIRED-WORD PCT		25.24	11.2	0.26 *	0.02			
	SINGLE-WORD PCT	3, 88	54.93	11.98	0.52 ***	0.08	0.67	0.42	20.5 ***

Note. F-values for individual models in text (all models were significant)
(Data missing for three participants in single-word task, n=91)
[a]*p =.07* **p <.05* ***p <.01* ****p <.001*

3.2.3 The contribution of decoding skill rate

Variance associated with complementary accuracy and speed/rate pairs

As noted, the decoding skill accuracy tasks showed ceiling effects for the College group, truncating the variance predicted by these tasks at the high end of the ability scale. This effect was confirmed. A series of regression models were run with WRAT as the dependent variable and the component skill task variables as the predictors. Each set of models consists of 1) the accuracy variable alone, 2) the rate variable alone, 3) the complementary task variables together (e.g., WORD accuracy and response rate), and 4) the task and the digit naming rate (DIGIT). The results can be summarized as follows. All of the component skill variables were significant predictors of the WRAT scores by themselves (F-values p <.001). In each of the component complementary pair models, both the accuracy and response time variables were significant and predicted unique variance in the WRAT (F-values p <.001), resulting in a statistically significant change in the adjusted correlation coefficient (see *R* 2 and F-values). In each of the complementary pair models, the DIGIT variable was not significant and did not add additional unique variance to the model, resulting in a statistically non-significant change in the adjusted correlation coefficient (see *R2* and F-values). DIGIT did capture some of the unique variance attributable to the rate variable. For example, WORD response time went from contributing 13% unique variance to 6% unique variance in the presence of DIGIT, suggesting an overlap of about 7%.

For the naming tasks (WORD and PSEUDOWORD), each of the rate variables was about as strong a predictor as the accuracy variables, accounting for about 49% to 54% of the variance each. For the two other decoding tasks (SINGLE-WORD and PAIRED-WORD), the accuracy scores were much stronger predictors of the WRAT scores than the response rate variables, though the rate variables continued to contribute small, but significant unique variance. Even in the SINGLE-WORD task, in which there was no ceiling effect, rate contributed a small amount of unique variance. For the SENTENCE level decision task, the rate variable was the stronger independent predictor of word recognition rate. Again, when combined in one model, both variables accounted for unique variance. (See Table 4.)

Table 4. Summary of regression analysis for variables predicting WRAT scores: word and decoding response rate measures PSEUDOWORD, WORD, SINGLE- & PAIRED-WORD decision percentage correct PCT and RATE

Model	**Variable**	*df*	*β*	*SE*	β_{std}		sr^2	adj. R^2	$\bullet R^2$	F ($\bullet R^2$)	
					PSEUDOWORDS						
1a	PCT	1, 93	56.66	5.44	0.73	***		0.54	0.53	-	-
1b	RATE	1, 93	62.28	0.26	0.71	***	0.50	0.49	-		
1c	PCT		38.52	5.41	0.50	***	0.18				
	RATE	2, 92	1.55	0.25	0.44	***	0.14	0.67	0.14	37.39***	
1d	PCT		38.55	5.45	0.50	***	0.18				
	RATE		1.57	0.32	0.44	***	0.09				
	DIGIT	3, 91	-0.03	0.41	###	ns	0.00	0.67	0.00	0	ns
					WORDS						
2a	PCT	1, 93	87.26	9.18	0.70	***	0.49	0.49	-		
2b	RATE	1, 93	2.37	0.25	0.70	***	0.49	0.48	-		
2c	PCT		55.62	9.79	0.45	***	0.13				
	RATE	2, 92	1.49	0.27	0.44	***	0.13	0.61	0.12	28.70***	
2d	PCT		55.79	9.85	0.45	***	0.13				
	RATE		1.41	0.36	0.42	***	0.06				

	DIGIT	3, 91	0.16	0.46	0.03 ns	0.00	0.61	0.00	0 ns
				PAIRED-WORD Decision					
3a	PCT	1, 93	72.48	6.37	0.76***	0.58	0.58	-	-
3b	RATE	1, 93	3.51	0.77	0.43***	0.18	0.17	-	
3c	PCT		66.97	5.93	0.70***	0.48			
	RATE	2, 92	2.32	0.51	0.28***	0.08	0.65	0.07	18.98***
3d	PCT		66.11	6.83	0.70***	0.35			
	RATE		2.26	0.57	0.27***	0.06			
	DIGIT	3, 91	0.10	0.39	0.02 ns	0.00	0.65	0.00	0 ns
				SINGLE-WORD Decision					
4a	PCT	1, 90	85.03	6.77	0.80***	0.64	0.63	-	
4b	RATE	1, 90	1.80	0.64	0.29***	0.08	0.07	-	
4c	PCT		83.70	6.23	0.79***	0.62			
	RATE	2, 89	1.55	0.37	0.25***	0.06	0.69	0.06	17.03***
4d	PCT		79.78	7.02	0.75***	0.44			
	RATE		1.37	0.40	0.22***	0.04			
	DIGIT	3, 88	0.42	0.35	0.08 ns	0.00	0.69	0.00	0 ns
				SENTENCE Decision					
5a	PCT	1, 93	56.37	9.68	0.52***	0.27	0.26	-	
5b	RATE	1, 93	10.17	1.03	0.72***	0.51	0.51	-	
5c	PCT		34.37	7.59	0.32***	0.09			
	RATE	2, 92	8.70	0.99	0.61***	0.34	0.59	0.34	75.09***

Note. F-values for individual models in text (all models were significant)
[a]*p =.07* **p <.05* ***p <.01* ****p <.001*

3.2.4 Best fit models of decoding accuracy, rate and higher level processing variables

To test the association of higher level variables on word recognition ability, a set of hierarchical regression models were run. Model 1 (WRAT=SINGLE-WORD + WORD response time) represents the best fitting model using the lexical level accuracy and rate variables ($F(2,89)= 131.12$, $p <.001$). Adding the sentence accuracy variable (SENTENCE, Model 2a) does not add any significant amount of variance (Change in $R2=.01$, $F=1.31$, $p >.50$). Adding the SENTENCE response time variable (Model 2b) does add a small, but significant amount of variance ($F(3,88)= 97.17$, $p <.001$, change in $R2=.02$, $F=6.92$, $p <.01$). Adding the WIAT reading comprehension variable (Model 2c) also adds a small, but significant amount of variance ($F(3,88)= 108.89$, $p <.001$, change in $R2=.04$, $F=15.52$, $p <.001$). (See Table 5)

To summarize, there appears to be a small, significant contribution to word recognition ability that is not accounted for by lexical and sublexical accuracy and rate measures, that is captured by the sentence level rate and comprehension task variables. The contribution of reading comprehension could be due to the fact that the more skilled readers see more print and therefore have greater sight word knowledge. The relationship of the sentence rate task is more difficult to interpret. Perhaps it is best, for now, to draw the conservative conclusion that sublexical variables, though important, are not the only factors that enter into word recognition ability.

Table 5. Summary of regression analysis for variables predicting WRAT scores: best fit models

Model	Variable	*df*	*β*	*SE*	*βstd*		sr^2	*adj.* R^2	$\bullet R^2$	*F* $(\bullet R^2)$	
1	SINGLE-WORD PCT		62.66	6.73	0.59	***	0.25				
	WORD RATE	2, 89	1.33	0.21	0.39	***	0.11	0.74	0.14	37.39	***
2a	SINGLE-WORD PCT		57.06	7.62	0.54	***	0.16				
	RATE SENTENCE		1.32	0.21	0.39	***	0.11				
	PCT	3, 88	10.62	6.94	0.10	ns	0.01	0.74	-	1.31	ns
2b	SINGLE-WORD PCT		56.09	6.87	0.53	***	0.18				
	WORD RATE		0.92	0.25	0.27	**	0.04				
	SENTENCE RATE	3,88	3.16	1.11	0.22	**	0.02	0.76	0.02	6.92	**
2c	SINGLE-WORD PCT		50.53	6.85	0.47	***	0.13				
	WORD RATE		0.94	0.22	0.28	**	0.05				
	WIAT	3,88	0.29	0.07	0.28	***	0.04	0.78	0.04	15.52	***

Note. F-values for individual models in text (all models were significant)
(Data missing for three participants in LPCT task, n-91)
$^a p = .07$ $*p < .05$ $**p < .01$ $***p < .001$

3.3 *Word recognition and comprehension relationship*

The first aim of the study was to explore word recognition and comprehension relationships. Specifically,

(a) Are there threshold levels of either ability above or below which no further variance in the other is evident?

(b) Are there poor decoders who are good comprehenders and are there good decoders who are poor comprehenders? Which is more prevalent?

We found a weakening of the linear relationship between word recognition and comprehension toward the high end of the scale and some evidence of threshold levels around which the relationship between comprehension and word recognition begin to change. The correlation between WRAT and WIAT for the AL group was $r = .64$, but only $r = .50$ for the college group. The overall correlation when groups were combined was stronger yet at $r = .74$.

Only one individual that scored below 85 (one standard deviation below the mean of 100) in word recognition (WRAT) also scored above 85 in comprehension (WIAT) (93 was the score) (see Figure 1). On the other hand, 14 individuals scored better than 85 in word recognition and scored less than 85 in comprehension. If we look at the range from 85 to 100 in word recognition, we see only 4 individuals who scored over 100 in comprehension. On the other hand, of those who scored 85 to 100 in comprehension, only 1 scored lower than 85 in word recognition, and 9 scored above 100. High levels of word recognition skill is not a guarantee of high levels of reading comprehension, at least as operationalized in the WIAT test. This provides some evidence for the concept of threshold levels of word recognition, beyond which little variance in comprehension ability can be predicted. The converse was not as strongly supported. Of the 23 individuals scoring better than 100 in comprehension, only 4 had WRAT scores below 100 and none below 85. A score of 100 in word recognition is necessary (hence the evidence does not support the existence of top-down compensation strategies in word recognition), though not sufficient (hence, word recognition scores do not account for the entire variance in word comprehension data). The results also illustrate the importance that restricting range can have on generalizations, since the strong linear relationship and discrepant individual patterns in this study emerge only when looking across the full set of scores. This result is contrary to the results of those studying college-level dyslexics who evidenced higher comprehension despite low word recognition ability (Bruck, 1990; Pennington et al., 1990). Thus, among adult literacy learners in our sample, compensating for poor decoding with high comprehension is a less prevalent characteristic.

The nature of the items that make up the word recognition scale on the WRAT suggest that experience or familiarity with the test words, in contrast to application of basic decoding skills measured in the decoding tasks in this study, is important to achieving higher WRAT scores. Word complexity by any metric of length, syllables, or frequency increases substantially after the first 16 items of the WRAT measure. An individual cannot score in the range of 85 to 100 without recognizing and pronouncing a number (7) of complex, multi-syllabic, infrequent words. One cannot score above the group mean of 100 without recognizing and pronouncing a substantial number (14) of such words.[2] Note also that these words contain complex sight to sound structures, that is, there are multiple legal pronunciations given the spelling, but only one correct pronunciation for purposes of scoring. This implies that word "recognition" in the literal sense of pronouncing a word known and seen or heard before is probably the skill most directly assessed. Simple pseudoword decoding skills or even relying on letter clusters, orthographic patterns, or morphemes, would not be sufficient. Experience or familiarity with the more complex WRAT items would be more characteristic of high verbal, college-level disabled readers as studied by Bruck (1990), less so the typical adult literacy program attendee.

Like in the Bruck (1990) study of adult college dyslexics, there are certain threshold levels of word recognition beyond which it is difficult to predict variance in comprehension. But unlike that study, only a few individuals were found to be compensating for poor word recognition with higher-level comprehension skills. The data pattern shows that more individuals developed high levels of word recognition in the absence of high levels of comprehension, at least as measured by the WIAT. Note that comprehension on the WIAT is a power and not speed or memory test. Passages are generally short, always in view of the respondent, and a single question per passage is administered and answered orally. Thus, the test requires focused critical analysis, with less import put on fluent reading. In addition, less demand is put on propositional processing in working memory, as would be the case in a longer passage. Longer passages and multiple questions, as in some standardized comprehension tests, put more emphasis on constructing a model of the text-base and situational model in working memory (van Dijk & Kintsch, 1983).

3.4 Component skills and speed/rate of processing

A second aim was to explore the relationship of measures of speed/rate of processing and accuracy in component reading skills to overall word recognition ability using hierarchical regression. Specifically: (a) Is there significant variance in word recognition ability accounted for by basic speed/rate of processing (PERC-RT, DIGIT) after accounting for AGE? (b) How much variance in word recognition ability is accounted for by decoding skill accuracy? (c) Is there significant variance in word recognition ability accounted for by speed/rate of response in decoding tasks (e.g., WORD naming) and is this the same as the basic speed/rate measures (e.g., DIGIT naming)? (d) What is the best fitting model of component skills for predicting word recognition ability? (e) Is there significant variance in word recognition ability accounted for by the sentence level and comprehension measures (SEN, WIAT) after the variance accounted for by the best set of lexical level variables is removed?

(a) There was significant variance in word recognition ability accounted for by basic *speed/rate* of processing and age. DIGIT naming *speed/rate* accounted for the most unique variance (24%), capturing the smaller percentages of variance of PERC-RT response time and AGE. PICTURE naming, which had been identified as a potential indicator of *speed/rate*, was not a significant predictor. DIGIT naming *speed/rate* was not an independent, unique predictor of variance in the presence of more direct measures of decoding and word naming.

(b) Each of the decoding tasks predicted a considerable amount of the variance in real English word naming performance. This result is consistent with the reading research literature, though there is often less attention paid to the importance of this persistent result in the adult literacy literature. The accuracy task that best predicted word recognition ability was the SINGLE-WORD pseudohomophone decision task. The single-word task requires decoding, then matching to the sound of a word separate from the spelling. The complexity of items across all three variants of component skill decoding tasks was limited to one-syllable pseudowords of three to six letters. Nonetheless, the mean performance in the AL group was about 75% correct on average across these task variables. This is confirmation of the many studies that show that many adult learners with comprehension problems are poor at simple decoding, somewhat independent of specific task demands (i.e., naming or decision paradigms).

(c) In addition to the predictive power of the decoding accuracy measures, *speed/rate* of skill application was a strong predictor of word recognition ability on its own, and contributed unique additional variance in addition to accuracy. The *speed/rate* with which a reader names sight words, or pronounces pseudowords, or decided whether a pseudoword sounds like another real word, was associated with the ability to name real words accurately across a wide range of abilities. Measures of oral responses (voice onset), however, were much stronger predictors of word recognition than key pad responses, which is suggestive of a specific influence of the requirement to articulate the response. Also, speed/rate variance was not discriminating solely at one or another end of the word recognition ability distribution. We could have found, for example, that decoding task accuracy is the sole predictor for adults with low word recognition ability, whereas both accuracy and rate information contribute to predicting performance for the higher ability adults, supporting a hypothesis of consolidation of procedural skills into automatized performance at that higher level. Examination of 3-dimensional cross-plots do not support this interpretation. Rather rate was a linear component distinguishing a dimension of word recognition ability different than decoding accuracy across the entire range of adults in the study. Put another way, two individuals with the same decoding accuracy scores (high or low) could be distinguished (in terms of their overall word recognition ability) by differences in their naming rates. The speed relation (msec/item) was curvilinear, that is small differences in speed at the high end were as meaningful as large differences at the low end of the ability spectrum. Inverting the speed scores to rates (items/msec) transformed the curvilinear relationship to a linear one.

(d) Seventy-two percent of the variance in the WRAT could be accounted for by the accuracy in deciding whether a single-syllable pseudoword sounded like an English word and the naming rate (inverse transformation) of relatively frequent words. Recall that most of the words at the high end of the WRAT have letter patterns that are at a minimum ambiguous, and usually misleading with regard to the sight-to-sound correspondences (e.g., assuage, omniscient). The majority are also four syllables or more.

(e) Higher level measures of sentence processing and reading comprehension also contributed a small but significant variance in predicting word recognition. Recognizing complex words in word recognition requires prior exposure to the words in meaningful texts. One hypothesis is that these higher level reading measures were indicators of this aspect of the task.

4. CONCLUSIONS

4.1 Methodological and measurement issues

First, we discuss methodological and measurement issues they may have broader relevant to reading research. One issue concerns the use of restricted ranges of reading abilities when studying adults. Most studies of adults have sampled and compared subgroups across a restricted range of reading comprehension abilities, using reading-level match designs. This strategy is derived from studies of children, but need not be applied in studying adults. In studies of children, it is more difficult to generalize across wide age-grade ranges because the nature of constructs may change qualitatively across ages. Also, interpretation of speed/rate variables with children must take into account the six standard deviation change in basic speed/rate of processing observed from 6 to 18 year olds, which then stabilizes through the age of 35 before starting a gradual decline (Kail & Salthouse, 1994). The strength of the multiple regression results in the present study would not have been as evident had a wider range of reading abilities not been examined.[3]

A second issue concerns the transformation of the response speed measures to normalize the data distributions. Transforming response speeds was necessary to understand the strength of their effects in linear model (i.e., multiple regression). Large differences in speed were evident in group mean comparisons (AL vs. college-level readers), but the relationship would have been dropped as insignificant in multivariate regression models when compared with the stronger linear relationships of accuracy measures. We would have underestimated predictive power of response times in regressions without transformations. A third related issue concerns the component skills that are embedded in outcome measure tasks (discussed further below). The WRAT is an untimed measure of word reading ability that requires pronunciation of complex, infrequent words in order to attain high ability scores. The WIAT is an untimed reading comprehension test that puts less demand on fluency and integration of information as do comprehension tests with longer passages and multiple questions per passage. In both of the tests used in this study, power is favored over efficiency. Still, effects of response rate were found on these tests. One might hypothesize that measures of response time on component skills would show an even stronger relationship to outcome measures that included tasks with a time limit, thus requiring greater reading efficiency.

4.2 Major findings

One aim of this study was to examine the relationship of word recognition to comprehension across a broad range of abilities in both domains, extending results found with specific reading-disabled and adult literacy subgroups. One general finding was a tendency to see more discrepancies between word recognition and comprehension scores toward the high end of the ability scales. In contrast to the studies of adult dyslexics by Bruck (1990) and Pennington et al., (1990), there was tendency in this sample for participants to have higher word recognition scores relative to their comprehension scores. Participants in this study were a mix of learners in adult literacy classes and college level students, so familiarity with an academic test does not fully explain the trend.

Achieving scores at the high end of the WRAT requires the recognition of multiple, complex, infrequent and irregular words. One way to achieve such high levels is through broad exposure to print through frequent reading (Stanovich et al., 1991). Such reading, if it were for personal and entertainment reasons, may not require the development of deep understanding and critical thinking comprehension skills demanded by the WIAT items. Future studies that include measures of exposure to print and reading habits could test this relationship more directly.

Another aim of this study was to draw further attention to the importance of considering the many implications that speed/rate may have on performance and acquisition processes. With children, the interpretation of the relation of speed/rate to ability is complicated by differences in general speed/rate of processing associating with age versus skill-specific experiences (Kail & Salthhouse, 1994). The present study begins to refine our understanding of that relationship by examining adult performance, where developmental differences in speed/rate of processing are minimal. After reviewing adult reading and disabilities research Fowler & Scarborough (1993) noted that speeded naming scores have not usually been correlated in any systematic way with individual differences in reading skills. This study provides more detail, if not more answers, about the relationships of speed/rate to word recognition across different levels of readers.

In hierarchical, multiple regression models it was found that more distal measures of speed/rate such as aging, perceptual speed/rate, and picture naming were weak predictors of word recognition scores, with all the variance captured by a measure of digit naming. The variance attributed to digit naming speed/rate in turn was captured by the more proximal measures of word recognition speed/rate, either pseudoword or real word naming. Measures of speed (inversely transformed to rate) of naming frequent words or simple pseudowords were significant predictors of word recognition abilities in addition to the most powerful accuracy measures on decoding, together accounting for 74% of the variance.

The results are consistent with a theoretical model that emphasizes the use of implicit learning and memory for phonologic and visual-orthographic patterns to undergird rapid, automatic word *learning*. This process has the effect that skilled word readers process and perceive complex words much differently than less skilled readers relying on decoding or other strategies. Although poor pseudoword decoding is a symptom of lacking such skill, the more direct impact is not so much the inability to generate legal pronounceable options for self-teaching, but rather the disruption to procedural processing and learning of higher order sublexical patterns, resulting in decreased learning of and therefore recognizing of complex words. Although the relationships of speed/rate to higher level word recognition in the current study is consistent with this line of reasoning, future studies are needed to more directly test word learning as well as recognition, to help tease apart different theoretical relationships between speed/rate and knowledge in the acquisition process.

The large proportion of variance predicted by a simple decoding and the real word naming speed/rate measure do not directly address the role of other aspects of word and text structure that may affect word reading processes such as morphology or other linguistic codes. This study more directly addressed issues of lexical access, less of semantic understanding and syntactic and propositional integration of text. Future studies of adults that include more measures of these aspects will be critical in better understanding the sometimes discrepant patterns found here and in other studies with regard to comprehension and word recognition.

5. NOTES

This sample of adult literacy learners was drawn from a larger sample (102) of adult learners who participated in a longitudinal research project designed to measure the development of component reading skills of adults enrolled in instructional programs over a six to nine month period.The full test battery was administered across multiple sessions.Of the 102 participants who completed the initial battery, 52 completed the full battery. Other measures not reported here included vision and auditory screening, rapid automatized naming, vocabulary knowledge, a listening version of the sentence processing task, silent reading rate, and a think aloud decoding task. See Sabatini, Venezky, Kharik, & Jain, 2000 for a full description of measures.

The theoretical implications of this transform from speed (msec/item) to rate (item/msec) warrant more attention in the future.A large non-linear difference in speed per item, such as seen in this data, could have moment to moment processing implications such as a break-down in working memory and attention, resulting in impaired learning and suggesting an intervention strategy focused on the nature of items and tasks. On the other hand, a fixed rate of processing difference across ability groups might imply a simple quantitative intervention of doubling the number of practice trials, exposures, or learning time available to slower learners.Either or both could operate to influence acquisition.

Of the first 16 word items, all are 7-letters or less, 3-syllables or less, and part of the corpus of the 10000 most frequent words in print according to Kucera and Francis (1967).The next sixteen words are range from 5 to 13 letters each, most between 2-4 syllables, and only 3 in the corpus of 10000 most frequent words.The remaining 10 are even more complex.To get a score of 85, one would need to name all of the first 16 correct and at least 7 of the next 26 items correct.To get a score of 100, one would need to name 14 of the next 26 correct.

6. REFERENCES

Abadzi, H. (1996). Does age diminish the ability to learn fluent reading? *Educational Psychology Review, 8*(4), 373-396.

Ackerman, P. L. (1989). Individual differences and skill acquisition. In P. L. Ackerman & R. J. Sternberg & R. Glaser (Eds.), *Learning and individual differences: Advances in theory and research.* (pp. 164-217). New York: W. H. Freeman and Company.

Bell, L. C., & Perfetti, C. A. (1994). Reading Skill: Some adult comparisons. *Journal of Educational Psychology, 86*, 244-255.

Booth, J. R., Perfetti, C. A., MacWhinney, B., & Hunt, S. B. (2000). The association of rapid temporal perception with orthographic and phonological processing in children and adults with reading impairment. *Scientific Studies of Reading, 4*, 77-100.

Bowers, P. G., Sunseth, K., & Golden, J. (1999). The Route between Rapid Naming and Reading Progress. *Scientific Studies of Reading, 3*(1), 31-53.

Breznitz, Z. (1997). Effects of Accelerated Reading Rate on Memory for Text among Dyslexic Readers. *Journal of Educational Psychology, 89*(2), 289-297.

Bruck, M. (1990). Word-recognition skills of adults with childhood diagnoses of dyslexia. *Developmental Psychology, 26*(3), 439-454.

Bruck, M. (1992). Persistence of dyslexics' phonological awareness deficits. *Developmental Psychology, 28*, 874-886.

Bruck, M. (1993). Component spelling skills of college students with childhood diagnoses of dyslexia. *Learning Disabilities Quarterly, 16*, 171-184.

Byrne, B., & Ledez, J. (1983). Phonological awareness in reading-disabled adults. *Australian Journal of Psychology, 35*(2), 185-197.

Clark, H. H., & Chase, W. G. (1972). On the process of comparing sentences against pictures. *Cognitive Psychology, 3*, 472-517.

Coltheart, M., Curtis, B., Atkins, P., & Haller, M. (1993). Models of reading aloud: Dual-route approaches and parallel-distributed-processing approaches. *Psychological Review, 100* , 589-608.

Das-Smaal, E. A., Klapwijk, M. J. G., & van der Leij, A. (1996). Training of perceptual unit processing in children with a reading disability. *Cognition and Instruction, 14*(2), 221-250.

Denckla, M. B., & Rudel, R. G. (1976). Rapid "automatized" naming (R.A.N.): Dyslexia differentiation from other learning disabilities. *Neuropsychologia, 14*, 471-479.

Ehri, L. C. (1991). Development of the ability to read words. In R. Barr & M. L. Kamil & P. Mosenthal & P. D. Pearson (Eds.), *Handbook of reading research* (Vol. 2, pp. 383-417). New York: Longman.

Ehri, L. C. (1992). Reconceptualizing the development of sight word reading and its relationship to recoding. In P. B. Gough & L. C. Ehri & R. Treiman (Eds.), *Reading acquisition* (pp. 107-144). Hillsdale, NJ: Erlbaum.

Fowler, A. E., & Scarborough, H. S. (1993). *Should reading-disabled adults be distinguished from other adults seeking literacy instruction?* (Technical Report TR93-7): National Center on Adult Literacy, University of Pennsylvania.

Frederiksen, J. R., Warren, B. M., & Rosebery, A. S. (1985). A componential approach to training reading skills: Pt. 1. Perceptual units training. *Cognition and Instruction, 2*, 91-130.

Gilbert, L. M. (1996). Use of Assisted Reading to Increase Correct Reading Rates and Decrease Error Rates of Students with Learning Disabilities. *Journal of Applied Behavior Analysis, 29*(2), 255-258.

Goswami, U., & Bryant, P. (1992). Rhyme. analogy, and children's reading. In P. B. Gough & L. C. Ehri & R. Treiman (Eds.), *Reading acquisition* (pp. 49-64). Hillsdale, New Jersey: Gough, Philip B., Ehri, Linnea C., Treiman, Rebecca.

Greenberg, D., Ehri, L. C., & Perin, D. (1997). Are word-reading processes the sme or different in adult literacy students and their -fifth graders matched for reading level? *Journal of Educational Psychology, 89*, 262-275.

Harm, M. W., & Seidenberg, M. S. (1999). Phonology, Reading Acquisition, and dyslexia: Insights from connectionist models. *Psychological Review, 106*, 491-528.

Jastak & Associates. (1993). *Wide Range Achievement Test: Reading Level 2*. Wilmington, DE: Author.

Kail, R., & Salthouse, T. A. (1994). Processing speed as a mental capacity. *Acta Psychologica, 86*, 199-225.

Kirsch, I. S., Jungblut, A., Jenkins, L., & Kolstad, A. (1993). *Adult literacy in America: A first look at the results of the national adult literacy survey* (Report 16-PL-02): Princeton, NJ: Educational Testing Service.

Kucera, H., & Francis, W. N. (1967). *Computational analysis of present-day American English*. Providence, RI: Brown University Press.

Logan, G. D. (1988). Toward an instance theory of automatization. *Psychological Review, 95*, 492-527.

Manis, F. R., Seidenberg, M. S., & Doi, L. M. (1999). See Dick RAN: Rapid Naming and the Longitudinal Prediction of Reading Subskills in First and Second Graders. *Scientific Studies of Reading, 3*(2), 129-157.

Moustafa, M. (1995). Children's productive phonological recoding. *Reading research Quarterly, 30*(3), 464-476.

Olson, R. K., Kliegl, R., Davidson, B. J., & Foltz, G. (1985). Individual and developmental differences in reading disability. In G. E. MacKinnon & T. G. Waller (Eds.), *Advances in theory and practice* (Vol. 4, pp. 2-65). New York: Academic Press.

Oney, B., Peter, M., & Katz, L. (1997). Phonological processing in printed word recognition: Effects of age and writing system. *Scientific Studies of Reading, 1*(1), 65-83.

Pennington, B. F., Van Orden, G. C., Smith, S. D., Green, P. A., & Haith, M. M. (1990). Phonological processing skills and deficits in adult dyslexics. *Child Development, 61*, 1753-1778.

Perfetti, C. A. (1992). The representation problem in reading acquisition. In P. B. Gough & L. C. Ehri & R. Treiman (Eds.), *Reading acquisition* (pp. 145-174). Hillsdale, NJ: Erlbaum.

Pratt, A. C., & Brady, S. (1988). Relation of phonological awareness to reading disability. *Journal of Educational Psychology, 80*(3), 319-323.

Psychological Corporation. (1990). *Wechsler Individual Achievement Tests: Reading Comprehension*. San Antonio, TX: Author.

Read, C., & Ruyter, L. (1985). Reading and spelling skills in adults of low literacy. *Remedial and Special Education, 6*(6), 43-52.

Ross-Gordon, J. M. (1998). Literacy education for adults with learning disabilities: Perspectives from the adult education side of the mirror. In S. A. Vogel & S. Reder (Eds.), *Learning Disabilities, Literacy, and Adult Education* (pp. 69-88). Baltimore, MD: Brookes Publishing.

Sabatini, J. S. (1997). *Is accuracy enough? The cognitive implications of speed of response in adult reading ability*. Unpublished Dissertation, University of Delaware, Newark, DE.

Sabatini, J. S., Venezky, R. L., Jain, R., & Kharik, P. (2000). *Study of Adult Reading Acquisition (SARA): Test Development and Technical Data*: National Center on Adult Literacy at the University of Pennsylvania.

Salthouse, T. A. (1991). *Theoretical perspectives on cognitive aging*. Hillsdale, NJ: Erlbaum.

Salthouse, T. A. (1992). *Mechanisms of age-cognition relations in adulthood*. Hillsdale, NJ: Erlbaum.

Shankweiler, D., Lundquist, E., Katz, L., Stuebing, K. K., Fletcher, J. M., Brady, S., Fowler, A., Dreyer, L. G., Marchione, K. E., Shaywitz, S. E., & Shaywitz, B. A. (1999). Comprehension and decoding: Patterns of association in children with reading difficulties. *Scientific Studies of Reading, 3*, 69-94.

Share, D. L. (1995). Phonological recoding and self-teaching: Sine qua non of reading acquisition. *Cognition, 55*, 151-218.

Stanovich, K. E. (1990). Explaining the differences between the dyslexic and the garden-variety poor reader: The phonological-core variable-difference model. In J. K. Torgesen (Ed.), *Cognitive and behavioral characteristics of children with learning disabilities* (pp. 7-40). Austin, TX: Pro Ed.

Stanovich, K. E., West, R. F., & Cunningham, A. E. (1991). Beyond phonological processes: Print exposure and orthographic processing. In S. A. Brady & D. P. Shankweiler (Eds.), *Phonological processes in literacy: A tribute to Isabelle Y. Liberman* (pp. 219-236). Hillsdale, NJ: Erlbaum.

Tressoldi, P. E., Lonciari, I., & Vio, C. (2000). Treatment of Specific Developmental Reading Disorders, Derived from Single-and Dual-Route Models. *Journal of Learning Disabilities, 33*(3), 278-285.

Underwood, G. (Ed.). (1996). *Implicit cognition*. New York: Oxford University Press.

van Dijk, T. A., & Kintsch, W. (1983). *Strategies of discourse comprehension*. New York: Academic Press.

Venezky, R. L. (1999). *The American way of spelling: The structure and origins of American English orthography*. New York: The Guilford Press.

Wagner, R. K., Torgesen, J. K., Laughon, P., Simmons, K., & Rashotte, C. A. (1993). Development of young reader's phonological processing abilities. *Journal of Educational Psychology, 85*(1), 83-103.

Wilson, B. A. (1998). Matching student needs to instruction: Teaching reading and spelling using the Wilson Reading System. In S. A. Vogel & S. Reder (Eds.), *Learning Disabilities, Literacy, and Adult Education* (pp. 213-236). Baltimore, MD: Brookes Publishing.

Wimmer, H., Mayringer, H., & Landerl, K. (1998). Poor reading: A deficit in skill-automization or a phonological deficit? *Scientific Studies of Reading, 2*(4), 321-340.

Wolf, M. (1997). A provisional, integrative account of phonological and naming-speed deficits in dyslexia: Implications for diagnosis and intervention. In B. Blachman (Ed.), *Foundations of reading acquisition and dyslexia: Implications for early intervention* (pp. 67-92). Mahwah, NJ: Erlbaum.

Wolf, M. (1991). Naming speed and reading: The contribution of the cognitive neurosciences. *Reading Research Quarterly, 26*(2), 123-141.

Wolf, M., & Bowers, P. G. (2000). Naming-Speed Deficits in Developmental Reading Disabilities: An Introduction to the Special Issue on the Double-Deficit Hypothesis. *Journal of Learning Disabilities, 33*(4), 322-324.

Wolf, M., Bowers, P. G., & Biddle, K. (2000). Naming-Speed Processes, Timing, and Reading: A Conceptual Review. *Journal of Learning Disabilities, 33* (4), 387-407.

7. ACKNOWLEDGEMENT

This research was conducted with the support of the National Center on Adult Literacy through a grant from the Office of Educational Research and via fellowship support at the University of Delaware. Some of the results here first appeared in the author's dissertation research (Sabatini, 1997). Thanks to Richard L. Venezky, and staff and students at Educational Technology Laboratory at the University of Delaware, as well as the adult educators and students who participated in the study.

8. ADDRESS OF CORRESPONDENCE

John P. Sabatini
National Center on Adult Literacy
University of Pennsylvania
Graduate School of Education
3910 Chestnut Street Philadelphia, PA 19104-3111
United States of America
Phone: (215) 898-2100
Fax: (215) 898-9804

LUDOVIC FERRAND AND JUAN SEGUI

READING ALOUD POLYSYLLABIC WORDS

1. INTRODUCTION

Although a great deal is known about the naming process of *monosyllabic words* (see for instance Coltheart, Curtis, Atkins, & Haller, 1993; Norris, 1994; Plaut, McClelland, Seidenberg, & Patterson, 1996; Seidenberg & McClelland, 1989; Zorzi, Houghton, & Butterworth, 1998), very few studies have been devoted to the naming process of *polysyllabic words* (see however, Ans, Carbonnel, & Valdois, 1998; Jared & Seidenberg, 1990). Indeed, most of the studies on word naming concern monosyllabic words. This is a paradox since monosyllabic words represent less than 10 % of the lexicon and therefore can be considered as the exception, whereas polysyllabic words should be studied more extensively. The present chapter addresses explicitly the processes involved in generating the pronunciations of polysyllabic words from their written forms. In particular, the focus of the present chapter is not lexical access per se but is the process of producing a phonological code for polysyllabic words. In this chapter, we will argue that the syllable is a likely processing unit of reading aloud polysyllabic words. We will present empirical evidence and then we will discuss different models of polysyllabic words.

2. PREVIOUS STUDIES ON THE ROLE OF THE SYLLABLE IN VISUAL WORD RECOGNITION

The seminal work of Spoehr and Smith (1973; see also Spoehr, 1978, 1981) suggests that syllable-sized units play a role in visual word recognition. Subjects were presented with five-letter English words that were either one or two syllables long and that were matched in pairs for other variables such as frequency and number of vowels (e.g., PAINT and PAPER). These authors showed that report accuracy was significantly higher for one- than for two-syllable words. These results suggest that processing in this task proceeds syllable by syllable (see also Mewhort & Beal, 1977).

Printzmetal, Treiman, and Rho (1986; see also Millis, 1986; Printzmetal, Hoffman, & Vest, 1991) also reported evidence that syllables are functional units in perceptual grouping of letters in a string. In their study, subjects had to report the color of a pre-specified target letter which appeared in the middle of a bisyllabic word. This target letter could be the last letter of the first syllable (e.g., the letter D in VODKA) or the first letter of the second syllable (e.g., the K in VODKA). Two colors were always used to present the letter strings but in some items the change in color did not occur at the syllable boundary but one letter before (e.g., VOdka) or after that boundary (e.g., VODKa). Subjects tended to make errors which reflected perceptual grouping of letters in terms of syllabic units, i.e., they would report the *d* of VOdka as a *D* or the *K* of VODKa as a *k*.

Seidenberg (1987, 1989), however, questioned the psychological role of syllables. He pointed out that bigram frequencies show a sharp decline at syllable breaks. Therefore, these *bigram troughs* can explain the effects attributed to syllables. This position has been challenged by Rapp (1992), and Carreiras, Alvarez and De Vega (1993), who reported syllable effects in the absence of bigram troughs. Indeed, the recent work of Carreiras et al. (1993) does suggest that syllable-sized units play a role in visual word recognition. These authors found that Spanish words containing syllables that occur frequently in Spanish were harder to recognize than words containing low frequency syllables. Since this inhibitory syllable frequency effect was obtained in both the lexical decision and word naming tasks, it is likely to reflect lexical access processes that are sensitive to syllable-sized units. According to Carreiras et al. (1993), all words that have one syllable in common with the target word will be partially activated upon target presentation and subsequently interfere in the recognition process.

Overall, these studies suggest that sub-lexical units such as syllables play a role in visual word recognition.

3. PREVIOUS STUDIES ON THE ROLE OF THE SYLLABLE IN READING ALOUD

While it seems plausible to assume that units smaller than syllables (phonemes, onsets, rimes) have independent status as units (see for instance Bowey, 1990; Grainger & Ferrand, 1996; Treiman, 1986, 1990; Treiman & Chafetz, 1987; Treiman & Kessler, 1995; Treiman & Zukowski, 1988), this does not negate the possibility that syllable-sized units are also units of performance.

Tousman and Inhoff (1992) have reported that the naming of a target word is facilitated by the prior presentation of clearly visible primes that corresponded to the first syllable of the target. For example, they showed that the naming latencies of the word GLUCOSE were significantly faster when preceded by the prior presentation (for 250 msec) of a prime that corresponded to the first syllable (e.g., GLU) compared to the prior presentation of a neutral prime (e.g., ---). One problem in interpreting the results of this research using long onset asynchronies is the possible use of predictive strategies by subjects on noticing the relationship between certain prime-target pairs. One means to avoid any contamination by strategic factors is to reduce prime visibility drastically through shorter presentation durations and massive forward and backward masking.

In a more recent study, Ferrand, Segui, and Grainger (1996) demonstrated that French subjects responded faster in word and non-word naming tasks when a masked orthographic prime corresponded to the first syllable of the stimulus than when it corresponded to a longer or a shorter segment than the first syllable. The classical masked priming technique (Forster & Davis, 1984) used in Ferrand et al.' study involves presenting very briefly a masked prime stimulus followed immediately by a given target stimulus that remains visible until subjects respond. In the Ferrand et al. (1996) study, target words were paired such that a given prime corresponded to a complete syllable only in one of the two words (e.g., BA is the first syllable of BA.LADE, but less than the first syllable of BAL.CON; and BAL is the first syllable of BAL.CON, but more than the first syllable of BA.LADE). Thus the word BA.LADE was named faster when preceded by the prime BA than by BAL, whereas the word BAL.CON was named faster when preceded by the prime BAL than by BA. Note that French is usually described as a syllable-timed language having clear syllabic boundaries and stress is typically word-final. These syllable priming effects were obtained for bisyllabic and trisyllabic word naming, as well as for non-word naming and picture naming. However, the effect disappeared with the lexical decision task that does not require overt articulation (the overall results obtained by Ferrand et al. (1996) are summarized in Table 1). The fact that very similar syllabic priming effects were observed in picture, word, and non-word naming but not in a lexical decision task strongly suggests that they are indeed located at the level of output phonology (articulatory encoding) where presumably the same processes are involved in naming these different types of targets. An alternative explanation of the results would be that initial syllables are access codes for visual word recognition (see, e.g., Spoehr & Smith, 1973; Taft, 1979) and that the presentation of a prime stimulus that corresponds to a word's initial syllable facilitates the retrieval of the corresponding lexical representation. The access code involved could be either visual (cf. Taft, 1979) or phonological in nature (Spoehr & Smith, 1973). In either case, activation of the access process by the syllable unit would lead to faster word naming latencies as long as word naming is at least partly dependent on lexical retrieval. However, this alternative explanation in terms of syllabically structured visual or phonological access codes in visual word recognition (Spoehr & Smith, 1973) fails to account for the absence of syllabic priming effects in the lexical decision task. In all cases in which a syllabic effect was observed, subjects had to produce an articulatory output, implying that it is the units involved in generating such an articulatory output that are structured syllabically.

The fact that we did not observe syllabic priming effects in the lexical decision task does not, of course, imply that this task is insensitive to either visual or phonological priming from masked letter strings. With monosyllabic word targets, Ferrand and Grainger (1992, 1993, 1994, 1996; see also Grainger & Ferrand, 1996; Ziegler, Ferrand, Jacobs, Rey, & Grainger, in press) have consistently observed masked orthographic and phonological priming effects (primes were pseudo-homophones of the target) in lexical decision. However, whereas orthographic priming effects appeared with prime exposures similar to those used in the present experiments, phonological priming effects required longer prime exposures (see Ferrand & Grainger, 1993). Therefore, it is possible that phonologically based syllabic priming effects would appear in the lexical decision task with longer prime exposure durations, if such sub-lexical input phonology is structured syllabically. The point, however, in demonstrating that there is no syllabic effect in the lexical decision task when one is using exactly the same presentation conditions that allowed the effects to emerge in word naming is to rule out an access code account of our word naming results.

Table 1. Mean latencies (ms) obtained in different conditions. Data from Ferrand, Segui & Grainger (1996)

	CV targets	*CVC targets*
Experiment 1A (Bisyllabic word naming)		
CV primes	567	589
CVC primes	599	558
Experiment 1B (Trisyllabic word naming)		
CV primes	608	626
CVC primes	632	604
Experiment 2 (Bisyllabic non-word naming)		
CV primes	612	656
CVC primes	646	616
Experiment 3A (Lexical decision task for words)		
CV primes	587	588
CVC primes	591	590
Experiment 3B (Lexical decision task for non-words)		
CV primes	715	711
CVC primes	719	718
Experiment 4 (Picture Naming)		
CV primes	715	750
CVC primes	755	706

In a later report, Ferrand, Segui, and Humphreys (1997) extended these results to British English. In a word naming task, they showed a syllable priming effect for English words with clear initial syllable boundaries (such as BAL.CONY). Furthermore, they demonstrated that for words with clear initial syllable boundaries, naming latencies were faster only when primes formed the first syllable of the target compared to a neutral condition (composed of percent signs such as %%%%%%). In another experiment, they showed that the two possible initial syllables of ambisyllabic words (such as BALANCE, where the /l/ belongs both to the first and the second syllable) facilitated word naming to the same extent, relative to the neutral condition. In a final experiment they observed a syllable priming effect for CV words with clear initial syllable boundaries (such as DI.VORCE). This result demonstrated that the previous syllable effect obtained in the first experiment for CVC words was not due to increased phonological and/or orthographic overlap. The overall results obtained by Ferrand et al. (1997) are presented in Table 2.

Thus, the results obtained in French and English suggest that syllables are functional units in word naming. In these studies the syllable played an important role (but see Schiller, 1998, for a failure to replicate in Dutch).

Table 2. Mean latencies (ms) obtained in different conditions by Ferrand, Segui, & Humphreys (1997)

	CV[C] targets	*CVC targets*	*CV targets*
Experiment 1 (Word naming)			
CV primes	546	549	
CVC primes	545	524	
Experiment 2 (Lexical decision)			
CV primes	627	638	
CVC primes	628	640	
Experiment 3 (Word naming)			
CV primes		559	
CVC primes		524	
Neutral primes		560	
Experiment 4 (Word naming: Ambisyllabicity)			
CV primes	528		
CVC primes	528		
Neutral primes	570		
Experiment 5 (Word naming)			
CV primes			551
CVC primes			586
Neutral primes			590

4. FRENCH AND DUTCH DATA

Schiller (1998) reported a series of experiments in Dutch using the same masking procedure and naming task but failed to replicate the syllable priming effect. A possible reason for the absence of syllable priming effects might be that syllables are not involved in the visual word recognition of Dutch. A parallel can be drawn with findings in auditory word recognition where one finds syllable effects in languages like French, but not in languages like Dutch (Cutler, Mehler, Norris, & Segui, 1986). Cutler et al. (1986) argued that in French with its clear syllable boundaries, the syllable is an important unit used for the segmentation of continuous speech (see also Segui, Dupoux, & Mehler, 1990). In contrast to French, Dutch is a stress language, characterized by a stress-rhythm, with large differences in syllable weight between strong and weak syllables. According to Cutler et al. (1986), stress-based procedures make the information from syllables superfluous. However, some syllable effects have been reported for Dutch by Zwitserlood, Schriefers, Lahiri, and van Donselaar (1993); although other studies have failed to find such an effect (e.g., Cutler, 1997). Differences between Dutch and French do not come as a surprise therefore, since the two languages belong to different language families, Germanic and Romance languages respectively.

5. ORTHOGRAPHIC AND PHONOLOGICAL SYLLABLES

In Ferrand et al's (1996, 1997) experiments, orthographic and phonological overlap between the prime and the target was confounded. In the conditions where the prime and the target shared syllabic structure, they shared both orthographic *and* phonological information (such as in bal/BALCONY). Therefore, the syllable priming effects observed in these experiments (Ferrand et al., 1996, 1997) could be mediated by orthographically defined syllable representations, phonologically defined syllables, or both.

In recent experiments, Ferrand, Grainger, Von Petzinger, and Jacobs (in preparation) examined the influence of masked primes sharing either the first or second *phonological* syllable with bisyllabic target words, while controlling for orthographic overlap. In other words, the shared syllables in this study were pronounced identically but had different written forms. For example, in the bi-syllabic French word DIN.DON (turkey), the initial phonological syllable can be re-written DAIN. This was added to a totally different second syllable to form the prime DAIN.PER. The same manipulation was applied to the same syllables occurring at second position in a different set of words (e.g., ME.DAIN/RON.DIN). The effects of phonological syllable primes were tested against orthographic control primes (sharing the same number of letters with targets such as DOIN.PER/DIN.DON and ME.DOIN/RON.DIN), and unrelated primes that had no letters in common with the target.

In a first experiment, we used the classical masked priming technique with a large group of subjects and a single prime duration of 57 msec. In a second experiment, we used a new technique recently introduced by Jacobs, Grainger, and Ferrand (1995), namely the *incremental priming technique*. This technique allowed us to evaluate the facilitatory or inhibitory nature of priming effects with respect to a within-condition baseline in addition to the traditional across-condition baseline (the unrelated condition). To obtain a within-condition baseline, prime duration was set at a level sufficiently low to yield a null priming effect. The zero point was thus defined as the level of prime duration at which no influence on target processing is observed. Prime duration was then gradually increased (i.e., incremental priming). If performance improves with respect to this within-condition zero point, then the prime can be said to have facilitated target processing. If performance decreases, then the prime has inhibited target processing. Thus, priming is defined with respect to two baseline conditions: the new within-condition baseline, and the traditional across-condition baseline. This double-baseline approach makes measuring of priming effects more reliable and imposes stronger constraints on interpretations of these effects. Exactly the same stimuli were used in both experiments. The results are presented in Tables 3 and 4.

In the first experiment, the time to read aloud bi-syllabic words was significantly speeded by masked primes that shared their initial phonological syllable with targets, compared to orthographic control primes and unrelated primes. No effects were observed for the second syllable. In the second experiment, these initial syllable priming effects were shown to increase in size as prime exposure duration increased.

Table 3. Mean correct response latencies (in milliseconds) with standard errors (in brackets) for word targets in the naming task as a function of prime type (PS=phonological syllable, OC=orthographic control, UR=unrelated) and syllable position

Prime Type			
1st syllable		2nd syllable	
PS	535 (10.3)	PS	553 (10.6)
OC	549 (10.5)	OC	545 (9.1)
UR	556 (9.8)	UR	553 (10.8)
Means	546		550

On the contrary, orthographic similarity in the absence of phonological identity (the OC primes) only produced significant within-condition and across-condition facilitation at the 29 and 43 msec prime duration. The small degree of overlap between OC primes and their corresponding targets was sufficient to facilitate target naming at these prime durations, but not at the shorter 14 msec or longer 57 msec prime duration.

In addition to the traditional across-condition baseline (the unrelated prime condition), the incremental priming technique provides a straightforward way of determining facilitatory and inhibitory priming effects by taking the shortest exposure duration (14 msec) as the within-condition baseline for each priming condition. Pilot work established that at duration of 14 msec the prime has virtually no effect on target processing. Therefore, all values above the zero-line indicate that target processing was inhibited relative to the within-condition baseline, whereas values below that line indicate that target processing was facilitated relative to the within-condition baseline.

Figure 1 gives the amount of net priming obtained in the three priming conditions as a function of prime duration for both the first syllable and the second syllable. Net priming effects were calculated with respect to the within-condition baseline (i.e., the shortest prime duration, 14 msec). As can be seen in Figure 1 (upper panel), for initial syllables there is a steady increase in the size of within-condition priming by phonological syllables (PS) as prime exposure duration is increased. Orthographic control primes (OC) facilitated target processing up to the third prime duration (43 msec) and then dropped back to the zero baseline at the longest prime duration. The unrelated condition showed no reliable (facilitation or inhibition) within-condition priming effect on target processing. As shown in Figure 1 (lower panel), for the second syllable all three priming conditions inhibited target processing relative to the within-condition baseline. Neither the phonological syllable primes nor the orthographic control primes showed any across-condition priming.

Table 4. Mean correct response latencies (in milliseconds) with standard errors (in brackets) by prime type (PS=phonological syllable, OC=orthographic control, UR=unrelated) and prime duration for word targets in the naming task

	Prime Duration			
Prime Type	1	2	3	4
1st syllable				
PS	494 (8.3)	460 (7.9)	438 (7.1)	433 (7.0)
OC	490 (7.0)	461 (9.4)	449 (5.0)	480 (10.3)
UR	495 (7.4)	491 (11.0)	486 (9.0)	487 (6.9)
2nd syllable				
PS	485 (9.0)	498 (11.2)	501 (10.0)	499 (9.2)
OC	482 (8.7)	504 (10.8)	490 (6.7)	496 (6.1)
UR	484 (9.4)	502 (11.4)	504 (11.0)	505 (8.6)

Note. 1 = 14 msec; 2 = 29 msec; 3 = 43 msec; 4 = 57 msec.

The results of these experiments clearly demonstrate that priming from initial syllables can be obtained when the prime syllable is not orthographically identical to the corresponding syllable in the target word. The initial syllable priming effects were robust relative to orthographic control primes, attesting once more to the purely phonological nature of the effect. These results therefore add to the growing literature demonstrating rapid activation of phonological information from printed strings of letters (e.g., Ferrand & Grainger, 1992; 1993; 1994, 1996; Grainger & Ferrand, 1996; Perfetti & Bell, 1991).

Nevertheless, it should be noted that Grainger and Ferrand (1996) failed to observe fast masked phonological priming effects with monosyllabic words in the naming task when all primes shared their initial phoneme with targets. Replacing the initial letter of prime stimuli with a percent sign reinstated the priming effects.
Grainger and Ferrand argued that naming latencies to monosyllabic words in the masked prime paradigm are particularly sensitive to shared onsets. The present experiments demonstrate that with bisyllabic words this sensitivity extends to the

initial syllable. Increasing word length (and therefore the number of syllables) might force subjects to wait for a larger number of articulatory units to be sufficiently activated before triggering a naming response. Moreover, the orthographic control (OC) primes shared the same initial phoneme as target words, whereas the unrelated (UR) primes did not. The fact that no significant difference was observed between these two types of prime at 57 msec prime exposures provides further evidence that bi-syllabic words are not subject to the onset priming effects observed in the speeded naming of monosyllabic words (Forster & Davis, 1991; Grainger & Ferrand, 1996).

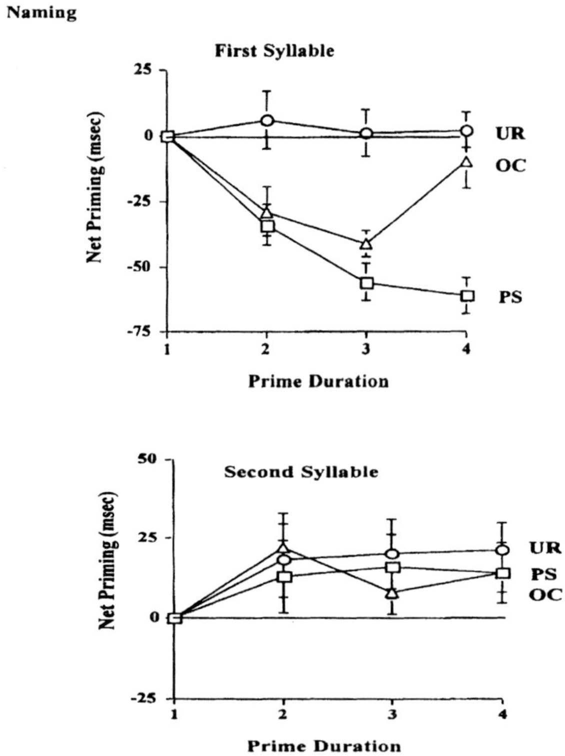

Figure 1. Net facilitatory and inhibitory priming effects with respect to the within-condition baseline (the 14 msec prime duration) for phonological syllable (PS), orthographic control (OC), and unrelated (UR) primes at prime exposures of 29, 43, and 57 msec in Experiment 2. Standard error bars are provided around each data point, following Loftus (1993). The upper panel shows priming with the first syllable, the lower panel shows priming with the second syllable.

The time-course of priming effects from initial syllables (see Figure 1) reveals early orthographic effects generated by letters shared between prime and target, followed by phonological effects determined uniquely by prime-target phonological overlap. We have recently proposed a model of orthographic and phonological processing in printed word recognition (Ferrand, Grainger, & Segui, 1994; Grainger & Ferrand, 1996; Jacobs, Rey, Ziegler, & Grainger, 1998) that provides one possible account of this pattern of effects. A printed string of letters first activates a set of letter representations which simultaneously send activation on to whole-word orthographic representations on the one hand and, more important for the present purposes, to sub-lexical phonological /articulatory representations on the other. It is hypothesized that responses in the word naming task are mainly governed by activity in articulatory output units which become active in the appropriate serial order. It is also hypothesized that subjects can trigger a speeded naming response when articulatory representations corresponding to the initial part of the word (the first syllable in the case of bi-syllabic words) reach a critical activation level.

The time-course of information flow in the model means that at the shortest prime exposures only letter representations are significantly activated by prime stimuli, giving rise to orthographic priming effects. With longer prime exposures, prime stimuli significantly activate phonological/articulatory codes, thus giving rise to priming effects uniquely determined by prime-target phonological overlap. Both of these effects are restricted to the first syllable since activity in representations corresponding to the second syllable does not influence the time to reach the naming response criterion. The fact that orthographic priming effects start to diminish as phonological effects begin to emerge (at the 43 msec and 57 msec prime exposures) can be explained by the orthographic control primes activating the wrong initial syllable representation. Thus inhibition at the phonological/articulatory level will start to cancel the benefits of shared letters.

6. THE SYLLABIC LENGTH-EFFECT RE-EXAMINED

6.1 Empirical findings

A large number of studies have examined whether the number of syllables in a word is related to naming latencies, but these studies have yielded inconsistent results (see Henderson, 1982, and Bachoud-Lévy et al., 1998, for a review). In their seminal study, Eriksen, Pollack, and Montague (1970) presented subjects with monosyllabic and trisyllabic words that were matched so that each monosyllabic word was the first syllable in a trisyllabic word (e.g., cab/cabinet). They found a significant effect of number of syllables on naming latency. However, the number of syllables was confounded with word length. In a later study, Klapp, Anderson, and Berrian (1973) found a significant effect of number of syllables when number of letters was constant. In the present context it is worth noting that Klapp's evidence comes also from picture naming and Arabic numeral naming (see Klapp & Wyatt, 1976, for a review of their work). Klapp et al. (1973) argued that the syllabic length effect was not due to visual input process but to the preparation of the articulatory response. This effect could not have been due to a difference in word perception times since the difference disappeared in a semantic categorization task where no articulation is required. Using a delayed naming task, Klapp et al. found no difference in naming latency between one-syllable and two-syllable words, suggesting that the syllabic length effect is a phonological encoding effect, not an articulatory effect. In a subsequent study, Klapp and Erwin (1976) measured the duration of the one- and two-syllable words of the 1973 study. They found no difference, suggesting that response duration can not have been the cause of the syllabic length effect.

However, other studies have reported no effect of the number of syllables on the initiation of word naming (e.g., Forster & Chambers, 1973; Frederiksen & Kroll, 1976; Mason, 1978; Richardson, 1976). More recent research conducted by Jared and Seidenberg (1990) indicates, however, a possible source of discrepancy between the results mentioned above. According to Jared and Seidenberg, studies examining the effects of number of syllables on naming have yielded inconsistent results because none of these studies examined the interaction of word frequency and number of syllables on naming. In their Experiment 3, Jared and Seidenberg showed that the number of syllables in a word influenced naming latencies only for low-frequency words. The authors interpreted this syllabic effect within the framework of the Parallel Distributed Processing model (PDP) developed by Seidenberg and McClelland (1989). According to Jared and Seidenberg (1990), an effect of number of syllables in naming does not necessarily mean that words are decomposed into syllables. The PDP model was used to describe how one might get syllable effects without explicit syllable units. They suggested that syllable effects might actually be spelling-sound consistency effects. Because each syllable must have a vowel, words with a greater number of syllables also have a greater number of vowels. In English (contrary to French) vowels are the greatest source of spelling-sound inconsistency. So words with more vowels have more sources of inconsistency than words with the same number of letters but fewer vowels. High frequency words may not show a syllable effect either because the effects are attenuated by frequent exposure to the word, or because the high frequency words have less inconsistent vowels than the low frequency words used in Jared and Seidenberg study.

One of us recently re-examined whether there are equivalent or differential effects of number of syllables on the latency to name high-frequency words, low-frequency words, and non-words in French (Ferrand, in press). The first experiment was a replication of Jared and Seidenberg's finding but with better controls in terms of initial syllable (items matched on the first syllable were used since Carreiras, Alvarez, & De Vega, 1993, found a syllable frequency effect on the initial syllable on naming), number of orthographic neighbors (hermits were used, i.e. words with no orthographic neighbors; Grainger, 1990) and syllabification (French words with clear syllable boundaries were used). Furthermore, in order to rule out the possibility that the syllabic length effect is due to ease of articulation rather than the time taken to generate a phonological code, we conducted a control delayed naming task. In the second experiment, non-words were used instead of words.

The results obtained by Ferrand (in press) extend those of previous studies by showing that there are differential effects of number of syllables on word and non-word naming latency. In the first experiment (see Table 5), number of syllables had an effect only on low-frequency words (thus replicating Jared & Seidenberg's result). However, there was no effect of number of syllables for high-frequency words.

In the second experiment (see Table 6), the syllabic length effect was also observed with non-word stimuli. These effects were observed when items were matched for number of letters, number of phonemes, number of orthographic neighbors, bigram frequency, initial phoneme and initial syllable.

Table 5. Mean naming latencies (in milliseconds), standard deviations (in brackets) and percentage of errors in Experiment 1of Ferraud (immediate and delayed word naming)

Immediate Naming	High-Frequency		Low-Frequency		Means
Word Type	M	%	M	%	
Two syllables	520 (73)	1.9	540 (80)	3.6	530
Three syllables	524 (78)	2.6	564 (76)	3.6	545
Means	522		552		
Delayed Naming	**High-Frequency**		**Low-Frequency**		**Means**
Word Type	M	%	M	%	
Two syllables	328 (32)	0.5	332 (38)	0.9	329
Three syllables	330 (35)	0.9	335 (40)	0.6	332.5
Means	329		333.5		

Table 6. Mean naming latencies (in milliseconds), standard deviations (in brackets) and percentage of errors in Experiment 2 of Ferraud, in press (immediate and delayed non-word naming)

	Immediate Naming		Delayed Naming	
Non-words	M	%	M	%
Two syllables	651 (102)	3.0	433 (54)	1.0
Three syllables	686 (108)	5.1	435 (59)	1.0
Difference	+35	+2.1	+2	0

Some recent studies have investigated the length effect in word and non-word reading aloud in order to assess whether the effect was driven by the number of letters in a string or by the number of phonemes in a string (Rastle & Coltheart, 1998; Weekes, 1997). It is important to note at this point that our syllabic length effects can not be confounded with the number of letters since all the stimuli had the same number of letters. It could be argued that our syllabic effects are confounded with the number of phonemes since three-syllable words had on average one more phoneme than two-syllable words. However, Rastle and Coltheart (1998) recently showed that there was a *disadvantage* for 5-letter words having three phonemes compared to 5-letter words having 5 phonemes. If anything, the phoneme length effect is facilitatory and it can not explain our syllabic length effect which is slowing down naming latencies.

The results reported here are compatible with any model of reading which postulates that reading aloud depends upon the joint activity of two procedures: (1) a procedure which operates in parallel across a letter string (and does not generate a strong syllabic length effect) and which is the predominant process in generating responses to high-frequency words; (2) another procedure which operates serially across a letter string (and generates a strong syllabic length effect) and which is the predominant process in generating responses to low-frequency words and non-words.

6.2 Models accounting for the syllable-length effect

The syllabic length effect constitutes an interesting challenge for current models of word naming. In principle, the Dual-Route theory of word naming (Coltheart, 1978; Coltheart, Curtis, Atkins, & Haller, 1993) should be able to explain the syllabic length effect with minor modifications. Traditional Dual-Route theory (Coltheart, 1978) assumes that normal readers have two methods at their disposal for converting print into speech: a lexical route and a non-lexical route. For the lexical route, words are represented in an orthographic input lexicon and are read aloud by retrieving the IR pronunciation. The lexical route is the equivalent to a dictionary look-up procedure (Forster & Chambers, 1973). The non-lexical route converts the graphemic representation of a letter string into phonemes piece by piece. In other words, the lexical route processes letter strings in parallel, whereas the non-lexical route processes letter strings sequentially. The Grapheme-Phoneme Conversion approach may have been motivated by properties of the English language. In English, syllabification of words is quite complex, while the resulting syllables show little consistency with respect to their phonological interpretation. Therefore, this theory has perhaps chosen to bypass the explicit use of syllables, and assumes that groups of graphemes from the visual input trigger conversion rules (Coltheart, 1978). However, if we consider English words with clear syllable boundaries (such as DIVORCE) or French words (i.e. French is usually described as a syllable-timed language having clear syllable boundaries; see Ferrand & Segui, 1998), and if we replace phonemes with syllables when polysyllabic word naming is considered, then the Dual-Route model could easily explain the syllabic length effect. One reason why number of syllables might affect human naming latency, compatible with the Dual-Route theory, is that the number of syllables reflect the operation of a sequential reading mechanism. A sequential reading mechanism will show an effect of number of syllables because the more syllables there are to process, the longer it will take to generate the phonological code for the letter string. The Dual-Route theory predicts that the number of syllables will affect naming latency for non-words and (very) low-frequency words more than for high-frequency words. This is because non-words and (very) low-frequency words are read via a length-sensitive non-lexical mechanism.

Recently, Ans, Carbonnel, and Valdois (1998) proposed a connectionist Multiple-Trace Memory model (MTM) explicitly devoted to polysyllabic word naming. This model is related on some specific aspects to both the Dual-Route model (Coltheart et al., 1993) and the PDP model (Seidenberg & McClelland, 1989) but is unique in a number of respects. In contrast to the PDP model, it does not postulate that a single uniform procedure is used for generating the pronunciation of both words and non-words. Rather, it is assumed that two types of procedures, a global and an analytic one, are required for processing all kinds of letter-strings. However, it can not be viewed as simply another version of the Dual-Route model since the global and analytic procedures do not work in parallel: global processing always proceeds first, the analytic procedure applying only secondarily when global processing has failed. And contrary to the Dual-Route model, this model does not retain the assumption that knowledge about spelling-to-sound correspondences is represented in terms of orthography-to-phonology conversion rules and that the pronunciation of non-words is generated by application of these rules. Rather and more in line with the PDP model, it assumes that mapping from orthography to phonology only emerges from the integrated activation of previously experienced whole words and word syllabic segments. An interesting property of the model is that it contains explicit syllable units. This model predicts that naming latencies should be longer for analytically than for globally processed printed stimuli since the analytic mode only applies after the global mode has failed. Therefore, an increase in naming latencies with syllabic length is predicted for non-words since analytic processing is sequential, each syllable requiring a new visual capture of information. The MTM model also predicts a syllabic length effect for very low frequency words since the analytic process might apply to these words.

In the MTM model, 97.52% of the words (on 12,839 words) were processed globally, the remaining (n = 326; 2.48%) were processed in the analytic mode. According to Ans et al. (1998), analytic processing essentially applies to words of the lowest frequency (median = 1.31 occurrence per million; range = 0.04-5.36 occurrences per million), the probability that a word will be processed globally increasing with its frequency. Our very low-frequency words had on average 2.63 occurrences per million (range = 0.08-7.95), so it seems probable that these words would be processed analytically in the model. Concerning non-words, 22.65% were processed globally (out of 830 non-words), although most were read analytically (77.35%; n = 642). Ans et al. (1998) showed that the probability that a non-word would be processed globally increased with its number of neighbors. More specifically, they show that non-words with a single neighbor were mainly processed analytically (it was the case for 68% of their non-words). Therefore, since in our Experiment 2, our non-words had only one orthographic neighbor (corresponding to the base word from which they were derived from), it seems reasonable to suggest that most of our non-words were processed analytically.

Our finding that the number of syllables has a clear effect on naming latencies for very low-frequency words and for non-words, but not for high frequency words supports models of naming that assume that a sequential process can be used to read aloud (Ans et al., 1998; Coltheart, 1978; Coltheart et al., 1993).

7. VARIABLE RESPONSE CRITERIA AND NAMING

In Ferrand's (in press) experiments, words and non-words were not presented in a mixed-list, so that subjects knew whether an item would be a word or a non-word prior to presentation. Under these conditions, use of the non-lexical route may have been maximized in Experiment 2 (non-words only) but minimized in Experiment 1 (words only) and use of the lexical route may have been minimized in Experiment 2 and maximized in Experiment 1. Despite this, the syllabic length effect was observed in Experiment 1 (words only) for very-low frequency words. It is also possible that the effect was slightly overestimated for non-words (since these items were blocked in Experiment 2).

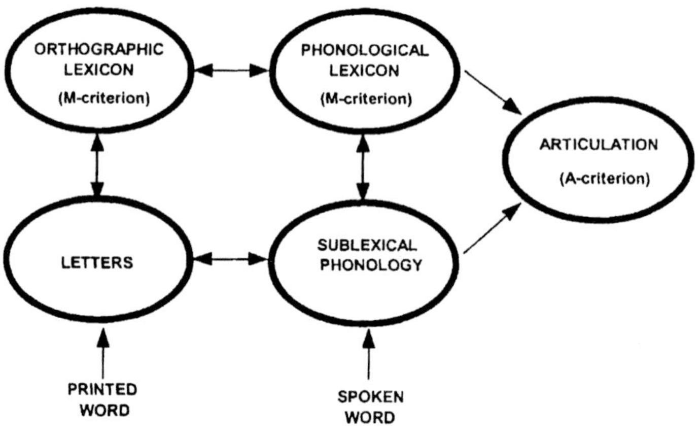

Figure 2. Extended architecture of the multiple read-out model with phonology (Jacobs et al., 1998) including a pool of articulatory output units. Criteria used for triggering a speeded naming response are set on activity in whole-word phonological representations (M criterion) and activity in articulatory output units (A criterion).

Speeded naming RTs might be triggered by response criteria that flexibly adjust with variations in list-context. These criteria are used by participants to determine the earliest possible moment that a naming response can be triggered with minimum risk of making an error. Criterion models have been proposed in many different areas of cognitive psychology in order to capture list-context effects. Lupker, Brown, and Colombo (1997) proposed a time criterion model of speeded naming (see also Jared, 1997). According to these authors, the average difficulty in naming the stimuli in a given list will modify the setting of a time criterion that subjects use to initiate their articulatory response.

The architecture presented in Figure 2 is an extension of the model described by Jacobs, Rey, Ziegler, and Grainger (1998) for the purposes of the naming task. The architecture is very similar to the recent connectionist two-process model of Zorzi, Houghton, and Butterworth (1998). In the complete version of the model presented by Zorzi et al., the phonological decision system (i.e., articulatory output units) receives activation from a system that computes retrieved phonology (i.e., the phonological lexicon) and a system that computes assembled phonology (i.e., sub-lexical phonology). Within this general framework, we hypothesize that a speeded naming response can be generated using two distinct response criteria: one based on unit activity in the phonological lexicon (the phonological equivalent of the M criterion set on whole-word orthographic representations in the Multiple Read-Out Model, Grainger & Jacobs, 1996, see also Ferrand & Grainger, 1996); the other based on activity in articulatory output units (the A criterion). The M criterion is sensitive to word frequency, in that high frequency words reach this criterion earlier than low frequency words (see Grainger & Jacobs, 1996). The A criterion is sensitive to the number of activated word units that have pronunciations that are compatible with the target pronunciation, and to the frequency and consistency of the target's sub-lexical spelling-to-sound correspondences (Jared, McRae, & Seidenberg, 1990).

With respect to influences of list-context, the presence of word stimuli will increase use made of the M criterion, particularly for high frequency stimuli, while the presence of non-homophonic non-words will lead to increased use of the A criterion. In other words, criterion shifts replace the relative involvement of processing routes as an explanation of list-context effects (see also Stone & Van Orden, 1993). The criterion adjustment account of list-context effects is independent of any specific model architecture, as long as the architecture contains some form of whole-word representation of phonology. It will be therefore interesting to examine applications of these response criteria in other computational models of word naming such as the dual-route cascaded model of Coltheart et al. (1993), and the recent MTM model proposed by Ans et al. (1998).

8. REFERENCES

Ans, B., Carbonnel, S., & Valdois, S. (1998). A connectionist multiple-trace memory model for polysyllabic word reading. *Psychological Review, 105,* 678-723.

Bachoud-Lévi, A-C., Dupoux, E., Cohen, L., & Mehler, J. (1998). Where is the length effect? A cross-linguistic study of speech production. *Journal of Memory and Language, 39,* 331-346.

Bowey, J.A. (1990). Orthographic onsets and rimes as functional units of reading. *Memory & Cognition, 18,* 419-427.

Carreiras, M., Alvarez, C.J., & De Vega, M. (1993). Syllable frequency and visual word recognition in Spanish. *Journal of Memory and Language, 32,* 766-780.

Coltheart, M. (1978). Lexical access in simple reading tasks. In G. Underwood (Ed.), *Strategies of information processing* (pp. 151-216). London: Academic Press.

Coltheart, M., Curtis, B., Atkins, P., & Haller, M. (1993). Models of reading aloud: Dual-route and parallel-processing-distributed approaches. *Psychological Review, 100,* 589-608.

Cutler, A. (1997). The syllable's role in the segmentation of stress languages. *Language and Cognitive Processes, 12,* 839-845.

Cutler, A., Mehler, J., Norris, D., & Segui, J. (1986). The syllable's differing role in the segmentation of French and English. *Journal of Memory and Language, 25,* 385-400.

Eriksen, C.W., Pollack, M.D., & Montague, W.E. (1970). Implicit speech: Mechanism in perceptual coding? *Journal of Experimental Psychology, 84,* 502-507.

Ferrand, L. (in press). Reading aloud polysyllabic words and non-words: The syllabic-length effect re-examined. *Psychonomic Bulletin & Review.*

Ferrand, L., & Grainger, J. (1992). Phonology and orthography in visual word recognition: Evidence from masked non-word priming. *Quarterly Journal of Experimental Psychology, 42A,* 353-372.

Ferrand, L., & Grainger, J. (1993). The time-course of orthographic and phonological code activation in the early phases of visual word recognition. *Bulletin of the Psychonomic Society, 31,* 119-122.

Ferrand, L., & Grainger, J. (1994). Effects of orthography are independent of phonology in masked form priming. *Quarterly Journal of Experimental Psychology, 47A,* 365-382.

Ferrand, L., & Grainger, J. (1996). List context effects on masked phonological priming in the lexical decision task. *Psychonomic Bulletin & Review, 3,* 515-519.

Ferrand, L., & Segui, J. (1998). The syllable's role in speech production: Are syllables chunks, schemas, or both? *Psychonomic Bulletin & Review, 5,* 253-258.

Ferrand, L., Grainger, J., & Segui, J. (1994). A study of masked form priming in picture naming and word naming. *Memory & Cognition, 22,* 431-441.

Ferrand, L., Segui, J., & Grainger, J. (1996). Masked priming of word and picture naming: The role of syllabic units. *Journal of Memory and Language, 35,* 708-723.

Ferrand, L., Segui, J., & Humphreys, G.W. (1997). The syllable's role in word naming. *Memory & Cognition, 25,* 458-470.

Forster, K.I., & Chambers, S. (1973). Lexical access and naming time. *Journal of Verbal Learning and Verbal Behavior, 12,* 627-635.

Forster, K.I., & Davis, C. (1984). Repetition priming and frequency attenuation in lexical access. *Journal of Experimental Psychology: Learning, Memory, and Cognition, 10,* 680-698.

Forster, K.I., & Davis, C. (1991). The density constraint on form-priming in the naming task: Interference effects from a masked prime. *Journal of Memory and Language, 30,* 1-25.

Frederiksen, J.R., & Kroll, J.F. (1976). Spelling and sound: Approaches to the internal lexicon. *Journal of Experimental Psychology: Human Perception and Performance, 2,* 361-379.

Grainger, J. (1990). Word frequency and neighborhood frequency effects in lexical decision and naming. *Journal of Memory and Language, 29,* 228-244.

Grainger, J., & Ferrand, L. (1996). Masked orthographic and phonological priming in visual word recognition and naming: Cross-task comparisons. *Journal of Memory and Language, 35,* 623-647.

Grainger, J., & Jacobs, A.M. (1996). Orthographic processing in visual word recognition: A multiple read-out model. *Psychological Review, 103,* 518-565.

Henderson, L. (1982). *Orthography and word recognition in reading.* London: Academic Press.

Jacobs, A.M., Grainger, J., & Ferrand, L. (1995). The incremental priming technique: A method for determining within-condition priming effects. *Perception & Psychophysics, 57,* 1101-1110.

Jacobs, A.M., Rey, A., Ziegler, J., & Grainger, J. (1998). MROM-P: An interactive activation, multiple read-out model of orthographic and phonological processes in visual word recognition. In J. Grainger & A.M. Jacobs (Eds.), *Localist connectionist approaches to human cognition.* Hillsdale, NJ; Lawrence Erlbaum Associates.

Jared, D. (1997). Evidence that strategy effects in word naming reflect changes in output timing rather than changes in processing route. *Journal of Experimental Psychology: Learning, Memory, and Cognition, 23,* 1424-1438.

Jared, D., & Seidenberg, M.S. (1990). Naming multi-syllabic words. *Journal of Experimental Psychology: Human Perception and Performance, 16,* 92-105.

Jared, D., McRae, K., & Seidenberg, M.S. (1990). The basis of consistency effects in word naming. *Journal of Memory and Language, 29,* 687-715.

Klapp, S.T., & Wyatt, E.T. (1976). Motor programming within a sequence of responses. *Journal of Motor Behavior, 8,* 19-26.

Klapp, S.T., & Erwin, C.I. (1976). Relation between programming time and duration of the response being programmed. *Journal of Experimental Psychology: Human Perception and Performance, 2,* 591-598.

Klapp, S.T., Anderson, W.G., & Berrian, R.W. (1973). Implicit speech in reading reconsidered. *Journal of Experimental Psychology, 100,* 368-374.

Loftus, G.R. (1993). A picture is worth a thousand p values: On the irrelevance of hypothesis testing in the microcomputer age. *Behavior Research Methods, Instruments, & Computers, 25,* 250-256.

Lupker, S.J., Brown, P., & Colombo, L (1997). Strategic control in a naming task: Changing routes or changing deadlines? *Journal of Experimental Psychology: Learning, Memory, and Cognition, 23,* 570-590.

Mason, M. (1978). From print to sound in mature readers as a function of reader ability and two forms of orthographic regularity. *Memory & Cognition, 6,* 568-581.

Mewhort, D.J.K., & Beal, A.L. (1977). Mechanisms of word identification. *Journal of Experimental Psychology: Human Perception and Performance, 3,* 629-640.

Millis, M.L. (1986). Syllables and spelling units affect feature integration in words. *Memory and Cognition, 14,* 409-419.

Norris, D. (1994). A quantitative, multiple levels model of reading aloud. *Journal of Experimental Psychology: Human Perception and Performance, 20,* 1212-1232.

Perfetti, C.A., & Bell, L.C. (1991). Phonemic activation during the first 40 ms of word identification: Evidence from backward masking and priming. *Journal of Memory and Language, 30*, 473-485.

Plaut, D.C., McClelland, J.L., Seidenberg, M.S., & Patterson, K. (1996). Understanding normal and impaired word reading: Computational principles in quasi-regular domains. *Psychological Review, 103,* 56-115.

Prinzmetal, W., Hoffman, H., & Vest, K. (1991). Automatic processes in word perception: An analysis from illusory conjonctions. *Journal of Experimental Psychology: Human Perception and Performance, 17,* 902-923.

Prinzmetal, W., Treiman, R., & Rho, S.H. (1986). How to see a reading unit. *Journal of Memory and Language, 25,* 461-475.

Rapp, B.C. (1992). The nature of sub-lexical orthographic organization: The bigram trough hypothesis examined. *Journal of Memory and Language, 31*, 33-53.

Rastle, K., & Coltheart, M. (1998). Whammies and double whammies: The effect of length on non-word reading. *Psychonomic Bulletin & Review, 5,* 277-282.

Richardson, J.T.E. (1976). The effect of stimulus attributes upon latency of word recognition. *British Journal of Psychology, 67,* 315-325.

Schiller, N.O. (1998). The effect of visually masked syllable primes on the naming latencies of words and pictures. *Journal of Memory and Language, 39*, 484-507.

Segui, J., Dupoux, E., & Mehler, J. (1990). The role of the syllable in speech segmentation, phoneme identification, and lexical access. In G.T.M. Altmann (Ed.), *Cognitive models of speech processing: Psycholinguistic and computational perspectives*. Cambridge, MA: MIT Press.

Seidenberg, M.S. (1987). Sub-lexical structures in visual word recognition: Access units or orthographic redundancy? In M. Coltheart (Ed.), *The psychology of reading*, Vol. XII of Attention and Performance (pp. 245-263). Hillsdale: LEA.

Seidenberg, M.S. (1989). Reading complex words. In G. Carlson & M. Tanenhaus (Eds.), *Linguistic structure in language processing* (pp. 53-105). Boston: Kluwer Academic Publishers.

Seidenberg, M.S., & McClelland, J.L. (1989). A distributed, developmental model of visual word recognition and naming. *Psychological Review, 96,* 523-568.

Spoehr, K.T. (1978). Phonological encoding in visual word recognition. *Journal of Verbal Learning and Verbal Behavior, 17,* 127-142.

Spoehr, K.T. (1981). Word recognition in speech and reading: Toward a single theory of language processing. In P.D. Eimas & J.L. Miller (Eds.), *Perspectives in the study of speech* (pp. 239-282). Hillsdale, NJ: Erlbaum.

Spoehr, K.T., & Smith, E.E. (1973). The role of the syllables in perceptual processing. *Cognitive Psychology, 5,* 71-89.

Stone, G.O., & Van Orden, G.C. (1993). Strategic control of processing in word recognition. *Journal of Experimental Psychology: Human Perception and Performance, 19,* 744-774.

Taft, M. (1979). Lexical access via an orthographic code: The Basic Orthographic Syllabic Structure (BOSS). *Journal of Verbal Learning and Verbal Behavior, 18,* 21-39.

Tousman, S., & Inhoff, A. (1992). Phonology in multi-syllabic word recognition. *Journal of Psycholinguistic Research, 21,* 525-544.

Treiman, R. (1986). The division between onsets and rimes in English syllables. *Journal of Memory and Language, 25,* 476-491.

Treiman, R. (1990). To what extent do orthographic units in print mirror phonological units in speech? *Journal of Psycholinguistic Research, 23,* 91-110.

Treiman, R., & Chafetz, J. (1987). Are there onset- and rime-like units in written words? In M. Coltheart (Ed.), *Attention and Performance XII: The Psychology of reading* (pp. 281-298). Hillsdale, NJ: Erlbaum.

Treiman, R., & Kessler, B. (1995). In defense of an onset-rime syllable structure of English. *Language and Speech, 38,* 127-142.

Treiman, R., & Zukowski, A. (1988). Units in reading and spelling. *Journal of Memory and Language, 27,* 466-477.

Weekes, B.S. (1997). Differential effects of number of letters on word and non-word naming latency. *Quarterly Journal of Experimental Psychology, 50A,* 439-456.

Ziegler, J.C., Ferrand, L., Jacobs, A.M., Rey, A., & Grainger, J. (in press). Visual and phonological codes in letter and word recognition: Evidence from incremental priming. *Quarterly Journal of Experimental Psychology.*

Zorzi, M., Houghton, G., & Butterworth, B. (1998). Two routes or one in reading aloud? A connectionist dual-process model. *Journal of Experimental Psychology: Human Perception and Performance, 24,* 1131-1161.

Zwitserlood, P., Schriefers, H., Lahiri, A., & van Donselaar, W. (1993). The role of syllables in the perception of spoken Dutch. *Journal of Experimental Psychology: Learning, Memory and Cognition, 19,* 260-271.

9. ADDRESS FOR CORRESPONDENCE

Ludovic Ferrand
Laboratoire de Psychologie Expérimentale
CNRS and Université René Descartes
71, Avenue Edouard Vaillant
92100 Boulogne-Billancourt
France
Email: ferrand@psycho.univ-paris5.fr

DOMINIEK SANDRA

HOMOPHONOUS REGULAR VERB FORMS WITH A MORPHOGRAPHIC SPELLING: SPELLING ERRORS AS A WINDOW ON THE MENTAL LEXICON AND WORKING MEMORY

1. INTRODUCTION

In contrast to all previous contributions to this book, the present chapter is not concerned with reading complex words. Rather, it focuses on the spelling of a subset of words which are complex at the morphological level, i.e., regularly inflected verb forms. The reason for including this chapter in a book on reading is to show that one can also learn interesting issues with respect to the mental lexicon by studying spelling rather than reading. This is not what one would think when going through the psycholinguistic literature on visual word processing. The literature indeed shows an immense imbalance between the attention for reading processes on the one hand and spelling processes on the other hand. Virtually no attention has been given to the latter (but see work by Assink, 1985, 1987; Fayol, Largy, & Lemaire, 1994; Largy, Fayol, & Lemaire,1996). The present chapter shows that some interesting research issues arise exactly in the context of spelling and that a complete picture of processing *visual* words requires insight in spelling processes as well as reading processes.

The linguistic object to which we will turn our attention are regularly inflected verb forms in Dutch. A particular subset of these forms causes considerable spelling problems for even highly experienced writers. Studying the causes of these problems sheds light on issues pertaining to the mental lexicon. This paper consists of three parts. Firstly, I will describe the major spelling principles of Dutch with an emphasis on the principles governing the spelling of the verb forms under study. This description will lead to an understanding why a particular set of regularly inflected verb forms is more error-prone in Dutch than others. Secondly, I will describe some experimental results obtained in the Centre for Psycholinguistics at the Antwerp University. These results reveal some of the factors determining spelling errors on these forms. Finally, I will situate these findings in a theoretical framework where both the nature of the stored information in the mental lexicon and computational limitations of working memory play a role.

2. PRINCIPLES OF THE DUTCH SPELLING

Each writing system is a visual representation of the words in a language. As is well known, what is actually represented (encoded) considerably varies across writing systems. On the one hand, some writing systems directly represent the meaning of the words, such that the written signs code for meaning in much the same way as spoken words do. In these so-called logographic systems, the orthography does not reflect the pronunciation of the word (or only very few aspects of it). On the other hand, other writing systems do not directly encode a word's meaning but reflect its pronunciation, such that written words are representations of sound rather than meaning. In a syllabic writing system, like Japanese Kanji, the written signs represent syllables in the speech signal. In an alphabetic system (the writing system of many European languages, like English, German, Dutch, French, Italian, Spanish) the orthographic units correspond to the small segments in the speech signal. Each of these sounds is represented by a single letter or a letter cluster (often digraphs, like *ea* or *oa* in English). The letters making up the basic representational code form a so-called alphabet, which is why these writing systems are generally referred to as alphabetic writing systems. Dutch spelling makes use of such an alphabetic system. Even though many languages rely on such a system, they vary considerably among each other with respect to the transparency between the graphemes and the sounds in the spoken language on the one hand (relevant for reading) and between these sounds and the graphemes on the other hand (relevant for spelling). In some languages there is a fair amount of transparency, which means that a grapheme is on average "sounded out" in the same way across the set of words in the lexicon, or, when spelling is concerned, the same sound is generally spelled in the same way. In other languages there is much more inconsistency in these mappings of graphemes to sounds or sounds to graphemes. English, for instance, is well known for using an alphabetic writing system with a conspicuous lack of transparency between graphemes and sounds (compare the pronunciation of the *a* in *car, call, bar*). Dutch, the language which this paper is concerned with, has a rather transparent spelling, but it is not so transparent that spellers can apply sound-to-grapheme correspondences mechanistically to arrive at the correct spelling. Exactly because they cannot do this, leads to the research issue discussed in section 3.

Because of the relatively high transparency between sounds and graphemes, the major Dutch spelling principle is generally referred to as the phonological principle. This can shortly be summarized as 'write what you hear'. Because this mapping from sound to written forms is quite reliable, Dutch does not have a so-called 'deep' orthography (as English). However, as already mentioned, its orthography is not entirely 'shallow' either, because in quite a few cases the mapping from sounds to their orthographic representation is not straightforward. Sometimes this is due to the fact that a single sound can be mapped onto several graphemes and spellers simply have to memorize which words contain one grapheme and which words contain the other, because there is no rule involved (e.g., the sound [au] can be written as *ou,* as in *koud* (cold), *goud* (gold), but also as *au,* as in *rauw* (raw), *blauw* (blue)). However, more interestingly for our present purpose, there are also cases where a single sound can be spelled with different graphemes but where the correct spelling can be derived on the basis of a rule. This is where the morphological spelling principle of Dutch comes in.

The morphological principle is founded on the intuition of spelling designers that it may be good to spell the same morpheme identically across all word forms in which it appears. Thus Dutch orthography has been designed in such a way that it quite transparently reflects the morphological make-up of a word. As a matter of fact, the principle is not consistently applied but let us focus on how it functions when it is needed to spell a word form correctly. There are two subdomains in spelling where the morphological principle is applied. One of these concerns the spelling of a stem-final sound. Consider the Dutch words *taart* (cake) and *paard* (horse) as examples in case. These words are pronounced as [ta:rt] and [pa:rt] respectively. In other words, the pronunciation of their phonological rime is identical, i.e., [a:rt]. Still, despite the prominance of the phonological principle in the Dutch spelling system, the spelling of these two words does not reflect their shared pronunciation. The reason is that the plural of the first word is [ta:rtən] whereas the plural of the second word is [pa:rdən]. The rationale behind this spelling convention is that the addition of a suffix which begins with a sjwa (here the plural suffix) reveals the underlying stem-final phoneme. The underlying phoneme /d/ in words like [pa:rt] is not heard in the words' pronunciation due to the process of final devoicing in Dutch: a voiced [d] is pronounced as the unvoiced [t], i.e., the same sound which is heard in final position in [ta:rt], but where it is not an underlying phoneme. So, when hearing a stem-final [t] spellers cannot tell "by ear" what the correct spelling is and cannot appeal to the dominant spelling principle "spell what you hear". But since the spelling encodes this so-called underlying phoneme, they must retrieve it if they want to avoid spelling errors and the only way to do so is to rely on the morphological principle, i.e. by creating a morphologically related form through the addition of a suffix with an initial sjwa sound. A second domain in which the morphological principle manifests itself is the spelling of verbal suffixes. Lets consider the two verb forms *bied* and *biedt,* which are inflected forms of the verb *bieden* (E. offer) in the first and third person present tense, respectively. These two verb forms have exactly the same pronunciation, i.e., [bit], but have a different spelling. Given the above-mentioned principle that a stem-final [t] is spelled as *d* if adding a suffix with initial sjwa turns the stem-final [t] sound into a [d], we can now understand why [bit] is spelled as *bied* rather than *biet.* However, why is there also a form like *biedt?* Again, the morphological principle is involved. In the spoken language it is clear that when the stem does not end in a [t]-sound, a [t] sound is added in the third person singular tense to encode this grammatical information. An example is *hij lacht* (E. he laughs), where the [t] sound fulfills the same function as English [s] in the same person and tense: an inflectional suffix encoding grammatical information. The reasoning, then, goes as follows: given that the [t] sound is the inflectional morpheme to encode third person singular in the present tense in the verb form when the suffix is audible, and given that the phonological principle requires spellers to spell that suffix for the latter verb category, it follows that the grapheme *t* must be spelled in all instances of third person singular present tense, whether it is audible in the spoken word form or not. In other words, the Dutch equivalent of written English *he offers* is *hij biedt* with a final *t* grapheme in analogy with forms like *hij lacht.* The result is that forms like *biedt* reflect two applications of the morphological principle of Dutch spelling: even though only a single [t] sound is heard, two graphemes are spelled: a *d* because a [d] sound is heard in morphologically related forms where the stem is followed by a sjwa (*bieden*) and a *t* in analogy with third person singular forms where the suffix in the spoken language can be heard (*lacht*).

The above description of a crucial aspect of Dutch spelling reveals that the morphological principle in the spelling system overrides the phonological one. This has an important consequence for a characterization of the nature of the Dutch spelling. If only the phonological principle were applied or if the morphological principle were not applied at the suffix level, many word forms would be homographic between the first and third person singular present tense. Quite a few Dutch verb forms in these grammatical functions indeed have the same pronunciation. As a matter of fact, this is the case for all verbs whose stem-final sound is [d] in the infinitive (Dutch infinitives are the stem followed by the phonological sequence [∂n]; e.g., bid∂n). It appears from a rough estimate on the basis of the verbs listed in CELEX (Baayen, Piepenbrock, & Gulikers, 1995) that ten percent of the Dutch verbs have this homophony in the spoken language. However, as a result of the morphological principle the written language diverges from the spoken language and does not reflect this homophony, i.e., the homophones are not spelled as homographs. Figure 1 demonstrates how the spelling relates to the pronunciation and the morphological structure of the word forms:

	1ST PERSON		3RD PERSON
MORPHOLOGY	antwoord + null	≠	antwoord + t
PRONUNCIATION	[antwo:rt]	=	[antwo:rt]
SPELLING	antwoord	≠	antwoordt

Figure 1. The relationship between the spelling of Dutch regularly inflected verb forms in the present tense, their pronunciation and their morphological structure

As can clearly be seen, the Dutch spelling of inflected verb forms in the present tense (but this generalizes to other instances of the verbal paradigm) reflects their morphological structure and not their pronunciation. In other words, Dutch has a morphographic spelling system.

This raises an interesting question for psycholinguists that are interested in aspects of lexical representation and processing. How do spellers cope with verb forms whose morphological structure differs but whose pronunciation is the same? The answer to this question depends on the question which kind of information drives the process leading to the spelling of the word form. If the major driving force is the pronunciation of the word form, then one would expect problems in the form of intrusion errors. As a single pronunciation is linked to two spelling patterns, the possibility arises that both are activated and that occasionally the speller selects the wrong form. If the morphological structure of a word form is an important driving principle during spelling, one would not expect this homophony to cause many problems, as the orthographic form is the simple concatenation of the spelling patterns corresponding to the constituent morphemes.

Informal observations of the written language produced by many people are already sufficient to show that these homophonous verb forms do cause problems. Even highly experienced writers, who have to write very often and may safely be assumed to know the underlying spelling rules, make the intrusion errors mentioned above. Such errors can be found in papers of university students, in e-mails of university professors, and even from time to time in magazines and newspapers. The occurrence of these errors testifies to the difficulty involved in spelling these verb forms. So the question to address in experimental research is not so much *whether* these verb forms present spelling difficulties but *when,* i.e., under which circumstances? In other words: are there specific determinants of these spelling errors or do they randomly occur in a proportion of the cases where spellers have to spell these words? And what do we learn from this with respect to the spelling process and the information which is stored in the mental lexicon?

3. EXPERIMENTAL FINDINGS ON DUTCH VERB SPELLING ERRORS

In our experimental research (cf. Sandra, Frisson, & Daems, 1999; Sandra, Frisson, & Baayen, in preparation) we focused on two memory-related factors: *lexical memory* (i.e., the mental lexicon) and *working memory.* Since the inflected verb forms under study cannot be spelled correctly by a simple process of mapping sounds onto graphemes, i.e., by applying the phonological principle, it seems plausible to assume that their correct spelling pattern must be *computed* on-line. This means that sufficient computational resources will be required in working memory and that each factor which imposes limits on working-memory space will cause errors. In situations where working memory limitations increase the error risk, the nature of the error patterns will depend on the information which is actually stored in the mental lexicon (the long-term memory component). If regularly inflected verb forms are always derived on-line and have no orthographic representation of their own for the purpose of spelling, two situations may arise. Since spellers will be unable to compute the suffix on a proportion of the cases (due to working memory limitations), they will either randomly choose between the spelling for the first and third person suffixes (no overt spelling and *t* spelling, respectively) or be biased to spell the stem only (i.e., not spell the suffix which they cannot compute). In the former case the intrusion errors will be equally distributed between first and third person singular. In the latter case the large majority of the errors will be made in the third person (as the first person form is homographic with the verbal stem). However, in the situation where regularly inflected verb forms do have their own orthographic representation in the mental lexicon – despite the fact that their spelling pattern can be derived by rule and storage would introduce redundant information in the mental lexicon – an important determinant of spelling errors might be the occurrence frequency of the two homophonic forms in the written language. It is a well-known fact that occurrence frequency is an important non-linguistic property of word forms, which strongly determines their accessibility in the mental lexicon (Andrews, 1989; Forster & Chambers, 1973; for a review of the frequency effect, see Monsell, 1991). It is such a reliable determinant of lexical processing that frequency manipulation has become a diagnostic for demonstrating the importance of particular units in lexical processing during reading (morpheme frequency: Baayen, Dijkstra, & Schreuder, 1997; Colé, Beauvillain, & Segui, 1989; Taft, 1979; syllable frequency: Carreiras, Alvarez, & de Vega, 1993; rime frequency: Bowey & Hansen, 1994; Geudens & Sandra, in press). Hence, if the orthographic patterns of regularly inflected verb homophones are represented in the mental lexicon, one would expect their frequency to modulate the error patterns. More particularly, one would predict that the higher-frequency form would cause intrusion errors on spelling the low-frequency form more often than vice versa.

Since the goal of our research was to study the distribution of errors in the first and third person singular present tense, we wanted to create circumstances which would be likely to give rise to sufficiently large numbers of errors. When spellers have lots of time to reflect on the spelling of a verb form, those who know the rules will make no errors. Hence, we decided to use a speeded dictation task in order to maximize the error risk. Participants in the experiment were provided with a sheet on which a set of sentences was printed. In each sentence two word forms were missing: one inflected verb form and one other word which presented spelling difficulties for entirely different reasons (i.e., forms which are hard to memorize). The experimenter read the sentences at a speed which made it possible for the participants to write down the words but limited the available working-memory resources for reasoning out the correct verb spelling or for performing a spelling check (dictation speed had been pretested before the actual experiment). If we had left the participants ample opportunities for checking their spelling, errors that initially appeared in their responses could have been corrected, which would have masked the information targeted by the study.

Given these experimentally induced limitations on working-memory we manipulated four factors in different speeded dictation experiments: Grammatical Person (1st - 3rd), Homophone Frequency Relationship (D-dominant - DT-dominant), Subject-verb Distance (adjacent – distant), and Interfering Morphosyntactic Information (present – absent). The first factor reflects the fact that the homophones under study involve these two grammatical persons. The frequency relationship between the two homophones allows us to address the question whether spellers are guided by the frequencies of homophonic but morphographically different forms or whether the error pattern is unaffected by this factor and, for instance, more related to the grammatical person (e.g., more errors for 3rd persons). The frequency factor allows us to address the question whether these spelling forms have their own orthographic representations in the mental lexion. If they have, the prediction is that the factor will shape the error patterns. The remaining two factors are related to aspects of working-memory. When the distance between the grammatical subject and the verb form increases spellers are expected to have more problems with the retrieval of the relevant morphosyntactic features from the subject. In order to select the correct suffix spelling one must identify whether the grammatical subject is a first or third person. However, if the inflected verb form appears a number of words further down the sentence than the subject, this information may be lost (e.g., through information decay in working memory) and hence less accessible than when the grammatical subject and verb forms are close to each other. The presence of intervening morphosyntactic information which conflicts with the information encoded by the grammatical subject is also a factor in working-memory that is expected to determine the error rates. More particularly, conflicting information is expected to increase the error risk. Spellers could err because they rely on the more proximal, misleading information in a sizeable proportion of cases (and forget about the subject) or because they have a conflict to resolve under conditions of time pressure and weigh the proximal singular noun information more heavily than the distant subject information (due to memory decay) and accordingly select the wrong form. We tested this hypothesis by studying whether the presence of a singular noun object between the grammatical subject and the verb form would affect the error rates. Since a singular noun can appear in subject position as a third person singular, it is expected to signal these grammatical features. When this information conflicts with the information carried by the grammatical subject – more particularly, when the subject is first person singular – more errors may occur than when such conflicting information is absent (subject is third person singular).

3.1 The contribution of lexical (long-term) memory

Rather than describing the experiments in detail here, I will focus on the theoretically most important effects, such that the overall picture becomes clear. The crucial finding relates to the nature of the representations in the mental lexicon (long-term memory). This finding is a significant interaction between the factors Relative Homophone Frequency and Person. More particularly, for verbs which appear more often in the third than in the first person (henceforth: DT-dominant verbs, because they end in the orthographic cluster *dt*), the homophonic intruders appear more often in the first person – the *dt* pattern of the third person imposes itself more on the *d* pattern of the first person than vice versa – whereas for verbs which appear more in the first person than in the third one (henceforth: D-dominant verbs) exactly the opposite occurs (Sandra, Frisson, & Daems, 1999, Experiment 1). In the condition where neither the *d* nor the *dt* form was dominant, the error risk did not differ between the first and third persons. Figure 1 illustrates this finding. We interpret this outcome as evidence supporting the storage of regularly inflected verb forms in the mental lexicon, even though these forms are not "needed" from an analytic, descriptive perspective, as they can be calculated by rule (but see the section below on Theoretical Implications).

This finding is quite reliable as we replicated it across different experiments and with a different type of homophony within the verbal paradigm of some verbs. Independently of our wish to replicate the pattern we had observed for the *d/dt* homophony, we also had a theoretical reason to move to another type of homophony. When using the *d/dt* contrast, all items are characterized by the fact that it impossible to hear the suffix as distinct from the stem in the spoken language. This is due to the fact that in spoken Dutch words any voiced underlying phoneme is devoiced in stem-final position (e.g., /d/ in /bid/ is pronounced as a [bit]). This so-called final devoicing rule results in a final [t] in the spoken word, independently of the suffix. Because we wanted to find out what would happen when the final [t] results from the suffix, i.e. when the pronunciation of stem and suffix are both audible, we ran another experiment with a speeded dictation task (Sandra et al, 1999, Experiment 2). In this experiment verbs without a stem-final *d* were selected (type *versieren* [E. decorate], where the stem is *versier*). For such verbs the homophony exists between the third person singular present tense (suffix *t*) and the past participle (suffix *d,* which is devoiced, thus causing homophony). We found the same interaction between Relative Homophone Frequency and Person, and could thus generalize the finding for the *d/dt* homophony to another type of homophony within the verbal system.

We were not only in a position to generalize our finding to a different type of verbal homophony but also to different tasks (I will describe only one of them). In addition to dictation of the *d/dt* verb forms in a list of sentences, we used another variant of the dictation task. In Frisson and Sandra (submitted) we dictated the verb forms as items embedded in a larger list of inflected verb forms only. The crucial aspect of the experiment was that we provided no grammatical context, i.e. participants heard the verb form only. They were told to spell the homophone which they "preferred" (i.e., they had to make a forced choice between *d* and *dt*). Of course, from the perspective of a normal writing context this task is quite unnatural, as inflected forms are precisely those forms whose suffix can only be spelled on the basis of grammatical information. However, we were interested how spellers would spell if the crucial information for distinguishing between the spelling patterns was withheld. One possibility is that, if they have no clue, they randomly choose between the *d* and *dt* homophones, such that relative homophone frequency does not play a role. Another alternative is that they use the frequency relationship between the two homophones as a guide in this unusual spelling situation. The experimental list contained the set of *d*-dominant and *dt*-dominant forms that was used in the speeded dictation experiments with sentence material. They were intermixed with a list of filler verb forms. All forms had been tape-recorded at a speed which allowed participants to spell a form within the interval between two items, but did not allow time for making up a problem solving strategy. It turned out that, in the absence of a grammatical subject, spellers were affected by the frequency relationship between the two homophones. More particularly, for *d*-dominant verbs more *d* responses were given than *dt* responses, whereas the opposite distribution was obtained for the *dt*-dominant forms. This is again evidence that spellers represent frequency information for regularly inflected verb forms.

3.2 *The contribution of working memory*

Two other design factors in the dictation experiment with sentences – Subject-verb Distance and Interfering Morpho-syntactic Information – concerned the role of working memory. As the distance between the verb and its subject increases, the grammatical features of the subject in working memory will decay and more errors are predicted. If there is a decrease in the availability of grammatical information (adjacent versus distant conditions) the probability increases that more intrusion errors are made and that the frequency relationship between the homophones leaves a clear fingerprint on the error distribution. This is exactly what happened. Significantly more errors were made in the distant condition than in the adjacent one, reflecting the limited capacity of working memory and the time-consuming nature of spelling the suffix correctly. However, the errors followed essentially the same pattern as in the adjacent condition: the three-way interaction between Distance, Homophone Frequency Relationship and Grammatical Person was not significant. Hence, the limitations of working memory cause more errors when subject and verb form are separated in the sentence than when they are adjacent by giving more opportunity to the homophone factor to manifest itself. However, the nature of the error pattern does not change, only the number of errors.

The factor Interfering Morpho-syntactic Information is another factor affecting working memory. When the morpho-syntactic features of the grammatical subject conflict with those of a local singular noun which occurs in-between the subject and the verb form, this may result in a conflict in working memory as well. The procedure which has to determine the suffix spelling is confronted with inconsistent information and since the features from the local noun may be more salient than those of the more distant subject, this may lead the speller in a proportion of cases to write down the verb form which fits the local noun (i.e., third person singular) rather than the grammatical subject. Note that in our experiments this conflict occurred only with first person singular subjects. The grammatical features of a local singular noun cannot conflict with third person singular subjects. We indeed observed that the conflict resulted in more errors. Conflict resolution takes time and since the experimental conditions did not offer the required time, because of limited attentional resources, spellers relied on the proximal singular object noun rather than on the singular subject first person pronoun. So, they spelled the *dt*-form more often than the *d*-form compared to a control condition without such conflicting information.

4. THEORETICAL IMPLICATIONS

Even though spelling research is not very popular in psycholinguistics, our research demonstrates that the study of spelling errors can shed light on the nature of the information which is encoded in the mental lexicon and on the contribution of working memory in this language modality. The idea to use error data for the study of a language modality is not new in psycholinguistics. As a matter of fact, analyses of different error types and their occurrence frequency were the first source of information used to study the nature of the speech production system (Fromkin, 1971, 1993; Garrett, 1980, 1982). Moreover, the current use of other dependent measures besides speech error data (like reaction times) has not led to a rejection of the speech error evidence, which is still considered important for building models of the language processor (e.g., Levelt, Roelofs, & Meijer, 1999). Error data are important in studies of language impairment too, like aphasia or dyslexia, where researchers also build on the assumption that the nature of the errors can reveal important information on how the non-impaired system functions. So, by applying this rationale to the study of written language production, we adopt a familiar paradigm in the field of psycholinguistics.

What have we learnt from our results? We set out from the observation that even experienced spellers still make errors on regularly inflected Dutch verb forms, despite the descriptive simplicity of the rules, their knowledge of these rules, and the high educational attention for these rules. The persistence of these errors suggests that it can be no coincidence the written word production system so often stumbles produces these errors and that there must be a principled explanation. In short: this particular spelling issue can illuminate aspects of the underlying nature of what is involved in written word production. Any model on written word production will have to be able to account for these errors. The error patterns which we obtained in controlled experiments suggest that the errors are not randomly distributed but reflect the joint operation of two memory systems: a long-term memory component (the mental lexicon) and a short-term memory component (working memory). In addition, two other factors play a role: the nature of the spelling rules involved and the relative importance of form and meaning in language communication. As we shall see below, the latter two factors are related to the characteristics of working memory.

The most important result pertains to the information which is stored in the mental lexicon and which is activated during spelling. The crucial finding is the effect of relative homophone frequency on the error rates. When spellers have little time to apply a spelling rule or to use analogical reasoning (i.e., compare homophones to non-homophones; e.g., *hij biedt* to *hij maakt*), they tend to write the most frequent homophone. This implies that the mental lexicon contains the information which homophone is the most frequent one. Accordingly, the theoretical significance of this finding is that the mental lexicon keeps track of the frequency with which it encounters individual inflected forms, even though these are fully regular and the existence of a rule obviates the logical need for keeping track of frequency information. Research on spelling errors in French (Largy, Fayol, and Lemaire, 1996) has shown that similar phenomena play a role in that language. In a sentence like (1) below, participants often wrote errors like *filtres* instead of the correct form *filtre*. This was not due to the preceding pronoun *les* triggering the *–ent* plural verb suffix (errors which also occur and which Fayol, Largy, & Lemaire, 1994, have called proximity errors) but was due to the form *les* being homographic with the frequent French definite article, which induced a noun reading of the form *filtre* in cases where the noun occurred more frequently than the verb. Hence the homophone frequency effect which we found with Dutch inflected verb forms was obtained in French across lexical categories (noun/verb).

(1) Le chimiste prend des liquides. Il les filtre.
(Word-for-word translation: The chemist takes liquids. He them filters.)

A second implication following from the observed errors for homophonous verb forms is that phonology drives the spelling process. This is perhaps not surprising in a language whose spelling applies the alphabetic principle. However, the phonology does not only play a role in a computational process which maps phonemes onto graphemes (compare this to the letter-to-sound conversion rules in Coltheart's, model for reading aloud; e.g., Coltheart, 1978; Coltheart & Rastle, 1994). It also plays a role at the level of full-form retrieval of stored orthographic representations in the mental lexicon. Otherwise we would not have found the homophone frequency effect.

The claim that there is full-form storage of regularly inflected verb forms might be challenged by the remark that the data do not require such an account. One might, for instance, propose a model in which a stem lexicon is linked somehow to a suffix lexicon and where the system learns over time which stem-to-suffix connections occur most frequently. As a matter of fact, this is exactly the account which Fayol and his co-workers (1994) proposed. However, there are two reasons why this counter-argument is not compelling and certainly does not invalidate an account of the data in terms of whole-word representations. Firstly, whereas the architecture behind the two accounts is quite different – whole word representations in our account, no such representations in the other account – it seems that the very notion of connections strength is almost equivalent to the notion of a whole word representation. What is being asserted in both cases is that the suffix letter is very strongly associated to the stem, hence creating a pattern. So, in a model where stems and suffixes are stored in separate modules, the very existence of associative links between elements from the two comes very close to the notion of a whole-word representation. At the very least, a strict separation between the modules must be given up in order to account for the data. Apart from this theoretical argument, there is also an empirical argument to be made. The model that makes use of stem and suffix modules predicts that errors must always be morphologically legal, i.e. those errors can only occur as the result of wrong stem and suffix combinations. However, in Dutch some error types cannot be explained in this way. More particularly, errors like *wastte* for *waste* (E. washed) cannot be explained. Since the past tense is formed by concatenating the stem *was* and the past tense suffix *te,* this error type cannot be accounted for in such a model. The model does not predict these errors, as they cannot be stored as whole-word forms (non-existing forms, hence no storage) nor assembled through stem plus suffix combination. Still, errors of this type regularly occur in writings of even 18-year old university students. How does the model that makes use of whole word representations fare in light of this error type? Does it offer a possibility for explaining them? The answer is positive. The form *waste* is not homophonous with another form at the whole word level, but homophony does exist at the subword level. The rime *astte* occurs more frequently (both type and tokenwise) than the rime *aste.* As a result, the same mechanism that is operational at the whole-word level may be operational at the sublexical level as well. This can naturally be accounted for within the model we propose: within the mental lexion connections are made between a single phonological pattern and the two orthographic representations instantiating this phonological pattern. Moreover, the system keeps track of the frequency of these orthographic patterns. The principle is a general one, obtaining both at the lexical and sublexical level, and can thus naturally account for error data at the whole-word level (*bied/biedt*), where the intrusion error is caused by a homophonic competitor at the level of orthographic representations for words, and at the subword level (*waste/wastte*), where the intrusion error is caused by a homophonic competitor at the level of sublexical orthographic representations.

Another important finding is that working memory plays an important role during spelling the homophonic verb forms studied in the experiments. Since working-memory makes use of attentional resources, it has only a limited capacity for storing and processing information. The nature of this memory system makes a prediction. If the conditions are such that the problem to be solved cannot be solved given the resources it can allocate to the problem, the error risk will increase. More particularly, the risk that disturbing factors will cause intrusion errors will be considerably enhanced. There are several different reasons why this was the case in the spelling experiments. A first factor is that the nature of the problem to be solved indeed did require the allocation of attentional resources. Participants had to spell a homophonic verb form correctly, i.e. decide which suffix combined with the stem. Since errors abound in non-experimental situations and errors can easily be elicited in experimental conditions, it is clear that we are not dealing with a highly automatised mental process here. Of course, even automatised processes can generate errors (e.g., speech errors), but the relatively frequent error rates on these homophonic verb forms in ordinary writing situations, the learning difficulty that is involved, and the strong intuition of Dutch spellers that they consciously have to solve the problem of how to spell a verb homophone all testify to the fact that we are dealing with a kind of rule that is represented in the form of declarative knowledge. This knowledge must be retrieved when the problem is encountered. This is not entirely surprising, given the fact that the dominant principle in Dutch is to spell what one hears. Note that this is also the case for the majority of inflected verb forms like *hij maakt* (E. he makes), *hij werkt* (E. he works), *zij kent* (E. she knows), *zij droomt* (E.she dreams). As a matter of fact, the homophony problem occurs only for about ten percent of the Dutch infinitives. Put differently, it does not often occur that the morphological principle overrides the phonological one in the spelling of present tense verb forms. If a different spelling had existed for Dutch, in which *hij treedt* was not spelled with a *t*-suffix on the basis of the analogy with *hij maakt,* the problem would not have occurred. However, spelling committees who have decided how the spoken language should be spelled, have opted for a consistent, hence analytical, spelling. This means that metalinguistic skills, i.e. conscious analysis of the language, are required in order to spell correctly. This, together with the low percentage of forms requiring such an analysis, makes it inevitable that attentional resources have to be allocated to solve the verb spelling problem correctly. However, by allowing very little time for writing up the verb forms, the experimental conditions in the speeded dictation task had been set up to make the process of conscious problem solving quite difficult. As a result, errors were bound to arise and these errors were necessary to be able to study their distribution. However, the observation that limiting the capacity of working memory caused sufficient errors, underscores the importance of working memory when it comes to the spelling of homophonic verb forms. By minimizing the attentional resources of the participants in the dictation experiments, we were able to bring out the role of stored representations in the mental lexicon. The role of working memory was demonstrated in these experiments in two ways: by showing that increasing the distance between subject and verb form increases error rates and by showing that the insertion of a singular noun causes between a first person subject and the verb form causes more errors than in a control condition.

The experiments on spelling errors shed light on the nature of what is stored in the mental lexicon. Do they also shed light on the processing course? Strictly speaking, they do not, as the task was an off-line one. Still, the effect of relative homophone frequency narrow down the number of possible processing models. One possibility is that if the spelling problem is not solved within time (or spellers are not even aware that there is a problem and hence do not mobilize their knowledge) the highest frequency orthographic representation reaches threshold activation first and is the form that is spelled. A variant on the above scenario is that both forms in the mental lexicon are activated simultaneously and that the most salient one (the higher frequency one) is eventually selected. However, it is also possible that working memory does manage to solve the problem within time. Even so, there may be an effect of the information stored in the mental lexicon. If the form to be spelled is the same as the high frequency homophone, no error will occur, as the output of both procedures will be identical. However, if the form to be spelled is the low-frequency one, the output of the mental lexicon will differ from the output of working memory, and this conflict may be the source of errors.

A final question to address is whether the results obtained in these experimental contexts and the interpretive framework are also valid to account for the errors which experienced spellers make in their daily writings. There is good reason to believe that this is indeed the case. In normal writing situations spelling is only a subcomponent of the writing process. Issues like meaning and sentence construction are also crucial and especially meaning is central to all forms of linguistic communication. Because language users must attend to meaning in language if they want their communication to succeed, they cannot allocate all their attentional resources in working memory to formal aspects of the language. As a result, not all "space" in working memory can be allocated to spelling during the writing process of an ordinary text. Given the relative importance of meaning and form in writing (and the ensuing allocation of working memory space), writers risk to make errors on those forms which require most attentional resources. This is the case for Dutch homophonic verb forms. As a result, the focus on meaning in writing texts in real-life situations can be compared to the limited time conditions which we imposed on our participants in the speeded dictation experiments. In both cases the effect is that working memory does not leave sufficient processing resources for solving the spelling problem in time. Thus considered, the data we obtained experimentally can be argued to be valid in the context of written word production in text writing.

An interesting avenue for follow-up research, which I have just begun, is to find out whether the same factors that cause spelling errors also play a role when readers have to read texts including these errors. For instance, the factor of relative homophone frequency may have a role both in spelling and in reading. When a verb form is spelled incorrectly in a text, the reading time of this form may be more delayed when the wrong form that appears in the text is the lower frequency homophone than when it is the higher frequency homophone.

To summarize. The spelling research that has been done by Frisson & Sandra (in press), Sandra et al (1999), Sandra et al (in preparation), and related studies in the Antwerp research team results in a number of claims. Fully regular verb forms are stored in the mental lexicon, even if there is no logical need for such storage. Spelling homophonic Dutch verb forms requires attentional resources – it mobilizes declarative knowledge – and is not an automatic process. If conditions are such that few attentional resources can be allocated to the spelling problem (speed in experiments, meaning focus in ordinary writing situations), the stored information in the mental lexicon will have the largest opportunity to determine the spelling of the verb form. As long as the high-frequency form in the mental lexicon matches the target form, no error will occur. When the high-frequency form mismatches the target form, an error may result. This demonstrates that when spellers are confronted with analytic rules, which are perfectly logical from a descriptive point of view, they may still be inclined to spell the most probable form given their past experience with written language – at least when the problem is complex enough that it takes too much attentional resources in working memory for being solved in time. Hence, if someone were to defend the idea that spellers naturally follow analytic, straightforward rules, our data show that this idea would be ill-taken. With respect to Dutch homophonic verb forms at least, spellers' spontaneous behavior is to a high extent probabilistic (spell the most frequent form) and is not that what one would expect if rule-application was a skill which they excell in. As such, a study of spelling errors and their distribution can inform us on the nature of the stored information in the mental lexicon, different kinds of memory systems and their interplay.

5. REFERENCES

Andrews, S. (1989). Frequency and neigbourhood size effects on lexical access: Activation or search? *Journal of Experimental Psychology: Learning, Memory, and Cognition, 15,* 802-814.

Assink, E.M.H (1985). Assessing spelling strategies for the orthography of Dutch verbs. *British Journal of Psychology, 76,* 353-363.

Assink, E.M.H (1987). Algorithms in Spelling Instruction: the Orthography of Dutch Verbs. *Journal of Educational Psychology, 79,* 228-235

Baayen, R.H., Dijkstra,T. & Schreuder, R. (1997). Singulars and plurals in Dutch: Evidence for a parallel dual route model. *Journal of Memory and Language, 37,* 94-117.

Baayen, R.H., Piepenbrock, R. & Gulikers, L. (1995). *The CELEX lexical database* (CD-ROM). Linguistic Data Consortium, University of Pennsylvania, Philadelphia, PA.

Bowey, J.A., & Hansen, J. (1994). The development of orthographic rimes as units of word recognition. *Journal of Experimental Child Psychology, 58,* 465-488.

Carreiras, M., Alvarez, C.J., & de Vega, M. (1993). Syllable frequency and visual word recognition in Spanish. *Journal of Memory and Language, 32,* 766-780.

Colé, P., Beauvillain, C. & Segui, J. (1989). On the representation and processing of prefixed and suffixed derived words: A differential frequency effect. *Journal of Memory and Language, 28,* 1-13.

Coltheart, M. (1978). Lexical access in simple reading tasks. In G. Underwood (Ed.), *Strategies of human information processing.* London: Academic Press.

Coltheart, M. & Rastle, K. (1994). Serial processing in reading aloud: Evidence for dual-route models of reading. *Journal of Experimental Psychology: Human Perception and Performance, 20,* 1197-1211.

Fayol, M., Largy, P., & Lemaire, P. (1994). Cognitive overload and orthographic errors: When cognitive overload enhances subject-verb agreement errors. A study in French written language. *The Quarterly Journal of Experimental Psychology, 47A,* 437-464.

Forster, K.I., & Chambers, S.M. (1973). Lexical access and naming time. *Journal of Verbal Learning and Verbal Behavior, 12,* 627-635.

Fromkin, V.A. (1971). The non-anomalous nature of anomalous utterances. *Language, 51,* 696-719.

Fromkin, V.A. (1993). Speech production. In J. Berko Gleason & N.B. Ratner (Eds.), *Psycholinguistics,* (pp. 272-301). Fort Worth: Holt, Rinehart, & Winston.

Garrett, M.F. (1980). Levels of processing in sentence production. In B. Butterworth (Ed.), *Language production (Volume 1): Speech and talk,* (pp. 177-220). London: Academic Press.

Garrett, M.F. (1982). Production of speech: Observations from normal and pathological language use. In A.W. Ellis (Ed.), *Normality and pathology in cognitive functions,* (pp. 19-76). London: Academic press.

Geudens, A., & Sandra, D. (in press). Orthographic subsyllabic patterns in Dutch beginning readers: The case of a transparent orthography. In L. Verhoeven, C. Elbro, & P. Reitsma (Eds.), *Precursors of Functional Literacy.* Amsterdam, Philadelphia: John Benjamins Press.

Largy, P., Fayol, M., & Lemaire, P. (1996). The homophone effect in written French: The case of verb-noun inflection errors. *Language and Cognitive Processes, 11,* 217-255.

Levelt, W.J.M., Roelofs, A., & Meyer, A.S. (1999). A theory of lexical access in speech production. *Behavioral and Bain Sciences, 22,* 1-75.

Monsell, S. (1991). The nature and locus of word frequency effects in reading. In D. Besner & G.W. Humphreys (Eds.), *Basic processes in reading: Visual word recognition,* (pp. 148-197). Hillsdale, NJ: Lawrence Erlbaum.

Sandra, D., Frisson, S., & Baayen, H. (in preparation). Interference effects of regular verb storage in the spelling of highly experienced readers and writers: Psycholinguistic evidence and simulation data.

Sandra, D., Frisson, S., & Daems, Fr. (1999). Why simple verb forms can be so difficult to spell: the influence of homophone frequency and distance in Dutch. *Brain and language, 68,* 277-283.

Taft, M. (1979). Recognition of affixed words and the word frequency effect. *Memory and Cognition, 7,* 263-272.

6. ADDRESS FOR CORRESPONDENCE

Dominiek Sandra
University of Antwerp
Centre for Psycholinguistics
Prinsstraat 13 (D-109)
2000 Antwerp
Belgium
Email: dominiek.sandra@ua.ac.be

INDEX

AAM: *see* Augmented Addressed Morphology (AAM) Model
Adults
  Italian readers, 54
  lexical decision tasks, performance, 27–28
  morphological analysis, 53
  Serbian readers, 54
  sublexical frequency and meaning, Dutch language, 198*t*
  word reading processes, 265–293
    basic processing rate, 277
    basic speed measures, 272
    best fit models of decoding accuracy, rate and higher level processing variables, 281–282
    college-level readers and adult literacy learners, comparisons, 273–274
    component skills and speed/rate of processing, 284–285
    component task, measures, 275
    decoding skill accuracy, 278–279
    decoding skill rate, 279–280
    dyslexics, 265–267
    expert word recognition ability, acquisition and nature of, 268–270
    hierarchical, multiple regression analysis, 277
    lexical decision decoding tasks, 272–273
    low literate adults, 265–267
    major findings, 286–288
    measurement issues, 286
    methodological issues, 286
    PAIRED-WORD task, 272
Adults (*cont.*)
  word reading processes (*cont.*)
    pseudoword naming, 272
    research questions, 270–271
    sentence-processing, 273
    SINGLE-WORD task, 272
    standardized measures of word recognition and reading comprehension, 274
    study method, 271–273
    study results, 273–285
    word naming, 272
    word recognition and comprehension relationship, 282–284
Affixes
  morpheme-based lexical reading, 246–250
    selectional restrictions, 254–255
  root frequency, 246–247
  trimorphemic words, English, 224
AGE, 277, 284
Arabic
  numeral naming, 305
  verbs, 100
Artificial Morpheme Boundary Experiment, 228–234
Augmented Addressed Morphology (AAM) Model, 193–194, 212
Autosegmental Phonology, 96

Base Family Frequency, 161, 170–172, 176
Base Family Size, 161, 170–172, 176
Base Lemma Frequency, 164, 170, 172, 176
Basic Reading and Reading Comprehension, 40
Binyan, 97

Binyanim, 97
Bound morphemes, representation of, 117–122
"Branding," opacity, 159–162, 168, 169*f*, 170

CA-Match, 40
CDT: *see* Character Decision Task (CDT)
CELEX lexical database, 171
Character Decision Task (CDT), 124–126
Chinese
  formal and functional processing, distinguishing, 125–126
  homophony, 132
  word composition, 123
College-level readers and adult literacy learners, comparisons, 273–274
College-level reading-disabled populations, 267
Concept units, form and meaning, 114–115
Consonants, Hebrew, 96
Constituent Frequency, 160, 163–164, 165, 170–175, 180–186
Core trimorphemic stimuli, 236–237

Danish adolescents
  dyslexic, 30
  reading-disabled, metalinguistic factors, 57–58
Decoding skill accuracy, 278
Derivational morphology
  French: *see* French
Derived words, effects of morphological structure on children's reading of, 27–52
  skilled word recognition, 27–28
  third and fifth graders, study on, 31–38
    word list, 48
  transparent derived words, study, 38–45
    word list, 49
  word reading, 28–29, 30–31
Digit and picture naming (DIGIT), 272, 277, 278–279*t*, 284
Disabled children: *see* Learning disabled children; Reading disabled children
Disabled readers
  college-level, 267
  morphological insensitivity, 56
Dual-Route model, 308
Dutch
  polysyllabic words, reading aloud, 300–301
  prefix reliability, 194–201
  pseudoprefixed words, 83
  semantic opacity, 159
    Germanic and Romance strata, comparison of complex words, 170–175
    low-frequency morphologically complex words, processing of, 160–164
Dutch (*cont.*)
  semantic opacity (*cont.*)
    semantic priming design, 164–170
  spelling principles, 316–319
  sublexical frequency and meaning, 194–216
    prefix reliability, 194–201, 211
    semantic processing, 201–205
  verb forms, 315–330
    regularly inflected, 318*f*
  verb spelling errors, 319–323
    d/dt verbs, 322
    homophonous verb forms, 325
    lexical (long-term) memory, 321–322
    working memory, 319, 322–323, 326
Dyslexics
  adults, word reading processes, 265–267
  Danish adolescents, 30
  phonological, morpheme-based lexical reading, 242–245

Elementary school students
  sublexical frequency and meaning, Dutch language, 199*t*
English
  decoding ability: *see* English decoding ability
  formal and functional processing, 123–124
  morphological structure, effect on children's reading of derived words, 27–52
    skilled word recognition, 27–28
    third and fifth graders, study on, 31–38, 48
    transparent derived words, study, 38–45, 49
    word reading, 28–29, 30–31
  trimorphemic words
    affixes, 224
    Artificial Morpheme Boundary Experiment, 228–234
    core trimorphemic stimuli, 236–237
    generally, 222–223
    hierarchical structure in existing words, 225–226
    left-branching and right-branching and illegal nonsense stimuli, 224*f*
    left-branching novel stimuli, 231
    left-branching words with bound/fused roots, 230
    lexical networks, as, 226–228
    morphological network effect, 234–235
    morphological structure, 223–224
    nonsense words, 223, 231
    nonsense word stimuli, 234
    pseudoprefixed stimuli, 230
    real-word stimuli, 232–234
    right-branching novel stimuli, 231

English (*cont.*)
trimorphemic words (*cont.*)
right-branching words, 230
structurally ambiguous words, 230
English decoding ability
first graders
phoneme- and syllable segmentation tasks, 3–4
morphological awareness and, 5–11
words varied in frequency and phonological complexity, 11–21
phonological awareness and vocabulary, 7–11
age, function of, 9*f*
suffixes and, 1–25
variance in, morphological awareness and, 5–11
Ethiopian language, roots, 100
Expert word recognition ability, acquisition and nature of, 268–270

Family Frequency, 161
Family Size, 161
FLH: *see* Full Listing Hypothesis
Formal and functional processing, experiment distinguishing, 123–126
Form and meaning, morphological representation as correlation, 113–137
bound morphemes, representation of, 117–122
concept units, 114–115
depiction of connection, 114*f*
formal and functional processing, experiment distinguishing, 123–126
lemma, 130–131, 132
morpheme frequency, 129–131
morpheme retrieval, 122
morphological transparency, 127–128
phonology, 131–132
polymorphemic words, representation of, 115–117
polysyllabic words, 115–116*f*
French
derivational morphology, 139–157
derivational affixes, 148–151
lexical decision latencies, 150*f*
masked morphological priming, 141–142, 144–148, 152*t*
prefixes and suffixes, differences, 151
prime word frequency, 146–148
priming with simple and complex words, 143–145
printed word perception, 141–142
pseudo-prefixation effect, 148–149
supralexical hypothesis, 142–143, 148
variants, 140*f*
polysyllabic words, reading aloud, 300–301
French (*cont.*)
prefixes, 151
priming
masked morphological priming, 152*t*
masked priming paradigm, 141–142, 144–148
simple and complex words, 143–145
suffixes, 151
syllabic length-effect, 308
Full-Form Frequency, 165
Full Listing Hypothesis, 82
Full-listing model, 192

Germanic and Romance strata, comparison of complex words with Dutch lexicon, 170–175
Grapheme-Phenome Conversion, 308
Grapheme-to-phoneme rules, 1

Hebrew
binyan, 97
binyanim, 97
consonants, 96
CVCCVC structure, 99
GLGL, 98
mishkalim, 98
morphemes, 93
MSM consonants, 95
nouns, 98
priming, 102, 106, 107
repetition priming, 102, 106
roots, 93–97
centrality, 99–100
final gemination, 104–105
priming, 107
psycholinguistic evidence, 101
traditional approach, 106
segment shifting, 103
SSM consonants, 95–96, 98
stems, 107–108
templates, 93–94, 97–98, 107
centrality, 99–100
verbs, 93–94, 97, 104
vowels, 96
word composition as semitic language, 93–111
psycholinguistic evidence, 101
High frequency derived forms, 41
High frequency mock derived forms, 41
High surface frequency, words with, 12
High vs. low frequency bases, 14, 16–17, 19
High vs. low frequency derived words, 15, 17
Homophonous verb forms, 315–330
Homophony, 132
Hybrid models, 192–193

Incremental priming technique
polysyllabic words, reading aloud, 301
Inflected pseudowords, reading aloud (Italian), 245–246
Inflections, awareness of, 29–30
Intelligence measures, reading and, 6
Interactive Activation model, 193–194
Interactive models, 192–194
Italian
adult readers, 54
morpheme-based lexical reading, 241–264
affixes' selectional restrictions, 254–255
inflected pseudowords, reading aloud, 245–246
list context, 257–258
non-semantic reading, 255–257
phonological dyslexia, 242–245
prefixed pseudowords, 250–254
quantitative properties of affixes and, 246–250
prefixes, 259
reliability, 195

Japanese
Kana words, 256
Kanji, 316

Learning-disabled adolescents
morphological insensitivity, 57
Learning disabled children
transparent derived words, study, 38–45
high frequency derived forms, 41
high frequency mock derived forms, 41
low frequency derived forms, 43, 45
performance by reading group, 40*t*
performance on real and mock derived forms, 42–43
word length and base frequency, 43–44*t*
word list, 49
word reading, 40–41
Left-branching novel stimuli, 231
Left-branching words with bound/fused roots, 230
Left-to-right processing
Turkish, 83
Lemma, 130–131, 132
Letter sequences, 1–2
Letter-Word Identification, 40
Lexical decision tasks
decoding tasks, 272–273
performance of adults, 27–28
Lexicalization, 268–269
Lexical memory, 113, 319
Dutch, verb spelling errors, 321–322
Lexical networks, trimorphemic words as, 226–228
Lexical processing, transparency, 127
Lexical reading, morpheme-based, 241–264
List context, morpho-lexical reading and, 257–258
Low frequency derived forms, 43, 45
Low frequency derived words
high vs. low frequency bases: *see* High vs. low frequency bases
word length and base frequency, contributions of, 35–36*t*
Low literate adults, word reading processes, 265–267
Low surface frequency, words with, 12

Masked morphological priming
French, 141–142, 144–148, 152*t*
Meaning: *see also* Form and meaning, morphological representation as correlation
prefixed words and, 191–219
Metalinguistic factors influencing morphological awareness, 57–59
Micro Experimental Laboratory, 197
Mishkalim, 98
Moroccan Arabic, verbs, 100
Morpheme-based lexical reading, 241–264
affixes' selectional restrictions, 254–255
inflected pseudowords, reading aloud, 245–246
list context, 257–258
non-semantic reading, 255–257
phonological dyslexia, 242–245
prefixed pseudowords, 250–254
quantitative properties of affixes and, 246–250
Morpheme Reading List (MRL), 13–14
discussion, 17–18
error analysis, 16
reproduction of, 22
Morphemes
awareness: *see* Morphological awareness
frequency, 129–131
Hebrew, 93
retrieval, 122
Morpheme-sized units, 2
Morphological awareness
age, function of, 9*f*
age, impact of, 70
English decoding ability and
multiple regressions, 17*t*
factors influencing, 55–59
hierarchical regressions, 8*t*
influences, 54

Morphological awareness (*cont.*)
metalinguistic factors influencing, 57–59
phonological factors influencing, 56–57
real word version of task, 16
semantic factors influencing, 55–56
Test of Morphological Awareness (TMA), 7, 33–34
words varied in frequency and phonological complexity, 11–21
written language, exposure to, 70–71
Morphological families, 143
Morphological insensitivity, 56–57
adolescents, 57
Morphological knowledge
suffixes, English decoding ability and, 1–25
Morphological network effect, 234–235
Morphological parsing, 221–239
Morphological Race Model, 193
Morphological representation
form and meaning, as correlation between, 113–137
Morphological structure, 221–239
effect on children's reading of derived words, 27–52
decomposition task, 36
oral production task, 36
skilled word recognition, 27–28
third and fifth graders, study on, 31–38, 48
transparent derived words, study, 38–45, 49
uncommon transparent forms, reading, 35–36
word list, 48, 49
word reading, 28–29, 30–31
Morphological transparency, 127–128
MRL: *see* Morpheme Reading List (MRL)
Multiple read-out model, 310*f*
Multiple-Trace Memory Model (MTM), 309, 311

Naming, 247–248
prefixed pseudowords, 250–251
semantic information, 257
variable response criteria and, 310–311
word and pseudoword, 272
National Adult Literacy Survey, 265
Nijmegen University, 161, 165, 171
Nominal compounds, 177
Nonsense words
trimorphemic words, English, 223, 231
Nouns
Hebrew, 98
Serbian, 59

Obligatory Contour Principle (OCP), 96–97
OCP: *see* Obligatory Contour Principle (OCP)
Opacity: *see* Opaque vs. transparent words; Semantic opacity
Opaque vs. transparent words, 14, 16, 18–19
Oral language
reading achievement, 29, 30
Orthographic information, 132

Parsing
morphological: *see* Morphological parsing
semantic opacity and, 159–189
Passage Comprehension, 40
Peabody Picture Vocabulary Test-Revised, 8, 39, 40
PERC-CT, 277, 278*t*
Phoneme- and morpheme-based tests, 4
Phoneme- and syllable segmentation tasks, 3–4
Phoneme deletion test, 7–8, 16
Phoneme vs. morpheme awareness, 10
Phonological awareness
English decoding ability and, 7–11, 16
age, function of, 9*f*
morphological insensitivity, 56–57
Phonological dyslexia
morpheme-based lexical reading, 242–245
Phonology, 131–132
PICTURE, 277, 278*t*, 284
Polymorphemic words
form and meaning, 115–117
Polysyllabic words
form and meaning, 115–116*f*
bound morphemes, 120*f*, 122*f*
reading aloud, 295–314
Dutch data, 300–301
French data, 300–301
incremental priming technique, 301
masked priming technique, 301–305
mean latencies obtained in different conditions, 298–299*t*
multiple read-out model, 310*f*
orthographic syllables, 301–305
phonological syllables, 301–305
syllabic length-effect, 305–310
variable response criteria and naming, 310–311
visual word recognition, studies on role of syllable, 295–296
Prefixed words
sublexical frequency and meaning, 191–219
Augmented Addressed Morphology (AAM) Model, 193–194, 212
Dutch language, 194–216
full-listing model, 192
hybrid models, 192–193

Prefixed words (*cont.*)
sublexical frequency and meaning (*cont.*)
Interactive Activation model, 193–194
interactive models, 192–194
models of morphological complex words, 191–194
Morphological Race Model, 193
prefix reliability, 194–201
Prelexical Morphological Decomposition model, 191–192
progressive demasking technique, 206–211, 216
semantic processing, 201–205
Turkish, 81–83
Prefixes
French, 151
Italian, 259
reliability, 194–195
Prelexical Morphological Decomposition model, 191–192
Priming
French
masked morphological priming, 141–142, 144–148, 152*t*
simple and complex words, 143–145
Hebrew, 102, 106, 107
polysyllabic words, reading aloud, 301–305
semantic priming design, 164–170
Progressive demasking technique, 206–211, 216
Pronunciation, 2
Pseudo-prefixation effect, French, 148–149
Pseudoprefixed stimuli, 230
Pseudoprefixed words, Dutch, 83
Pseudoword naming, 241–264
affixes' selectional restrictions, 254–255
inflected pseudowords, reading aloud, 245–246
list context, 257–258
non-semantic reading, 255–257
phonological dyslexia, 242–245
prefixed pseudowords, 250–254
quantitative properties of affixes, 246–250
Pseudowords
morphologically complex, 259
prefixed, 250–254
suffixes, 248–249

Racial identity, 96
RA-Match, 40, 44
RAN: *see* Rapid automized naming (RAN)
Rapid automized naming (RAN), 270
Reading disabled children
7.5 to 9.5 years of age
phoneme- and morpheme-based tests, 4
Reading disabled children (*cont.*)
phonological and morpheme awareness tests, 20
Real-word stimuli, 232–234
Redundancy, 129–130
Regression analysis, 16
Repetition priming, Hebrew, 102, 106
Right-branching novel stimuli, 231
Right-branching words, 230
Roots
Ethiopian language, 100
Hebrew, 93–97
centrality, 99–100
final gemination, 104–105
priming, 107
psycholinguistic evidence, 101
traditional approach, 106
Rosner phonological awareness test, 20S

Second- and fourth-grade children
Turkey, recognition of morphologically complex words, 84–91
Segment shifting, Hebrew, 103
Semantic opacity
Germanic and Romance strata, comparison of complex words with Dutch lexicon, 170–175
low-frequency morphologically complex words, processing of, 160–164
nominal compounds, 177
parsing and, 159–189
semantic priming design, 164–170
Semitic language
roots, 93–97
semitic morphology, experimental studies of, 102–108
word composition as: *see* Hebrew
Sentence-processing, 273
Serbian
adult readers, 54
correlations, 63*t*, 69
derivational morphology, 69
English, differences, 68
morphological and phonological analysis, beginning readers, 59–64
morphological awareness, 55
morphological production, 73–75
nouns, 59
phoneme deletion items, 75–76
sentence frames, 62*t*
Short-term memory, 5
Skilled word recognition, 27–28
SLI: *see* Specific language impairment (SLI)

Specific language impairment (SLI), 55
Spelling errors, 315–330
Stems, Hebrew, 107–108
Structurally ambiguous words, 230
Sublexical frequency
  prefixed words and, 191–219
Suffixes
  English decoding ability and, 1–25
  French, 151
  pseudowords, 248–249
  Turkish, 82–88
Supralexical hypothesis
  French, derivational morphology, 142–143, 148, 151–152
Surface Frequency, 164, 166, 171, 172, 175
Syllabic length-effect, 305–310
  Dual-Route model, 308
  Grapheme-Phenome Conversion, 308
  mean naming latencies, 307*t*
  models accounting for, 308
  Multiple-Trace Memory Model (MTM), 309, 311
Syllable, 117–120; *see also* Polysyllabic words
  psychological role of, 296
  reading aloud, studies on role of, 296–299
  visual word recognition, studies on role of, 295–296

Templates
  Hebrew, 93–94, 97–98, 107
    centrality, 99–100
Test of Morphological Awareness (TMA), 33–34
Third and fifth graders
  morphological structure, effect on children's reading of derived words, 31–38
    word list, 48
Third to sixth grade children
  English decoding ability
    accuracy on reading, vocabulary, and linguistic skills, 15*t*
    derivational morphology, 3
    morphologically complex words, accuracy in decoding, 14*t*
    words varied in frequency and phonological complexity, 13–20
TMA: *see* Test of Morphological Awareness (TMA)
Transparency
  derived words, effects of morphological structure on children's reading of, 38–45
    word list, 49
  high frequency derived forms, 41
  high frequency mock derived forms, 41
Transparency (*cont.*)
  lexical processing, 127
  low frequency derived forms, 43, 45
  morphological transparency, 127–128
  opaque vs. transparent words, 14, 16, 18–19
  performance by reading group, 40*t*
  performance on real and mock derived forms, 42–43
  word length and base frequency, 43–44*t*
  word list, 49
  word reading, 40–41
Transparent derived words, study, 38–45
Trimorphemic words, English
  affixes, 224
  Artificial Morpheme Boundary Experiment, 228–234
  core trimorphemic stimuli, 236–237
  generally, 222–223
  hierarchical structure in existing words, 225–226
  left-branching and right-branching and illegal nonsense stimuli, 224*f*
  left-branching novel stimuli, 231
  left-branching words with bound/fused roots, 230
  lexical networks, as, 226–228
  morphological network effect, 234–235
  morphological structure, 223–224
  nonsense words, 223, 231
  nonsense word stimuli, 234
  pseudoprefixed stimuli, 230
  real-word stimuli, 232–234
  right-branching novel stimuli, 231
  right-branching words, 230
  structurally ambiguous words, 230
Turkish
  base forms, 69–70
  correlations, 69
  derivational morphology, 69
  English, differences, 68
  morphological and phonological analysis, beginning readers, 65–68
  morphological awareness, 58–59
  morphological production, 76–77
  phoneme deletion task, 77
  recognition of morphologically complex words, 81–92
    left-to-right processing, 83
    prefixed words, 81–83
    suffixed words, 82–88

Variable response criteria and naming, 310–311
Verbs
  Arabic, 100

Verbs (*cont.*)
  Dutch, 315–330
  Hebrew, 93–94, 97, 104
  homophonous verb forms, 315–330
  Moroccan Arabic, 100
Vocabulary, morphological skill and, 5, 7–11, 16
Vowels, Hebrew, 96

WDT: *see* Word Decision Task (WDT)
Wechsler Individual Achievement Test (WIAT), 40, 271–272, 274
  correlation with WRAT, 283
  explained, 286
  plot of, 276*f*
  scores, 287
Wide Range Achievement Test-3, 40
Wide Range Achievement Test-Reading (WRAT), 272, 274, 277, 278–280*t*
  correlation with WIAT, 283
  explained, 286
Wide Range Achievement Test-Reading (WRAT) (*cont.*)
  plot of, 276*f*
  predicting scores, 282*t*
  variance, 284
WISC Blocks, 62
WISC-R Vocabulary and Digit Span, 5–6
Woodcock-Johnson Psycho-educational Battery, 40
Woodcock Word Identification, 5
Word Attack, 5
Word composition as semitic language: *see* Hebrew
Word Decision Task (WDT), 124–126
Word naming: *see* Pseudoword naming
Word Reading Test (WRT), 32–35
Word recognition, Turkish, 81–92
Working memory, 319, 322–323, 326
WRAT: *see* Wide Range Achievement Test-Reading (WRAT)
WRT: *see* Word Reading Test (WRT)

NEUROPSYCHOLOGY AND COGNITION

The purpose of the Neuropsychology and Cognition series is to bring out volumes that promote understanding in topics relating brain and behavior. It is intended for use by both clinicians and research scientists in the fields of neuropsychology, cognitive psychology, psycholinguistics, speech and hearing, as well as eduction. Examples of topics to be covered in this series would relate memory, language acquisition and breakdown, reading, attention, developing and aging brain. By addressing the theoretical, empirical, and applied aspects of brain-behavior relationships, this series will try to present the information in the files of neuropsychology and cognition in a coherent manner.

1. P.G. Aaron: *Dyslexia and Hyperlexia*. 1989 ISBN 1-55608-079-4; Pb. ISBN 0-7923-3155-9
2. R.M. Joshi (ed.): *Written Language Disorders*. 1991 ISBN 0-7923-0902-2
3. A. Caramazza: *Issues in Reading, Writing and Speaking: A Neuropsychological Perspective*. 1991 ISBN 0-7923-0996-0
4. B.F. Pennington (ed.): *Reading Disabilities: Genetic and Neurological Influences*. 1991 ISBN 0-7923-1606-1
5. N.H. Hadley: *Elective Mutism: A Handbook for Educators, Counsellors and Health Care Professionals*. 1994 ISBN 0-7923-2418-8
6. W.C. Watt (ed.): *Writing Systems and Cognition: Perspectives from Psychology, Physiology, Linguistics, and Semiotics*. 1994 ISBN 0-7923-2592-3
7. I. Taylor and D.R. Olson (eds.): *Scripts and Literacy: Reading and Learning to Read Alphabets, Syllabaries and Characters*. 1994 ISBN 0-7923-2912-0
8. V.W. Berninger (ed.): *The Varieties of Orthographic Knowledge: I: Theoretical and Developmental Issues*. 1994 ISBN 0-7923-3080-3
9. C.K. Leong and R.M. Joshi (eds.): *Developmental and Acquired Dyslexia: Neuropsychological and Neurolinguistic Perspectives*. 1995 ISBN 0-7923-3166-4
10. N. Gregg: *Written Expression Disorders*. 1995 ISBN 0-7923-3355-1
11. V.W. Berninger (ed.): *The Varieties of Orthographic Knowledge: II: Relationships to Phonology, Reading, and Writing*. 1995 ISBN 0-7923-3641-0
    Set (Vols. 8 & 11) ISBN 0-7923-3081-1
12. Y. Lebrun (ed.): *From the Brain to the Mouth: Acquired Dysarthria and Dysfluency in Adults*. 1997 ISBN 0-7923-4427-8
13. J. Rispens, T.A. van Yperen and W. Yule (eds.): *Perspectives of the Classfication of Specific Developmental Disorders*. 1998 ISBN 0-7923-4871-0
14. C.K. Leong and K. Tamaoka (eds.): *Cognitive Processing of the Chinese and Japanese Languages*. 1998 ISBN 0-7923-5479-6
15. P. Reitsma and L. Verhoeven (eds.): *Problems and Interventions in Literary Development*. 1998 ISBN 0-7923-5557-1
16. I. Lundberg, F.E. Tønnessen and I. Austad (eds.): *Dyslexia: Advances in Theory and Practice*. 1999 ISBN 0-7923-5837-6
17. T. Nunes (ed.): *Learning to Read: An Integrated View from Research and Practice*. 1999 ISBN 0-7923-5513-X
18. T. Høien and J. Lundberg: *Dyslexia: From Theory to Intervention*. 2000 ISBN 0-7923-6309-4
19. H.J. Hartman (ed.): *Metacognition in Learning and Instruction: Theory, Research and Practice*. 2001 ISBN 0-7923-6838-X
20. E. Witruk, A.D. Friederici and T. Lachman (eds.): *Basic Functions of Language, Reading and Reading Disability*. 2002 ISBN 1-4020-7027-6
21. K. Hugdahl (ed.): *Experimental Methods in Psychology* ISBN 1-4020-7210-4
22. E.M.H. Assink and D. Sandra (eds.): *Reading Complex Words: Cross-Language Studies* ISBN 0-306-47707-6